Implementing Qlik Sense

Design, Develop, and Validate BI solutions for consultants

Ganapati Hegde

Kaushik Solanki

Packt>

BIRMINGHAM - MUMBAI

Implementing Qlik Sense

Copyright © 2017 Packt Publishing

First published: October 2017

Production reference: 1171017

Published by Packt Publishing Ltd.
Livery Place
35 Livery Street
Birmingham
B3 2PB, UK.
ISBN 978-1-78646-044-8

www.packtpub.com

Credits

Authors
Ganapati Hegde
Kaushik Solanki

Reviewers
Karl Pover
Julian Villafuerte

Commissioning Editor
Veena Pagare

Acquisition Editor
Tushar Gupta

Content Development Editor
Tejas Limkar

Technical Editor
Danish Shaikh

Copy Editor
Alpha Singh

Project Coordinator
Manthan Patel

Proofreader
Safis Editing

Indexer
Tejal Daruwale Soni

Graphics
Tania Dutta

Production Coordinator
Deepika Naik

About the Authors

Ganapati Hegde is an engineer by background. He carries an overall IT experience of over 16 years. He is very passionate about technology and is always looking out to learn newer technologies.

He started his IT career with SK International where he headed Software Services and worked with myriad of technologies, including programming, databases, IT security, application virtualization, and cloud services. During his stint with SK International, he was involved in lot of integration projects and thus has good knowledge on API/SDK. He was instrumental in setting up practices such as RSA, Citrix, Oracle, and Salesforce.

He is currently working with Predoole Analytics, an award winning Qlik partner in India, in the presales role. He has worked on BI projects in several industry verticals and works closely with customers, helping them in their BI strategies. His experience in other aspects of IT, like application design and development, cloud computing, networking, and IT Security, helps him to design perfect BI solutions. He conducts workshops to increase user awareness and drive adoption.

He works on analysis of unstructured time stamped data and IOT as well, allowing customer to get business insights and help improve efficiency. This is being done with the help of big data platform Khika, which does real time co-relation of log data across sources. This helps customers mitigate risk and help in IT Audit and Compliance.

Ganapati is now working on improving his knowledge of advanced analytics using technologies like R and phython.

I would like to thank my wife Seema and my parents for standing by me and providing constant encouragement. The conducive environment they created for me to write this book is commendable.

I would like to thank Mr. Hemant and Mr. Vasudev, founders of SK International, who put immense faith in me and helped me to work on several technologies.

Special thanks to Amit, founder of Predoole Analytics, who gave permission to work on this book and who provided guidance to me during my initial days at Predoole. I take this opportunity to thank my co-author Kaushik and my other colleagues, who helped me when I was new to Qlik and shortened my learning curve. Also, the team at Qlik India has been phenomenal and has helped improve my knowledge through ongoing partner training. I thank each one of the members. I wish to thank all my school and college teachers and mentors who have helped me to be the person I am today. Thanks to Packt team for giving this great opportunity. Last but not the least I thank The Almighty.

Kaushik Solanki has been Qlik MVP(most valuable player) for years 2016 and 2017. He has been playing with Qlik technology for more than seven years. He started his career being a Qlik developer and currently works with Predoole Analytics, an elite Qlik partner in India, as Qlik Project Delivery Manager. He is also a certified Qlikview administrator.

Kaushik loves to share his experience and educate others. He is an active member of Qlik community, where he helps in solving problems.

He has a great understanding of project delivery, right from business requirement to final implementation. His experience in various domains has helped businesses to take valuable business decisions.

Kaushik is an Information technology engineer by profession. He also holds the master degree in finance.

I would like to thank Tushar Gupta, Sr. Acquisition Editor of Packt, for giving me the opportunity to write this book. I thank my co-author Ganapati Hegde, without whom this book would not have finished.

A special thanks to Amit Gadkari, Director of Predoole Analytics Pvt Ltd, for finding talent in me and giving me opportunity to grow with him. He is responsible for whatever standing I have today.

I would like to thank my parents and my wife Megha for understanding me and helping me beyond limits. I would also like to thank all my colleagues for helping me with the topics of this book.

I thank all our editors for giving their valuable time in reviewing the book and helping in making this book more fruitful. Finally, I thank Tejas and the team from Packt publication for their continuous support and publishing of this book.

About the Reviewers

Karl Pover is the owner and principal consultant of Evolution Consulting, which provides QlikView consulting services throughout Mexico. Since 2006, he has been dedicated to providing QlikView pre-sales, implementation, and training in more than 50 customers. He is the author of Learning QlikView Data Visualization and a Qlik Luminary since 2014.

Twitter: @karlpover

LinkedIn: https://mx.linkedin.com/in/karlpover

Blog: http://poverconsulting.com/

First and foremost, thanks to my wife, Pamela. I owe you several long weekends.

Thanks to the team at Evolution Consulting, especially to Julian Villafuerte, Carlos Reyes, and Jaime Aguilar for taking on more responsibility. A special thanks to Julian for taking the time to review the final version of the book, and Alejandro Morales for helping me to develop a few extensions.

As always, thanks to my parents, Judy and Bill, for their love and support throughout my life.

I am grateful to all the technical reviewers, and especially to Ralf Becher, who contributed material to the book. I also appreciate the work done by Rohit Kumar Singh and the rest of the Packt team, who gave me a little extra time to make this a great book.
Last, but not the least, thanks to all the customers, past and present, who have always asked for the impossible.

Julian Villafuerte is a founding member of Evolution Consulting, a Mexican firm which provides QlikView consulting services throughout the Americas. Since 2010, he has helped several companies to define effective strategies for data management and business analysis. As a consultant, he has worked in application development, project management, pre-sales, and training for many industries, including retail, manufacturing, and insurance. In October 2015, he published *Creating Stunning Dashboards with QlikView*, a practical handbook focused on developing useful and engaging analytical applications. He has a Master's degree in Information Technology Management and teaches at Tecnológico de Monterrey in Mexico City. Recently, he has started a blog called QlikFreak (https://qlikfreak.wordpress.com/), where he shares tips and tricks about data visualization, scripting, and best practices.

www.PacktPub.com

For support files and downloads related to your book, please visit www.PacktPub.com.

Did you know that Packt offers eBook versions of every book published, with PDF and ePub files available? You can upgrade to the eBook version at www.PacktPub.com and as a print book customer, you are entitled to a discount on the eBook copy. Get in touch with us at service@packtpub.com for more details.

At www.PacktPub.com, you can also read a collection of free technical articles, sign up for a range of free newsletters and receive exclusive discounts and offers on Packt books and eBooks.

Mapt

https://www.packtpub.com/mapt

Get the most in-demand software skills with Mapt. Mapt gives you full access to all Packt books and video courses, as well as industry-leading tools to help you plan your personal development and advance your career.

Why subscribe?

- Fully searchable across every book published by Packt
- Copy and paste, print, and bookmark content
- On demand and accessible via a web browser

Customer Feedback

Table of Contents

Preface

Implementing Qlik Sense is a book intended for readers who wish to do a great project implementation on Qlik Sense. This book will give readers all the information, right from strategy to requirement gathering to implementing BI solution using Qlik Sense. Various scenarios in the book will empower the readers to take right decisions in tricky and difficult situations while developing analytical dashboards.

What this book covers

Chapter 1, *Consultant – An Introduction*: This chapter will give the readers an understanding about what is consultancy, how it differs from being a developer, and the importance of consultancy in making a project successful. The readers will learn about what they are supposed to do as consultants, the importance of their role in making a project successful, expectations that are there from a consultant, and the roles they need to play.

Chapter 2, *Preparing for the Project*: This chapter will give the readers an understanding about how to prepare for a project and the homework they need to do. The readers will learn about the initial homework they need to do, how to understand the customer better, and how to accordingly plan the strategy. The readers will also understand what is expected from a consultant and the roles they need to play being consultants.

Chapter 3, *Prerequisites to start a Project*: This chapter will enlist the various aspects needed to start a project. It will help to understand the various aspects along with their importance, and the tactics to handle them. The readers will learn about the important aspect of starting the project which is often missed and can lead to failure of project. They will also learn about scoping the project along with learning about documentation and its importance.

Chapter 4, *Requirement Gathering*: The focus of this chapter is to start the project execution with requirement gathering. Requirement gathering plays an important role in successful project execution. The take away for the readers from this chapter will be the tactics about requirement gathering and getting acquainted with the common mistakes which are done by most of the developers and project managers while executing this phase of a project.

Chapter 5, *Architecture Design*: This chapter is about architecture design where the focus will be to design infrastructure architecture and data architecture. This chapter will teach the readers about the importance of architecture design and the various aspects which will help to design architecture. The chapter will touch upon strategies to be used to ensure easy scaling and expansion.

Chapter 6, *Development*: This chapter talks about the actual execution of a project, where business requirement starts taking shape in form of dashboards and interactive analysis. The readers will learn the best practices of data modeling and visualization. They will also learn about handling tricky situations in this phase in an effective manner.

Chapter 7, *Validation, UAT and Go Live*: This chapter will focus on data validation and visualization validation. The chapter will help the readers understand how validation can be done quickly and how to ensure that the dashboard displays correct results. The readers will take away the skills to perform validation of the data as well as visualization. They will learn about the way to conduct the UAT with the business users and take the project to Go-live Stage.

Chapter 8, *Post Go-Live*: This chapter will teach the readers about the post Go-live activities which are required to make a project successful. It will talk about the adoption strategies, maintenance, auditing and documentation. The readers will learn about the importance of post Go-live activities and how they can make a difference to make project successful.

Chapter 9, *Avoiding Common Pitfalls*: This chapter will teach the readers about the most common mistakes and the steps to avoid them. They will learn about the importance of post Go-live activities and how they can make a difference to make a project successful.

Chapter 10, *Knowledge Sets*: This chapter will make the readers aware about some of the domain terminologies. It is important for any developer to have a basic understanding of domain. The readers will learn about the importance of various modules under each domain, which will help them to provide value added services to their customers, to improve customer satisfaction.

Chapter 11, *A real life case-study*: This chapter will make the readers understand how to apply the earlier learnt concepts in a real-life scenario. The names used in the chapter are not real but scenarios are real. The chapter will make the readers go through a real-life example to understand the challenges faced and the ways to handle them.

What you need for this book

The examples provided in the chapter will require you to have Qlik Sense Desktop installed on your PC. The Qlik Sense Desktop is a free software available for download from Qlik web site. The software runs on 64 bit Windows 7, 8.1, or 10 operating system. Recommended config is 4GB Ram or more with Intel i3 or higher processor.

The examples provided use Microsoft Access database. The user just needs Microsoft Access odbc driver to connect to the mdb file from Qlik Sense Desktop.

Who is this book for

This book contains guidelines for Qlik Sense developers who wish to become Qlik Sense consultants and ensure successful project implementations and drive greater adoption. The readers are advised to know the basics of Qlik Sense, starting from installation to basic configuration, like licensing the product, allocating roles to users, allocating the licenses to users, and so on.

Conventions

In this book, you will find a number of text styles that distinguish between different kinds of information. Here are some examples of these styles and explanations of their meaning.

A block of code is set as follows:

```
REM Full Load from Excel file "Sales" ;

Sales:
LOAD
    Region,
    SalesID,
    Product,
    SalesAmt,
    LastModifiedDate
FROM [lib://Chapter 6/Sales.xlsx]
(ooxml, embedded labels, table is Sheet2);

REM Store the data into Qlik Data Mart i.e QVD;

Store Sales into [lib://Chapter 6/Sales.qvd];

Drop table Sales;
```

In-text code is highlighted in font and color as here: LOAD. The file and folder names are also shown in the same style, for example, Chapter6/Sales.xlsx.

At several places in the book, we have referred to external URLs to cite source of datasets or other information. A URL would appear in the following text style: http://finance.yahoo.com.

New terms and **important words** are shown in bold. Words that you see on the screen, for example, in menus or dialog boxes, appear in the text like this: In order to download new modules, we will go to **Files | Settings | Project Name | Project Interpreter**.

Warnings or important notes appear like this.

Tips and tricks appear like this.

Reader feedback

Feedback from our readers is always welcome. Let us know what you think about this book-what you liked or disliked. Reader feedback is important for us as it helps us develop titles that you will really get the most out of. To send us general feedback, simply email feedback@packtpub.com and mention the book's title in the subject of your message. If there is a topic that you have expertise in and you are interested in either writing or contributing to a book, see our author guide at www.packtpub.com/authors.

Customer support

Now that you are the proud owner of a Packt book, we have a number of things to help you get the most from your purchase.

Downloading the example code

You can download the example code files for this book from your account at http://www. packtpub.com. If you purchased this book elsewhere, you can visit http://www.packtpub. com/support and register to have the files emailed directly to you. You can download the code files by following these steps:

1. Log in or register to our website using your email address and password.
2. Hover the mouse pointer on the **SUPPORT** tab at the top.
3. Click on **Code Downloads & Errata**.
4. Enter the name of the book in the **Search** box.
5. Select the book for which you're looking to download the code files.
6. Choose from the drop-down menu where you purchased this book from.
7. Click on **Code Download**.

Once the file is downloaded, make sure that you unzip or extract the folder using the latest version of:

- WinRAR / 7-Zip for Windows
- Zipeg / iZip / UnRarX for Mac
- 7-Zip / PeaZip for Linux

The code bundle for the book is also hosted on GitHub at `https://github.com/PacktPublishing/Implementing-Qlik-Sense`. We also have other code bundles from our rich catalog of books and videos available at `https://github.com/PacktPublishing/`. Check them out!

Errata

Although we have taken every care to ensure the accuracy of our content, mistakes do happen. If you find a mistake in one of our books-maybe a mistake in the text or the code-we would be grateful if you could report this to us. By doing so, you can save other readers from frustration and help us improve subsequent versions of this book. If you find any errata, report them by visiting `http://www.packtpub.com/submit-errata`, selecting your book, clicking on the **Errata Submission Form** link, and entering the details of your errata. Once your errata are verified, your submission will be accepted and the errata will be uploaded to our website or added to any list of existing errata under the Errata section of that title. To view the previously submitted errata, go to `https://www.packtpub.com/books/content/support` and enter the name of the book in the search field. The required information will appear under the **Errata** section.

Piracy

Piracy of copyrighted material on the internet is an ongoing problem across all media. At Packt, we take the protection of our copyright and licenses very seriously. If you come across any illegal copies of our works in any form on the internet, do provide us with the location address or website name immediately so that we can pursue a remedy. You can contact us at `copyright@packtpub.com` with a link to the suspected pirated material. We appreciate your help in protecting our authors and our ability to bring you valuable content.

Questions

If you have a problem with any aspect of this book, you can contact us at `questions@packtpub.com`, and we will do our best to address the problem.

Consultant - An Introduction

1

In this chapter, we'll talk about consultancy and its importance, and how wearing the hat of a consultant helps in delivering successful projects. This chapter is useful for developers who aren't aware of who a consultant is, and what is expected from a consultant.

This chapter assumes the reader is conversant with basic Qlik development and is aware of terminologies used in business analytics. The BI market is growing at a phenomenal rate, and hence it is natural that consultants will play a big role. The figures quoted by Gartner for Analytics are mind-boggling indeed.

> Gartner says that the Worldwide Business Intelligence and Analytics Market will reach $18.3 billion in 2017.

This chapter will be covering the following topics:

- Understanding who is a consultant
- Importance of being a consultant
- Difference between a developer and a consultant
- Roles and responsibility of a consultant
- Strategy which a consultant must follow

Understanding who is a consultant

Before we start the discussion on who a consultant is, let's take an analogy. Though the analogy has nothing to do with Information Technology, it helps you to relate the point which we are trying to make.

For a moment, let's assume you are sick. The sickness is causing you a lot of discomfort. It is decreasing your efficiency and your ability to work effectively and doesn't allow you to focus.

For obvious reason, you go to a doctor. You wait for your turn. When it is time, you enter the doctor's room, but you see that the doctor is impatient and looks in a hurry. You complain about your ailment (say, stomach pain) and lo and behold, the doctors writes a prescription, collects the fees, and you are out of the clinic feeling disappointed. You might take the medicine or rush to another doctor. You would agree that the experience was not pleasant.

Let's take the same example, but say that instead of an impatient doctor, you come across a doctor who is calm, composed, and welcomes you with a smile. He makes sure you are comfortable. He starts asking you questions. You complain of stomach pain. He asks you detailed questions, such as:

- Is it the first time you are facing this or does it happen regularly?
- What time of the day does it bother you?
- Do you have any allergies to any specific foods?
- What did you eat in the last 24 hours?

Plus, more questions which help in correct diagnosis.

As he asks these questions, you feel comfortable and that you are in safe hands and with the right doctor. The doctor proceeds with examining you and checks your pulse and blood pressure. Only then does he prescribe medicine. The doctor shows genuine intent to make you well and asks you for a follow-up visit to ensure that you are fully fit again.

Did you note the contrast in the approaches?

This is exactly what happens in IT world. If we equate it to the doctor-patient analogy, we can say the patient is similar to a customer who has business challenges and is looking for a doctor, who is, in this case a consultant to overcome the challenges and provide the right solution.

Just like every patient is different with a different constitution, similarly every business is different. In fact, the situation varies drastically across different industry verticals and across geographies.

Moreover, in the real world the situation is more complex, as a consultant must deal with multiple teams in an organization and each team has its respective set of challenges and different expectations.

A consultant is a person whose approach is to understand the business challenges and find solutions to them.

A consultant is the one who does a lot of ground work before he/she starts working on a project. The consultant brings in the best practices during various stages of the project. (The details will be covered in subsequent chapters.) A consultant must the business of the customer, understand the process, and the way existing reporting/analytics are done.

A customer will always prefer a person who understands his concerns, thinks proactively, and gives suggestions. A consultant needs to play an important role in all the aspects of a project. The book will take you through each of these aspects and help you in your transition towards becoming a consultant. The various aspects are mentioned as follows:

- Preparation
- Getting ready with the prerequisites
- Requirement gathering
- Architecture
- Modeling
- Designing
- UI (User Interface)
- UAT (User Acceptance and Training)
- Go-live
- Post Go-live steps

Each of these steps is important in its own way and each of them will have its own challenges. The book will also cover a consultant's journey in each of these steps. We have tried to give examples to make it easy for you to relate to the points which we are making.

Importance of being a consultant

After having understood who a consultant is, let's look at the importance of being one.

Before we get into the importance of a consultant, it's important to understand the power of analytics and the role it plays in any business organization.

Business users are no longer looking only at just reporting. They now want analytics which helps them to look at data in a more scientific way. In fact, analytics has now become a decision-making system. As businesses become dynamic and competition fiercer, the window for making decisions is also shrinking.

With changing technology, companies no longer have an ERP as a data source. The information is now spread across different applications. The applications too are no longer on-premise; some of them have moved to the cloud. Even social media applications like Facebook and Twitter are now considered sources of information for companies. Big data is one of the buzz words, and Microsoft Excel still remains one of the prevalent data sources! It's important for customers to get the best from all the data sources.

Companies look at Analytics in multiple areas, such as:

- Sales
- Marketing
- Finance
- Operations
- HR
- Supply Chain
- IT

Analytics brings great value to the company in each of these areas. We will delve deeper into these areas in further chapters, but for a brief understanding, let's look at why these areas consider analytics so valuable:

- Sales looks for increasing profitability and increasing revenue
- Marketing wants to up-sell and cross-sell, and improve **Return on Investment (ROI)** on campaigns
- Finance wants to find ways of reducing cost
- Operations wants to streamline the process
- HR wants analytics for talent retention, succession planning, reward management, and performance monitoring
- The supply chain wants better sourcing and better vendor management
- Information Technology looks for better asset management, service delivery, and IT project performance management

Let's take an example of a fictitious company, say PQR Corp, which is a manufacturing company. PQR has a turnover of 150 million USD and has all the previously mentioned functions of sales, finance, operations, HR, supply chain, and IT.

If PQR Corp invests one million USD in Analytics (with the help of a good consultant, of course!), then a good consultant can not only recover the cost for PQR but can also make the investment turn substantially beneficial:

- If he/she can help improve sales revenue by 10 percent, a company's revenue can grow from say 150 million USD to 165 million USD, which is an increase of 15 million USD in revenue USD
- If he/she can help in reduction of the inventory cost from 30 million USD to 20 million USD, it is a savings of 10 million
- Similarly, if the consultant can help improve sourcing strategies and help save 5 percent in sourcing cost from 60 million USD to 57 million USD, a saving of 3 million USD can be achieved

The statistics are amazing. Considering the preceding example, one can easily see an overall benefit of 28 million USD. If one adds other benefits from other functions, like HR, IT, and/or operations, these numbers will grow.

When you look at the **Key Result Area** (**KRA**) of each of these functions, you can understand the mammoth implications of getting the BI strategy right. KRA are areas in business for which an individual or group is responsible.

You will appreciate how analytics plays a crucial role for a company and how you as a consultant can influence the success of an organization. The power of analysis helps organizations to understand their data better and to take better business decisions. A poorly executed Analytics implementation gives no added value to the organization and the investments go waste.

After being a developer, a natural progression in one's career is to look at becoming a consultant. Organizations look at consultants as trusted advisors. A good consultant always commands great respect from a client.

After years of development experience, a person is expected to want a more challenging role. A consultant carries tremendous responsibility on his/her shoulders. The approach which a consultant takes will have a direct impact on the fortunes of a company. Any company which invests heavily into an analytical software, like Qlik, will expect a good Return on Investment and a low cost of ownership.

Difference between a developer and consultant

In the previous sections, we looked at who a consultant is and the importance of being one. In this section, we will look at the difference between a developer and a consultant.

Being a consultant is a natural progression for a developer. It is always good to start your analytical journey by being a developer. In the lifecycle of a developer, one gets to learn the technical aspects of Business Intelligence(BI). A strong technology base is a very critical aspect that makes a developer a good developer. This phase exposes the developer to the execution phase of the project.

Let's say someone is planning to build a great building. He/she may hire the best of the people to build it and the people may put in their best efforts for that. A lot of time, effort, and money will be spent for this building to come up. It will take years for this effort and the building will be built. But when it's time to occupy the building, the person may realize that there are a lot of design flaws which make the building difficult to use. The people who moved in will then slowly start moving out, simply because it's tough for them to live there.

This analogy holds true for many BI projects, where huge investments are made and the best of developers are hired, but the adoption of software is not up to the mark. The reasons could be many but the situation is certainly not the ideal one.

For a moment, in the preceding example, let's say the person hires a fantastic architect. The architect spends a lot of time to understand what the person expects from the building, what purpose it is meant for, who the people are who will be living there, and what kind of lifestyle they will expect.

He/she then starts working on a detailed plan, going in to the minutest details of planning everything, such as the depth of the foundation, the number of gates in the building, the location and size of car parking, the number of elevators, the size of apartments, safety measures, and all other important aspects.

Now, when this meticulous planning is executed by a a set of experienced people, the result will be amazing, won't it? The project is bound to be successful and will deserve all the applause and accolades.

No doubt, a developer is an important part of a BI project; it's important that the direction is right. Hence, it's imperative that a developer, after a certain years of development experience, transitions himself/herself in to being a consultant. This is the precise reason why we are writing this book for budding developers--to help them move into a consultant role and contribute to and own project success.

Roles and responsibilities of a consultant

The previous section gave an idea about being a consultant and why a developer must look at progressing towards being a consultant.

This section will cover the overview of the roles and responsibilities of a consultant. The subsequent chapters will cover these in greater detail.

Roles of a consultant

The roles of a consultant can be summarized as:

- Interacting with business users
- Understanding the data sources
- Setting the expectations correctly
- Designing the perfect solution
- Planning the Go-live
- Planning for the future road-map

Interacting with business users

This is one of the most crucial phases of any BI project. This phase involves spending time with end users, understanding the business challenges, and the goals of the function and organization at large.

Usually, it's not possible to get everything in a single meeting and several follow-up meetings will be required. Business users will fall in to various categories. There will be senior management, middle management, and regular users. Each of these profiles of business users will have different sets of expectations and KRAs. It's important to map all these users as their buy-in is important for a project's success.

Understanding the data sources

One of the reasons people look at implementing BI solutions is to have a single source of truth. The technological advancements have made data spread across different applications. It's important for the consultant to understand all the data sources. There could be Excel sheets, ERPs, cloud CRM, social media applications, big data, and legacy applications.

Qlik can usually connect to most of the data sources, but a recheck is important to ensure that it does. If a direct connection is not possible, alternate ways need to be explored. It could be as simple as taking CSV dump from that data source, or it could be using the SDK to write a custom connector.

Setting the expectations correctly

This is an often-neglected factor which later leads to disgruntlement among the users, and can lead to feeble adoption and project failures. It's important to discuss with the users what is possible and what is not. Any workarounds which are possible should also be discussed. If a non-Qlik solution is being used, the business users may be accustomed to the way the earlier software worked.

The way a functionality worked in earlier software may be different in Qlik. Alternately, a consultant may need to look at other ways to achieve the exact functionality using extension objects. All of these need to be discussed, so that the users know what to expect and you can avoid backlash at a later time. Most of the non-Qlik BI solutions are query based and the reports developed in such solutions may show near real-time data. The consultant should discuss these aspects as well and prioritize which data needs to be refreshed at frequent intervals and which can be done at a periodic intervals.

Designing the perfect solution

A perfect foundation is required to build a structurally strong building. Similarly, a consultant has a crucial role to play in planning the solution. The solution architecture must be robust, scalable, and flexible. One of the important reasons for lower adoption is poor performance. Business users will not have the patience to wait for data to be refreshed when they select something.

The consultant must take this into account and understand all the factors which affect performance. For multi-geographical deployments, ensure multi-node deployments. The business users are always paranoid about security aspects. Qlik is very good at governance and security, and offers powerful ways to meet the security requirements. Modeling and design also play important roles.

The UI should be simple and intuitive. Since Qlik is based on responsive HTML 5 design and offers single development for laptops and handhelds, the design too should be well-thought of to make it easy for the users to use in multiple form factors.

Plan the Go-live

The consultant must properly plan the Go-live stage. The users, being new to the system, will be anxious and will expect a lot of support. This part of the project can be made easy with a planned UAT phase.

The consultant takes care of the minutest details to ensure client satisfaction. Simple factors like single sign-on can make the initial experience satisfying for the users. The queries raised should be addressed as soon as possible. Make the documents/manuals easily accessible to the users. Users accessing during non-office hours should also be able to refer to the same.

Plan for the future road-map

This, too, is an important point which gets missed out. Organizations start with functions which are high priority for them and subsequently roll it out to other functions. A function that potentially has a large user base may not have been considered and then suddenly the architecture may run into performance issues.

The consultant must also make a note of the rate at which data is growing and plan accordingly. The Qlik platform approach makes it a very versatile solution, allowing it to be used as embedded analytics as well. Hence, the consultant must plan if the organization is wanting to extend analytics to external users.

A consultant carries huge responsibilities, as he/she must implement the solution from start to end. A consultant must get involved in all the phases of development.

Responsibilities of a consultant

The responsibilities of a consultant can be summarized as :

- Doing value adds
- Documentation
- Implementing best practices
- User Acceptance and Training (UAT)
- Post Go-live

Doing value adds

Business users broadly fall into two categories:

- Users who are new to Analytics
- Users who have been using an existing solution

The consultant must have different approaches for both the sets of users.

The consultant, while doing the requirement gathering, should also come up with suggestions which will be beneficial to the client. Any alternate approach which may better the end result should be proactively suggested. The value add should happen in UI aspects and even future road-maps.

Documentation

A great way to ensure that all major and minor points are noted is in the form of documentation. Documentation must happen in all the phases of projects. The consultant must ensure that he/she is prepared for requirement gathering stage by having a proper questionnaire.

This approach ensures nothing gets missed out. The requirements must be scoped, and if required, be broken into functional and technical parts. A project plan with timelines and a responsibility matrix helps both of the parties and avoids confusions. All prerequisites and system requirements from an infrastructure perspective should be documented and sent to the client.

A good approach is to run through the documents jointly with the concerned stakeholders and then take acceptance. Before the actual development starts, it's important for the consultant to ensure that he/she and the client are on the same page. The documentation part takes some time, but shouldn't be ignored or taken lightly. A consultant must ensure that timely communication is sent out to the client during the development phases and that regular reviews are done to avoid last minute surprises.

Implementing best practices

Once a solution has been designed and agreed to by the client, the implementation process starts. Implementation has various stages, including the installation of Qlik Sense software, connection to the data sources, data modeling, user interface, validation, and testing. Using the best practices plays an important role in the performance of the software and helps with ease of use. The best practices also improve the flexibility and help increase adoption.

Best practices include writing perfect logic to do incremental data loads. Incremental loads help with faster data refreshes and at same time ease the load on the source systems. If multiple options are available, choose the one which gives better performance; for example, if you have the option of using ODBC or OLEDB, choose OLEDB, as OLEDB gives better performance.

A good approach is to make development as modular as possible. This approach makes the code flexible and easily manageable. The data modeling should be optimized to ensure performance even with an increase in data volumes.

The UI is another critical piece which has a direct impact on how the end user perceives the software. Ensure the Qlik Sense application is neatly categorized and the **Dashboarding Analysis and Reporting (DAR)** approach is followed. A sheet should be pleasing to the eyes. Too many objects make it difficult for the end users to comprehend.

Aspects like comments in code and brief descriptions of logic shouldn't be ignored. Validation and test cases should be done thoroughly. Nothing irritates the user more than seeing incorrect data.

User Acceptance and Training (UAT)

Once the development is over, the crucial phase of **User Acceptance and Training** (**UAT**) starts. Just like a good trailer propels user interest and adds to the value of a movie, the UAT phase is where the consultant starts creating excitement in the end users. A lot of effort is required to make this phase successful.

A lot of time needs to be spent with the end users to make them comfortable. After validation from the consultant side, validation must also be undertaken by the end users. Any deviations should be noted and promptly fixed. Validations should be done thoroughly. Security aspects such as role based access, application rights, and data level security should be taken care of. On completion of the validation part, significant time should be allocated for user training.

The creation of an easy and user friendly manual must be done beforehand. Always remember that though you know the system thoroughly, the system is new for the user. Trainings should be conducted with small user sets. The size of batches for training should be such that every end user can be given attention. Record the sessions, thus making it easy for the user to refer back to it whenever required.

Simple, self-explanatory how-to videos (for example, how to make selection) make the user comfortable. Seeing a video is always easier than going through lengthy paragraphs! The training, if required, should be repeated. Ensure that the users are comfortable and can do the basic stuff easily. Allow the users to use it on both their laptops and handhelds. Also, publish a FAQ document.

Post Go-live

Once the project goes live, it's not the time to relax! This phase will decide the adoption of the software and the overall success of the project. Use the Qlik Monitoring application to check all critical parameters, such as System performance.

Ensure all reload jobs are executing properly and that users see the correct data. Look for users who aren't using the system. This can be infectious and spread to other users. Address their concerns and ensure a positive word spreads about the software. Plan an adoption strategy with the stakeholders.

At some organizations, the carrot and stick approach may be required. One good way to drive adoption is to ensure senior management uses it regularly; educate them on the benefits of doing their reviews on the Qlik application. Once the seniors start using the software, the other users are bound to start using it too. Identify your internal champion who will keep up the adoption drive once your job is over.

Qlik keeps releasing newer versions. Lot of times, new functionalities are introduced. A consultant must also plan for these upgrades. This gives an additional opportunity for the consultant to touch base with the end users by conducting a follow-up workshop/training.

Strategy that a consultant should follow

Though the topic mentions the strategy that a consultant should follow, in reality, there is no particular strategy which will work. Why is this so? Read on to find out.

Let's again use an analogy. Consider that three obese people, who wish to lose weight, go to a dietitian. Will the dietitian prescribe the same diet plan for all the three? The probability of this happening is very remote. Why? Simply because the same plan will not work for all three!

The dietitian must look at several parameters before he/she can decide the plan. The factors he/she has to look at could be the age of the person, BMI, height, weight, ethnicity, medical history, diet preferences, the temperament of the person, food allergies, and so on.

Only after doing this study will the dietitian be able to make a diet plan which suits the patient. The plan may have to be fine-tuned a few times once the dietitian gets feedback from the patient. The diet plan may have to be coupled with exercise plans to meet the objective of weight loss in a scientific manner.

The BI consultant also faces similar situations when he/she has to plan the strategy. Every organization is different, and so the same strategy will not work every time. Let's look at the parameters which can affect the strategy.

Size of the company

The size of company matters when deciding the BI strategy. A large organization is very different from a small organization. In a smaller organization, one person may perform multiple tasks. The C-level executives (CEO, CFO, COO, and CMO) can be accessed relatively easily. They will be willing to spend time with the consultant during the requirement gathering session, making the exercise simpler and faster.

Compare this to a large organization, and there is a huge level of hierarchy. The C-level executives are almost impossible to be reached. The people in the lower level of the hierarchy may have different thoughts, and hence, the consultant must spend a lot of time doing the requirement gathering sessions. The subsequent phases requiring user interaction will require a lot of detailing.

What system do they use currently?

How does this matter? It matters a lot because accordingly the approach and strategy of the consultant would vary. For example, a company which largely uses MS Excel would need a different approach; the users will be new to analytics, and hence the strategy for the roll-out would need to deliver a mix of analytics and reporting, and then gradually move to analytics.

The users of an organization who use a traditional BI system, like Business Objects, would already be exposed to some amount of Analytics, and so the excitement would be more towards data discovery and self-service. There could also be another category where the organizations are shifting from a new age BI solution, like Tableau or Power BI.

These will require different approaches and the users will largely be looking at bringing in multiple data sources and co-relations between different sources. The training for these different sets of users must be done according to the BI maturity levels.

Why do they want a new system?

This question is important, as the success of the project will depend on this. If the client is already using a BI system, there will be a strong reason to look for a change. The consultant needs to understand the bottlenecks faced by the end users and ensure that the new system overcomes them, and that it also delivers a lot of additional benefits.

What are the objectives and goals?

If the end user is not sure about the objectives and goals, the project is likely to suffer. Many a time, the users may not be able to express the requirements correctly. This is where the skill of a consultant will be tested thoroughly. The consultant has to ask the right questions and get the answers. It's best to proceed only when the objectives are clear.

Are the stakeholders identified?

No one likes to board a ship without a captain. Similarly, the stakeholders play an important role in the success of a project. There could be one stake holder or there could be multiple. The stake holder takes responsibility for a project from the client end and the consultant must work closely with the stake holder.

Is there a project champion?

A project champion is an important link in the BI cycle. The champion is usually the one who will get the credit for implementation of a project and who works very closely with the consultant to make the project successful. He/she helps the consultant to get interviews with the business users, helps to define the scope of the project, and plays an active part till the roll out. The champion becomes most valuable when the role of the consultant ends.

What are the data sources?

Though Qlik can connect to most of the data sources, this point is important. While planning a strategy for known data sources, such as SAP, Navision, or say, Oracle Business Suite, these being known data sources, there is a good amount of predictability. However, some customers have legacy applications or custom developed applications. The consultant needs to be aware of the potential challenges these systems may throw and plan the strategy accordingly.

Is the data clean?

Clean data is a consultant's delight. This helps with implementation, and even the validation process gets easy. The challenge usually comes when the data is not clean and the consultant must also work on the strategy to clean the data.

Future road map

The consultant needs to know if the project will be extended to other functions in the future, whether external people will also be a part of it in the future, and whether any additional data sources are being planned. The solution design can be bettered once the consultant gets these details.

Summary

In this chapter, we looked at some important aspects. The BI market is looking extremely upbeat, and as more and more businesses start adopting analytics in a big way, the need for a trusted advisor who can help organizations in their analytical journeys, is strongly felt.

The chapter looked at understanding who a consultant is and the various aspects of consultancy. We also looked at the roles and responsibilities of a consultant. We also looked at strategies a consultant must adopt for a successful project.

The analogies provided in the chapter try to make you understand, in simple terms, the importance of being a consultant. The main intention of writing this chapter is to make you aware of the larger picture, and to help them understand the need to look at progressing to the role of a consultant.

Now that you have an idea about being a consultant, it's time to move to the next level. A good preparation is important for you to be successful. The next chapter will focus on how a consultant can prepare himself/herself for a project.

2
Preparing for the Project

In the previous chapter, we talked about defining a consultant. We also looked at why consultants are valued and what a client expects from a consultant.

This chapter is about the importance of preparing for a project. Before starting, let me put before you some powerful quotes:

> *A man who does not plan long ahead will find trouble at his door.*
> *-Confucius*

> *By failing to prepare, you are preparing to fail.*
> *-Benjamin Franklin*

> *Planning is a process of choosing among those many options. If we do not choose to plan, then we choose to have others plan for us.*
> *-Richard I. Winwood*

These quotes may have been made several years ago, but they still hold true. A very critical aspect of the project, often neglected, is the preparatory phase. This is the phase where a consultant should invest a good amount of his/her time.

In our childhood, we heard about the story of two wood cutters. Though the nature of work was the same for both, the first wood cutter had an efficiency problem. The first wood cutter initially was able to cut a lot of trees. As time progressed, his efficiency came down drastically. The second wood cutter kept on cutting the same number of trees. This was perplexing to the first wood cutter, and when he approached the second wood cutter to understand the reason, a simple question from the second wood cutter was an eye opener. You must know the question. For readers who may not be aware, the question was--When was the last time you sharpened your axe?

Similarly, sports enthusiasts would agree that a sports person doesn't jump into a game directly. If we take an example of a runner, never will a champion jump into a track and start competing. Experts strongly advocate a warm-up routine before you start your run. What is the reason for this?

If a runner starts running without a warm-up, there are huge risks of damage to the body, in the form of injuries like muscle breakdown or torn ligaments. The warm-up routine prepares an athlete's body. The muscles get stretched and joints are exercised. This helps the runner perform better.

Great people always prepare and practice hard. When you prepare well, you mitigate the uncertainties. Your confidence levels go up and your approach becomes extremely positive. The customer, too, can sense this, and becomes more cooperative. These preparatory steps also help you to do value additions.

We urge you to inculcate this habit of preparation before the actual work starts. Over the course of the next few pages, let's look a bit in-depth at how a consultant can prepare himself/herself. The topics we will cover are:

- Knowing about the company
- Understanding the existing landscape
- Understanding organizational hierarchy
- Knowing what to study and prepare
- Identifying your champion

Knowing about the company

An important step in preparation is spending time understanding your customer better. Unless this happens, you will be delivering a standard project and nothing more.

> *You can acquire some measure of knowledge from various research techniques, but nothing beats living, breathing, and feeling the same things your prospect (customers) do.*
> *-John Jantsch*

Every company has a different way of functioning. Since businesses are extremely dynamic; lots of companies keep adapting themselves. A consultant must be aware of how a particular industry functions.

Let's take an example. If your client is from an insurance industry, it's important to know how the insurance industry is performing and what direction it is taking. Are there any announcements which are going to change the dynamics? Is there any new government order in pipeline that may alter the functioning? A consultant must be aware of all this.

Though analytics spread across various functions, companies will start with areas which are important to them. Taking the preceding example, if there is a new regulatory compliance which needs to be adhered to, the energy of the company will be focused on implementing that. If the compliance requires certain data to be sent across to the regulatory body, the company will try to get that information set to be made available in the dashboard first.

Try to understand all these factors so that you are better prepared and can relate to the client requirements. This also helps to build the initial trust the client has in you, and the business users in the organization then become comfortable discussing their requirements.

Understanding the existing landscape

One of the important aspects a consultant must look at is about the existing landscape. When we say landscape, it essentially means understanding how the client is managing analytics currently. It also means understanding the existing datasources and the existing BI tools. It also means understanding why the company is looking at changing their software. Let us look at each of these.

Existing data sources

Knowing the existing **data sources** helps you to plan better. It is good to know all the data points. It does matter if the systems are known software or are custom built. Known software are easier to tackle, but custom or legacy applications can pose lot of challenges. For known software which the consultant may not have encountered, it's a good idea to go through available documentation and try to get as familiar as possible. Let's take an example of a consultant who is new to an application, like **Salesforce**. He/she can study the documentation and look at the ER(entity relations) diagrams to understand different objects and relationships.

An example of the sales objects of Salesforce is given next:

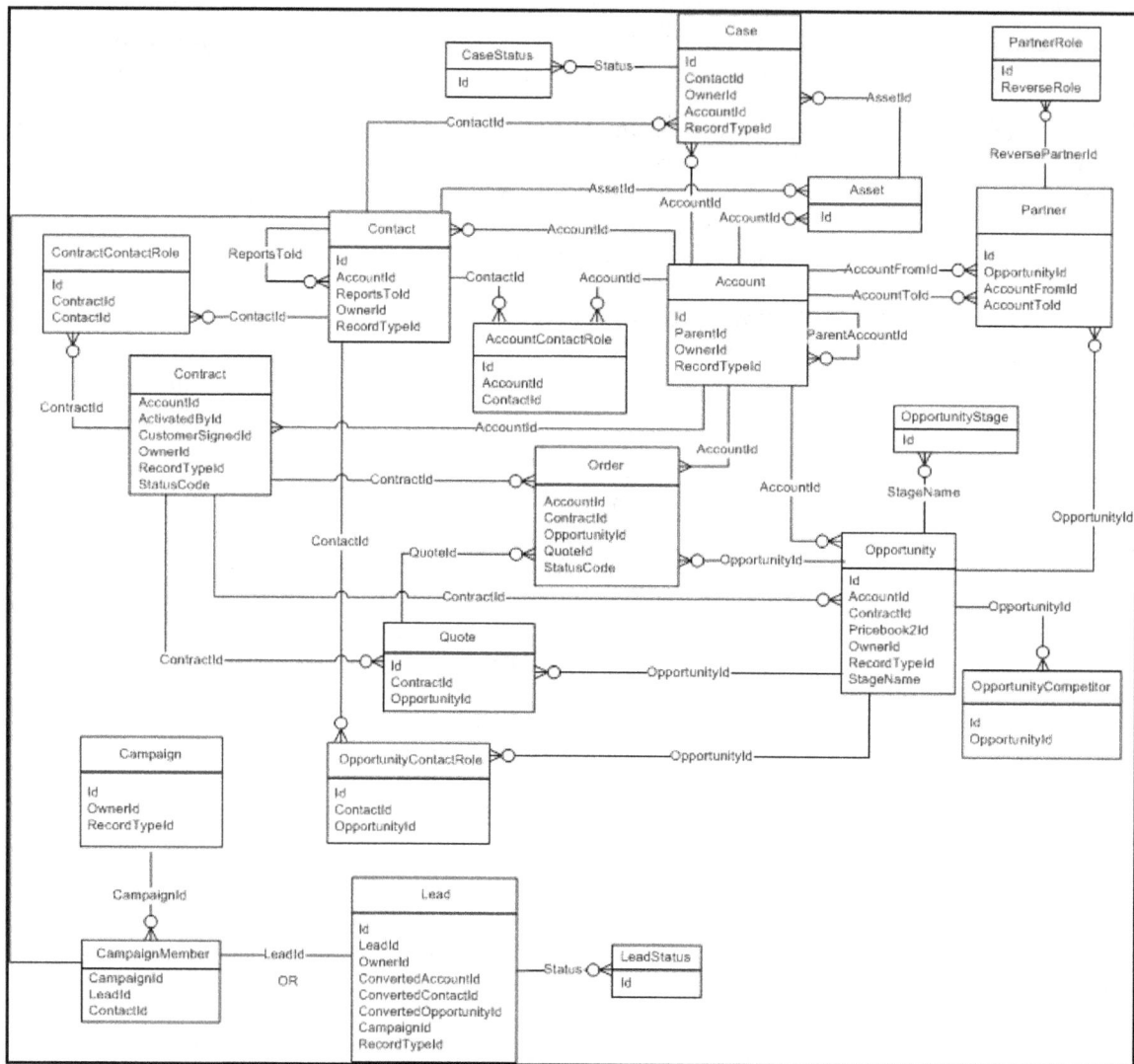

ER diagram for Salesforce

You can find more on this at https://developer.salesforce.com/docs/
resources/img/en-us/206.0?doc_id=dev_
guides%2Fapi%2Fimages%2FSforce_major_objects.pngfolder=api

If a consultant studies this diagram, he/she can easily become familiar with the new system. This also familiarizes him/her with terms like leads, accounts, and contacts, for when business users talk about them. The consultant can similarly look at other applications and start preparing and getting accustomed. We will try to cover some frequently used applications which a consultant may often encounter.

Let's take a look at some of the most commonly used applications:

- Customer relation management (CRM)
- Help desk applications
- Human resource systems
- Enterprise resource planning
- Social media
- Data-warehouses
- Miscellaneous

Customer Relation Management

These applications usually take care of **Sales** and **Marketing**. You should have some basic understanding of these software when you interact with the Sales and Marketing functions. Some of the commonly used software are:

- Salesforce
- Microsoft CRM
- SugarCRM
- Oracle Fusion CRM
- Other CRMs (VTiger, Siebel, Talisma, and Zoho)

Help desk applications

These applications are post sales and take care of service related issues. Knowledge of these applications is required when you interact with customer support and service functions.

Commonly used support applications are:

- Zen Desk
- Lan Desk
- Service Cloud

- ManageEngine Service Desk
- Other software (Desk.com, Kayako, FreshService, and Vision)

Qlik has ready connectors to a lot of these applications. Some of the applications are on cloud only, while some are available both on-premise and on cloud. If ready connector is not available, the consultant can plan alternate mechanisms, like the Rest API or SOAP API, to connect and extract data.

Human resource systems

This software is used for employee management. The usage covers recruitment and on-boarding, payroll, rewards, and performance management. Other non-core HR systems also fall under HR, such as **Learning Management Systems (LMS)**. The following are some of the prominent HR software:

- Success Factors
- SAP
- Oracle
- HRMS
- Cornerstone
- SABA

These systems can be connected via OLEDB/ODBC connectors. Some cloud based systems can be connected via REST/SOAP API.

Enterprise Resource Planning

Enterprise Resource Planning (ERP) is the core application for most of the companies. Some companies use all modules covering all functions in ERP. Alternatively, some modules may be used from other companies. We recommend that the consultant gets familiar with them. Some of the popular ERPs are:

- SAP
- Oracle
- Microsoft (Navision and Dynamics)
- Others (Infor, JD Edwards, Sage, and Lawson)

Qlik has connectors for SAP. Other applications can be connected via traditional OLEDB/ODBC connectors. Cloud based apps can be connected via APIs.

Social media

Social media has become an important data source for many companies. With the explosion of social media, customers are more expressive online, and hence it becomes all the more reason for companies to know what the customers are saying there. Some commonly used social media apps are:

- Facebook
- LinkedIn
- Twitter
- Google Analytics
- YouTube

Customers will also want sentiment analysis to understand customers better. Qlik has multiple connectors to connect and extract data from these sources.

Data warehouses

Data warehouses make the job of a consultant simpler. The data warehouse is generally used in large organizations. It is designed to get data from all the sources in a company and make it available for reporting and analytical software. The data warehouses are denormalized and meant for **Online Analytical Processing (OLAP)**. Some of the leading systems are:

- Terrada
- Netezza
- Vertica
- Actian

The data warehouse helps the consultant to get all the organizational data from one single source. The validation phase also becomes easier in customers have invested in a data warehouse.

Miscellaneous

Apart from commonly used applications, there are custom developed applications and lots of applications which are domain specific. It's not possible to list all of them, but some of them are:

- Microsoft Excel
- Accounting (QuickBook, Tally, Freshbooks, and so on)
- Core banking applications (Finacle, Flexcube, BaNCS, and so on)
- Insurance applications (CSC, Policy Works, and so on)
- SIEM (ArcSight, QRadar, and Khika)
- Bigdata (Hadoop, Cassandra, and MongoDb)

Existing BI systems

Just like it's good for a doctor to study the medical history of a patient before prescribing a medicine, a consultant must be aware of the existing BI systems being used.

If a doctor is not aware of the medical history, it can be dangerous. The patient may be allergic to certain drugs or the prescription may need to be altered if the patient has high blood sugar or high blood pressure. If the patient is already on medication, a prescription may have adverse reactions if the doctor hasn't taken due diligence.

The existing BI software can be traditionally broken down further.

Manual reporting

Manual reporting is still prevalent in many companies. Yes, we too were initially surprised! The top management of such companies is used to someone preparing reports in Excel and sending them over email. Excel is quite a powerful tool and can show some graphical reports.

The consultant must treat such companies in a different way, as the exposure of the business users to analytical systems will be limited. From what we have experienced in such organizations, a good approach is to automate the reporting process and then gradually move to analytics.

Traditional BI tools

Traditional BI tools are found in many companies and are largely used for operational reporting. A lot of companies that are using earlier versions of ERP will have these tools. Some of the notable traditional BI tools are **Business Objects, Microsoft SSRS, Crystal Reports,** and **Cognos.**

These tools are query based and are heavily dependent on the IT team. They are difficult to customize and may become slow over the years. Normally, you will find hundreds of reports which have been developed by IT. These tools are prone to lower adoption over time and make business users usually switch to Excel. They prefer taking dumps (or exporting data) and preparing reports in Excel. These users have a reporting and analytical background, and are going to be looking at the next level. The consultant must work out a different approach in such companies. The approach needs to be based on the usage and expectations of the users.

Next generation tools

The next generation tools are more graphical and extremely analytical. The objectives of these next generation tools are **data discovery** and **self service.** They have collaboration capabilities. Mobility, too, is an important aspect which a lot of these types of tools provide.

Some of the prevalent tools are **Qlik, Tableau, Microsoft Power BI, Lumira, Tibco**, and a few more.

The way every tool works is different and architecture varies a lot. These tools are now being looked at very keenly. Right implementation of such tools will be most challenging for the consultant.

The challenges will vary with each customer, and even with the type of tool the company uses. The best approach in such a circumstance is to get into the details of the reason a client is wanting to do a switch to Qlik. Each reason must be carefully studied and the consultant must be prepared to address them all in the Qlik solution he/she will develop.

Understanding the need for change

This is the most crucial aspect a consultant must look at. Spend a good amount of time in studying the reasons why client is looking to change the BI software. These parameters will be crucial aspects of your project's success.

If a company wants to change to a newer system, the reasons can be many. They can vary depending on the existing system. Let's look at some of them now.

Challenges with manual reporting

Manual reporting, as mentioned in an earlier section, is largely based on Excel reports. Substantial efforts are required by the **Management Information System (MIS)** team in preparing the reports. These efforts are repetitive in nature, depending on whether there are daily, weekly, monthly, quarterly, or yearly reports.

Because the reports are manual, there are chances of human errors creeping in and the numbers being wrong, thus giving the wrong picture to the senior management. The downside could be incorrect decisions, leading to losses.

The other challenge with this approach is the amount of time taken to prepare the reports. By the time the management gets the reports, a significant amount of time has elapsed and the data is not current and may even be two or three weeks old. This also hampers an effective decision making process.

As data starts growing, the performance of Excel drops. Vlookups, if used, take several hours to complete and may fail to complete leading to repetitive work. As an organization grows, the number of Excel sheets starts becoming unmanageable and can lead to chaos.

Organizations pay a lot of attention to security of data these days. Excel sheets have very limited security, and the information which is meant for certain users may knowingly/unknowingly go to unintended audiences.

Another downside is that the manual approach becomes people dependent and any absenteeism or attrition causes further delays. There could be other reasons for the company to look for a new system as well, and the consultant must understand them.

Challenges with traditional reporting

Traditional systems are better than manual systems. They are not people dependent and the reasons why a company is looking for a new solution will vary.

Most of the traditional systems are query based systems. Over time, as data size grows, the query based tool takes more time to fetch data and a report which used to take few seconds to open starts taking several minutes to open. The business users will not have too much patience to wait for a report to open. Assuming that they do wait for a report to open, once they see the report, they may need to open a few more reports to start analyzing. If the overall time shoots up, the business users are unlikely to use the systems.

Businesses have become dynamic. The traditional dashboards were developed when requirements were different. As time progresses, business users' requirements change, too. Traditional systems are complex and heavily IT dependent. The change request may take several weeks or months to develop, and by the time the reports are ready, it's likely that the requirements have changed again.

Business users today consider mobility an important parameter. Many of the business applications are available on mobile, and this improves productivity. The users expect analytics to also be available on mobile. The traditional systems may not be capable of delivery analytics over mobile. In case some of them do, any changes needed by business users consumes humongous time.

Self-service and advanced analytics are becoming important for the users, too, and so the companies are looking out for newer systems.

The consultant must be aware of all the factors which are making the companies change to newer system, and prepare accordingly.

Challenges with new age tools

Companies which have shifted to new age tools may still have some challenges, thus hindering adoption and making users shift back to Excel. The reasons can be multiple; a consultant needs to be aware of the limitations of the other tools to better understand the reasons.

One common challenge the companies face in the absence of a data warehouse is that some new age tools struggle to connect to multiple sources and bring data in single dashboard. One example we can think of is that when companies have a sales information in CRM tool, finance information is on another system, and some information may be in Microsoft Excel. For example, the budget may be in Excel and the actual revenue in CRM. The customer order information may be in CRM and the account receivables in ERP. The users want to see a consolidated dashboard. The dashboard needs data from all the sources. If the business users are unable to get this information (for example, Budget vs Actual, customer-wise dues outstanding) in a single dashboard, their purpose will not be served.

Some of the new age systems may be unable to connect to certain applications due to a lack of connectors and will need constant manual intervention to covert data in a readable format. There could be some functionality which is important for the users but the tool is unable to deliver it. An example could be mapping and geo-analytics.

Large organizations may be a mix of analytical and non-analytical users. They may want the tool to have reporting capabilities as they may not be able to give licenses to all the users.

Other reasons could be the customer looking for advanced analytics, like statistical analysis and predictive analysis, which the tool is not capable of. As mentioned earlier, this scenario is one of the most challenging aspects for a consultant and he/she should look at it very carefully.

Understanding organizational hierarchy

We briefly covered this in the Chapter 1, *Consultant - An Introduction*. Let's look at why this can be a make or break situation for a consultant. A consultant needs to work with several functions in an organization. Every organization will have a hierarchy for each of these functions. A hierarchy is a structure in an organization where each level has a different role and responsibility. The hierarchy often reflects the different decision-making structures. The following is an example of the Sales hierarchy for a **Multi-National Company** (**MNC**):

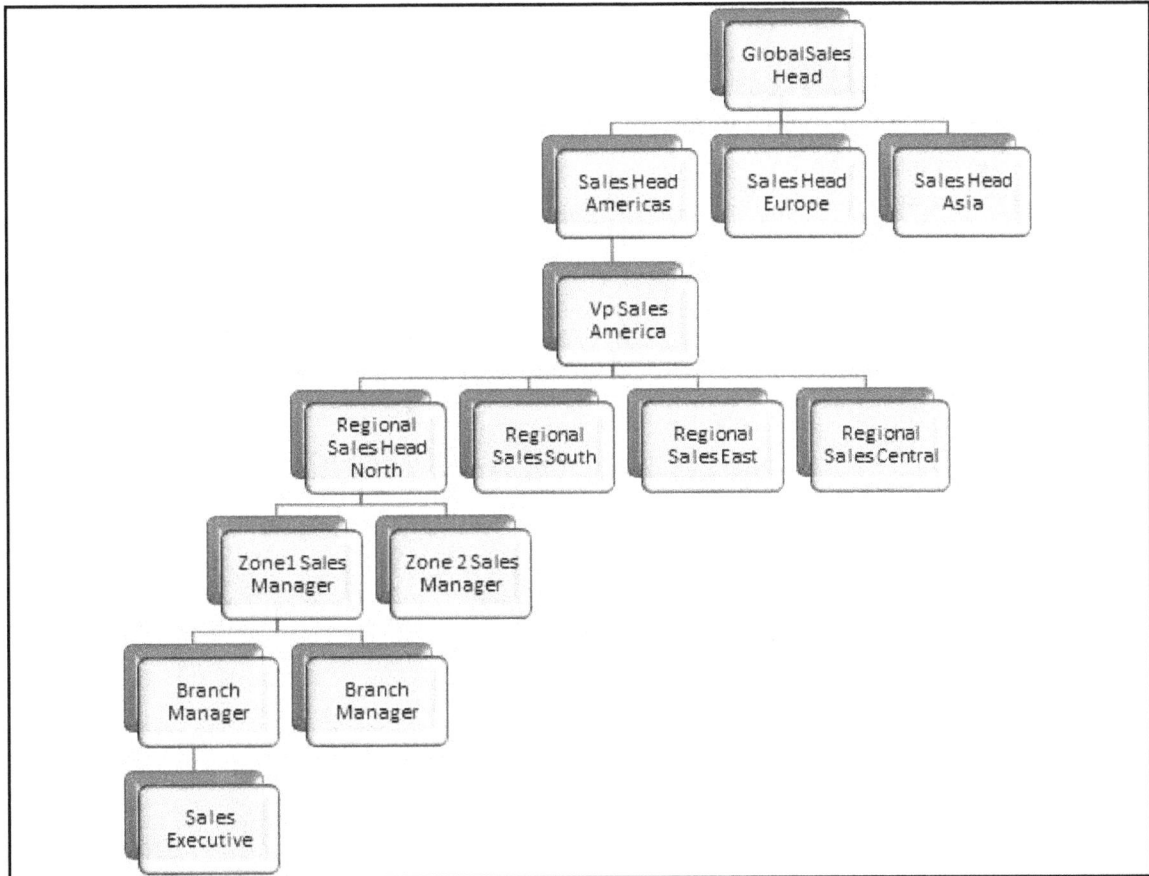

Sales hierarchy for a MNC

If we look at preceding figure, it shows the Sales hierarchy for a large MNC. Though self-explanatory, we will try to cover in brief the different people involved. The structure is partial as it only covers America. The others, Europe and Asia, will also have similar hierarchies. The following is a brief explanation of the hierarchy:

- **Global Sales Head**: He/she looks at the entire organization's sales and is responsible for delivering the sales revenue targets.
- **Sales Head Americas**: He/she looks at the American continent sales. So, this person is responsible for sales in America, Canada, and Latin American countries.
- **VP Sales America**: He/she looks at the entire sales in the United States of America.

- **Regional Manager**: A country is divided into several regions and there is a person to manage each of these regions.
- **Zonal Manager**: A region is further divided into several smaller zones and each zone is managed by one person.
- **Branch Manager**: Each of these zones has several branch offices and each office has a branch manager.
- **Sales Executive**: Each of these branches has several sales executives who interact with the end consumers.

Now that we have seen who the users are in the sales function, let us now bifurcate them into various levels. This is called a **pyramid structure** in an organization. Let's see how we can depict this in the form of a diagram:

Pyramid Depiction of Organization Roles

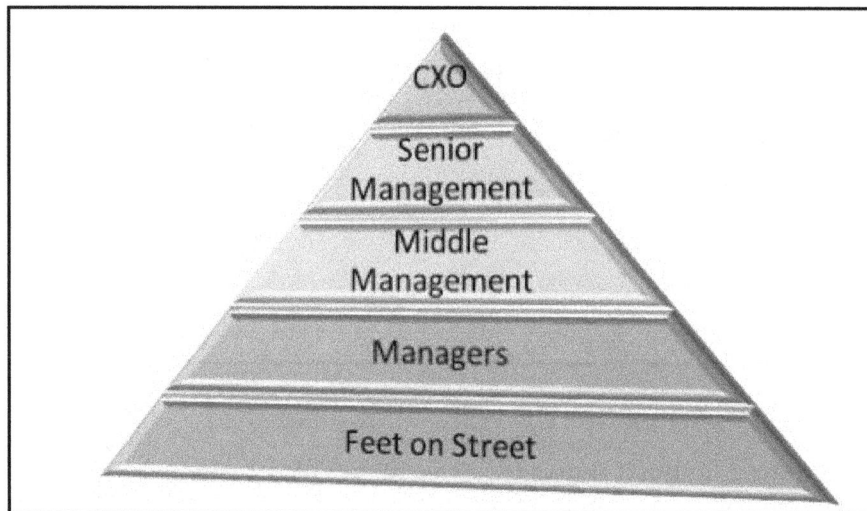

Organization pyramid

The preceding figure explains the hierarchy in the context of an organizational pyramid. The pyramid puts people from Sales Hierarchy in various roles. What the pyramid essentially shows is how the organization classifies different people and bifurcates the roles and responsibilities.

Let us look at each of the layers in the pyramid, from bottom to top:

- **Feet on Street**: They form a large chunk of sales functions. These people are the ones who interact the most with the customers. The organization may or may not consider them as analytical users. Co-relating with *Figure 02*, we can say that this layer maps largely with sales executives.

- **Managers**: These are the people who manage teams of sales executives. They are usually considered for analytical purposes, and some of them could be people whom the consultant interacts with during the requirement gathering phase. Co-relating with *Sales Hierarchy* figure, we can say that this layer maps largely with branch managers.

- **Middle Management**: The middle management is an important link between the senior management and the manager level in the pyramid. These people are analytical users for sure. This layer plays an important role in strategy executions and also plays a role in providing inputs which help in defining the strategies. Co-relating with *Sales Hierarchy* figure, we can say that this layer largely maps with zonal managers and regional managers.

- **Senior Management**: The senior management includes key people in the pyramid. These people are the ones largely responsible for the sales revenues in their respective countries and continents. They are key analytical users and it's important for the consultant to vet all the requirements from them. These people are influencers and can drive adoption. When we look at *Figure 02*, we can associate the VP sales, the continental head, and the global sales head with this layer of the pyramid.

- **Top Management (CXO)**: The top management comprises of CXO (typically, the Chief Executive Officer, the Chief Financial Officer, and the Chief Operating Officer). They form the top most layer and are responsible for the overall functioning of the company. This layer comprises of users across various functions, like Sales, Marketing, Human Resources, Operations, Supply Chain, Plant Operations, and Finance. The consultant will have to treat these users separately. They will have different sets of requirements, and usually the consultants will have to build a CXO dashboard for these sets of users.

The reason for explaining this in detail is to make the consultant aware of the different users who will be using the software. A generic approach may not work, as the needs of people in every layer of the pyramid will be different.

The way they look at data is also different, as the roles and responsibilities change across the layers. The consultant must also look at how he/she can provide information to the lower levels of the pyramid if the organization does not have budgets to extend licenses to all the users.

A consultant should remember that the lower layers in the pyramid are also equally important. If the company is not able to give licenses to everyone, the consultant can work on alternate mechanisms. Qlik NPrinting is a good option in such cases, since the information required at these layers can be disseminated easily by sending out reports via email.

What you need to study and prepare

The basic and crucial factor you need for preparation is the study of the website of your client. These days, the websites are very detailed and a lot of messaging is conveyed by them.

Studying a website helps you understand the nature of the business, the products/services the client sells, and the geographies in which it is present. Go through all the sections of the website in detail. The vision and mission statements will give you an idea of what the company is wanting to be. Make notes, and this will help you ask relevant questions in the requirement gathering phase.

> *The first step in exceeding your customer's expectations is to know those expectations.*
> *- Roy H. Williams*

Look at the preceding quote. How can you achieve this? Preparation is the key again. As you go through the website, look at the management team. Go through the profile of each of them. Some of them would be the stake holders and it's critical to know what their thought process is. Try to search which organizations they have worked with before and how they helped their earlier companies grow. These points can be used to break the ice when you meet these key people.

Social media can be an effective way to know about them. You can look at their Twitter handle to understand their goals. Go through the interviews which are published. You are sure to find some key points about what they want to do and what matters to them the most.

Identifying your champion

Another crucial link for a consultant is to identify a project champion. A project champion is someone from the customer organization. Let's look at what a project champion does in a BI project:

- Gives you an overview
- Helps you in understanding organizational hierarchy
- Helps you to identify organizational goals and objectives
- Helps you to identify and meet key people
- Helps you in defining KPI and helps in getting sign-offs
- Helps to set the right expectations in the project
- Helps you to understand the business challenges
- Helps you to identify factors driving business adoption
- Helps you to define success factors
- Helps in the UAT phase
- Drives the BI initiative after the consultant's role is over

As you can see, a project champion plays a critical role. For a project champion, rolling out the BI solution could be the most important factor, and a KRA, to help him grow in the organization.

A champion may not always be present, and a consultant may have to identify a suitable person and convert him/her to a champion. This is again a challenge, but can be met once a consultant starts meeting business users. The champion could have an, analytical background, or not, if a company is largely in the manual reporting category.

A consultant must work closely with the champion to ensure success.

Summary

This chapter focused on the importance of preparing for the project and explained the reasons why preparation is extremely important for a consultant before he/she starts actual work.

The chapter also covered what kinds of preparations a consultant must undertake. It's good for a consultant to know about the company, how it operates, and its goals and objectives.

We also looked at how a consultant should understand the different types of business users and the roles they play. The other aspects we looked at are important for a consultant in terms of understanding the data sources and various tools the client uses. The chapter also focused on what challenges the companies usually face, and lastly, the importance of a project champion and why it's important to work closely with him/her.

In the next chapter, we will look at the prerequisites before a consultant can start his/her work. We will also look at scoping a project and planning for risks.

3
Prerequisites to Start a Project

In the previous chapter, we looked at aspects relating to preparing for a project. In case you skipped the chapter, we recommend going through it before reading this chapter. It is intended to do the preparatory work which will be put to effective use.

In this chapter, we focus on prerequisites for a project. Prerequisites are important for both the client and the consultant. This is the crucial link after your preparatory steps and before you start the actual work with detailed requirement gathering.

Similar to how one is supposed to look at prerequisites before installing software (to avoid installation failures), look at the prerequisites for a project below before starting. The topics which we will cover in this chapter are:

- Understanding the business process
- Gathering requirements in brief
- Risk and mitigation plan
- Documentation
- Example

Understanding business process

In the previous chapter (Chapter 2, *Preparing for a Project*), we touched upon the importance of going through the client's website as a preparatory step. Completing this preparatory step will help you to get the details of how the client's business operates and help you understanding their business process easily.

Before we start, for readers who may be unfamiliar, business process is nothing more than the way a company functions to meet its business objectives. Every organization is formed with some purpose and is meant to achieve certain things. One of the definite objectives is making profits.

An organization can be big or small, and have its own way of doing business. If we take two companies, say A and B in a similar industry, it's quite likely that the way sales are done in Company A will be very different from the way they are done in Company B. The reasons could be multiple.

So, what does a consultant need to know? The answer can't be explained in a single sentence. Let's briefly look at the various functions in an organization and touch upon some aspects.

Looking at the sales function

Though considered simple, sales can be one of the most complicated functions. Companies can be divided into different categories. There are multiple models which are explained next. Refer to the following *Sales mechanism* figure and its explanation thereafter:

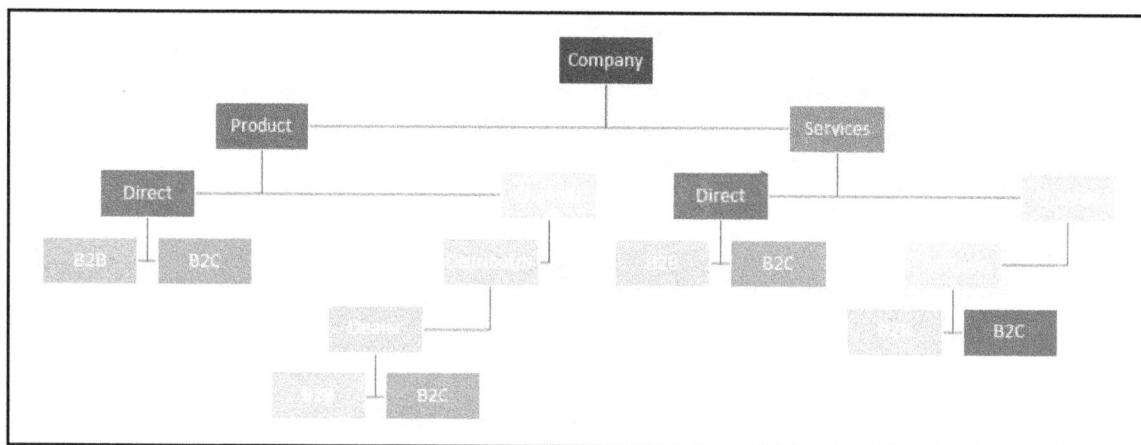

Sales mechanism

Business to business

Business to business is often referred to as **B2B**. The companies that are in B2B space sell to other companies and not to individual customers. Examples of these types of organizations can be software companies such as Qlik or companies such as Boeing, who manufacture airplanes. We can divide B2B type of businesses into further sub-sections. Let's have a look.

Direct sales

Direct sales is the model where an organization sells directly to another organization. To cite an example, Boeing may sell directly to Lufthansa.

Indirect sales

Indirect sales is the model where an organization sells to a distributor or a business partner. The distributors/business partners in turn sell to end users in an organization. There could be one more level, wherein the distributor sells to a partner and then the partner to their clients. An example for this model can be Qlik selling to a partner and the partner in turn selling to an organization.

Business to consumer

Business to consumer is also referred to as **B2C**. This set of companies sell to the end customers (or individuals). In this scenario the organization will have to cater to a substantial number of customers and the model will be slightly different compared to B2B.

The selling mechanism can be similarly divided into further sub-sections.

Direct sales

This is the mode in which an organization sells directly to consumers. An example can be an organization running an e-commerce platform for the end customer to login and buy directly.

Indirect sales

In this model, a company sells to a distributor. The distributor sells to a store and the store to an end consumer. The easiest example to relate to this can be of a perfume manufacturer who sells to a distributor. The distributor sells to a perfume store and finally you, as a consumer, get the perfume from the store.

Mixed mode

Mixed mode is where companies have both models of B2B and B2C. There are several examples for this. One example which we can relate to is that of a financial institution like a bank. Banks can do business with companies and consumers. They usually have a corporate division and a retail division. The sales can happen both directly and indirectly. The indirect way is sales by agents who sell on behalf of the bank to the end consumer.

Companies can also be categorized on the basis of what they sell. Let's look at this in the next section.

Product companies

These companies sell products. The products can be anything: software, hardware, automobiles, machines, pencils, or anything similar. Product companies look at different sets of parameters when it comes to matters of profitability, sales, growth, and so on.

As explained earlier, a product company can be B2B or B2C, and can do its business in both direct and indirect ways.

Services companies

These companies provide services that a lot of products need. Some examples which we can relate to easily are software development and customization services. Others are automobile garages, electrical services, transportation services, and other similar ones.

The services can be provided to both companies and individuals.

Product and services mix

There could be some organizations that offer both product and services. An example could be of a company that manufactures a machine and also provides installation and maintenance services. This can be true for software companies that sell software and provide implementation and customization services.

New age companies

This set of companies can't be classified into the previously defined categories. So we define them as new age companies. They can be companies such as Uber, who are **aggregators**. They are neither selling a product nor are they doing pure services. They are providing a platform for the end customer to hire services from cab drivers.

Given this background, what should a consultant explore? The consultant must understand the process of how these companies sell and what methods they follow. This is a must to enable a consultant to understand the flow and to know what the parameters are, which can make a difference to an organization.

We recommend you engage with the customer to get into the finer details. The consultant must be ready to understand what an organization is looking for from **Business Intelligence (BI)** and how these parameters affect the sales.

As a consultant, you must also do value-adds and help your client get the best from the BI project. A simple example can be the use of Qlik DataMarket for a company which has multiple outlets. The data available from Qlik DataMarket can help your clients to bring in demographic or weather data. This data can enrich the clients existing data and help them take better business decisions. In this example, looking at the demographics, the economic data will help the company to decide on the feasibility of opening a new store.

Even for a simple sales process, a consultant can make a big difference. A good implementation can help the client to improve forecasting, perform up-selling and cross-selling, focus on regions which are weak, or identify which sales people are better equipped to sell a product. The consultant should help the client in utilizing Qlik's biggest strength, namely, using Qlik for data-discovery and for helping make better decisions.

Understanding finance

Finance and sales are usually the early adopters of **Business Intelligence (BI)** software. So we will describe these two functions in detail.

Finance is an important function in any organization and it performs multiple functions. They play a big role in budgeting, planning, and forecasting. Another important area which the `finance` function looks at is streamlining cash flow.

Finance also focuses on expenditure and spend management. Risk and compliance is another parameter which can make or break companies. Finance looks at **accounts payable (AP)** and **accounts receivables (AR)** as well.

Let us look at these areas briefly.

Financial planning

Unless the finances are planned and budgeted, an organization will find it very difficult to continue normal operations. There are several **General Ledgers** (**GL**) which need to be managed. Identifying key trends will help in better forecasting. The budgets can also be planned accordingly.

A consultant must help the finance guys by doing value adds. Building dashboards which highlight the trends, and identifying forecasts and variations will help the companies to plan better. You can also think of including **what-if** analysis to help the cause. Predictive analysis will also take this to the next level.

Spend analytics

The biggest KRA for a finance professional is to reduce expenditure, thereby helping the company grow and improving profitability in a big way.

Expenditure occurs in several areas, such as salaries, travel, hotel stays, operational costs, mobiles, food, and several others. This too is spread across various departments. It's important to understand how the expenditure has happened in the past and identify the areas where savings can be made.

The consultant can help to highlight the parameters easily for the finance professionals. Value addition can happen by collating external data with internal data. An example can be understanding market trends for airfares and comparing it with how the company is spending.

A consultant can also help the companies bargain better with hotels, airlines, and other vendors. Once the companies start seeing trends and can commit certain business volume, it will help them get better prices. Non-budgeted expenditures often cause financial plans to go haywire and all this can easily be managed via analytics.

Cash flow management

Maintaining working capital and cash flow is very important in the day-to-day working of any company. The important areas of maintaining cash flow are **account receivables** (**AR**) and **account payables** (**AP**). To explain in simple terms, AR is managing the income and AP is the expenditure.

The consultant must enable the finance professionals to easily get this information and make this analysis extremely simple for end users.

A private company may also decide to go public. This calls for a huge exercise and involves several external entities, such as lead managers, underwriters, registrars, and investment bankers. Analytics play an important role in such a scenario.

Decisions involving pricing and stake dilutions call for analysis on several parameters and requires lot of slice and dice. External data can also play a big role in deciding the timing and other economic factors which can make an **Initial Public Offering** (**IPO**) a success.

A consultant must be aware of such scenarios and be prepared to provide next level analytics to make it very easy for the companies.

Profitability analysis

Profitability and revenue management is another area which finance looks keenly at. There are some common overlaps with the `sales` function in revenue management.

Profitability analysis can become very cumbersome in the absence of a system, since the data can be huge and can come from multiple sources. Companies always look to improve profitability. Improving margins can help this. Market dynamics and competition also play key roles in this.

Consultants should help the finance guys with what-if analysis and predictive analysis, and help to make decisions easy for end users. Again, external data can help enrich internal data. External data, such as geographic competition and product wise information, can help the companies perform better analysis.

Risk and compliance

Managing compliance is very important for finance. Listed companies must be very stringent in adhering to compliance. Mistakes can lead to loss of reputation and penalties.

Maintaining transparency becomes very important and helps build auditor and investor confidence. Mitigating risk helps the companies prepare for contingencies. A consultant must help the clients get all of this information at their fingertips.

Understanding human resources

Human resources (HR) is the department which has to manage employee related matters. This function becomes important from the perspective that employees make a company.

The HR function has to look at several important aspects (refer to *HR flows and functions* figure). Let's look at some of them:

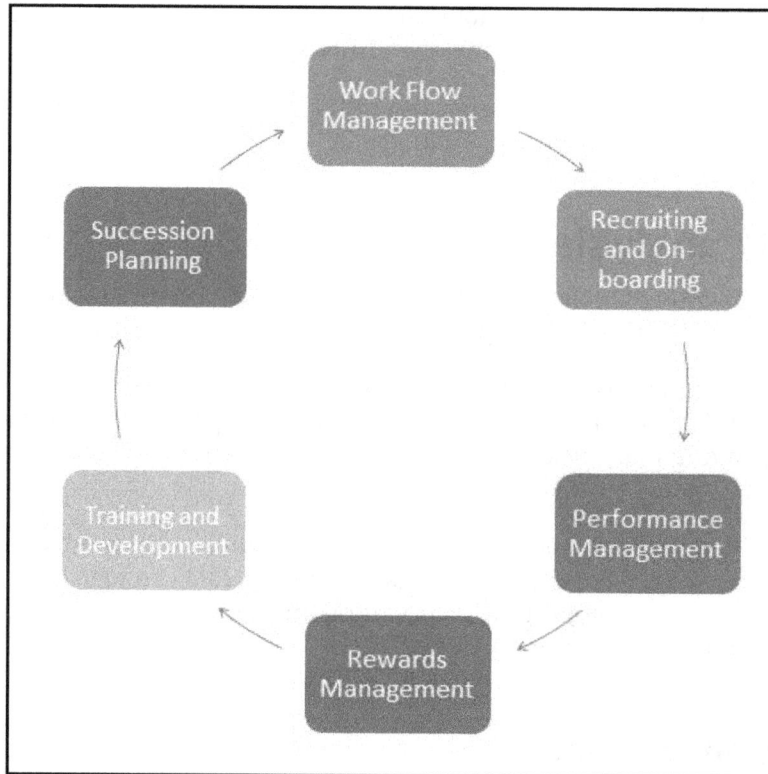

HR flow and functions

Hiring and on-boarding

Employee handling and managing attrition have become very important for the HR function. HR must be able to manage an effective work force. Forecasting becomes crucial to have optimum employee strength. HR should also be able to effectively analyze which of the hiring channels is most productive.

Succession planning is one area which, if not taken care of, can lead to lacuna in the organization. This becomes all the more important for senior management positions. If not planned in advance, there could be a large gap in finding an alternative, and by the time on-boarding happens, several months may just have been lost.

Similarly, attrition analysis is also another important area. A higher the attrition rate doesn't augur well for a company. HR must analyze the reasons if attrition rate is high.

Maintaining diversity, that is having right balance of age groups and gender ratio, plays an important role in the success of a company.

A consultant should focus on understanding the HR's recruitment needs and help the HR function to manage the key metrics. Value-add can be in the form of comparing the attrition rates with external similar industry benchmarks. The consultant can also suggest doing social media analysis to understand what people are saying about the company. Any negative comments will have a direct impact on recruitment.

Reward management

Employee compensation and payroll is another crucial area for HR. Other compensation related parameters include incentives, overtime, variable pay and more.

HR also needs to, on an ongoing basis, keep track and analyze compensation versus performance. There is some overlap with finance where in HR needs to analyze costs per full time employee, that is labor cost as a percent of total revenue. Variable compensation is often tied to the profitability of a company and this analysis is very valuable to HR.

HR will also need to analyze the optimum number of HR people required to serve the entire workforce. Human capital **Return on Investment (ROI)** is another factor which needs to be looked in to.

A consultant should plan a relevant application to cater to these HR needs. Data security will be an area which will need to be given a lot of priority. The consultant can do value-add and suggest automation wherever possible to save time. Payslip generation and scheduling can be suggested using **Qlik Nprinting**. This will take away a significant burden from HR.

Workforce management

Workforce is one of the biggest and most important assets for any company. The HR function will have to work with several functions to understand the utilization of employees, understand performance, and plan for recruitment.

A company has to make the right decision regarding whether to recruit a **full-time employee** (**FTE**) or look at contracting or outsourcing. The HR function will need all the parameters which can help them take the decisions. If outsourced or contracted, contract management and legal and regulatory compliance also becomes a part of HR strategy.

Manager index is one area which is considered crucial in achieving overall employee satisfaction. Lot of people who leave companies do so because of their manager. HR has to be on top of this to ensure this is managed properly and taken due care of.

Without a system in place, the HR function has to struggle to get the data points, and then strategics and make those crucial decisions. A lot of time gets wasted in manual reporting, and delayed decisions can significantly hamper the growth of the company.

Of late, we have seen HR becoming another early adopter, along with the `sales` and `finance` functions. The consultant will need to be aware of the challenges and help provide HR with the ability to analyze these key points and rapidly arrive at decisions.

Training and development

A good HR department will always value the importance of training. With changing market dynamics and changing technology, companies must invest in training their people.

Different functions will have different needs and thus HR has to manage this part well. A lot of analysis needs to be done before HR decides to invest in training. The past training courses and benefits resulting from them need to be analyzed. The performance of an employee will also depend on the effectiveness of earlier training.

Training options will be many but identifying effective training methods and identifying the right trainer is a task in itself. The consultant should strive to make this analysis easy for the HR team. If external data is available, it should be used effectively to compare it with internal data.

Employee development plays a key role in the happiness of an employee. Companies have lots of mechanisms to keep collecting regular feedback. In the absence of a system, the HR department struggles to do this analysis. The employee grievance redressal can then get delayed, leading to attrition.

Thus, when we look at the HR function, we can easily see the huge challenges the function faces and how a good consultant can make lives easy and do their bit in helping the organization grow.

Understanding supply chain management

Supply chain management (**SCM**) is a term largely prevalent in the manufacturing and retail industry. SCM is one of the key functions for such companies. In simple terms, we can define SCM as a function which extends from procurement of raw materials from suppliers, manufacturing the product and then distribution of the finished product to consumers (directly or via distributors/dealers):

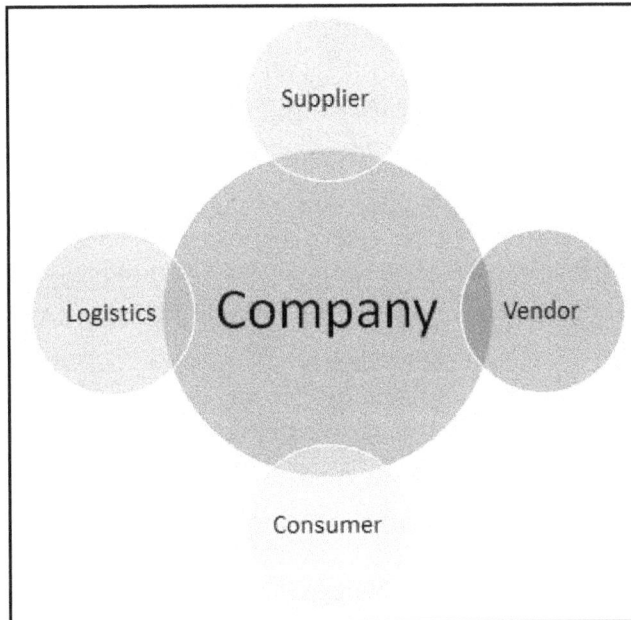

Supply chain players

Supply chain is associated with inventory (stock). This can be inventory of raw materials, semi-produced goods, or finished goods. Excess of inventories or shortage of inventories, both will have repercussions on profitability. Excess of inventories increases the cost significantly, and if a product has a shelf life, then it can be counterproductive. Having small inventory increases the waiting time for the end consumers, thereby increasing the risk of the consumer shifting loyalties to competition.

Analytics can be great for the SCM function by helping them maintain optimized inventory; helping the company to arrive at the optimum inventory is a complex process. The SCM professional will need to look at the past trends and demands, and thereby plan the optimum inventory. Predictive analysis will also be needed to do forecasting and demand planning.

SCM also involves transportation and logistics. This is another area where SCM looks for better efficiency and cost reduction. The consultant should be aware of the business process and help design the BI solution optimally. At every sub-function, the consultant can do value-additions to make the proposition more attractive and useful.

Since SCM involves several players (refer to *Supply chain players* figure), such as your client, your client's suppliers, logistics partners, distributors, and customers, the consultant can suggest value-add by thinking of improving collaboration between all these players.

You must have come across one of the Qlik products, **Qlik Analytical Platform (QAP)**. The QAP is a great way to extend analytics to external entities, such as to vendors, suppliers, end-consumers, and logistic partners. The users in those companies can also, via a vendor portal or a customer portal, log in and get their bit of analytics.

The approach of the consultant by embedding the Qlik application in external portals reduces possibilities of errors and brings all the players on to a single platform. This brings in greater transparency for everyone and allows them to be better prepared for demand peaks.

The steps involved in an SCM can be many. Let's look at some of them:

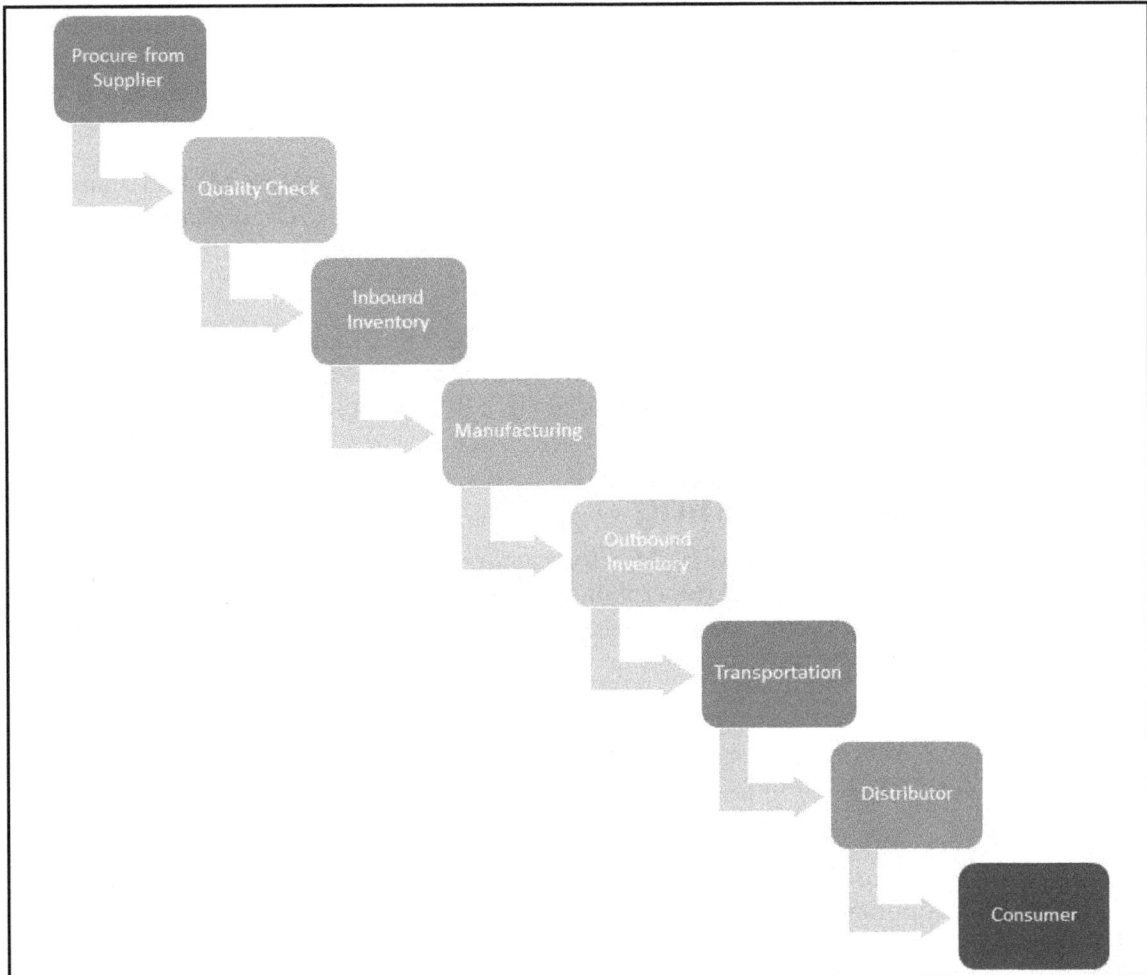

SCM flow

Material sourcing

For any product to be manufactured, raw materials are required. The process of buying raw materials from a supplier is called **sourcing**.

The cost of raw material is directly proportional to the manufacturing cost of a product. A minor change could impact cost in a big way, thereby drastically affecting the profitability of a company. The quality of raw materials plays an important role in the quality of the finished product.

For SCM, sourcing is important. To arrive at the right decision, analytics is important. For a company which operates in different geographic areas, the situation becomes all the more complex. The same raw materials in different regions may be bought at different rates, and thus cause reduced profits and bring in a certain amount of unpredictability.

The consultant must help the SCM professionals in looking at the past trends and analyzing supplier performance. Understanding the past trends and analyzing the demands can help with better forecasting, and this helps the organization to negotiate better and get the optimum deals from the suppliers.

Analyzing supplier performance helps in sourcing the best raw materials from the right supplier, thus enabling the company to maintain standards. The contract management and payment terms, all can be looked at as parameters in a BI system.

Forecasting and planning

One of the important components of SCM is forecasting and planning. As mentioned earlier, the inventory planning will depend on forecasting. The other aspect is demand planning. The demand planning exercise helps SCM to look at sourcing the right quantity at the right time and from the right supplier.

This aspect also affects the working capital and cash flow of a company. An effective BI system will help SCM to forecast and do demand planning in a better way. They can also plan for short duration demand peaks or plateaus.

A consultant must work towards the objectives of the SCM function and design the right set of dashboards. Value add can be done via automation. Reports on delivery and payment schedules can be automated for the suppliers. The consultant can also look at integrating predictive analysis to help forecast and plan demand in an effective way.

External data, such as economic and financial data (such as currency rates), can help SCM to better analyze and plan for contingencies.

Production

Production pertains to the actual manufacturing of a product. There are several parameters which fall under production. These are self explanatory:

- Product defect and quality issue
- Machine efficiency and output analysis
- Wastage (Scrap) analysis

- Maintaining standards
- Monitoring costs per job

A consultant will have to work with multiple data points and help the SCM personnel in to do the analysis. Reducing wastage is crucial as it saves costs and improves efficiency.

Warehouse

A warehouse is an area where materials are kept. These could be raw materials or finished goods. SCM has to plan the activities properly. Space optimization is the key. Also, labor is required to process the raw materials, and manufacturing has to be planned meticulously to improve efficiency.

The process is elaborate, starting typically with quality checks against the raw materials, processing and planning the jobs, and scheduling them as per machines and shifts.

The consultant should design dashboards to help SCM manage this. Consultants should look at adding values, for example by creating exception reports. This can help SCM immensely.

Transportation

Transportation efficiency and costs are important aspects in the SCM cycle. Delays will escalate costs and also have an impact on the manufacturing cycle.

Perishable raw materials and finished goods need to be managed well. This directly impacts production and the quality of the product. On time shipments help to build a good reputation for the company. Transportation delays affect customer satisfaction and have the potential of impacting sales in a negative way.

The consultant must effectively help SCM to monitor all the aspects of transportation and logistics. There can be value-add done by using Qlik GeoAnalytics. This will help with route planning and find optimum routes. Easy slice and dice in Qlik application can help SCM choose the right logistics partner based on service delivery parameters.

Material returns

Returns are just when a product of yours is not accepted by a consumer. The reason for returns could be several, one of them being the product not meeting customer expectations. It could be due to a product fault or a difference in specifications.

Delayed shipments may also get rejected as many end consumers may consider it as a lost opportunity. There are financial repercussions for a company due to returns. Companies often have products under warranty and may have to send back replacements.

The SCM professionals have to consider these factors and manage this process well. A good BI can, to a large extent, help the companies mitigate this risk and help track warranties. The SCM professionals should perform analysis on the reasons for returns and try to minimize the risk in future.

The consultant should get into the nitty-gritties of the process and help SCM to get deeper insights for better management of the returns.

Others

There are several other functions which too need analytics. We will not be able to cover all of them, but we would like to summarize some of them.

Understanding marketing

Marketing does demand generating activities to help sales. Marketing teams undertake various measures to create product awareness among the consumers and increase interest in the product. They do activities such as:

- Placing advertisements
- Participating in trade shows
- Conducting seminars
- Running email campaigns
- Doing telecall campaigns
- Conducting public relations activities
- Handling social media contents and campaigns

The marketing team spends money on each or some of the channels. For them it's very important to measure the success of the campaign and get ROI. There is a bit of overlap with the `sales` function. A consultant should help the client in understanding consumer sentiment for its brand and help the marketing team calculate ROI.

Understanding information technology

Information Technology (**IT**) is a support function helping all the functions with technology to manage their routine activities. For this they need several technology aspects, like laptops, servers, applications, networking and security devices. Any new implementation is a project and so this too needs a detailed level of management.

Some of the things IT look at are:

- Project management
- Asset management
- Governance and security
- Help desk management
- Software and license management

The `IT` function requires interaction with almost every function. The consultant can prepare several interesting dashboards for the `IT` function, enabling them to monitor all the areas in an optimum fashion. IT also needs to do presentations on the up-time and face IT audit and compliance.
The consultant thus has to help IT in all these areas and help them with insights to manage the show.

Understanding procurement

Procurement is also referred to as the purchasing department. This department interacts with the other departments. They need to check with finance for budget allocations before they can procure.

The procurement has its own business process of getting prices from different suppliers. The procurement has to do analysis by different departments, geographies and look at spend categories. They also manage various contracts with the vendors.

A good BI system helps procurement rank the vendors and the suppliers against various products and services and helps track their performance, thus helping them make better decisions in the future.

Gathering brief requirements

The intention of writing this section is to make use of something which we call the **brief requirement gathering**. This is not to be confused with detailed requirement gathering, which we will be covering in the subsequent chapter.

We mentioned in the earlier chapter (Chapter 2, *Preparing for the project*) about the organizational hierarchy and the roles people play. We also mentioned that it's important to understand requirements at every stage of pyramid. This helps you achieve project success and also helps the adoption to go up substantially.

As you start meeting the stake holders at top layers of the pyramid, the amount of time they spend with you will go down as you go higher up the layers. The people on top of pyramids can help you drive adoption when they start using the software themselves.

The consultant must do this brief requirement gathering exercise when he/she meets the top executives. The requirement can be put in the form of a brief project scope (we will cover this in the next section).

In the previous sections, we covered the business process and the general requirements of multiple functions. You should use that knowledge and also build upon it based on your client's business. As a consultant, you should be ready to note down the requirements from top management. We have mentioned on several occasions the need for a consultant to do value additions, and so the consultant on his/her part too must be ready with questions which can bring out the requirements in the best possible way.

If the top management is not aware of what Qlik can do for them, do a quick demo which brings out the capabilities of the Qlik Sense tool and try to show them a demo which makes business sense to them. For example, for a CEO you can show an executive dashboard demo. You may refer to a sample at `https://demos.qlik.com/qliksense/ExecutiveDashboard?q=performance`.

Once the top management understands the functionality and power of Qlik Sense software, the consultant can start the brief requirement gathering exercise. The questions should be aimed at understanding the client goals, getting to know the current challenges faced, and clarifying how the consultant can help to solve the challenges.

An example question to the chief sales officer could be: Would you want your sales representatives to view their performance at any point of time against their targets, at the same time allowing them to look at what kind of incentives they could make by achieving the targets?

Another sample question for the chief financial officer could be: Would you want your finance managers to look at expenditure in a graphical way at any point in time and enable them to see function wise spends with breakup and with an ability to see variance depicted through colors (for example, red means negative variance and yellow a positive variance)?

Brief project scope

We advise you to have a brief project scope template ready. This document will capture the requirements in an overview.

This document can then become a base for the detailed requirement gathering exercise. The document should capture the essence of the project, the objectives, **Key Performance Indicators** (**KPI**), and the input sources. This document also helps you to get a rough idea about the complexity of the project, the time lines involved, and what kinds of developers will be needed to execute the project.

A template similar to the one that follows can be considered:

Project Name: Give a name to the project.

Version History:
The table consists of the following details:

Version	Description	Created by	Date	Approved by
1.0	Initial Project Brief Document	<your name>	01-June-2017	<Approver name>
1.1				

- **Project objectives:** Mention the project's objectives (what the organization wants to achieve from the project):
    - Increase revenue by 10 percent by increasing cross-sell and up-sell opportunities
    - Reduce inventory costs by 20 percent by optimizing inventory levels
- **References:** Give references on the interactions carried out:
    - Meetings held on 21 May 2017 in London with head of finance
    - Sample reports sent to us on 23 May 2017

- **Brief organization background:** Mention a few lines about the company, its nature of business, and any other important details
- **Project purpose:** This section can be used to describe the need for the BI project
- **Project benefits:** List the benefits the organization will get from implementation of the BI project:
    - Reduce reporting time from 10 days to near real time
    - Move to online reviews
- **Data sources:** Mention the data points from where data will be extracted for the dashboards:
    - Budgets and quota to be picked from `Master.xls`
    - Transaction data to be picked from SAP ERP

- **Application brief:** Mention the KPI which needs to be captured:
    - Sales analysis: value and volume
    - Revenue/Profitability by brand/product
    - Production cycle times

- **Application security:** Mention about security aspects in brief:
    - Application to be published in **Finance** stream
    - Access based on product(s) handled
    - No export of data rights to anyone

- **Project success criteria:** Define the parameters which will count towards the success of the project:
    - Elimination of manual reporting
    - High adoption
    - Online reviews

Planning risk and its mitigation

We have already stressed the importance of preparation, and in this chapter, we are focusing on the prerequisites. However well you may prepare, however strong your plan may be, things may change and give rise to risks.

A look at the following quote and you will know the importance of this subject:

If you've been in the software business for any time at all, you know that there are certain common problems that plague one project after another. Missed schedules and creeping requirements are not things that just happen to you once and then go away, never to appear again. Rather, they are part of the territory. We all know that. What's odd is that we don't plan our projects as if we knew it. Instead, we plan as if our past problems are locked in the past and will never rear their ugly heads again. Of course, you know that isn't a reasonable expectation.

- Tom DeMarco

Risks may come in various forms. The most commonly seen risks are:

- Time delays
- Low adoption
- Unclean data
- Deviations from planned scope of work
- Project champion leaving the company
- Inability to connect to data source
- Performance issues

Different phases of risk management are depicted in *Risk management phases* figure and let's look at each one of them:

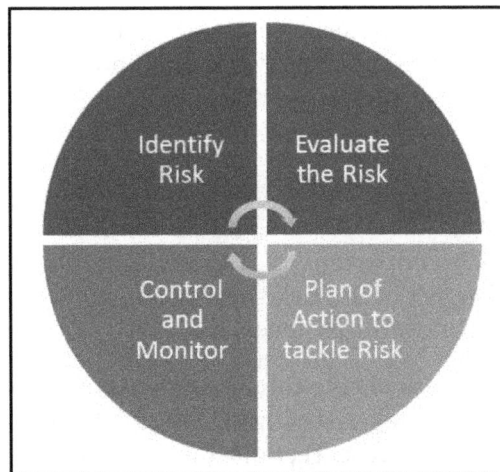

Risk management phases

Identifying risk

A good consultant should be prepared for risks. Risks can come from expected sources or they can be completely unforeseen. The risks can also be categorized as **technical risks** or **functional risks**.

The unforeseen risks are difficult to predict and the best remedy is to identify them early. The other risks can be anticipated much earlier (in fact, some can be looked at before you even start the project). The key to risk management is early identification.

Consultants during the course of implementation get visibility to the perceived risk. Time delay is one for the frequent reasons of risk and can hit project's success in multiple ways (time, cost escalations, and loss of opportunity). Timely reviews can easily help identify this risk at an early stage.

Low adoption is something which can occur only after implementation, but this too can be identified early if the consultant can understand the end user better.

Unclean data is hard to predict initially, but in a disciplined organization, the risk of this happening is rare. This risk can be perceived during the data extraction and modeling phase.

Technical issues too are hard to perceive early. However, some of them can be identified early, like connectivity to a non standard data source. There can be some issues which crop up after the system goes live. The other technical issues can be performance related, which can come as a surprise.

Changes in the scope of work is one reason for project delays and if not handled properly can become a big risk. A consultant must be aware of all potential risks, and in fact take all possible precautionary measures in advance.

Evaluating the risk

Once the risks are identified, it's important to carefully understand them. As a consultant, you should also look at the impact of the risk. Depending on their type, the risks can be categorized by the consultant and priority levels set.

Risks can have several implications. There can be financial implications for both the consultant and the client due to a delayed project. There can be other implications, such as loss of credibility or loss of user interest. Technical risks can also be the reason for low adoption and reduced user interest.

After prioritization, the impact of risks should be looked at and plans to overcome risks should be worked out. A good project plan which encompasses all factors like delivery times, technical architecture, validations, and other important parameters, will help the consultant to immediately see the impact of a risk across the project.

Plan of action to tackle risk

After you have identified and assessed the risk, look at all the aspects which the risk will affect. This will help you to plan the remedial actions and tackle the risk.

For example you came across unclean data during the extraction process, as a consultant, you should flag this by looking at different areas which will be impacted. A small dataset may not cause significant changes, but if it's a large dataset, it can impact several dashboards.

One of the important but most neglected aspects of risk is making the client aware of it. One of the aspects is the impact it will have on the existing project. The other aspect is what action can the client take to make newer data clean.

So, what could be the impacts of unclean data. Some areas which we can think of are:

- Data modelling issues
- Incorrect data on dashboards
- Reduced end user experience
- Time and costs in data cleansing
- Change in application logic for workarounds

As a consultant, start planning on actions which can help you control the risk. Some action points can be (not all may be applicable):

- Clean the data at source (this may be the toughest one)
- At **Extract, Transform and Load** (ETL) layer, write scripts to clean the data which goes in to Qlik data file (qvd)
- Create intermediate master, mapping the incorrect values with correct values
- Proactively engage with the users, make them aware of the issue, and make them aware of the action items

Control and monitor

Risk control and monitor essentially means that a consultant must, on an ongoing basis, proactively look at risks. This is an important aspect of monitoring. Control is quickly working on identifying the risk, classifying it, identifying its impact, and then working out a good plan to minimize and mitigate it.

Controlling and monitoring have to happen continuously and can be achieved through proper checks and balances. In the next section, we will talk about documentation which can help you achieve control. Frequent reviews allow you to monitor this.

An early contingency plan can help you to assess and respond to these risks in a much better way. Any new risk which a consultant comes across should be factored in for future projects, and this helps with the growth of the consultant.

> We strongly advocate that the consultant be aware of the risks and controlling them before they become unmanageable. Keep your client informed of the impacts and the plan of action to make them less anxious.

Documentation

Documentation consumes significant time in a project and is often considered monotonous and boring. However, neglecting this aspect will prove detrimental to your project.

Documentation starts from preparatory steps and extends until go-live. Change management post implementation will call for additional documentation. In an earlier section, we went through the project brief. There are several other areas where documentation needs to be maintained. They need to be visited often. This helps you to notice anomalies and also helps you to identify risks.

Some of the areas where a consultant should maintain documentation are:

- **Customer Info:** This is your internal document, based on your study of the customer. Refer to earlier chapter (Chapter 2, *Preparing for the project*) and based on the information gathered from the website, stake holder's goals, nature of business, current systems, and other relevant topics document the same.
- **Initial project brief:** This is the document that provides an overview of the project and is the base for other documents.
- **Requirement gathering template**: This template helps you to get all the information and also helps you to suggest value add.

- **Scope document**: It is a detailed document mentioning the scope of the project.
- **Solution architecture**: This document mentions details of your solution.
- **Deployment architecture**: This document mentions network and security aspects. This document also depicts the different components and the interaction between each of them.
- **UI wireframe**: The wire-frame helps you to discuss with stakeholders about how the application will look. This helps you cut down on re-works and helps you to set your client expectation much better.
- **Implementation methodology**: This document helps you to make clients aware of the different aspects in the implementation.
- **Project plan**: This documents helps you to break down the project into phases and milestones, and allocate work to people. This document also mentions task dependency.
- **Non-functional document**: This document captures all the technical aspects of the project, including hardware and software requirements. It also covers security and governance aspects, architecture, and backup plan.
- **User manual**: This document is a customized document. It acquaints the first time users with various aspects like details of the application, getting started with the software, and various features and functions.
- **Test cases for data validation**: It is important to do data validation, and the test cases must be kept ready to ensure the values match with the expected values.
- **FAQ document**: It helps the user to get quick answers and helps the adoption of the software.
- **Scope change template**: It helps you to document the changes in scope. This can impact other documents and they too should be revised accordingly.
- **Project review presentation:** This can be a weekly/fortnightly activity. This helps you to present to your client what was done, what is pending, what is the plan for next week/fortnight, and what, if any, are the dependencies impacting the project. This document also highlights risks which may occur due to some aspects not being taken care of or done in time.

The list looks big, but going through the process of maintaining these documents helps you to be in control of the project. Timely review is very essential and any deviations should be immediately assessed. This can also help early detection and control of risks.

Documentation also helps you to be prepared for unforeseen events, such as people moving out from the organization. We also recommend working with the client and preparing videos wherever possible. Training can be recorded and then they can be played for the new users to make them learn quickly. Developers too should be made to follow best practices and document their code, and provide comments to make the code more readable.

Example

In this section, we will look at a small example and try to relate it with what was explained in the earlier sections. The names are not real but the scenarios will be real. We will look at an example of a **retail chain**.

AB Fashions LLC has approached you to get benefits from implementation of a BI project.

First step is to go through the website of AB Fashion LLC and get to know more about the company. Looking at the website, the following observations were captured:

- AB Fashions LLC is headquartered in London and has operations across multiple countries covering Europe, Asia, Latam, and Americas
- AB Fashions LLC is a fashion retail chain and caters to clothing and accessories for men, women, and children
- AB Fashions LLC is a B2C company and has an omnichannel model
- AB Fashions LLC is a large format retail with presence in premium malls, and also has an e-commerce website selling directly to customers
- AB Fashions LLC procures apparel from leading designers and sells them via both online and retail stores
- AB Fashions LLC is active on social media and is always on the look out for newer ways to connect with their audience
- Their turnover is 200 million USD

It's also important to understand the objectives and goals of AB Fashions LLC. An initial ground work can be done by finding out about the key people in management and then following interviews given by them, visiting their Twitter handle, and also trying to get some more information from Linkedin regarding their past experiences.

Eric is the CEO of AB Fashions LLC. Eric is also the founder of the company and is well known in the industry. He is technology savvy and not averse to takings risks. A bit of research on him gives us more idea about what his plans are and the direction he is looking at for AB Fashions LLC:

- Eric is looking at expanding from 70 stores to 100 stores in the next 2 years
- Eric is wanting to improve the sluggish growth rate and is looking at revenue of 250 million USD for the financial year
- Improving store profitability and improving efficiency are other areas which Eric wants to focus on

- Eric wants to understand the customers better and wants AB Fashions LLC to be able to cater to them in a much better way
- Eric wants to spend more on marketing this year and have clients of AB Fashions LLC to have a greater recall value and improve customer loyalty

Lisa is the CFO of AB Fashions LLC. She's been with the company for more than three years. After studying her interviews and reading her tweets, the following points have come to the fore:

- Lisa is concerned about improving the profitability of the company.
- Considering Eric's plan for expansion, Lisa wants to focus on budgeting and having a good working capital. The expenditures in store openings and in increasing head counts have to be planned, and she wants a better visibility into expenses and wants to cut down on unwanted costs.
- She wants the employees to be better informed, even at the store level.

An initial study of the company can help us know so many things. This study has helped us get insights into the nature of the company, its business, and its vision.

Looking at the directions given by Eric and Lisa, you can start planning on how as consultant you can help them achieve their goals, and start thinking of the value adds.

You can also start gathering some initial inputs to help you understand the current systems in place. After a brief initial conversation with the CIO, Rob, we could get the following inputs:

- AB Fashions LLC has **SAP ECC 6** as their ERP. The point of sales(pos) data and the eCommerce data are captured in SAP.
- AB Fashions LLC has built a **Data-Warehouse** (**DW**) on SAP and is using **Business Objects** at their front end.
- Rob and his team end up spending a lot of time when a user requests changes in reports. There are cubes built on DW and changing these(cubes) takes considerable time. A lot of times they have to take external help.
- Over time the performance of the reporting tool has slowed down and the reports now take considerable time to open.
- Of late, the users have started asking Rob and his team for data exports in excel.
- Rob is keen to have a lot of current work offloaded to the business users.
- Rob also mentioned that the users are keen to get data from social media.

You now have good information about the existing systems and have understood some of the challenges. Next would be to get some more information from Eric and Lisa. To make it more interactive, we will try to present this in the form of a conversation (role-play):

You (Jay): Good Morning Eric. It's a pleasure to meet you. I was going through your various interviews and admire your vision for taking AB Fashions to the next level. As I understand, you are keen to increase the number of stores, increase the revenue, and provide a better experience to your clients. I would like to hear more on this vision from you.

> **Eric**: Good morning Jay. What you mentioned is right. We have big plans. One of the aspects we are trying to improve upon is making our brand stronger. We are investing more in our marketing efforts this year. We would like the BI software to help us in improving our sales. I would like to quickly understand which are my most profitable products across regions and for what time periods. Currently, crunching this is taking considerable time. I would also like to get more information about store profitability, optimizing store operations, and improving footfall. I will be happy to understand the breakup of my sales based on seasons and weekdays/weekends. I want to better understand my customers and want to do a detailed SKU level of analysis and understand user preferences.

You: Thanks Eric. Just want to understand from you how you are doing omni-channel analytics and would it help if we can also help you understand what your customers are saying about you on social media?

> **Eric**: We, for now, are finding it difficult to consolidate sales from different channels. If you can provide us an easy way, it will help us to up-sell and cross-sell, and also give a better experience to our clients. Social media is important to us, but for now we have to depend on an external agency for this input.

You: Great! This can be achieved very easily in Qlik. We can help you to get data from your various channels in a single dashboard and help you easily look at performance across the channels. You can also target customers through the most effective channels. What more are you expecting from the BI solution?

> **Eric**: I would want to analyze my sales trends and compare them month on month, quarter on quarter, year on year. I want to measure performance against targets at all levels (product category wise, product wise, store wise, and region wise). Managing returns is an important area. I want to understand which products have high returns. This will help me to decide whether to continue with the product or not. I also want to understand how my campaigns are performing and the ROI for each of them.

You: Eric, you had mentioned setting up new stores and also improving the customer experience.

    Eric: Yes, that's right.

You: We can help you make better decisions on store opening. We can help you with demographic details of a location, along with the spending power of the region, and also help you understand the age wise makeup of the population there. This will help you identify your target area easily and help you plan future stores.

    Eric: That will be great!

You: Thanks Eric. This was helpful. Who in your team will help me get detailed information on the KPI you mentioned?

    Eric: Please get in touch with Mark, our VP-sales.

You: Thanks Eric for the insights. Will interact with Mark to get more details. Have a great day!

A quick conversation will thus help you understand the broad level of expectation. This information will help you build a brief project document. This document can then be shared with Mark and a detailed requirement gathering can be taken up. We see how Jay could bring in value-add mentioning bringing in external data to make better business decisions. Jay could also have talked about Geo Analytics. This would have helped them understand how people from different areas are shopping, which of the stores they are going to, how much time does it take for them to reach a store, and how much of nearby the population is each store catering to.

Similar exercises can also be carried out with the CFO, Lisa. Like with Eric, try to bring in value-adds which can help them in their business. Some of other functions which this exercise can be carried out on are merchandising and inventory management. **Store operations** is another function for which a separate Qlik dashboard can be developed.

Summary

This chapter looked at various aspects that are prerequisites for starting a project.

It's tempting to jump into a project and start the work. However, a better approach is doing the ground work. We looked at the importance of understanding a client better. It's important to know the way business is done by your client and understand the flow of information as it occurs. Each function by itself is different and has its own way of working. We tried to briefly cover few of the functions which are early adopters, such as `sales`, `finance`, `HR`, and `SCM`.

Next, we looked at getting a broad overview of the project from senior stake holders. This ensures that you don't end up implementing a solution which is different from what the senior management is expecting.

Once you get the overview, document the same and get into the details with middle management. We also looked at several other documents which a consultant should pay attention to. The documentations are needed at every stage of the development.

Risk is a crucial aspect which a consultant must consider in a project. There is a lot of merit in quickly identifying the risks and working on action points to mitigate them. Documentation playsan important role and helps you to control and manage the risks better.

We also looked at a retail example and explored how we can initially approach the customer. We understood the ways to prepare and then went through a role play between the consultant (you) and the CEO.

With this chapter, we end the initial preparation phase. The next chapter will take off from where we end this chapter.

The next chapter marks the start of the execution phase of the project. It will take us through the process of detailed requirement gathering. The chapter will also talk about the strategy to be used and the documentation to be done. The chapter will also touch upon another real-life example.

4
Requirement Gathering

In the previous chapter, we looked at the initial preparation, and it is foundation to this chapter. We recommend that you go through the previous chapters before you start reading this chapter.

In this chapter, we will take you through the entire process of project execution, covering all the phases, starting with requirement gathering to and continuing to post-go live.

Before we start explaining the requirement gathering phase, let's look at a couple of powerful quotes:

> *If I had an hour to solve a problem I'd spend 55 minutes thinking about the problem and 5 minutes thinking about solutions.* — **Albert Einstein**

> *A problem well put is half solved.* — **John Dewey**

When we look at the preceding quotes, we can easily infer that if we spend time understanding the problem well, we can plan the solution in a much better way. This helps to better plan the implementation as well. This is true, because many industry experts have experienced this and they agree that unless we understand gravity of the problem is, we will never be able to find a good solution to that problem.

Let us look at the importance of understanding a problem (or a business challenge) better by revisiting an example which was mentioned in the first chapter of this book.

In Chapter 1, *Consultant – An Introduction*, we explained the concept of a consultant by using an example of a doctor and patient. If you recall, in the second approach, as the doctor started asking the patient relevant questions, the patient felt good about it and started to think that the doctor was trying to understand the problem that he/she was facing. So, with every question from the doctor, the patient felt more and more comfortable and started believing that the doctor would soon find out the root cause of the problem and suggest effective treatment.

From this example, you can infer that understanding the business challenge not only helps you deliver the best services to your clients, but also helps to build confidence in clients and creates trust, which eventually helps you to get things done by the client faster.

In a nutshell, and equating to the example of the doctor, we can say that understanding a problem is similar to understanding the business challenge of your client. The terminology for this is referred to as **Requirement Gathering**. We must also understand that requirement gathering is not just confined to understanding the problem. Requirement gathering can not only all the information that we need to understand the problem, but also, the same information that helps us to design and implement the best solution for the client.

Understanding requirement gathering

As the name suggests, requirement gathering is all about gathering the relevant information about the project, including the infrastructure information, technical information like data sources and connectivity, dashboarding and reporting requirements, and user and licensing information. In short, requirement gathering is all about an understanding of each and every aspect needed to design and implement the perfect solution.

Let us understand requirement gathering using a real life example.

Let us picture going for a vacation. Once you have taken the decision, the next question is-- *What are the various factors I need to ponder?*

Most of us will start making notes of basic questions, like the ones mentioned next:

- Where do I want to go for a vacation?
- What is the budget?
- What is the duration of the vacation?
- How will I travel to the location?
- Where will I stay?

Once you start answering these questions, there will be another set of questions which you will have to answer or try to get answers to, like:

- What are all the places to visit at that location?
- Which is the best hotel fitting my budget?
- Should I go for an American Plan or European Plan?
- How do I plan the local transportation?
- Where do I get Foreign Exchange (Forex) from?
- What will the weather be like, and what kind of clothes will be needed?
- Should I go for a packaged tour or should I explore on my own?

And so on.

The key to having a great vacation is to ask yourself as many questions as possible. Asking these questions and getting answers to them will make you well prepared for your tour and you will enjoy it for sure.

The process that you followed in this example was continuing to ask various questions to get clarity. The in-depth questions will definitely help you to plan the vacation and get the most out of it. This process of getting into details and trying to understand the problem statement is called requirement gathering.

When it comes to requirement gathering for the Qlik Sense implementation, you should take the brief scope document as the starting point for requirement gathering. The scope document is important for the BI projects. The scope document provides an overview of the project and the requirement gathering takes over from scope document and is all about detailing. If you don't have a scope document, things can go haywire.

A project could be executed as a fixed cost project or it could be based on time and material. Irrespective of the model chosen, it is important that you have the scope for the project defined, and the same should be documented.

If you have not created the scope document, then it is recommended that you define the scope of the project first. The sample format of a scope document has been covered in the previous chapter.

Importance of requirement gathering

The success of a project is strongly dependent on the quality and completeness of requirement gathering. Hence, it is important for the Qlik consultant to focus more on this phase of the project execution to deliver quality dashboards and reports to end users. A good requirement gathering not only helps deliver quality implementation, but also helps once the project goes live.

Requirement gathering helps a consultant to get details of aspects that are critical for the success of the entire project. This makes this process an important and integral part of the project. Let us look at these critical factors in brief.

Focused deliverables

The deliverable is the most important factor that decides the success of a project. Hence, it is very important for a consultant to have a clear definition of the deliverable. A clear list of deliverables helps the consultant decide many more things, which can directly or indirectly impact the overall project delivery.

Requirement gathering helps the consultant get a fair idea about what needs to be delivered to the client. It may not be possible to have crystal clear deliverables in first attempt of every project, but continuous requirement gathering helps you to get closer to the desired deliverables. This also helps the clients to refine their requirements in such a way that they get maximum output from the project.

Project timelines

Once you know what you need to do, the next step is to define the timelines required for it to be delivered. Though it sounds easy and simple, it is not. There are various other factors that a consultant needs to consider when deciding the timelines, because once you commit the timelines, you must adhere to them. Delays usually leave a bad impression with the client.

Requirement gathering helps you to get insight on those aspects which may impact the overall timelines. It is always good to know what the data sources are, if there is a direct connectivity available with these data sources, what the data linking fields are, what the complexities of the logic are, and so on. Misunderstanding any of these points can hamper the delivery. Thus, requirement gathering helps you to know all these points and finally decide the achievable timelines for the project.

Resource planning, roles, and responsibility

Resource planning is important for the delivery of a quality project. Depending on the complexity of the requirements and quality requirements, a consultant should decide what levels of skills are needed to get the delivery done according to the committed schedule.

Requirement gathering helps the consultant to know the complexity of the project. Depending on that, the consultant can identify the resource that can deliver the requirements. For example, if the requirements are complex, the consultant can deploy an experienced person who can write the complex logic and validate the same; however, if the requirements don't require much effort, then a relatively less experienced person can be deployed to develop the requirements.

Once the resource is decided, the consultant can easily assign the roles and responsibilities to them.

Milestone and task definitions

A milestone definition is important for a project to be executed successfully. This is the because milestone helps to gets answers to questions like what is to be delivered, when it should be delivered, what the current status of the development is, what the show stoppers are, and so on. These questions help the consultant and the client to keep an eye on the project and continuously measure its activities.

Requirement gathering helps the consultant to define these measurable milestones and individual tasks according to the known deliverables. Once the consultant knows what needs to be delivered, he can easily define the tasks which need to be carried out to execute the project. For example, a milestone can be *Data modeling*, within which the sub-tasks can be integration and connection to the data sources, data fetching (logic generally called the extraction process), incremental logic, QVD generation, data modeling, and so on.

Success criteria

It is important to define the success criteria for the project. How would one know that the project delivered is perfect and truly completed? Hence, it is important for a consultant to discuss with the client and agree upon the success factors of the project.

Requirement gathering helps to define a measurable success criteria, which also defines the quality of the project.

Thus, requirement gathering is an important phase of project execution and should never be neglected. You can say that requirement gathering is the pillar of a Business intelligence project; better the requirement gathering, more the likelihood of succeeding in the Business intelligence project. It becomes important for a consultant to get this phase conducted from a skilled person who has knowledge of the industry and has good communication skills, along with the ability of ask relevant questions to client and get the maximum information from them. Any information which is missed in this phase can lead to delays in the project or unsuccessful project implementation.

Executing requirement gathering

Now that you know what requirement gathering is and why it is important, the next question which will come to your mind is, how do you get started with requirement gathering? What is the kinds of information which you should gather? What are the various methods in which requirement gathering can be conducted? Let us understand them in detail.

When it comes to requirement gathering for the Qlik Sense, you should try to get information for three categories: functional, technical, and infrastructural.

Functional requirement gathering

As the name suggests, this type of requirement gathering involves discussion with the business users on the functional deliverables. The functional requirement mainly talks about the final output that the user wants to have as project delivery.

Functional requirement gathering should always start with the senior management, like the CEO, CFO, COO, and CIO. This will help you understand the BI strategy which the senior management is looking for. It is always the senior management which has the capability to influence the overall adoption of the BI reporting, thus understanding their requirements becomes an important factor.

When the project is large and multiple modules needs to be captured under the Qlik Sense project implementation, the functional requirement becomes little tricky, because there is always a challenge of deciding from where to start. In such a case, you as a consultant should select the requirement which seems to be the most critical and difficult for the business currently, the one which is consuming the maximum amount of time to generate the insights in data. The reason is, if you deliver that critical requirement on or ahead of time, you will set a positive impression with the client and that will be like a quick win for you. Additionally, it will give you more confidence to finish other deliverables ahead of time.

Once you choose what deliverables you want to pursue first, you have started with the functional requirement gathering. All you need to do is prepare the set of questionnaires and get into meetings with the business users (mostly the ones who are currently preparing those reports, or any business user who has given the requirement) to get a detailed understanding of the requirements, from the data sources to logics to final interactive visualizations.

You should also try to get information on security aspects from the business users, such as who should see what kind of data. Although this requirement can be taken up later, it is important to have a discussion with business users so that they can start thinking about it too.

While doing the functional requirement gathering, you are likely to face a tricky situation. The requirements can be of two types: requirements which are known to the business and requirements which are unknown to the business. **Known requirements** are the ones for which business users know what output they want, what the logic that needs to be applied is, and what the data sources are. This situation can be handled easily because the idea of requirements is clear. The difficulty starts when the requirements are not clear, that is, **unknown requirements.** Unknown requirements are the ones which the users are unable to clearly express and can not be documented. Most of the time, business users are unaware of the capabilities of the business intelligence tools. On seeing a small demo of the tool, and after looking at the functionality and its operations, they tend to get excited about it and they start thinking about all the possible sets of requirements.

Thus, it may become a little complicated for a consultant to understand them and think about the feasibility of those requirements. To understand unknown requirements, the consultants need to put themselves in the business users' shoes and think from their perspectives, and visualize the same thing as the business users. To do this, the consultants need to have thorough knowledge of the business, along with the working model.

Technical requirement gathering

Technical requirement gathering plays a key role in Qlik Sense implementation, because this requirement is mainly focused on the flow of data from various sources to Qlik Sense. This type of requirement gathering should be done only after the functional requirement gathering is over, because functional requirement gathering will give you a basic idea about the data and data sources. This phase of requirement gathering is mostly done with either the techno functional person or one who understands the database and its flow.

Technical requirement gathering should focus on the data and logic which are required to develop the reporting. You as a consultant should ask various questions of the concerned person, such as, how many data sources will be required? What are the various options available to connect them? What are the various tables and columns which should be considered? What are the various database logics, if any?

Along with the data information, you should also get an idea about the frequency at which the data should be fetched from the source system to Qlik Sense. This is very important, because if you are connecting directly to a transactional system, the data load should happen in such a way that it doesn't increase the workload of the production system. If you need to fetch data from the data warehouse, then you should know when the data warehouse finishes the **Extract, Transform, and Load** (ETL) process, and accordingly you need to schedule the data fetching for Qlik Sense.

If the business has given you any idea about the data refresh frequency in functional requirement gathering, you should convey the same to the technical person, to find the feasibility.

Infrastructural requirement gathering

Many of the Qlik consultants do not take this aspect seriously, because their focus in only on the delivery of the project. Ignoring this aspect of requirement gathering can lead to performance issues within a short period of Go Live.

The infrastructural requirement gathering consists of hardware and software requirements of the entire project, and thus getting an idea of this information becomes important. You should do this requirement gathering with the network team and the server team.

Hardware requirements mainly include about three components, which are, RAM, CPU, and Storage.

Estimating the correct RAM requirement is critical for Qlik Projects, because Qlik is an in-memory technology. There are couple of things which a consultant should consider before estimating the RAM of the hardware.

First, you should know what the size of the reporting data is, which may come from couple of data sources because it is a key driver. We also know that there will be a compression at the QVD level, but one should also know that when the application is loaded into the RAM, it grows about four to five times the application size. A consultant should also keep in mind that the compression depends upon the unique values in the data set, so more unique values will give you more compression and less unique values will give you less compression.

Another parameter is concurrency. This information is required because every concurrent user requires approximate 10 percent of the application RAM for storing user specific selections. A consultant should also look at number of applications which need to be developed and at same time judge the complexity of each application. Knowing the approximate reporting data size is another parameter which a consultant should find out .

For CPU estimation, a consultant should get an idea about the level of complexity each application will have, because all the calculations will be performed by the CPU.

The storage can be decided as per the reporting data size.

A consultant should consider at least three years ahead when estimating the hardware; frequent changes in hardware are not that easy.

There are few more aspects which a consultant should look at as a part of requirement gathering, such as the backup strategy, reverse proxy, connectivity from the internet, SSL security and certificates, end users geography(with respect to Qlik Sense server).

Now that you know what goes into requirement gathering and the different parameters to be considered, the next question which should be asked is how to conduct the requirement gathering?

There are various methods mentioned in hundreds of books; each one of them is effective for different types of requirement gathering and for different projects. For project implementation like Qlik Sense, the following are a couple of methods which can be followed to get maximum inputs from requirement gathering.

Brainstorming

Brainstorming is the methodology whereby a group of people meet in a room and discuss a problem statement to find the solution of the same. In general, you can call this an idea generation discussion, where each stakeholder gives the idea as per his/her understanding and skills.

Brainstorming as a topic is a big one, but I want to keep my focus on how it can be used for Qlik Sense project requirement gathering.

Brainstorming sessions are good to start with for requirement gathering, because they involve senior management and head of departments, who can participate in the discussion where everyone can discuss the high-level strategy for BI along with the final deliverables. All individuals can add value to the process by giving their feedback as per their domains of expertise.

As a consultant, you can drive this session by starting a small Qlik Sense demo(some good demos are available on `demo.qlik.com`), and showcasing the functionality and data discovery abilities of Qlik Sense. This will help the group of people to visualize the requirements, which can further help them to enhance their business operations using data discovery.

Once everyone sees the capability of Qlik Sense, they will automatically start giving ideas about what can be developed in Qlik Sense and define the success criteria of the project.

Requirement workshops

Requirement workshops are the discussions with the business users to understand the requirements in detail. The brainstorming session will give you a brief level of requirement gathering, whereas the requirement workshop will take you through the detailed requirement gathering.

Requirement workshops are generally done with an individual person or a group of people who are currently generating the reports or analyse manually or with semi automation.

Requirement workshops are an effective way of gathering the requirements, because they help you to interact directly with the business users who are currently developing the reports and analysis. It helps the consultant to have a look at the entire process of reporting and understand the complications of the same.

Requirement workshops not only help to get the requirement, but also help to have a discussion on couple of complex reports or requirements which the business users find difficult to develop. In such discussions, the consultant can take the business users through a couple of important KPIs or reporting matrices which are being used by the same industry.

Document analysis

Most of the time, the reports and analysis are already being developed by the business users fully or partially, on some or the other tool. While doing this, they may have some documentation which explains the entire process of the report development, including the data sources and the logic applied in the reports. Understanding such documentation is nothing but gathering requirements by document analysis.

Document analysis is one of the good ways of gathering the requirements, because it already has all the information which one should have in order to develop that requirement in a new tool. Such documents become important content, because they help the consultant to understand the current process of the report generation. This further helps the consultant to seek the optimized way to develop requirements and enable the business users to get good amount of analysis from them.

Another advantage of doing the requirement gathering by analyzing the document is that the consultant need not start everything from scratch. They can easily understand the document and get the required information in a much shorter time.

This type of requirement gathering can become complex when the documents are not updated. In such cases, it becomes complicated for the consultant relate to the documents with the actual reporting. Thus, if the documentations are not being updated regularly or when changes have been made, then they cannot be leveraged to the maximum.

Reverse engineering

As I said earlier, many times it happens that business users have already developed some or other parts of the requirements in some ERP system or in Excel. So in the business requirement gathering phase, the business users may ask a consultant to have a look at the already developed code, which can give him the idea about the logic and the data sources which can be used to redevelop the requirements.

The process of investigating and getting required information from already developed code is called **Reverse engineering.** Reverse engineering becomes an important way of requirement gathering when there is no techno functional person available who knows the business as well as the technical part of it, and who can help the consultant to understand the requirements. Also, if there are no documentations available to analyze it, then the reverse engineering can become handy.

For example, you can go through the various SQL queries/functions/procedures available, which are being used to fetch the data from the source system and which may have various logics applied in them; you can also have a look at the Excel formulas which are being used to generate the reports, and so on.

Questionnaires

One of the effective ways of requirement gathering is by way of questionnaires. In this type of requirement gathering, a consultant prepares a list of questions which can be asked to various groups of people to get the maximum information from them. This type of requirement gathering is helpful when you want to do a requirement gathering for unknown requirements.

It has been seen that the business users are more concerned about their business challenges, and keeping this in mind, they give requirements for business intelligence. However, they may not be able to visualize what more could be done with their data set, which could help them to analyze their data in a better way. It is a consultant's duty to help the business users understand the power of business intelligence tools like Qlik Sense by asking a series of questions which are related to their business or domain.

There is no specific type or format of questions which can be prepared to be asked. They can be optional types of questions, or they can be a questions with *yes* or *no* options, or they can be questions which require descriptive answers. Only thing to remember is that the questions should be specific and relevant to the domain for which the requirement gathering is going on; otherwise, they may not give the expected information.

Must have, should have, and good to have strategies

Once the requirement gathering is done with every group of people across departments and functions, you will have a long list of requirements from each of them. Among these requirements, not all the requirements will be important and urgent, but still everyone would like to get their requirement done at the earliest, probably because of their curiosity towards Qlik Sense or due to the pressure from senior management. In such situation, it becomes difficult to prioritize the requirements in such a way that every department gets some of their requirements implemented.

To handle this kind of situation, you need to be able to prioritize the requirements. There are various prioritization techniques available which can be used, but the one which I use and would like to talk about is the Must, Should, and Good to have strategy. The idea of this strategy is taken from the MoSCoW prioritization technique, which is used in agile methodology. This technique was developed by Dai Clegg.

The MoSCoW technique categorizes the requirements into four main buckets, which are Must have, Should have, Could have, and Wont Have. The MoSCoW methodology is more suited for software development projects, but to make an effective use of this methodology for BI projects like Qlik Sense, we can concentrate on the main three categories, which are Must Have, Should Have and Good to Have(could have).

Must have requirements

These are the requirements which are critical, highly important, and urgent for the business, which define the success criteria for the entire project. A project should have these must have requirements, because they signify the purpose for which the project has been initiated.

There should be a clear definition of the must have requirements so that one can define the success of the project basis. Thus, it becomes important for the consultant to define the requirement under this category to give a purpose to the project.

A consultant should gather all the required information for this requirement delivery. If a consultant is unable to get all the required information, or if more time is needed to fulfill this requirement on time, then it is good idea to wait to start the project. Failure to deliver this requirement may fail the entire project.

Should have requirements

This category should have the list of requirements which are important for the business but not urgent to deliver in the initial phase of the project. It is necessary to have the requirements in this category, because once the Must have category requirements are finished, businesses would like to see these requirements taking shape. For a consultant, this list becomes the second priority requirement, which should be taken for development once the Must have requirements are finished.

For a project to be successful, finishing this requirement is also as important as Must have requirements are, though the failure of delivering this requirement may not be considered as an entire failure of the project. However, a consultant should not ignore these requirements, because these requirements will be important for business.

Good to have requirements

Practically not all the requirements are always urgent and important. There will be many requirements which are desirable by the business but they may not be that important and urgent at that moment of time. Such requirements should be tagged as Good to have requirements.

Good to have requirements do not become part of the committed requirements, but a consultant can decide to deliver these requirements only if Must have and Should have requirements are developed and there is spare time available.

It is important to define this type of requirement, because if you deliver this requirement along with the other two requirements, to the business users, it will be an added service and it will create a good impression on them. It is like offering a full meal with dessert.

The MoSCow method also defines one more category of the requirement, which is **Won't Have.** At times this is also important, because a consultant needs to define clearly what can be delivered and what cannot be delivered. This helps businesses to have a clear idea about what they are going to get as a delivery of the project and what requirements won't be included in that. This helps the consultant to avoid any confusion about the delivery of the project.

Questionnaires

The core of any requirement gathering is the questionnaires. They play an important role in making the requirement gathering phase successful, because they help to get each and every detail about the requirements. The more questions asked in requirement gathering meetings, the more information and clarity will be available about the deliverables of the project, the risk involved in the projects, and so on, which in a way helps a consultant to execute the project and make it successful.

Preparing questionnaires can be called a preparation stage, which is needed to make the requirement gathering effective and complete. If a consultant is ready with the list of questions before going for a requirement gathering meeting, it will help him to get the exact answers of those questions and avoid any miscommunication and misperception. It will also help the consultant to document the discussion and get the signoff from the business users upon the same.

Most of the time, it has been seen that meeting without prior preparations results in an unsatisfactory meeting, because the discussions don't happen in the right directions, which delays the meeting and wastes the valuable time of the stake holders.

For a consultant, it is important to make sure that his time, along with the stakeholder's time, is utilized effectively, and this can happen only when you ask right question at the right time to the right person. Someone has said that *Knowledge is having a right answer, intelligence is asking a right question.*

Preparing and asking questions will not help a consultant unless they are framed properly and asked to the right person. You cannot ask a technical question to a functional guy and a functional question to a technical guy. If you do that, then they may give you incomplete or incorrect information, which may confuse you and waste everyone's time.

It is important for a consultant to keep the requirement gathering meeting crisp and clear by preparing proper questions and asking them at the right time to the right people. A consultant should focus on getting the requirement as soon as possible, so that he can invest more time in defining the solution for the same and finishing the project on time. Any delay due to reiterative meetings can lead to delay in the project.

Let us understand through an example the disaster of asking a wrong question to a wrong person by an example.

Once there was a man passing through a lane and he saw a boy standing next to a dog. The man immediately asked the boy, *Does your dog bite?* The boy answered, *No.* The man felt good knowing that the dog didn't bite and he tried to cross them. As soon as he crossed the boy, the dog bit him. He scolded the boy and said, *Why did you lie about your dog not biting?* And the boy said, *No I didn't lie. My dog doesn't bite, but this is not my dog.*

If you observe the conversation in the previous story, you will find that the man did ask a question, but the question was incomplete. He should have first asked, *Is it your dog?* THis mistake was that he assumed that the dog was the boy's, and this error caused him the dog bite. A wrong question got him in trouble.

The same applies to our requirement gathering meetings also. If you ask a wrong question to a wrong person at a wrong time, you may get incomplete answers or the answers may lead you to trouble. Thus, it is important for a consultant to do an initial preparation of the questions before going to the meeting, and to make sure that the right questions are asked to the right people.

Let us see what kind of questions need to be asked in the requirement gathering meetings.

The list of questions can be categorized, as follows.

Functional questions

You can prepare a list of functional questions, which you may need to ask while doing requirement gathering with respective business users. These questions can be further divided as per the modules and as per the business users with whom you are going to have meetings. It will not only help you to get clear answers and get you the right information, but can also help the business users to understand how they can best analyze their data and get insight from it.

Sales module

Let's have a look at some of the questions related to the sales module:

- **General Questions:**
  - What are the other KPIs along with sales trends?
  - Do you have quotas data?
  - What is the granularity at which you have quotas data?
  - Do you want to see the quota achievement?
  - Do you want to see the sales quantity?

- Do you have gross profit/margin?
- Do you have COGS (Cost of goods sold)?
- What are the different dimensions, like product, product category, location, region, and so on?

- **Question on Trends:**
    - How many years of data do you want to see in trends?
    - Do you want YTD(year till date)/QTD(quarter till date)/MTD(month till date) sales?
    - Do you want sales versus target and sales versus previous year sales?
    - Do you want to see the sales versus COGS/GP/margin trend?
    - Do you want to see rolling 12 months Sales?
    - Do you want period in cyclic dimension or drill down from year to quarter to month to day to hour?
    - Do you want to see the sales by financial year and financial quarter or calendar year and calendar quarter?
    - Do you want to see Sales by week?

- **Sales by Other Dimensions:**
    - Do you want to see the contribution of sales by region, product category, and others?
    - Do you want to see sales by customers?
    - Do you want to see the top N dimensions (product group, region, location, customers)?
    - Do you want to see the customers, products, and regions which contribute to 70 percent of the overall sales?
    - Do you want to do pareto analysis (80/20)?
    - Do you want to do what if analysis with sales?
    - Do you want to see the forecasting of the sales?

- **Order Management:**
    - Numbers of orders received month on month?
    - Pending Orders?
    - Cross sell to customers? Which products have been bought the most by the customers and which can be sold to them?
    - Orders received by sales man?

- **Inventory:**
  - Do you want to see the inventory at end of every month?
  - Do you also want to see the sales along with inventory to see how the inventory is supporting the sales?
  - Do you want to have market basket analysis?
  - Do you want to see the inventory valuation?
  - What pricing mechanism do you use for inventory valuation-weighted average or moving average, or simple average?
  - Do you want to see the inventory by expiry?
  - Do you want to see the inventory ageing?
  - How do you calculate the ageing?
  - Do you want to see inventory carrying cost?
  - **If it's a Manufacturing company, then:**
    - Do you have BOM (Bills of material) defined for your finished goods?
    - Do you have a tagging of finished goods and raw material?
    - Do you want to see the BOM versus actual consumption of the inventory?
    - Do you want to see days of inventory remaining?

- **Procurement:**
  - How many requisitions/indents/purchase orders are created month on month?
  - How many requisitions/indents/purchase orders are open and closed?
  - Do you want to see PO life cycle?
  - Do you want to see PO by vendor, product, region, location, and so on?
  - Do you want to compare the cost of material by vendor?
  - Do you want to do vendor analysis?
  - How many materials are pending to be received?
  - Do you want to see the numbers of vendors which consume 70 percent of overall spend?
  - Payments which are due to vendor/ pending purchase orders and so on?
  - Do you want to analyze discounts over period of time?

- **Accounts (GL):**
    - Do you want to create a PNL(profit and loss) and balance sheet statement?
    - Do you want to see actual versus budgeted expenses?
    - Do you want to see the top expenses by GL(general ledger) account?
    - Do you want to have what if analysis to plan the budget for next year?
    - Do you want to see the actual expenses over trend?
    - Do you want to see the actual expense by expense group, location, and so on?
    - Do you want to calculate the working capital?
    - Do you want to calculate the EBITA(Earnings Before Interest, Taxes, Depreciation and Amortization?

- **Accounts (Payable):**
    - Do you want to see payable over trends?
    - Do you want to see payables by vendor, product category, location, and so on?
    - Do you want to see the top vendor by outstanding payable?
    - Do you want to see the payments by payment terms?
    - Do you want to see the payment overdue ageing?
    - Do you want to see the means of payment (electronic, paper, and so on)?
    - Do you want to see the payment life cycle?
    - Do you want to see OTIF(on time in full) analysis for the payments done to vendor?
    - Do you want the visibility of payments overdue in next interval of days?

- **Accounts (Receivables):**
    - Do you want to see receivables over trends?
    - Do you want to see receivables by customers, orders, location, and so on?
    - Do you want to see the top customers by receivables amount?
    - Do you want to see the outstanding by payment terms?
    - Do you want to see the receivables ageing?

- Do you want to see the means of receivables (electronic, paper, and so on)?
- Do you want to calculate the customer payment index?
- Do you want to do OTIF analysis?
- Do you want visibility of receivables in next interval of days?

- **Human resource management:**
    - Numbers of Active Employees?
    - Numbers of New Joiners?
    - Numbers of Leavers?
    - Month on Month Active Employee Count.
    - Employee count by Age Group, Gender, Grade, Band, and Experience.
    - Numbers of Employees per department.
    - Salaries paid to employees month on month.
    - Salaries by the different salary components (Basic, HRA, DA, and so on.)
    - Highest paid employees.
    - Employee Profile.
    - Leave management.
    - Hiring Cost.
    - Training Cost.
    - Numbers of employees who have taken training.
    - Employee Performance Index.

- **Production:**
    - Number of Production orders released in a Month.
    - Production orders by stage in a production.
    - Production orders by equipment.
    - Total number of product quantities produced by equipment in a month.
    - Equipment efficiency percentage.
    - Overall Scrap percentage.
    - Scrap by Production order, Equipment, location, and so on.
    - Down time of an equipment.
    - Down time by reason.

- **Marketing:**
    - Number of campaigns done in an year.
    - Number of leads generated by each campaign.
    - Lead conversion ratio.
    - Leads by sources.
    - Loss leads ratio.
    - Numbers of loss leads by loss reason.
    - Cost per lead.

Technical questions (database)

These are the types of questions which will help you understand how to fetch the data from various sources and link it together to achieve what the users want. They are mostly asked to a techno functional person or a database guy who understands the data sources:

- What are the different data sources required to gather all information?
- Do you have a data warehouse where all the data is collated?
- What ERP(enteprise resource planning software) is being used?
- Is there direct connectivity with the data source available, in terms of ODBC or OLEDB connection?
- If the data source is a cloud based system, can data be fetched using the web services?
- Do you need to connect to the raw tables, the views, or a cube to get the data?
- Do you have prebuild queries which can help to understand the base tables and fields, along with the logics, if any?
- Are there any standard reports available which can give you the data required?
- What are the list of tables required for reporting?
- What are the fields which are required?
- What are the linking fields, that is, the primary keys, foreign keys, and composite keys?
- What is the granularity of each of the tables?
- Does each table have the last modified timestamp?
- What are the fact tables and how many are required?
- What are the dimension tables?
- Are there field description available if there are generic fields?

- What are the logics which can be applied or are already available in database, to reduce the duplication of work?
- Do you have any documentation available which can show the data flow diagrams to understand the flow of the data?
- What is the size of the database and what will be the size of the reporting data?
- What is the time when the data fetching can be scheduled, so that a minimum load can be put on the transactional data source?
- Is there any limitation on the number of sessions/connectivity in a database?
- Is a slowly changing dimension required?
- How is the slowly changing dimension handled in the database?
- If the data source is going to be CSVs or text files or Excel files, how will it be shared with Qlik?
- Can the csv/text/excel files be uploaded in the database and then Qlik get access to them through the database, or do you want to upload them directly in Qlik?

Technical questions (non-database)

Along with the functional and database information, you may also need information on the infrastructure and the network connectivity, so you may need to prepare another list of questions which will be asked of network guys or infrastructure guys. Following is a list of questions which you can ask:

- What is the size of the hardware in terms of CPU, RAM, and HDD?
- Is the hardware a physical server or a virtual machine?
- Is it going to be available on premise or on cloud?
- Are the server ports open? If not, then it may require opening a couple of ports.
- Is the server part of a domain?
- Is the server accessible from the internet?
- Can we give a DNS to the server?
- Is reverse proxy needed?
- Do you have a domain controller like Active Directory?
- Are there multiple domains?
- Is the domain accessible from the Qlik Server?
- Do you need to have a clustered environment for Qlik or a standalone installation?

- What will be the backup strategy be for the installation and data?
- Is any version controlling software, like tortoise, being used in the organization, like tortoise?

The previous listed are just sample questions which you can ask to respective user groups, but they are not the only questions. You may change them, add to them, or remove couple of them, depending on the industry or the organization for which you are implementing the Qlik solution.

As a consultant, you should always remember that to get maximum information from business users, you need to think as they think and see the data as they see. You may find it difficult to get the answers to your questions or any further help from a couple of business users, because they may feel insecure about the BI automation activity, but you need to make them understand and agree that it will help them to increase their productivity. For any business users, their **KRA (Key Result Area)** / **KPA (Key Performance Area)** is more important than anything, so you need to align your requirements and questions such that they see that their KRA is getting achieved by doing this activity.

Must ask information

A consultant is responsible for performing every single activity to make sure that the project is successful in every sense. That's the reason the detailed requirement gathering is conducted to make sure that a consultant knows and understands all the business requirements in detail, including the current way of report generation and the way the analysis is done for decision making by management.

Most of the time, the detailed requirement gathering discussion happens with the middle or the lower management, who are currently generating the reports and feeding the management with the analysis. But it is also important for a consultant to have a couple of meetings with the senior management or the respective management who can help to get the answers to the must ask questions.

Business objective

Any requirement, either for BI or software development for any other purpose is meant to get certain ouput. For example, you want to have a software solution like ERP to make sure that all transactional entries are automated and error free. You want to have a reporting system to make sure that better insights can be obtained from data and better decisions can be taken.

In the same way, it is important for a consultant to know the objective of the business behind implementing a BI project like Qlik, because it will help him/her to drive the Qlik project from the requirement gathering phase in the direction of achieving this objective.

If the consultants know these objectives, they can prepare a list of the right questions that should be asked of the business users in requirement gathering, which will give them the right information. They can keep their focus on getting the quick win requirements, which can help them to generate confidence in business about the Qlik project.

For example, in the previous chapter, we saw that a consultant met CEO Eric, CFO Lisa, and CIO Rob to know their vision and goal in near future.

Current business challenges

Many a times, the current pain point from the existing system of the business becomes a driving factor for the next technology or the improvement in the existing system. So if a client has started a project on Qlik, it means that the business has some pain point with the existing system, which may not be allowing them to grow or to get valuable output from it.

Thus, for a consultant, it becomes important to know this information to make the project successful, because this can be one of the criteria which can be used to define if a project is successful or not. If a consultant helps the business to resolve this pain point, using the dashboard or any other way of reporting or providing the relevant data set, the project can be called half successful.

Failure to address this problem may result in the dissatisfaction of the client and the client may consider the project unsuccessful.

For example, the major pain point is to collate data from various data sources and making a relation between them, like linking Salesforce data along with ERP data, or linking human resource data with sales data.

Success criteria

It is quite difficult to define if a project is partially successful or successful, or if it has failed, without any success criteria or measurable points. Thus, it is important that management defines the criteria upon which the project can be measured; successful delivery of those criteria defines the success of the project.

Because the nature of this information is critical, a consultant should try and get this information from management. If management has not defined this criteria, it is duty of the consultant to make them understand the importance of this information and get it defined by them.

The success criteria can be anything, like:

- The project should be delivered on time with the Must have requirements
- The project should not fail from the performance point of view and should provide good performance to business users
- The entire architecture of the project should be such that it can be scalable in future with more users and data coming in
- Training of business users, support, and maintenance can also be a success criteria

And so on.

Defining success criteria not only helps the consultant but also helps the management to keep an eye on the project and make sure that the project is going in right direction.

Key stakeholders

As the name suggests, key stakeholders are the people who initiated the BI project, or the ones who are responsible for the success of the project from the business side.

For a consultant, it becomes important to know the key stakeholders, because they will be the single point of contact for any help which is required by the consultant during the execution of the project. The consultant should contact them if he/she finds any such risks in the project which may result in a delay.

They will be the ones who will be deciding the success of the project, and thus, the consultant should keep them intimated about the project's progress.

If the key stakeholders are not aware of the current execution of the project, the consultant may face backlashes from them.

Common mistakes in requirement gathering

It is said that h*umans makes mistakes,* and requirement gathering is an activity performed by humans, so it is also prone to mistakes. Being a consultant, one should make sure that he/she tries to avoid common mistakes which happens during the requirement gathering for BI projects.

As we have learned since starting this chapter, requirement gathering is an important phase in the execution of a project, so any mistake made during requirement gathering may result in some risk to the project, which may cause the project to fail.

The following is a list of mistakes which are commonly made in the requirement gathering phase.

Lack of business understanding

Most of the times, the consultant starts requirement gathering without understanding the dynamics of that business. They may not be doing this intentionally, but they may skip this due to time factor or other pressure from the client or from the project manager, and at times due to overconfidence.

One common mistake consultants do is that they think that if you know one domain, you can easily understand any other domain. This is, however, not true; for example, sales may be analyzed differently in pharma company, retail company, and insurance company. Though it is sales function, but there are different ways of interpreting it in different type of organizations. Thus, it is important for a consultant to do basic preparation of understanding the business operation before starting requirement gathering.

Assumptions

A common but costly mistake that many consultants make is that they make assumptions while doing the requirement gathering. The sole purpose of requirement gathering is to get all the information from the business users about their expectations and their requirements. So, a consultant should not assume anything about a requirement without getting it approved by the business.

I call it a costly mistake because any assumptions made by the consultant may directly result in failure of the project. Any development or delivery made on the basis of such an assumption may get rejected by the business users, and it may result in the delay of the entire project and wastage of the man-months used for developing that requirement.

Communication problems

Requirement gathering is generally done by verbal communication between a consultant and a business user. So, it is important that a consultant is fluent in communication and has the skills to make his point crystal clear, so that the other person can understand and respond with correct information.

It is always recommended that a consultant know the native language of the business users and use that while doing requirement gathering, as that will help the business user to understand the points made by the consultant easily and avoid any misunderstanding. It will also help the consultant to build his reputation and trust with the business users.

No participation in meeting

It has been observed and experienced by many business analysts, while doing business requirement gathering, that not all business users know what they want, which makes requirement gathering little difficult. In such a case, if a consultant does not actively participate in requirement gathering meetings then the conversations made in such meetings may result in unclear requirements, and misunderstandings could arise.

If a consultant actively interacts and drives the meeting himself, then it becomes easy for him to get the correct information from the business users and to guide them in right direction to fulfill their requirements.

No recurring conversations

At times, a consultant thinks that requirement gathering can be done only at the start of a project, but it is not true. He may need to do requirement gathering while the project is halfway or when a small delivery is ready. This is because not all the business users know what they want; they may visualize their requirement only after a couple of rounds of discussions.

It is important for a consultant to know the exact needs of the business users, and for that he may also guide them, but that may or may not be possible in a single meeting.

A consultant should not assume that only one meeting with such business users will get him/her all the information and clarification about the needs of the business users. At times, the business users have clears idea about what they need, only after seeing the sample visualization of similar requirement relating to their industry. So, a consultant should conduct a recurring meeting with such users to make them visualize and think more about what they want.

Gap analysis

Many consultants fail to do gap analysis. Gap analysis is the identification of the pain areas of a business, which cannot be solved using the current system. This information helps a consultant to focus on such areas and to make sure that they can be addressed in the project delivery he/she is about to do.

Documentation

Documentation is another common mistake which business analysts make. At the time of requirement gathering, the consultants generally make a rough list of the discussions and the requirements given by the business users, but they rarely convert this into a detailed document. There is a tendency to assume that the listed points are for their understanding only, but that is not true.

There must be good documentation done on the given requirements. This helps the consultant to show-case it to the business users to get their confirmation on the requirement understanding. This helps the consultant to avoid any misunderstanding of requirements.

Sign off

Many times, a consultant prepares documentation of the requirements which he/she gathered during all the meetings, but fails to share it with the business users and get their sign off on the same. It may happen that a project needs to be kick started soon, but that doesn't mean that the requirement gathering sign off can be avoided.

Failing to get a sign-off may cause disagreement between the business users and the consultant. In the event of project failure, business user may put the responsibility on consultant for incorrect requirements gathered.

Thus, getting a sign off on requirement gathering documentation is an important task which a consultant should do.

It is always good to be prepared before the storm. A consultant should make sure that he doesn't make any of the listed mistakes to avoid any negative impact on the project.

Authentication and authorization

One important thing most of the consultants forget to talk during the requirement gathering stage is about the authentication and authorization.

Authentication is nothing but knowing if the user is the right and authenticated user. It is like asking the question *Who are you?* Someone should authenticate if the user is correct user. There are many systems available to do this job, where they save the passcode of the user and then they crosscheck the passcode when authentication is requested, and if the passcode is right then it allows the user to enter the system.

Authorization comes into picture only after the user is authenticated. It is like giving permission to access the data. Not all the users should have access to all the data; giving right permission to the users is necessary to maintain the security of the data.

Let us have a look at thefollowing example to understand the difference between authentication and authorization.

Let us assume that you are a supply chain professional and you have joined a manufacturing company. So, when you join a company, the company gives you an employee id. The employee id confirms that you are an authenticated user and that you are allowed to enter the company office.

Now that you are authenticated, it doesn't mean that you can enter every available department in the company. You may only be allowed to enter the supply chain department, or additionally, the procurement department, which is related to your work, but you may not be allowed to enter the manufacturing unit or any other unit which is not related to your work. This specifies your authorization.

In BI project like Qlik, the users are authenticated using Active directory or any third-party authentication services. The authorization part is taken care by using section access in Qlik.

Authentication and authorization are very important for any project. It is important for a consultant to get the authentication information from the IT team. The IT Team usually handles applications which can provide authentication to Qlik users. The authorization information should be taken from the business users who own the data and know what information should be shared with which user.

Documentation

Documentation is nothing but jotting things down on a paper or in a digital form. Almost every one of us knows this, but what we fail to know is that it is a very important task, which should be carried out in every single phase of the project life cycle.

Documentation holds the ability to solve most of the problems quickly, provided that it is a quality document which contains all the information about the project.

I am sure you must have heard the following proverb:

> *If it is not in written, it has never happened.*

The preceding proverb explains to us the importance of documentation in just couple of words. We also understand the importance of documentation, but most of us ignore it purposefully, because it takes time for preparation, and at times we don't know what should be documented and what should not be.

The following section will help you understand the main areas which should be captured and documented for Qlik projects, to make sure that a developer does not find it difficult to understand the requirement.

The documentation should have the following details.

Front page

This page captures the title for the document. If you are creating a separate document for every single requirement, then this page should contain the name of the report, along with the name of the entire project (if at all given) and the client name.

Introduction page

This section should contain brief information about the project and the requirement. The subsection of this section can be following it.

Introduction to document

The introduction should contain information about the document, such as what is the purpose of the document and what kind of information it is going to hold.

Scope of the document

This section should cover the scope of the document in brief, what information it will cover, and what information it won't cover.

Assumptions and constraints

Any assumptions are made for this requirement or any known constraints about the project should be clearly mentioned.

Meetings held

In this section, you can write down when the meeting was held for the gathering of this requirement. Also, you can mention the audience and the place of the meeting.

Abbreviations used in documentation

You can note down any specific short forms used in the document. This will help the reader to understand the document easily.

Requirement category

This section should specify the nature of the requirement: whether it is a must have, should have, or good to have requirement.

Functional requirement

In this section, you should jot down the details about the business requirement given by the business users in brief.

Business use case

This section should talk more about the business use cases which came up during discussion with the business users. This will help the reader to understand the purpose of this requirement and how it will help the business to make decisions.

KPIs

This section should list down the KPIs from the requirement which is given. This section should also list the logic used to derive that KPI.

Dimensions

This section should cover the list of dimensions required to slice and dice the data. You can also list down the dimension hierarchy, if any, to define the drill down requirement.

Functionality requirement

In this section, you should note down any specific functionality requirement of the business. For example, when a specific selection is made, then the data should be shown in a specific format.

Current reporting data flow

This section should cover the process that is being followed by the business users in the current environment to develop the given requirement. This step helps to know the complexity of the requirement and also helps to know what kind of logic needs to be applied to develop this report.

If possible, note the things step-wise, as follows:

1. Download the data from the source system
2. Transform the data
3. Create a pivot or any other chart

This is just an example. You may have n numbers of steps, depending on the requirement complexity.

Data sources

This section should list the various data sources which are needed to get all the necessary data. It should also list the connectivity parameters, such as, database server's IP address or DNS name, the port which will be used to connect to database, and so on. If there are flat files or Excel files, then their name and path should also be noted as parameters.

Various data sources have various parameters, so depending on the type of database, all parameters should be noted down in this section.

Tables and fields listing

Once you understand the database, you should delve deeper at the table level and further to field level. This helps to pick only the necessary fields for preparing the report.

This section should list all those tables from where the required data can be pulled in. At times, not all the fields from the table are required for report, and the fields which are considered should be listed down.

Other logic and mappings

This section should list any specific logic which is needed for developing the report. It could be anything like mapping logic, if statements, case statements, any other mapping which is used to derive any extra fields using the available fields, and so on.

Visualization requirement

While doing requirement gathering with the business users, if you have discussed on the visualization aspects and how the KPI would be presented and analysis done, the same should be noted in this section.

Authorization requirement

One of the key information which needs to be considered in requirement gathering is security with regards to authorization, that is, who will see what kind of data. This information needs to be taken from the business users.

This section should list such requirements and define who should see what kind of data.

Risk and mitigation plan

At times in requirement gathering, you may come across such notable points which could be a risk to your project. You may know how to mitigate these known risks though. It is important to note all such risks and mitigation plans for the same.

This section should note such risks and the plans to mitigate them.

User acceptance

This section should be used to take confirmation from the business users about all the points listed in previous sections. It is important to have this section in documentation, because it confirms from the business users that the noted points are the ones which they have discussed with the consultant.

Example

In this section, we will try to understand how the business requirement gathering happens in a real scenario. We will continue with the same example which we used in the previous chapter, where the CEO Eric and CFO Lisa of a retail company had a similar vision to increase the profitability of the company.

To convert their vision into reality, they want to analyze their sales along with the margin for various stores and various products. They want to do this using the Qlik BI tool and they have hired a consultant, Jay (you), to do the requirement gathering and implement the BI tool to help them achieve what they want.

You decide to have a requirement meeting with the business user, Mr. Ravi. Following is the conversation which they have while doing requirement gathering:

Jay (You): *Good morning, Ravi, thanks for joining this meeting. I am a Qlik consultant and our company has been asked to implement the Qlik project to analyze your data to achieve the vision of increasing the profitability of the company. Rob told me that you are the one who is currently preparing the analysis for Eric and Lisa to take respective decisions.*

Ravi: *Good morning Jay. Nice to meet you. I have already been informed by our CIO Rob about the Qlik project. And you are right, I am responsible for preparing the analysis for the management.*

Jay (You): *Glad to hear that you already know about Qlik. As you know, the management wants to have a near real time analysis of sales and margin, and they want to see that analysis on Qlik. I have been told to take the requirement from you and understand it thoroughly.*

Ravi: *Yes, even I want to get this report developed in Qlik.*

Jay (You): *That's great. Let us start the requirement gathering. I will be asking you a few questions related to the requirement and I request your help in getting my understanding right.*

Ravi: *Sure.*

Jay (You): *Can you tell me in brief what is this report all about? What kind of analysis do you present to the management?*

Ravi: *This report is mainly about analyzing the sales over the trends for all the 70 stores we have. I also show the margin along with sales, so that the management can compare them side by side, and see if the margin has increased with increase in the sales or not. I also show the targets to measure the over all progress.*

Jay (You): *What are the data sources for this report?*

Ravi: *The data comes from the SAP system which we have. So sales and margin comes from the SAP system and the targets are fed in by the Excel.*

Jay (You): *How do you get the data from SAP?*

Ravi: *I have access to the SAP system. We have developed a customized report which collects the sales and margin data from various inbuilt SAP tables.*

Jay (You): *Is there any TCode which you use to get this data?*

Ravi: *Yes, the TCode is ZMSales.*

Jay (You): *Is there any business logic applied in this report?*

Ravi: *Yes, we have used few masters which are linked to this data and we also do basic categorization as per our business needs.*

Jay (You): *Can you share those business logics with me? Do you have any documentation of those logics?*

Ravi: *No, we don't have any documentation, but I know those logic because I have developed those reports in SAP. I can explain to you the entire logic.*

Jay (You): *Thank you. Can you tell me who creates this target excel file and from where do you get it?*

Ravi: *I get this file at the start of every year from the finance team. The targets are decided by the finance team and management in their meeting.*

Jay (You): *Does this target file get updated during the course of the year?*

Ravi: *Yes, at times it does get updated in any month.*

Jay (You): *In such a scenario, how do you handle your report? Do you change the already reported numbers?*

Ravi: *It is simple, because the targets get updated only for the future months. So if the month is closed, its target doesn't get updated. So it doesn't have any impact on the data which is already reported.*

Jay (You): *The targets are defined at what level?*

Ravi: *Targets are defined for each product category for each month. Mainly, we have three categories: men's wear, ladies' wear, and kids' wear.*

Jay (You): *How many months of data do you show in your report?*

Ravi: *Typically, the management is interested to see the trends for the previous two years and the current running year.*

Jay (You): *What are the main KPIs which you have in your report?*

Ravi: *Mainly I show YTD, MTD, and FTD sales, margin and targets side by side, and also give the variance of the same. This gives an overview of the sales. Then I also show the top performing brands and the non-performing brands in another sheet. I also show the stores which have done more sales as compared to last year. I only show the like to like stores when I show comparison of the stores.*

Jay (You): *What do you mean by like to like stores?*

Ravi: *In our retail business, not all stores get opened at the same time. Stores may start operations any time in a year, so in this case, you cannot compare the sales of one store with other as they may have started operations at different time. So the store which is old may have more sales than the store which is newly open. To tackle this situation, we use the like to like logic. In this logic, we compare the store opening date, and we only consider the stores which were in operation during the time periods which are getting compared.*

So for example, if we are comparing the YTD sales data, assuming we are in the month of September 2017, with the previous year YTD, we will only consider the sales of the stores which were open before September 2016. This is so that we get a correct comparison. The stores which were opened after September 2016 will not be considered for this comparison.

I hope you understood the logic.

Jay (You): *Yes, I understood it. For this calculation, we would require the store opening date, right?*

Ravi: *Right, without that how will you know the tenure of the store?*

Jay (You): *Do you use any kind of color coding to showcase the KPIs?*

Ravi: *No I don't use any color in my report. This is one of the things which we are looking to get from Qlik reports.*

Jay (You): *On what basis do you decide the color?*

Ravi: *For example, if KPI is YTD Sales comparison, the color combination is as follows. If the YTD Sales of current year is 90 percent of the previous year then it should be in green. If it is in between 60 percent to 90 percent, it should be in yellow, otherwise it should be red.*

Jay (You): *What about the KPIs where you compare the sales with target?*

Ravi: *In that case also the color criteria will remain same.*

Jay (You): *Is there any specific challenge you face while making this report?*

Ravi: *Our business model is such that we might need to do some back dated entries in the system. In such cases, it becomes difficult to prepare report and thus I always take data at a cutoff date. After that, if there are any changes in the data, I do not consider it, which at times gives a wrong picture to the management.*

Jay (You): *In such cases, when back dated entries happen in system, what do you do in next month? Do you consider the reported numbers or do you show the updated numbers?*

Ravi: *I always show the updated numbers, irrespective of what I had shown earlier. I always give a disclaimer about the same while showing the report.*

Jay (You): *That's great. Qlik will also show the updated numbers always. Is there anything else which you feel may become show stopper?*

Ravi: *No, if you handle this situation, I feel you are half way through.*

Jay (You): *Have you ever come across the issue of slowly changing dimension while creating report?*

Ravi: *No, we don't have that situation, and even if that arises the slowly changing dimension has been taken care at SAP level.*

Jay (You): *Ok.*

Jay (You): *What is the frequency at which you prepare this report?*

Ravi: *I prepare this report on a weekly basis. At what frequency can Qlik provide this report?*

Jay (You): *Qlik can provide you the report on daily basis.*

Ravi: *Sounds good. If that happens then the management can see the data every day and take necessary decisions.*

Jay (You): *Yes, that's the power the BI tool has.*

Jay (You): *Last question, who are the users of this report? Is this report available to middle management also?*

Ravi: *The main users are Eric and Lisa. But I also prepare a subset of this report at brand level, so that it can be shared with the respective brand managers, who then take the decision of merchandizing.*

Jay (You): *Can you provide me the details, like who should see what kind of data? In Qlik, we just need to define that, and Qlik takes care of the security. Depending on the user who logs on the portal, Qlik will automatically hide the unauthorized data from them.*

Ravi: *Perfect. I am excited to see this report live as soon as possible.*

Jay (You): *Sure Ravi. I got most of the information which I was looking for.*

Jay (You): *Thanks for spending your valuable time with me to discuss this report. You have given me quite important information, which will help me to develop this report.*

Ravi: *Thanks Jay, it was a pleasure to talk to you. Feel free to contact me if you need any further help.*

Jay (You): *Thanks Ravi. Good day.*

This conversation is just a simple example of how a requirement gathering meeting happens between the consultant and the business user. In case of complex requirements, there will be many more questions needed to get all the details of the requirement.

Summary

So we have reached the end of the chapter, and in this couple of hours of reading, we have learned important aspects of requirement gathering. Following them will help increasing the productivity and deliver quality services to client.

In this chapter, we started with the basic understanding of what requirement gathering is. Just to rewind it, it is nothing but the way in which a problem can be understood and the solution that can be thought of. It is an important phase in the life cycle of project execution, and can have negative impact if we skip this phase in project implementation.

Moving ahead in the chapter, we learned how to execute requirement gathering and we saw that we can divide it into multiple categories, like functional requirement, technical requirement, and infrastructural requirement. Once you do this, you need to start the requirement gathering process and that you can do in various ways. You can do the brain storming sessions, requirement gathering discussions, document analysis, reverse engineering, and questionnaires. Each one of this method can be used to conduct good requirement gathering; at times you may use one or all of these methods together.

Then we understood the must have, should have, and good to have strategies and looked at how this strategy can help you to priorities the requirements given by the various business users. This is a very good strategy which is mainly used in agile methodology. Now a days, agile methodology is getting popular for software development and support projects.

Then we saw what are the different kinds of questions which should be asked in requirement gathering. We also learned the importance of asking questions. We ran through an example of a meeting and and questions to be asked to get the information.

Then moving ahead in our chapter, we learned about the important point, that is, the must ask information. These are the list of questions which one should ask, without fail, to the business. This information will help you to understand the reason behind starting the BI project and will help you to understand the success criteria based on which the project's success will be decided.

We also saw what the common mistakes which are likely to be done by a consultant while conducting requirement gathering. We went through most of the common mistakes and understood why they happen and what would happen if those mistakes were done. Those mistakes have a direct relation with the success of the project, and thus it is recommended that they should be avoided as much as possible.

Moving forward, we looked at the authentication and authorization part of the project; what these keywords stand for and why they are important. We looked at the way these security features are implemented in Qlik projects.

Then we learned what documentation and how it can help you in the future. We also looked at the different parameters which should be included in the requirement gathering document. From a consultant's perspective, this is a very important step which he shouldn't avoid. It can help you during both the phase of implementation and after the project is complemented. A proper documentation shows the quality of the work done.

At the end, we saw a small requirement gathering conversation between a consultant and a business user, where both of them discussed the requirement and the consultant asked many questions to get more and more information from the business user.

In the next chapter, we are going to learn how to architect the Qlik project. We will see various aspects of architecture, starting from the infrastructure architecture to data architecture. We will also see how to do Qlik Sense installation with two different options available. So stay tuned for the next chapter.

5
Architecture Design

In the previous chapter, we learned about requirement gathering. In this chapter, we will see the best methods to architect the entire project from an infrastructure point of view and from a data point of view. This chapter is even more important than other chapters, because the sustainability of a project depends on the topics covered in this chapter.

In this chapter, our primary focus will be about architecting a project in such a way that it can sustain for a long period of time. A project with highly flexible and robust architecture design tends to remain for a long time, and thus it is important to know how to build such architecture.

In this chapter, we will be covering these topics:

- An introduction and importance
- Hardware and software requirements
- Installation architecture
- Backup and restore design
- Data architecture
- Data flow diagrams

An introduction and importance

Architecting is nothing more than the art of designing the foundation of the building; the more powerful the designing, the more likely the building will stand strong in any circumstances. The same applies to projects in the IT world. If you design the most optimized architecture of a project, the project is likely to remain for a long period.

We come across cases where a project which started well, after a period, starts falling apart. The primary reason for this is often because it is not architected properly.

When it comes to architecting the Qlik projects, the project manager may not understand the importance of it and may not pay enough attention to architecting the project. There could be reasons for not taking architecting seriously. The main reason is that many project managers are non-technical guys; what matters to them is to finish the project on time and utilize the available resources to the fullest. So they never think of the future of the project, and thus they don't know how to make a durable project.

The second reason could be the time constraint because, in most of the cases, the Qlik projects are underestimated in terms of time. Everyone feels that Qlik projects can be delivered very quickly, which is true for small projects, but the big projects need proper planning and sufficient time for execution.

Thus, being a Qlik consultant, you should take architecting of the Qlik project seriously. Irrespective of the size of the project, you should do proper planning of infrastructure and other things, keeping at least three to four years in mind.

The importance of architecture designing can be understood by the following quote:

> *It is not the beauty of a building you should look at; it's the construction of foundation that will stand the test of time.* -- **David Allan Coe**

It is clear from the previous quote that you must focus on the foundation of a project because that is what is going to hold the project in all kinds of known or unknown calamities.

For a project in Qlik, architecting the project is nothing more than handling two important factors properly, which otherwise may make a successful project fail subsequently. One is proper hardware and software infrastructure and the other is data architecture.

Both parameters are most important for Qlik projects; they can be called the Qlik projects' two pillars. If anyone pillar is down, then the entire project may fail. As you know, Qlik is an in-memory tool and it does all the calculations and aggregations on the fly. It becomes very important that there is enough hardware and software infrastructure available for Qlik to perform as expected. The other pillar, data architecture, is important because it's the input for Qlik. Thus, it is important to create a proper design for the flow of data to get proper output from Qlik.

Parameters for infrastructure design

For Qlik infrastructure design, a Qlik consultant should consider the hardware and software requirements. Along with that, the Qlik consultant should also consider the way in which the Qlik Sense dashboards would be accessed by the end users, that is, whether they would access the Qlik Sense dashboard within the company network, which is intranet, or they would access them over the internet.

If it is within the intranet, there may not be much setting required, but when Qlik Sense needs to be accessed over the internet, then depending on the client's security policy, there might be additional configuration required to provide enhanced security.

Hardware infrastructure

As a Qlik consultant, you should know the Qlik architecture, how Qlik performs calculations and how it stores the data. If you know this well then you can estimate a better hardware infrastructure.

Let us have a look at the various parameters which are required to be considered to design a good hardware infrastructure.

RAM (Random Access Memory)

We all know RAM. In brief, it is the storage location on the machine which allows faster access to the data stored within and thus allows faster calculations to be performed on the data.

Qlik is an in-memory data discovery tool. When we say in-memory, it means it stores the data in RAM of the machine and does all the required calculations, like aggregations and other calculations, in RAM, which makes the response of the result of the calculation faster. That is the reason why Qlik gives a faster response even when the data size is huge.

Thus, while designing the architecture of the Qlik hardware, it is important that you know how much RAM will be required.

CPU (Central Processing Unit)

CPU can be called brain of the computers. It is responsible for performing all kinds of calculations. Because Qlik does all the calculations on the fly, it is important that you have enough CPU speed to perform all the calculations.

There are few things you need to consider while deciding the CPU for Qlik hardware:

- **CPU speed**: Speed in Gigahertz (GHz)
- **CPU cores**: Number of cores in processor
- **CPU brand**: Company like Intel or AMD, and so on

Note: It is a wrong perception that if you increase the RAM of the server, your performance will increase substantially. CPU is also as much important as RAM, because all the calculations done on front-end require sufficient CPU.

HDD (Hard Disk Drive)

HDD is the secondary storage device which is used to store all the file systems. Qlik stores everything as a file system and uses its own file extensions to store data, so that it can be retrieved faster.

Being a Qlik consultant, you should know that the data is not only stored in **QVD** (**qlikview datafile**) but also in Qlik Sense application which has an extension of `.qvf`. So you need enough available space to create a dashboard. Qlik also generates extensive logs, and for that also you need space on hard drive.

Thus, estimating HDD is also important; you should have sufficient hard drive to store all the data.

Number of concurrent Users

One may wonder why it is important to know the number of concurrent users while estimating the hardware for Qlik. However, a Qlik consultant should be aware about Qlik reserving approximately 10 percent of the RAM per application for every concurrent user. This RAM is allocated when user opens any application hosted on Hub. For example, if a sales application is consuming 2 GB of RAM and there are 10 concurrent users, the RAM needed will be 4GB (2 GB+ 200MB*10).

So the number of concurrent users plays an important role in deciding the RAM requirement for the Qlik hardware.

Number of Applications

Just like the number of users, the number of applications, along with the complexity, also plays an important role in deciding the hardware requirement for Qlik. More the number of applications with more concurrency, more RAM will be required.

Things to remember

- Qlik does data compression depending on the unique values in the dataset.
- When QVF is created and stored along with the data, it is in compressed format.
- When QVF is loaded in RAM, the size of the RAM taken by the application is almost four to five times the size of the application.
- For every concurrent user you need to make provision of 10 percent of RAM needed by the application.

Example calculation

Let us now look at a scenario which will help you to put the preceding learning into practice.

Sample Data:

Source data size	50 GB
Compression ratio	80 percent
File size multiplier	4
User RAM Allocation	10 percent
Number of Application	1
Number of Concurrent users	10

Based on the preceding example let us understand how we can do the calculation.

Calculation:

Application Size = Source Data Size * (1 - Compression Ratio)

$$= 50 \text{ GB} * (1 - 0.80)$$

$$= 10 \text{ GB}$$

RAM Required (Initially) = Application Size * File Size Multiplier

$$= 10 \text{ GB} * 4$$

$$= 40 \text{ GB}$$

RAM required (per User) = RAM Required (Initially) * 10%

$$= 40GB * 10\%$$

$$= 4\ GB$$

Total RAM Required = RAM Required (Initially) + (RAM Required (Per User) * No of Concurrent Users)

$$= 40\ GB + (4\ GB * 10)$$

$$= 80\ GB$$

Clients often ask the consultant for server recommendations. Qlik consultant should share the server white-list provided by Qlik. The white-list has the chipsets which have been tested by Qlik in their labs.

> **TIP**
>
> In case you are not aware, the white-list can be obtained from the URL: `http://www.qlik.com/us/resource-library/qlikview-tech-note-scalability-center`.

Software infrastructure

Along with the hardware, it is also important to decide which software will be required to run the different products of Qlik.

The following are the software which are required.

Operating system

An operating system is required to be installed on the server. Qlik technology is built to work on Microsoft operating systems only, thus, the operating system should be the Microsoft operating system.

You can choose any OS or the one recommended in the minimum software requirement document for the Qlik Sense version you are planning to install.

If your project involves multiple developers who are going to need simultaneous access to the Qlik Sense server, then you may also require Windows terminal licenses. By default, the server allows two logins, but if you need more, you will have to buy terminal licenses from Microsoft.

Microsoft office

If you are planning to use NPrinting along with Qlik Sense, then you may also need the Microsoft Office Suite to be able to do the designing of the reports on Excel, PPT, or in Word.

Microsoft .NET Framework

You will need the latest .net framework to be installed on the server so that Qlik Sense software can be installed successfully. Qlik Sense uses the .net framework to perform the internal operations and many other things.

Relevant ODBC/OLEDB Drivers

If your data source provides the ODBC/OLEDB connection, then you may also require separate drivers to be installed on the server, so that you can create an ODBC/OLEDB connection and connect to the relevant data source.

Qlik connectors

If your data sources do not provide the ODBC/OLEDB connection, then you may have to look for additional connectors which Qlik provides, like Qlik SAP connector, Qlik Salesforce connectors, and so on.

PostgreSQL

By default, PostgreSQL is installed along with the Qlik Sense install.

Security infrastructure

If you are planning to expose Qlik Sense to public network, that is, internet, then to secure the data and to access, you may want to use the HTTPS connection to your Qlik server. In such case, you will need trusted *digital certificates* for encrypted connection between Qlik Sense server and client machine.

As a Qlik consultant, you should know what *ports* are being used by Qlik Sense, so that you can have those ports open on the firewall, for Qlik to have successful connection. There are settings available in Qlik Sense to change the default ports to customized ports.

To be able to authenticate the users, you should have at least one third party authentication module, because Qlik Sense does not do authentication by itself. You may need Active Directory, Windows local directory, or any third-party authentication module. You can also use Salesforce, Facebook, or Twitter as authentication module.

Network infrastructure

When users want to connect to Qlik Sense over the internet, you will need a *static IP* for the Qlik Sense server. Also, you may need to provide a domain name mapped to your static IP address and also require a trusted digital certificate.

> If you want to implement reverse proxy, you will have to also think about the same and plan the resources and configuration accordingly.

You should also know that to access Qlik Sense from outside network, a couple of known ports need to be open on the firewall.

Hardware and software requirements

We have already seen what parameters are required for hardware infrastructure and seen the required software list. Let us have a look at the minimum hardware and software requirements for Qlik Sense:

CPU	Multi core x64 compatible processor. Recommended minimum 4 cores.
RAM	Minimum 8 GB (Additional as per the data volumes).
HDD	1.5 GB minimum for installation, and additional to store the data and apps. It can also be SAN or network drive.
Operating system	For Qlik Sense server, server operating system Microsoft server 2012 R2 64 Bit or above For Qlik Sense development, any operating system above Windows 7 64 Bit
.NET framework	4.5.2 or above
Security	Any third-party authentication module, like AD or Microsoft integrated windows authentication.
Repository Database	PostgreSQL (By default installed with Qlik Sense).

Installation architecture

Now that you know what hardware and software are required, you are good to start with the installation process. But before actually starting the installation process, you should also know what kind of installation will be required as per the requirement is given by the client.

Let us understand a some terminology before considering the types of installation.

Node

Node is nothing but a computer or server which is created to perform a specific role or a combination of roles.

When Qlik Sense is installed, it installs a series of services, which are used to perform respective tasks. For example, the proxy service will be used to do authentication, session handling, and load balancing, whereas scheduler service will be used to schedule the tasks to reload the applications, and so on.

So when you want to assign a specific task to a single server, you can configure the services on that node to make it perform only that specific task.

There are basically two types of nodes which can be created in Qlik Sense:

- **Central node**: Central node is responsible for controlling all the services, thus every install of Qlik Sense should have one central node
- **Rim node**: An additional node which is configured to host one or more services of Qlik Sense to share load of central node

You can also create a node for specific purposes. For example, you can configure a node to behave in one of the following ways:

- Production
- Development
- Both

Site

Qlik Sense site is nothing but the collection of one or more nodes connected to the central repository. Each node in a Qlik Sense site shares the same license. So you don't need a separate license for adding nodes to your site.

There are basically two types of Qlik Sense sites:

- **Single node site**: Single node site has only one node, which is central node, and it does not have any rim nodes connected to it. You can also call this a standalone installation. All the services and repository databases are installed on the same server.

- **Multi node site:** In this type of Qlik Sense site, you install one or more rim nodes which are connected to a central node. Each node is created with a specific role to perform and then they are connected to the control node.

Multi node site allows the following advantages over single node site:

- Scalability
- Increases the capacity
- Improves resilience
- Improves reliability

Single node architecture

Single node architecture contains the installation of single node Qlik Sense site. As we have seen, this is a configuration where all the services and repository databases are installed on a single server.

Single node architecture is useful when there is a small user base and the small amount of data is being used for analysis. Typically for small and mid-size companies, a single node architecture can suffice.

For example, a company which has a limited number of users and a couple of Qlik Sense dashboards with small data size can use single node architecture. A single node architecture is easier to manage. Based on the roles available in Qlik Sense management console, organization can assign the development role to specific users and to another set of users the role of publishing the final application to specific streams.

The following figure shows a single node architecture:

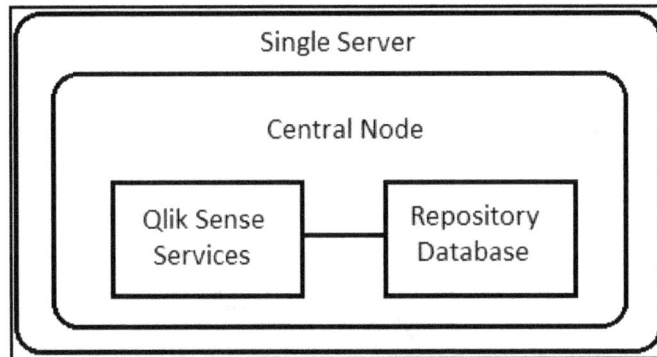

Advantages of single node architecture:

- Simple to install
- Faster access to the repository database

Disadvantages of single node architecture:

- Does not provide scalability option
- Failure of central node leads to application becoming unavailable to users.

Multi node architecture

Multi Node architecture is nothing but having multiple node in a Qlik Sense site. In this installation, there is one central node and one or more rim nodes which are created to perform specific tasks and roles. All these nodes are installed on different servers.

Multi node architecture can be used in two cases generally. The first being when you want to separate the development activity from the production server and have an automatic synchronization between the development server and the production server. The second being when you want to share the Qlik Sense server load across servers. This gives better performance to the end users by increasing the hardware of the server and doing the load balancing amongst them-in short, when you want to scale the Qlik Sense implementation.

The following diagram shows a multi node architecture:

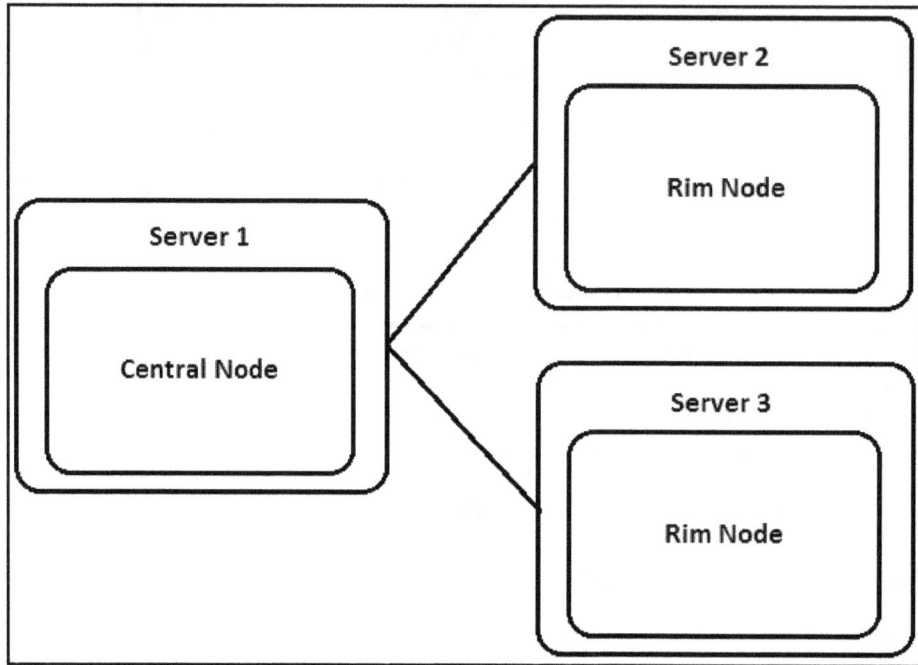

Advantages of multi node architecture:

- It is a scalable architecture
- It doesn't require additional licenses
- It adds resilience
- It helps in load balancing

Disadvantages of multi node architecture:

- Complex to implement
- Requires more hardware and software resources
- Requires continuous syncing of database from rim nodes to central node

Qlik sense repository database

When Qlik Sense is installed, the PostgreSQL database also gets installed on the server. This PostgreSQL is used to store the Qlik Sense apps along with other information. Depending on which node architecture you choose to install, you will also need to choose the option for installing the database repository. The two options which you get are **Shared Persistence** and **Synchronized persistence**.

From the latest version of Qlik Sense, that is June 2017 release, you won't find the option of synchronized persistence while installing the Qlik Sense, because shared persistence has been made compulsory from this version, but if you are installing prior version, you will get an option while installing to choose any one of them.

Let us have a look at both and their use cases.

Synchronized persistence

Synchronized persistence is nothing but installing a separate instance of PostgreSQL database on each of the machines where you are installing Qlik Sense, be it central node or rim node.

When you are planning a single node architecture installation, you will have only one instance of repository database on the central node, and the repository will be connected to this central node. In this case, all the data, along with app, will be stored in the local repository. Because there are no other nodes involved in this architecture, you don't need to sync the database.

Following image shows a synchronized persistence installation on single node architecture:

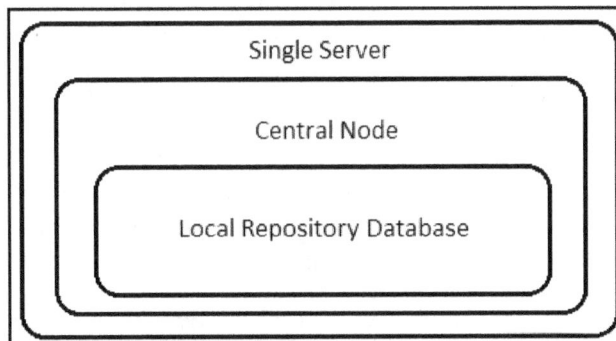

When you are planning a multi node architecture installation, then every installation of rim node, along with the central node, will have their own local copy of the repository database installed on respective servers. Every node will use its local copy of the database to create apps and make changes to them. All these changes are then synced with the central node at regular intervals.

Following image shows synchronized persistence with a multi node architecture:

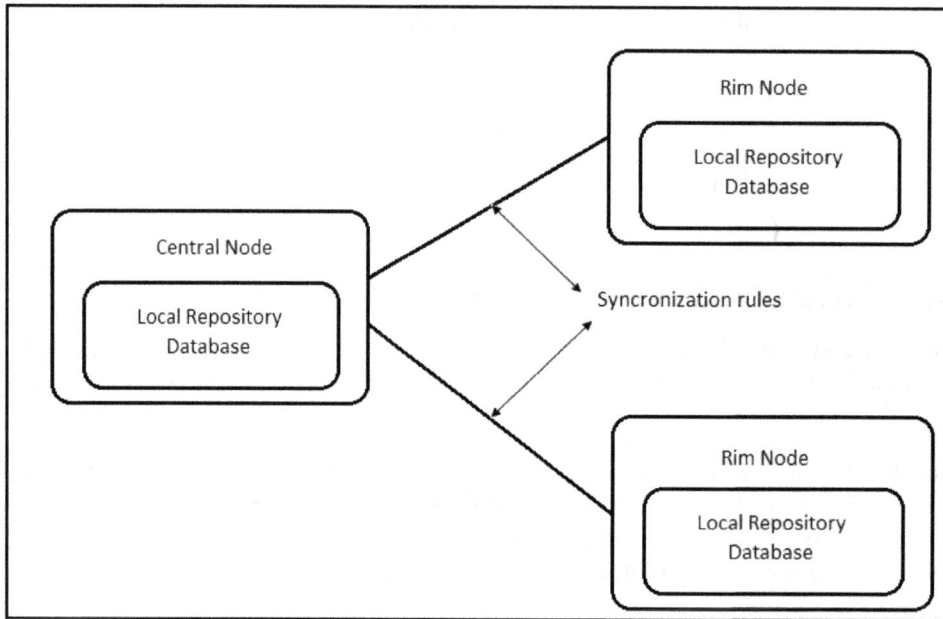

The advantage of using synchronized persistence is that it allows the database copy to be available on all the nodes. So if a rim node fails, you do not lose any data, because the same has been synced with the central node at set intervals, so you get all the data up to the last sync between the central node and the rim node. When the central node is down, you can still get data from the local database of the rim node, up to the last sync between the central node and the rim node.

The disadvantage of this persistence is that it requires time to sync the data from all the nodes to the rim node. Depending on the network speed between the central node and the rim node, it takes time. This activity will consume server resources for the sync.

Synchronized persistence was available only until Qlik Sense version 3.

Shared persistence

As the name suggests, it is the sharing of Qlik Sense repository database amongst all nodes. We have seen previously that the main drawback of synchronized persistence is that it takes time to sync the data, so to overcome this problem, shared persistence is used where the repository database is shared between all the nodes in the architecture. This helps to reduce the synchronization time required to sync the database and makes the data available faster.

Shared persistence in single node installation is shown next:

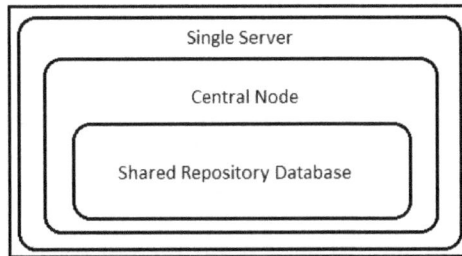

In single node architecture, because the installation is done only on single server and that too only on a central node, you can create a shared folder on a local computer to store the apps and install a local copy of repository database.

Shared persistence in multi node architecture is shown next:

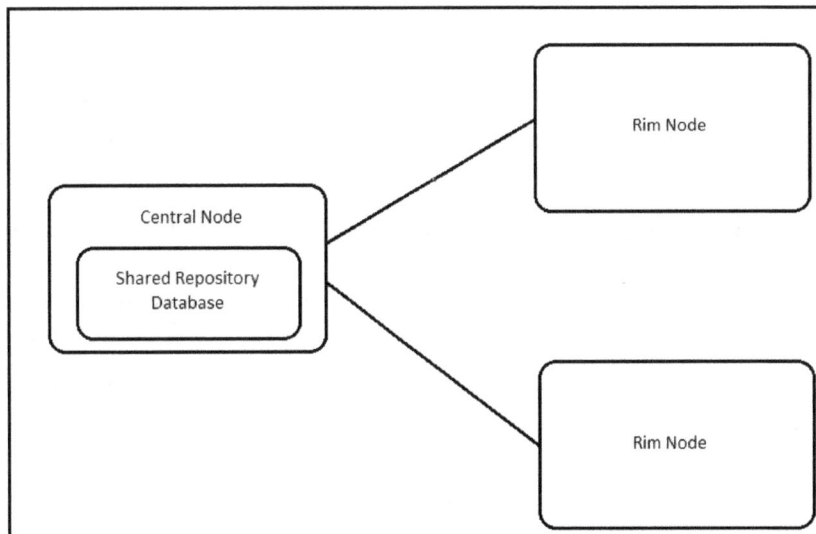

In multi node architecture, you can install the repository database and create a shared folder, which can be accessed by the other nodes in the architecture. All the rim nodes directly store the respective data and apps on the shared database and folder, which almost removes the synchronization time which was required in synchronized persistence.

The shared folder can be created either on the central node or it can be any other server which is in the same geographical area and same network.

Shared persistence has few limitations as of now, which you should be aware of:

- Shared persistence does not work when the node is in a different geographical location.
- It supports only eight nodes which can connect to the repository database.
- Because the folder is a shared folder and it can be accessed only over network, the network speed and the hardware speed play important roles. If they are not sufficient, a node may or may not work as expected.

As a Qlik Sense consultant, you should have a fair idea of what kind of Qlik Sense installation architecture will suit your client side, depending on their requirements. Also, you should know how to configure various settings for a Qlik Sense installation, before and after the installations.

I would recommend that you follow the steps given on the help site of Qlik for installation, upgrade, and uninstallation of Qlik Sense.

Backup and restore design

We all know what backup and restore means and their importance. Generally, it is done for data and systems which are very important and which need continual access.

Though Qlik Sense does not generate any data, it provides critical insights to businesses about their data. The business users depend on the Qlik Sense dashboards for business information and usually they want Qlik Sense to be continuously available. Hence consultant should plan the backup and restore mechanism for Qlik Sense server.

There are a couple of ways in which you can take the backup of the Qlik Sense site.

DR (Disaster Recovery) server setup

A disaster can be anything which causes the Qlik Sense server to go down and lead to a major impact on the business operations. Today, no one can assure that there won't be any kind of disaster. A disaster could occur for any reason, like natural calamities, human error, malfunction of software, and so on. Thus, it is important that the Qlik Sense installations, especially ones with large-scale usage should have a disaster recovery plan.

Disaster recovery in Qlik Sense is nothing but setting up a mirror copy of the production install, along with the configuration setting and the data, on another server, typically located at different geographical area or in different network. This DR (disaster recovery) server will be configured to sync data from the production site at regular intervals to get new data and updates. This helps to reduce the downtime caused by the disaster, as DR instance is replica of production. The DR setup can be made active if primary site goes down. The activity should be scheduled in such a way that the end user should not be impacted much.

In case your production architecture is single node architecture with either shared persistence or synchronized persistence, you don't need to worry much, because you have only a central node in the single node architecture, so creating a DR won't be that difficult.

When you have multi node architecture in production environment, with synchronized persistence, then you should create a backup for the machine where the central node is installed, because all the data from the rim node will be synced with the central node, and the central node is responsible for handling the repository database. With multi node architecture, if you have shared persistence, then you can take the backup of the node on which the repository database is installed and the shared folder.

This backup strategy is the most effective way of doing the backup, but it requires additional investments and the hardware needed is equivalent or at least half the size of the production site server. So the cost impact in this strategy is high.

This type of backup can be planned when Qlik sense dashboards are critical to business and any downtime of Qlik Sense server impacts business operations.

Physical backup

In this backup strategy, you will have to take the backup of the physical files and folders which have the data stored within them. You can schedule a regular backup of these files and keep them on some other server or on network drive.

In case of any disaster, you will need to install Qlik Sense and create the same architecture as the production server had, and then use this backup file and database to restore the data and settings.

This strategy won't require many resources, except the space on either hard drive or the network drive. The restoration of the data in this type takes longer than the earlier type.

This option can be used when the downtime doesn't impact the business operations. You can also use this option along with the previous type to make it more secure.

Now let us see what items you need to be backed up for Qlik Sense.

Applications

By applications we mean the Qlik Sense applications. These applications can be either dashboards or extractors (the applications which are used to fetch data from the source database or the QVD generation applications). Every application which is hosted or created on Qlik Sense server is stored either on the local drive of the server, on the shared drive on the server, or on the network drive.

These applications contain the data models created for each dashboard, and thus, it is important that you take the backup of the folder which contains these applications.

You can find the location of the folder from the Qlik Sense management console.

Application data

Application data is nothing but the base data which is used to create the dashboard on Qlik Sense site. Depending on the requirement, the dashboard may data present either in QVD and/or from Excel and/or text files.

Backup of the folder which contains this data is important because when you reload the Qlik Sense application, it will need all these files required to refresh the dashboard.

Log files

Log files are also important as they contain the history of various events which have occurred, starting from the installation day.

There are a couple of default Qlik Sense applications which are created by the administrator or the root admin to monitor the logs, and those applications use this log folder for base data. Thus, it is also important to take a backup of this folder.

Qlik Sense certificates

Qlik Sense certificates are used for secure communication between the users and the Qlik Sense services, and servers as mean of encryption of traffic between server and client.

So it is important to take a backup of the Qlik Sense certificates to make sure that you do not lose information like passwords used for the data connections.

Repository database

Qlik Sense Repository database is an important part of Qlik Sense installation. It is responsible for storing most of the Qlik Sense configurations. It stores user information, proxy information, and many more things.

Thus, it becomes important to take backup of this database, to make sure that when we restore the Qlik Sense, it works properly with all the old settings.

Qlik Sense uses the PostgreSQL database to store the configurations, so when planning a backup of this database, you should run some specific steps to take the database dump and store it as backup.

Implementations may have either a single node architecture or a multi node architecture. Irrespective of whichever persistence method used either synchronized persistence or shared persistence, you must take a backup of the repository database of the central node.

Example Scenario

Now that we have covered almost all the points which need to be taken care of when deciding the infrastructural architecture, let us look at an example scenario which will help us to understand the topics in more detail.

Let us continue with the same example we saw in the previous chapter, about the company AB Fashion. Requirement gathering has been done and now it is time to decide the architecture which will need to be implemented to make sure that Qlik Sense is available all the time with the high availability of data.

As a consultant, you ask some questions to business and to yourself and find answers to them to decide the architecture. Following are the questions and answers:

Q1: What is the actual data size of the data sources?

A1: The data source is SAP and the expected size is around 300 GB.

Q2: Out of the entire data, how much data will be used for analysis?

A2: The data which will be required for analytical reporting is around 80 GB.

Q3: What is the rate at which data will grow every year?

A3: With growing business, the data grows at a rate of 10-15 percent every year.

Q4: How many applications will be needed to give data insight to the business?

A4: To cater to all the requirements given by the business users, total 5-6 applications will be required.

Q5: How many overall users will be accessing the applications?

A4: Including the management, the company has decided to share the insight with some other users, like department heads and brand managers. So overall, the user base will be 35.

Q6: At any point of time, how many users will be accessing the application concurrently?

A6: Out of the total 35 users, we will have a maximum of 15 concurrent users, and that too at month end, when monitoring the sales is important.

Q7: What will be the complexity of the application?

A7: From the requirement gathering, it is expected that the complexity of the applications will be moderate.

Q8: Does the management need access to reports from the internet?

A8: Yes, because the management generally travels to multiple locations and they need continuous access to the dashboards.

Q9: Is additional security needed?

A9: Qlik itself will have a login mechanism and licensing, so we don₀t think we would need any additional security, apart from hosting Qlik Sense on HTTPS.

In addition to these questions and answers, there is some more information which is available:

- The company uses Active Directory to authenticate its users.
- The company wants to have the latest version of Qlik Sense installed.
- It doesn't have extra server for development. The development should happen from Qlik Sense browser.
- The company has a firewall installed on its network.
- The company has not bought NPrinting module.

Hardware requirements

With all the preceding information, you will first start with estimating the hardware. The calculation to decide the RAM requirement is as follows.

Calculation

Application size = Source data Size * (1 - Compression Ratio)

$$= 80 \ GB \ * \ (1 - 0.80)$$

$$= 16 \ GB$$

RAM required (Initially) = Application size * File size multiplier

$$= 16 \ GB \ * \ 4$$

$$= 64 \ GB$$

RAM required (per User) = RAM required (Initially) * 10%

$$= 64GB \ * \ 10\%$$

$$= 6.4 \ GB$$

Total RAM required = RAM required (Initially) + (RAM required (Per User) * number of concurrent Users)

$$= 64 \ GB + (6.4 \ GB \ * \ 15)$$

$$= 160 \ GB$$

So the required RAM for Qlik Sense hardware can be around 160 GB, but looking at the estimation for the next 5 years, you can suggest 196 GB upgradable to 256 GB. It is important that you tell the client that the server should be capable of upgrading in future.

Looking at the complexity of the application (assuming they are moderate in complexity), you can suggest a server with the latest CPU, with good clock speed and with at least 16 core processors.

Software requirements

Now that you have estimated the hardware for Qlik Sense, it is time to recommend the software for the server. The software requirement will be as follows:

Operating system	Windows server 2012 R2 and above with 64-bit architecture
Microsoft office	MS Office 2007 and above (optional)
.NET framework	.NET framework 4.5.2 and above
SAP connector	Qlik Sense SAP connector

Security requirements

Users are likely to face challenges if security requirements are not taken care of. Two main points which need to be taken care as mentioned as follows:-

- A Digital certificate with wild card or with specific domain name from trusted certificate provider.
- Active Directory information, like host name of the server which is acting as Active Directory.

Network requirements

Business users will face challenges in accessing Qlik Sense applications if network requirements are not take care of. Let us look at two important ones.

- Certain ports like 443 for HTTPS connection and 4244 for Qlik Sense authentication, need to be open for inbound connection on company's firewall.
- A static IP address and DNS should be configured to allow access to Qlik Sense from outside the company network.

User access requirement

For installation and connection to data sources, access requirements must be met. The two important ones are mentioned as follows:-

- One user with admin rights will be needed to install the Qlik Sense software on server.
- Connection details of SAP will be needed, along with the username and password, to get full access or access to specific modules of SAP.

Installation architecture

Now it's time to decide the Qlik Sense installation architecture.

Looking at the requirement, you can suggest that single node architecture is sufficient, as the user base is small and the number of applications which need to be developed is also less.

Because the client needs the latest version of Qlik Sense, you will have only one option, which is shared persistence.

So the overall architecture will look as follows:

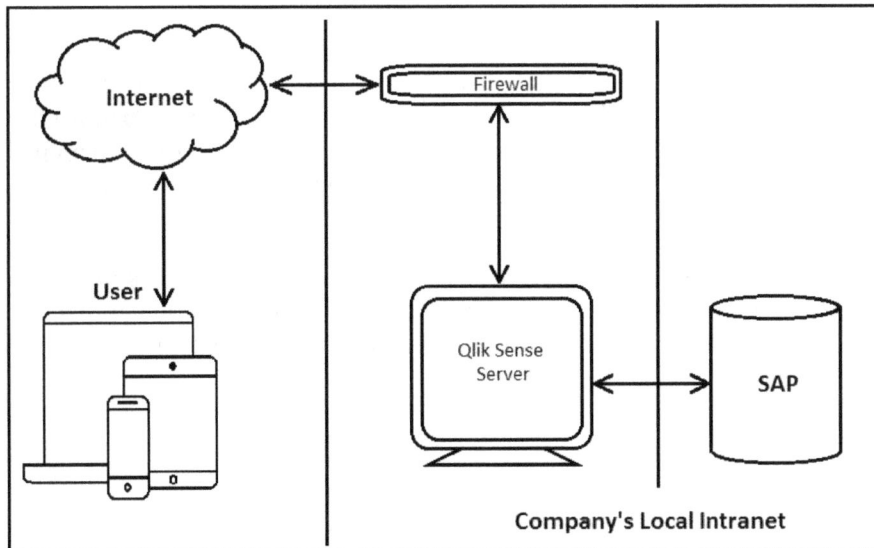

AB LLC - Qlik Sense Architecture

You can see from the preceding diagram that the users will try to access Qlik Sense over the internet and the request will be moved to the company's firewall and then the firewall will grant a link to the Qlik Sense server.

Backup and recovery

The client needs continual access to the Qlik Sense server, so the best option is to create a DR server, which can be used if any disaster happens.

Data architecture

Like infrastructure architecture, data architecture is also an important activity which you should plan before starting the project, or make changes as needed during the course of the project. Data architecture involves planning the data fetching from source system, data manipulations and transformation as per the requirement and storing the output in Qlik Data format. This becomes an input for the Qlik Sense application.

Before actually starting to design the data architecture, you should know a couple of important file formats, like **QVD (Qlik Sense application)** and **QVF (Qlik Data Files)**.

QVF

When you create an application on Qlik Sense Desktop, Qlik Sense creates a file on the machine with .qvf extension. QVF is a file format used by Qlik Sense to store the visualization and the base data which is used for visualization. The QVF format stores the data in compressed format. The compression depends on the numbers of unique values available in the final data.

QVF can be used for two purposes: first, to load the data from the data source using the relevant connection string and storing data in QVD, and secondly you can use the QVF for developing the data model (logical linking between data) and create a visualization on top of that.

QVD

Qlik Sense uses its own proprietary file format to store the data. QVDs are used to store one table at a time; it can be either a raw transactional table or it can be an aggregated table. The whole purpose of using the QVDs is to load the data into Qlik Sense faster than loading the data from the source system. The speed of data loading using QVD is 10 to 100 times faster. It can store data which has come from any source.

QVD allows you to create your own data warehouse, which can be then used for developing the Qlik Sense dashboards. It is recommended to use the QVDs when the Qlik Sense deployment is large and contains multiple data sources.

Now that you have a fair idea about the QVF and QVD, let us have a look at the parameters required for deciding the data architecture design.

Parameters of data architecture

To decision of choosing the right data architecture should be based on a few important parameters described as follows.

Data source

The core of data architecture is the source of the data. It is very important for you to know how many data sources will be used to get the required data for analysis in Qlik Sense. You should also know what kind of data each of this data sources has. This will help you to understand the logical relationship between those data sources and make your life easier while deciding on the relevant data architecture.

If you have multiple data sources like ERP and CRM systems, the same data may be present in both application. In such cases you should know which sources to connect and fetch the relevant data.

For example, an ERP system like Oracle Apps or Navision provides connectivity via the free ODBC drivers where as for an ERP system like SAP you will need separate connectors which might be paid connectors to extract the data from various modules of SAP like R3, BW, Cubes, Info providers, Reports, and so on. If it's a CRM software like Salesforce, you will need a separate connector.

Once you know the data sources, you should also know the various tables or views which will contain required data for analysis. If there are various tables needed, then you will also need to know the linking fields from those tables to be able to link them properly with the right fields.

Business logics

Business logic is also an important parameter to be known by a Qlik consultant to decide data architecture for Qlik. Knowledge of business logic helps to decide which logic should be applied at what level.

Qlik Sense provides a feature of **ETL (extraction load and transform)**, which helps to create a data warehouse with transformed data, which can be used for various analysis. Qlik also provides a way by which the transformation can be done at frontend, but as a best practice, all static transformation should be done at backend to provide better performance.

For example, it is better to do reporting against data which is aggregated at the month level whereas the base transnational data may be at the day level. Hence it is good to aggregate the data at the warehouse level or at the data modelling level, which will decrease the number of records and less data is moved to the RAM, which finally helps in improving the performance of the application.

Frequency

The frequency of data arrival and the frequency of reports needed help in deciding what kind of data architecture approach should be used. Most of the time, the data is required on either monthly, weekly, or daily basis. For analysis, the data needed is usually one day old in some specific cases, real-time data might also be needed.

The data fetching frequency can be decided based on the business users requirements. When the report frequency is not real time, then a multi-tier architecture works well, but when real time data is needed, the data architecture must be a very simple and contain one less tier, so that data can be populated in the report faster.

In Qlik Sense, you can create different types of architecture at QVD or QVF level. This is explained in next section.

QVD Tier Architecture

In this design, you load the data primarily from QVD for dashboard and visualization design. You can use various tiers of QVDs, such as one tier, two tiers, and three tiers. It is not limited to three tiers, but most of the scenarios can be achieved using three tiered architecture. Let us have a look at these tiered architectures.

One Tier

In this type of architecture, you do not create QVDs at all. Instead, you load the data directly from the data source into the QVF and create a dashboard on top of it.

This is the simplest architecture, but it is not recommended to use this architecture for a large development. The reason behind this is after you have developed the dashboard, any changes in script or whenever you want to refresh the data the application will always hit the data source and try to fetch data all the time, even though source data may not have changed. This creates a heavy load on the data source and it may cause performance degradation at the data source. Thus, it is not recommended architecture.

Also, this design doesn't provide flexibility and re-usability.

Following is diagram of one tier architecture:

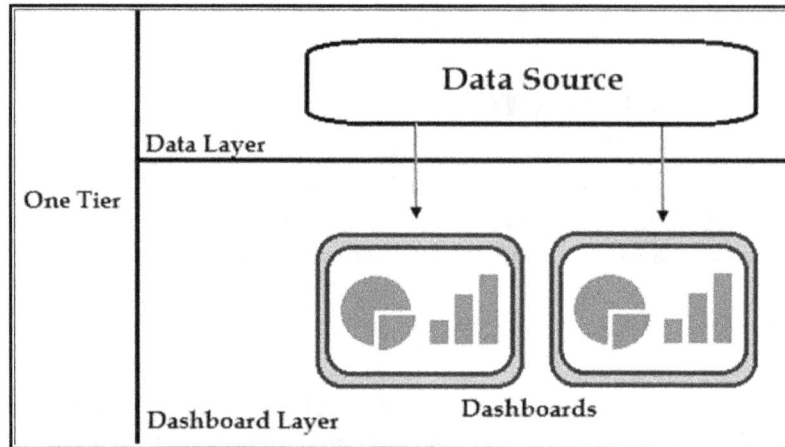

Data Layer is the one which contains the data sources.

Dashboard Layer is the one which contains the dashboards.

Two tier architecture

In this architecture, QVD layer has been added. Instead of using a direct connection to database for dashboard designing, the data is stored in QVD first and then QVDs are used to load the data into QVF, which is used to create visualization.

Architecture contains two additional layers, which are as follows:

- **Extraction layer**: In this we create an extraction layer by writing QVF applications which connect to data source tables and create QVD. The QVF will not be used to create visualization. The sole purpose is to take an extract of database table and store into QVD.

You can also do the transformation of data or apply business logics before storing the data into QVD.

- **QVD layer**: The QVDs which are created using the extraction layer will be used to load data into the dashboards.

The following diagram shows a two tier architecture:

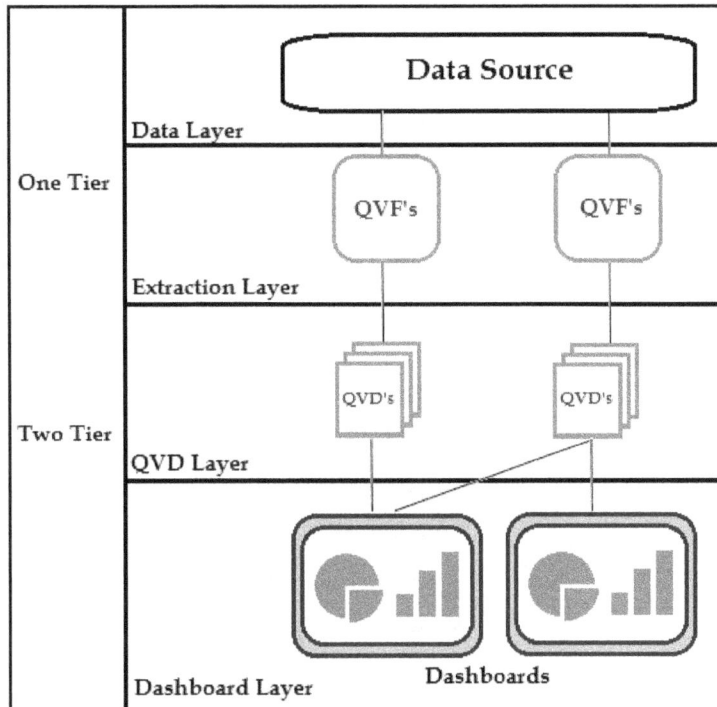

Two Tier QVD Architecture.

The advantage of using this architecture over one tier architecture is that it allows re-usability and consistency of data. Also, the fetching of data can be scheduled during non-peak works thereby reducing impact on source systems.

Three tire architecture

This architecture is used to make the data architecture more robust and flexible, and it increases the reusability of data.

In this architecture, one more layer of extraction and QVD is added to two tier architecture. The purpose of adding the additional layer of QVDs is that you can do aggregation of QVDs and add further business logic. For example from daily data we can do aggregation at the month level in this layer.

The following diagram shows three tier QVD architecture:

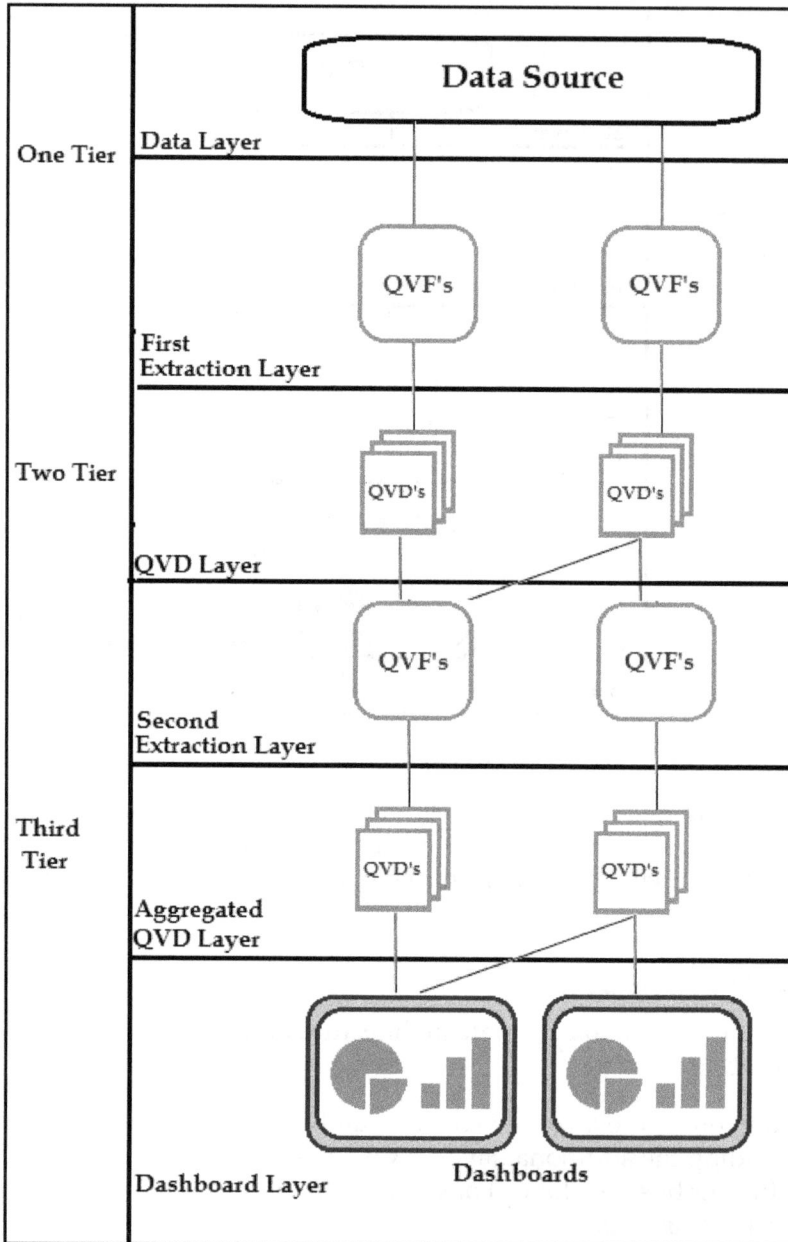

The first layer of QVD can be used to take the exact replica of the database table, and the second layer can be used as an aggregated or transformed QVD layer. The advantage of following this approach is that the same data may be required in different Qlik Sense applications and this approach allows the re-usability, provides the flexibility and reduces development time.

QVF Architecture

Like QVD, the QVF also stores the data within it, so it is also possible to load the data from the already created QVF which contains the data and the data model. Thus, you can also have a QVF architecture. But unlike QVD, which allows multiple QVDs to be loaded in one QVF, you cannot load data from more than one QVF.

Two Tier QVF Architecture

Just like QVDs, we can also use the data available in the QVF file. The business logic and the data model contained in one QVF can be leverage by another QVF
The following image shows a two tier QVF architecture:

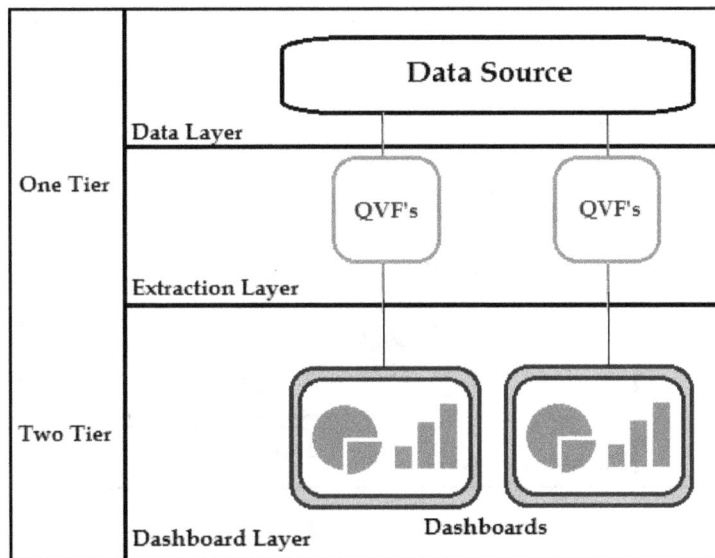

The advantage of following this QVF architecture is that data loading if much faster than the approach of using QVD load. It is always a binary load when you load data from QVF.

This architecture can be used for incremental loading and historical data loading. It is also used to keep the data modelling script secure from the other users who may have access to the dashboards.

Three tier QVF architecture

In this architecture, you create an additional layer of QVF to provide more security to your scripting and logics, and also to increase the reusability.
The following image shows a three tier QVF architecture:

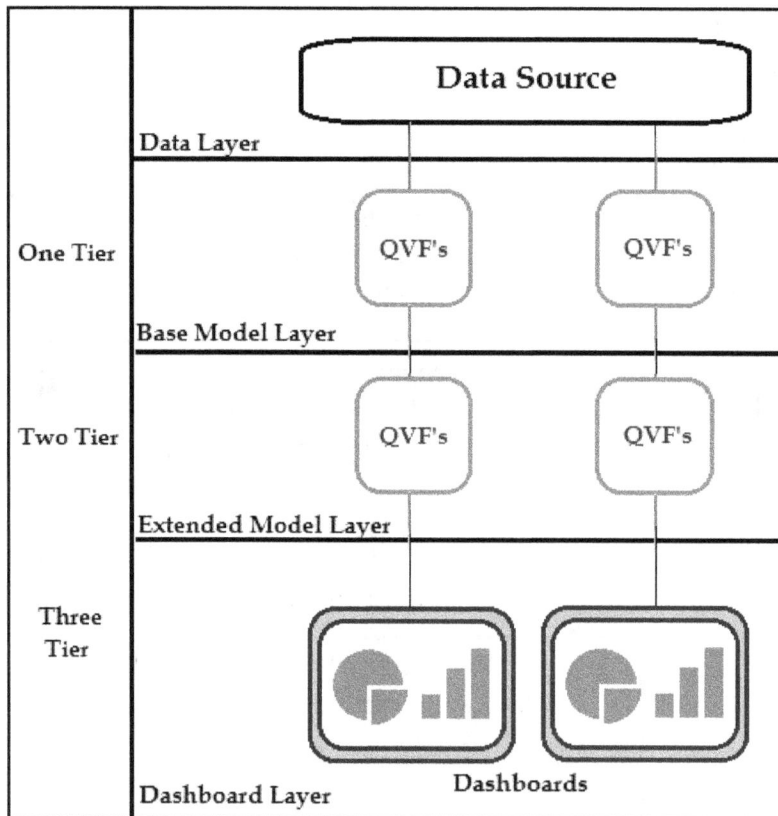

Three Tier QVF Architecture

Hybrid architecture

Depending on the complexity of the data and the requirement, you can also merge the QVD architecture and QVF architecture together, which makes a hybrid architecture.

The following diagram shows a hybrid architecture:

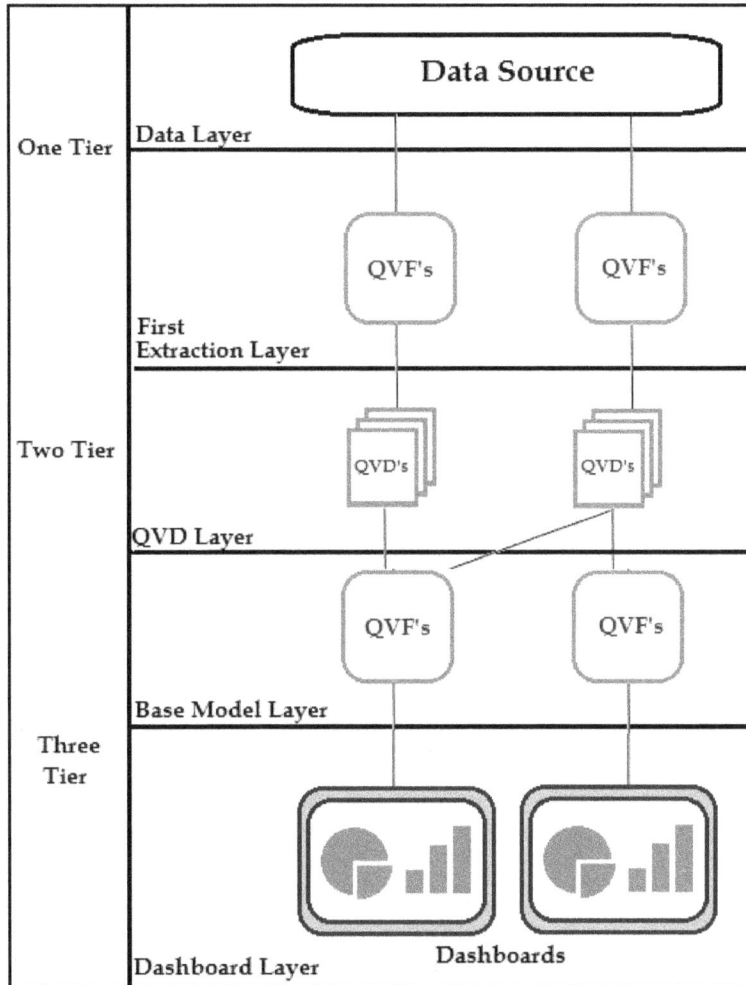

Example case study

Let us continue the same example of the fictitious company, AB LLC. In the previous step, we had given an estimate of hardware and software to the client. Depending on our input, the client has made available the hardware and all setup has been done successfully.

Let us look at the various input parameters from the client and the best approach for designing the data architecture.

Data Sources

The client has mentioned that they would need data input from multiple sources, like SAP, Excel, and few CSVs:

- **SAP**: Contains all the transaction data captured from various locations (stores). This data is at a daily level and has information of all the products which the company is selling
- **Excel**: Excel contains the budget data which is available at store level, month level, and product category level
- **CSV**: It contains mapping of various fields, such as customer categorization, store master, and so on

Business logic

The client has provided business logic which needs to be incorporated to get proper data for analysis. The logic contains the filters which will be needed to analyze the raw transactional data, and applying logic to visualize few key KPIs, and so on.

We also got an input from the client about the nature of the applications they want. They want to create an aggregated application for their top management and detailed application for their middle order management.

Frequency

There are couple of reports which the client analyzes only at month ends, so those dashboards should be refreshed only then. However, the dashboard which they require for their top management should get refreshed on a daily basis.

One report is needed by top management to analyze a few sales KPIs and they want to see fresh data every two hours.

With all these inputs, we can start on designing the data architecture.

If we analyze the previously listed inputs properly, we can easily make out that there are three basic points which we should look at:

- There is a need for a detailed transactional dashboard, which will be used by middle management. So for this requirement, we need to fetch the raw transactional data from the source system.
- For top management dashboards, the data needs to be aggregated. Thus, the aggregation layer is also needed, which should be created using the raw transactional data.
- A couple of tables which give data for sales **KPI (key performance indicators)** need to be refreshed at intervals of two hours.

So as per the analysis, the data architecture should be a three-layer QVD architecture.

The following is the data architecture for the requirement of AB LLC:

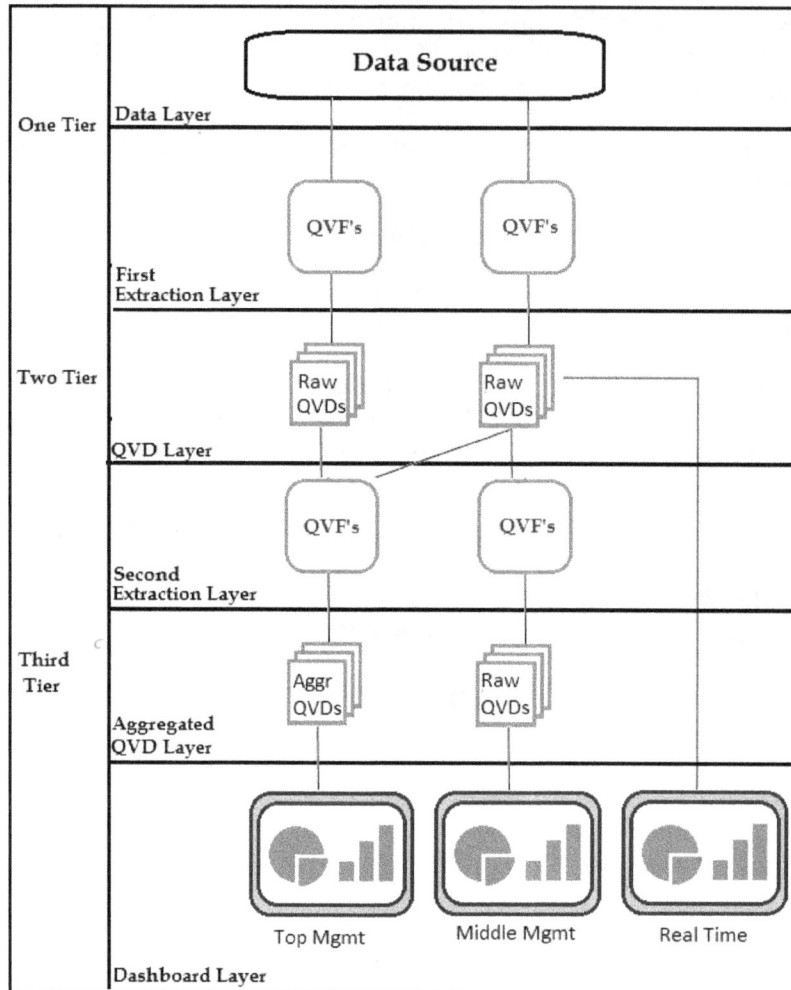

As you can see in the preceding diagram, there are three main applications: one for top management, which will take data from aggregated QVDs; second for middle management, which will take data from transformed raw QVDs; and third for top management, which will get data from the raw QVDs.

One thing to note here is that for real-time application, we have taken the data from raw QVD because an additional layer of aggregation QVD may take time, which may not fulfill the requirement of getting data every 2 hours. Thus we have taken the data from raw QVDs and we will aggregate them as per the dashboard requirements.

Note: The execution of data fetching is serial in nature, that is, at first layer 1 will generate QVDs, then layer 2, then layer 3, and so on.

Data flow diagrams

One of the graphical representations used to show the flow of data from source to destination is Data flow diagrams (DFD). DFDs are widely used for visual representation. When it comes to analyzing the process of data handling, DFDs are used to understand the entire structure of the data flow.

Let us understand the importance of DFDs using a simple example. Consider a case when someone decides to build a building. The very first thing he will do is hire an architect, who will analyze the building area and build the blueprint of the building structure. This blue print will be considered the base architecture of the building and the building will be built as per the blue print created by the architect. The importance of making the blue print before starting the actual building is to understand the various aspects of the building, to understand the risk involved in the construction, and to decide how will it look like. Doing this helps to understand everything on paper first, and if any changes are required, they can be done easily on paper rather than during construction.

A similar concept applies to data architecture. It is always better to build the architectural blue print of the data before starting data architecture. To do this, a data flow diagram is used.

A data flow diagram uses its own collection of symbols to show the flow of data. See the following diagram for the various symbols used in data flow diagrams::

	External entity
	Process

▭	Data store
──────────▶	Data flow

External entity

This entity is used when you want to show the external entity in your data flow diagram. The external entity can be anything which is external to your system, for example, the users, computers, any other system, and so on. The symbol used to represent the external entity is square with rounded corners.

External entity is used to show how the external entity is related to the data flow. For example, the user is an external entity who gives input and is shown accordingly in DFD.

Process

The process is nothing but any operation which is performed on the given input. The symbol used to show the process is a circle. The process can be anything; for example, any transformation done on the data set, any logical operation done on the data, linking of two or more datasets together, and so on. Anything which takes the input and gives the output can be called process.

Data store

Data store is an entity which is used to represent the database. If you want to show that the input is being taken from the database, or that the output is being stored in the database, then you should use the data store symbol. The symbol used for this is rectangle.

Data flow

Data flow is nothing but the symbol which is being used to show how the data travels from one entity to another entity.

Example of creating a DFD

Let us see an example of the DFD diagram and look at how to create it.

Assume that we want to show that how the data is extracted from source system and post that a basic transformation happens and we store the result to QVDs.

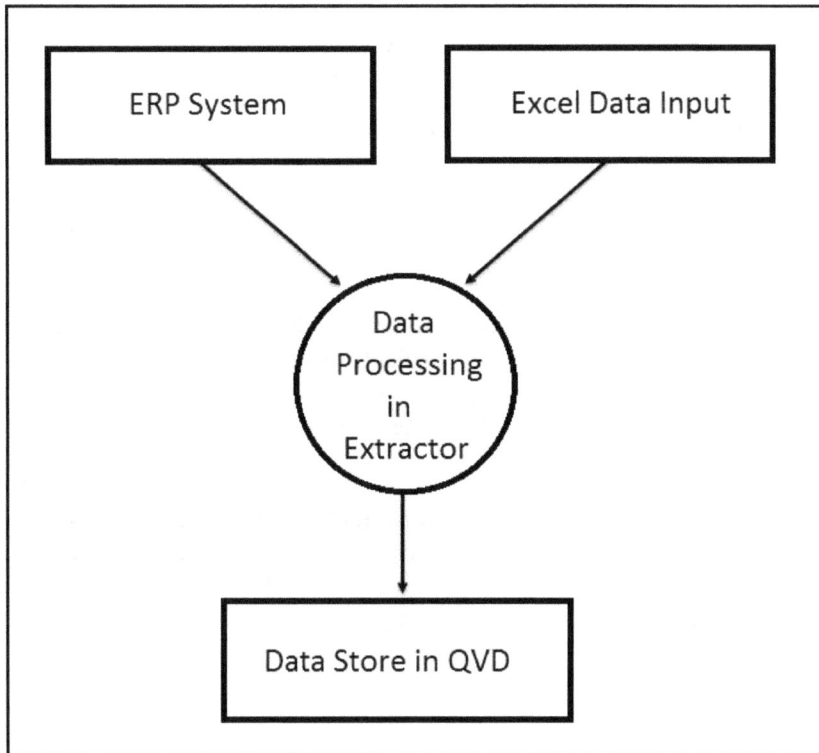

Summary

We learned various ways in which architecture designs for the Qlik Sense project can be taken care of.

We learned what is meant by architecture and why it is important, especially when it comes to Qlik Sense. We saw that there are two basic kinds of architectures, infrastructure architecture and data architecture. Diving in infrastructure architecture, we saw which parameters need to be considered when deciding the hardware requirement for Qlik Sense project. We also saw the basic software requirement.

Then we started with understanding the deployment architecture and its various aspects, which should be understood before starting architecture design. In this, we look at node, site, single and multi-node architecture and different persistences

Moving forward, we saw the backup and restore strategy. We looked at the various options of taking backups of applications and the data of Qlik Sense. We also understood the entire concept using an example.

After finishing the infrastructure architecture, we looked at the data architecture and various aspects which are needed for data architecture.

We learned about QVF and QVD, and looked at the parameters of data architecture, which should be known before deciding the data architecture. Then we saw the QVD architecture with one tier, two tier, and three tier architecture. Then we saw the QVF architecture with two tier, three tier, and the hybrid architecture. We also saw an example of data architecture and understood the entire concept.

Lastly, we learnt about data flow diagrams and with help from an example, learnt how it helps us visualize the data flow of an entire project. In the next chapter, we will look at the various best practices while doing development and this will cover data modelling techniques, security aspects, and visualization best practices.

In the next chapter we look at the important aspect of development. The major work of a project goes into the development and we will look at good practices a consultant needs to follow. We will cover topics such as different ways of data extraction, best practices one should follow in data modelling, security needs and visualization strategy. We will look at how a consultant should handle tricky situations.

6
Development

In the previous chapter, we looked at the importance of good architecture. We understood various aspects of architecture, both from infrastructure and data perspective. The chapter focused on other important aspects as well, such as backup and recovery design. In this chapter, we will learn about the best practices in dashboard designing and the art of developing a quality and user-friendly dashboard, which will cater to all the business requirements and provide business users with an ability to analyze their data, along with flexibility.

Along with this, we will see how to execute the project based on the data architecture we built in the previous chapter. We will also look at various best practices while developing dashboards.

This chapter is going to be the heart of the book as it will take you through the actual development once we have the requirements from the business users. In this chapter, you will learn how to develop quality code, tackle common coding challenges, and write easy maintainable code.

The project sustainability will depend on how best you code your scripts and design the visualization. A poorly coded project may initially look okay, but over a period will cause performance issues, leading to user dissatisfaction and ultimately the end of the adoption.

Let us start the chapter with couple of quotes which inspire us to write good code:

> *Any fool can write code that a computer can understand. Good programmers write code that humans can understand.* **- Martin Fowler**

Always code as if the guy who ends up maintaining your code will be a violent psychopath who knows where you live. - **Martin Golding**

Both the preceding quotes try to teach us the importance of coding. In the world of information technology, it is said that writing a fresh new code is much easier then changing or modifying an existing code. This is true because at times the codes are written without following the best practices. Same parameter applies to Qlik Sense projects, as it also involves scripting. We will learn how to write quality codes later in this chapter.

In this chapter, we will look at some of the areas in Qlik Sense where we follow good practices:

- Data extraction process
- Building data model
- Common challenges of data modeling
- Script management
- Best practices in data modeling
- Data modeling validation
- Security strategy
- Visualization strategy
- Choices of objects
- Use of extensions
- Visualization best practices
- Story telling

Data extraction process

The process of fetching the data from various source databases for further transformation and utilization in development of dashboard is the *Data Extraction Process* for Qlik Sense projects.

Data extraction is the starting step towards building the Qlik Sense dashboards. This process involves fetching the data from one or more databases, and merging and transforming them in such a way that it can be visualized graphically and an analysis can be done on that.

Qlik Sense uses the **Extract, Transform, and Load** (ETL) process to prepare the data for dashboard usage. Let us have a detailed look at the ETL process.

Extract, Transform, and Load (ETL)

ETL is the process used to create a data mart and data warehouse. In this process, the data is pulled from various data sources, then transformed into the required format by applying the business logic, and then stored back in the destination database, which could be the data warehouse.

> The main element of this process is the staging area, because the pulled data gets stored in the staging area first and then the required transformation happens on that data. Once the transformation is finished, the output is stored in the destination database. Thus, the staging area plays an important role in ETL, and for the same reason, the staging area needs to be of good capacity for processing and storage.

Following diagram shows the ETL process:

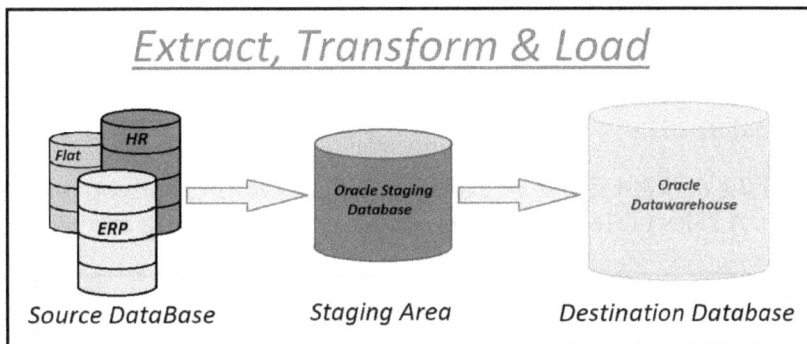

Extract

Extraction is the process of pulling the required data from available data sources. The sources can be any ERP (Enteprise resource planning) systems, such as Oracle Apps, SAP, Microsoft Dynamics, or Tally ERP, or it can be CRM system, such as Salesforce, Zoho, or Bitrix24. The sources can be flat file systems like excels, csv, text files, delimited files, or XML files, or normal databases like Oracle, SQL Server, Mongo DB, or MySQL; it can also be social media data from Facebook, Twitter, and so on.

The extraction from the database can be done in mainly following two ways:

- Full load
- Incremental load

Full Load

In this type of extraction, all the data from the source system is pulled using the extraction scripts. It is like creating replica of the required tables from the database in the staging area. The advantage of full load is that you do not need to worry about any changes happening in the source database, such as insert, update, or delete. Every time you extract the data, you pull the entire data from the source, and thus don't miss any data since the last extraction.

This process allows hassle free scripting, as there is no need to apply any logic while pulling the data. But on the other hand, it is a time-consuming process due to the full extracts of the data. The time required to finish the extraction process depends on the numbers of records and fields a particular table has.

> Full load of the data is generally performed on data marts which are small, mainly the dimension tables which have few millions of records, such as product master, customer master, and so on. Apart from this, full load is also done for fact tables at the initial stage of data warehouse, when there is no data in it.

Let us understand the concept using an example. Let us assume that you want to do a full load on sales table. A sales table with data is shown in the following image:

Region	SalesID	Product	SalesAmt	LastModifiedDate
A	1	P1	100	16-Mar-17
A	2	P2	150	20-Apr-17
A	3	P3	200	6-May-17
B	4	P1	100	31-May-17
B	5	P2	200	13-Jun-17
B	6	P3	300	9-Jul-17
C	7	P1	50	28-Jul-17
C	8	P2	150	3-Aug-17
C	9	P3	250	19-Aug-17

Assuming that the preceding data is stored in excel named `Sales.xlsx`, the full load script in Qlik Sense will be as follows:

```
19
20   REM Full Load from Excel file "Sales" ;
21
22   Sales:
23   LOAD
24       Region,
25       SalesID,
26       Product,
27       SalesAmt,
28       LastModifiedDate
29   FROM [lib://Chapter 6/Sales.xlsx]
30   (ooxml, embedded labels, table is Sheet2);
31
32   REM Store the data into Qlik Data Mart i.e QVD;
33
34   Store Sales into [lib://Chapter 6/Sales.qvd];
35
```

Once this script is reloaded, it will fetch the nine records. Now if new data gets added, modified, or deleted in the table, the same script will be used to get the entire data. Every time the script is reloaded, it will purge the old data which is already fetched and extract full data from the source system and store it in QVD.

Incremental Load

Another type of data extraction method is incremental load. As the name suggests, it extracts only the incremental (or changed) data from the data source, which is then concatenated with the last fetched data available in the data warehouse.

The important part of this process is the identification of changes made in the source tables. The last modified data is the field that helps to find the incremental data from the table. And thus, it is important that the table in the database has the last modified data for the records for us to use the incremental extract method. Generally, a time stamp is captured in database whenever any record is added/modified/deleted.

The incremental extraction is done on the tables which are huge in size. This is because fetching entire data at every extract is time consuming. Mostly it is done on fact tables, but at times it is done on dimension tables which have millions of records, like product tables in a retail industry.

There could be three kind of possibilities that can happen with a record in a table: new records get inserted in the table, an existing record is updated in the table, or a record is deleted from the table.

Let us see how to do incremental extraction in all the three cases:

- **Insert Only**: In this incremental extract, only the newly inserted data will be extracted from the source system and concatenated with the data available in the data warehouse. The logic used to write the incremental script for insert only option is as follows:

  1. Get the maximum date from the history data which is already loaded in the data warehouse table (for Qlik Sense, it will be QVD (Qlikview data file))
  2. Store the maximum date into variable (this variable will be used while comparing the last extract date in where condition).
  3. Fetch the data from the source system, where the date field is greater than the variable date.
  4. Concatenate the history data with the new records fetched from step 3.
  5. Store the appended data in the data warehouse table (QVD).

Let us take the previous example where we had done the full load of the Sales table. Now assume the table has got new records, as follows:

Region	SalesID	Product	SalesAmt	LastModifiedDate
A	10	P1	80	20-Aug-17
B	5	P2	160	20-Aug-17
C	12	P2	130	20-Aug-17

The script inserts only the incremental extraction, as follows:

```
1    REM Find the Maximum Date ;
2    MaxDate:
3    LOAD
4        Max(LastModifiedDate) as MaxDate
5    FROM [lib://Chapter 6/Sales.qvd]
6    (qvd);
7
8    REM Store the Max Date in variable using Peek Function;
9    Let vMaxDate = peek('MaxDate',0,'MaxDate');
10
11   REM Load the New Data from Source System where the Date is greater then Variable;
12   "Sales":
13   LOAD
14       Region,
15       SalesID,
16       Product,
17       SalesAmt,
18       LastModifiedDate
19   FROM [lib://Chapter 6/Sales.xlsx]
20   (ooxml, embedded labels, table is Sheet1) where LastModifiedDate > $(vMaxDate);
21
22   REM Concatenate the History Data With newly fetched Data;
23   Concatenate("Sales")
24   LOAD
25       Region,
26       SalesID,
27       Product,
28       SalesAmt,
29       LastModifiedDate
30   FROM [lib://Chapter 6/Sales.qvd]
31   (qvd);
32
33   REM Store the Data Back to QVD;
34   Store "Sales" into [lib://Chapter 6/Sales.qvd];
35
```

Once the preceding script is reloaded, a new QVD will be created, which will have history data along with the incremental data. Following image shows how the the data stored in QVD looks like:

Region	SalesID	Product	SalesAmt	LastModifiedDate
A	1	P1	100	3/16/2017
A	2	P2	150	4/20/2017
A	3	P3	200	5/6/2017
B	4	P1	100	5/31/2017
B	5	P2	200	6/13/2017
B	6	P3	300	7/9/2017
C	7	P1	50	7/28/2017
C	8	P2	150	8/3/2017
C	9	P3	250	8/19/2017
A	10	P1	80	8/20/2017
B	5	P2	160	8/20/2017
C	12	P2	130	8/20/2017

- **Insert & Update**: Many times, source databases are designed such that they also store the history of changes in the same table. In such scenarios, the **Insert only** method would fail, because the method assumes that the incremental data is new data and not an updated one, which leads to duplicate entries in the QVD files. For example, if you see the data stored in the Sales QVD in the previous section, the **SalesID** 5 was updated on 20-Aug-2017, but instead of updating the existing record, the **Insert Only** script just added that record considering it a new record, which is wrong. To handle this kind of scenarios, the **Insert & Update** method is used. The logic to insert and update the record in QVD is as follows:

1. Get the maximum date from the history data which is already loaded in the data warehouse table (for Qlik Sense, it will be QVD)

2. Store the maximum date into variable

3. Fetch the data from the source system, where the date field is greater than the variable date.

4. While concatenating the history data with the new records fetched from step 3, remove the older records from QVD and replaced with modified records fetched in step 3.

5. Store the data in the data warehouse table (QVD).

Following is the script for the insert and update method:

```
1    REM Find the Maximum Date ;
2    MaxDate:
3    LOAD
4        Max(LastModifiedDate) as MaxDate
5    FROM [lib://Chapter 6/Sales.qvd]
6    (qvd);
7
8    REM Store the Max Date in variable using Peek Function;
9    Let vMaxDate = peek('MaxDate',0,'MaxDate');
10
11   REM Load the New Data from Source System where the Date is greater then Variable;
12   "Sales":
13   LOAD
14       Region,
15       SalesID,
16       Product,
17       SalesAmt,
18       LastModifiedDate
19   FROM [lib://Chapter 6/Sales.xlsx]
20   (ooxml, embedded labels, table is Sheet1) where LastModifiedDate > $(vMaxDate);
21
22   REM Concatenate the History Data With newly fetched Data except the records which are already fetched in above step;
23   Concatenate("Sales")
24   LOAD
25       Region,
26       SalesID,
27       Product,
28       SalesAmt,
29       LastModifiedDate
30   FROM [lib://Chapter 6/Sales.qvd]
31   (qvd) where not Exists(SalesID);    This Logic used to remove the updated records from the history data.
32
33   REM Store the Data Back to QVD;
34   Store "Sales" into [lib://Chapter 6/Sales.qvd];
35   |
36
```

The records which got updated in QVD are as shown in the following screenshot:

Region	SalesID	Product	SalesAmt	LastModifiedDate
A	1	P1	100	3/16/2017
A	2	P2	150	4/20/2017
A	3	P3	200	5/6/2017
B	4	P1	100	5/31/2017
B	6	P3	300	7/9/2017
C	7	P1	50	7/28/2017
C	8	P2	150	8/3/2017
C	9	P3	250	8/19/2017
A	10	P1	80	8/20/2017
B	5	P2	160	8/20/2017
C	12	P2	130	8/20/2017

You can see that there is only one record for **SalesID** 5, which is of the latest date.

- **Insert, Update, and Delete**: Consider a case when a record is deleted from the database. In such case, it should also get deleted from the history data which is stored in the QVD, otherwise the QVD will give wrong data. To handle this scenario, the Insert, Update, and Delete method is used. The logic to delete the records from the QVD is as follows:

1. Get the maximum date from the history data which is already loaded in the data warehouse table (for Qlik Sense, it will be QVD)

2. Store the maximum date into variable

3. Fetch the data from the source system, where the date field is greater than the variable date.

4. While concatenating the history data with the new records fetched from step 3, remove the older records from the QVD which are fetched in step 3.

5. After concatenating table, use the Inner join on Primary Key from database with the concatenated data. (using Inner join).

6. Store the data in the data warehouse table (QVD).

In our dataset, let us assume that the **SalesID 7** is deleted from the source system. Let us see what will be the script:

```
1   REM Find the Maximum Date ;
2
3   MaxDate:
4   LOAD
5       Max(LastModifiedDate) as MaxDate
6   FROM [lib://Chapter 6/Sales.qvd]
7   (qvd);
8
9   REM Store the Max Date in variable using Peek Function;
10  Let vMaxDate = peek('MaxDate',0,'MaxDate');
11
12  Trace "The Max Value is $(vMaxDate)" ;
13
14  REM Load the New Data from Source System where the Date is greater then Variable;
15  "Sales":
16  LOAD
17      Region,
18      SalesID,
19      Product,
20      SalesAmt,
21      LastModifiedDate
22  FROM [lib://Chapter 6/Sales.xlsx]
23  (ooxml, embedded labels, table is Sheet1) where LastModifiedDate > $(vMaxDate);
24
25  REM Concatenate the History Data With newly fetched Data except the records which are already fetched in above step ;
26  Concatenate("Sales")
27  LOAD
28      Region,
29      SalesID,
30      Product,
31      SalesAmt,
32      LastModifiedDate
33  FROM [lib://Chapter 6/Sales.qvd]
34  (qvd) where not Exists(SalesID);
35
36  Inner join ("Sales")          <=== Inner Join condition is used to remove the deleted records from QVD.
37  Load Distinct SalesID
38  FROM [lib://Chapter 6/Sales.xlsx]
39  (ooxml, embedded labels, table is Sheet1);
40
41  REM Store the Data Back to QVD;
42  Store "Sales" into [lib://Chapter 6/Sales.qvd];
43
```

The data stored in the QVD is as shown in the following image:

Region	SalesID	Product	SalesAmt	LastModifiedDate
A	1	P1	100	3/16/2017
A	2	P2	150	4/20/2017
A	3	P3	200	5/6/2017
B	4	P1	100	5/31/2017
B	6	P3	300	7/9/2017
C	8	P2	150	8/3/2017
C	9	P3	250	8/19/2017
A	10	P1	80	8/20/2017
B	5	P2	160	8/20/2017
C	12	P2	130	8/20/2017

You can see in the previous table that the record with **SalesID 7** was skipped as desired, and the record which was updated, that is **SalesID 5**, is reflecting correctly.

Following table shows a comparison between full load and incremental load:

	Full Load	*Incremental Load*
Approach	It truncates the history data and pulls full data from the data source	It pulls only new data and concatenates that with the history data
Performance	It is time consuming when performed on transactional tables which have millions of records	It is much faster because it fetches only incremental data from the data sources
Use Case	Best for small tables like dimension tables	Suitable for transactional tables, which have the identifier for new records

Building Data Model

Before starting any development on Qlik Sense, it is very important to understand the concept of **Data modeling**. In layman language, you can say that Data modeling is nothing but the way in which different data tables are linked together to get the required analysis. There are various data modeling techniques available, each suited for a specific kind of requirement.

Data modeling is very important for any BI project, because in data modeling you explore the logical relationship between the various attributes of the business. It helps you to visualize the different aspects of the business and find correlation between them. Thus, modeling becomes an important part of BI projects, where business wants to see the correlation between the various attributes and their impact on each other.

Out of the many data modeling techniques available, the best suited technique for analytical projects is **Dimensional modeling**. Dimensional modeling is a technique where data is stored in de-normalized form. The reason for de-normalizing the data is that it gives better query performance when huge amount of data is used. That is the reason why Qlik Sense also uses dimensional modeling to get better performance from its apps.

Dimensional modeling is very simple to build as it involves lesser number of joins between a table compared to ER (entity relationship) data modeling. This makes it more effective and robust. In dimensional modeling, accommodating the unseen changes is also easy and this model can be easily expanded as and when required.

There are couple of terminologies which should be studied to get the best understanding of dimensional modeling. They are as follows:

- **Fact tables**: Fact tables are nothing but the tables which are used to store the business transactions. They store the measurement data which gets generated as a result of business operations. Fact tables hold some characteristics like:
  - Storing mostly the measurement values that are numeric in nature
  - Storing the foreign keys which link to the dimension tables
  - Being additive, semi-additive, and sometimes non-additive

- **Dimension tables**: Dimension tables are the ones that store the detailed information about the fact tables. Mostly, the data that is stored in the dimensional tables is descriptive in nature, describing the attributes of the fact table. The dimension tables are de-normalized in nature and thus contain more numbers of columns than fact tables. Following are the characteristics of dimension tables:
  - They store textual data (That doesn't mean that they cannot store numeric data; they can but which is descriptive in nature, like pincodes)
  - They store the attributes of the fact tables
  - They are small in size as compared to fact tables (in terms of number of rows)

There are mainly two types of dimensional modeling:

- Star schema model: This is the widely used dimensional modeling method in data warehouses. In this modeling technique, there are one or more fact tables which are surrounded and connected by the dimension tables. The following image shows a sample star schema model:

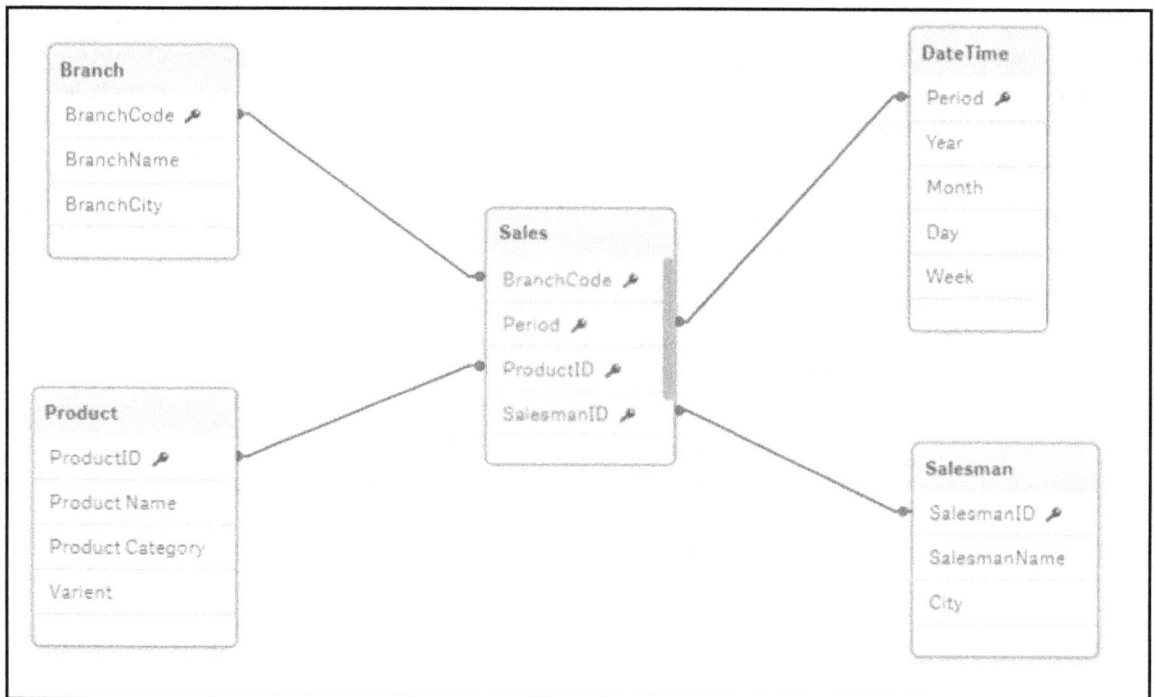

The name **Star schema** is given to this method because of the way it looks after linking of the fact tables with the dimension tables. As you can see in the preceding image, it looks like a star.

- **Snowflake schema model**: At times, there is a need to normalize the schema. In such cases, snowflake schema model is used. These are nothing but the star schema models with the dimension tables further normalized.

Following image shows a snowflake schema model:

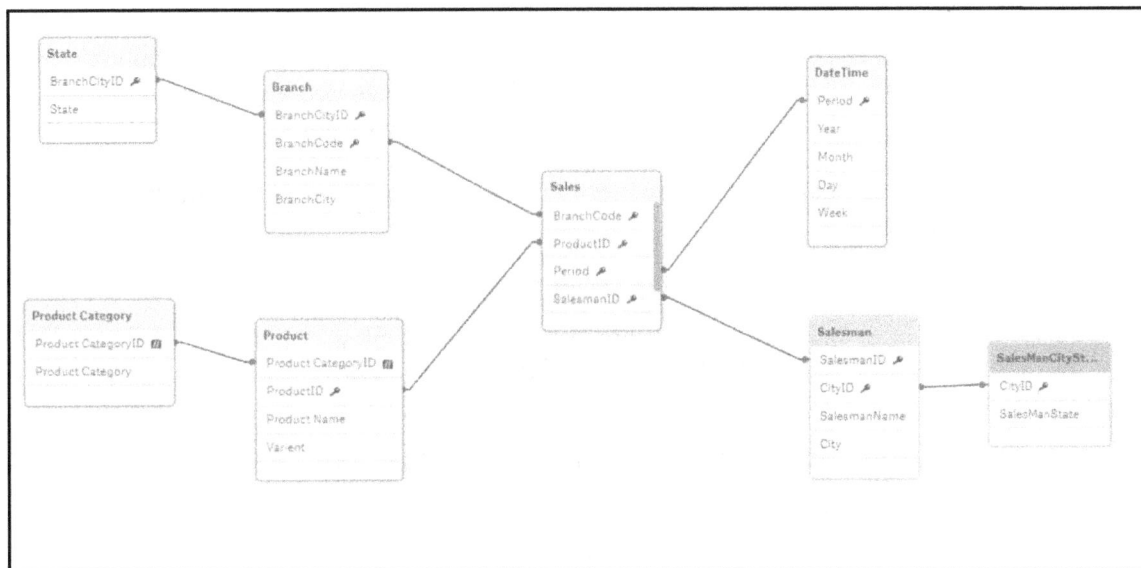

When it comes to data modeling for Qlik Sense, the best suitable schema design is the star schema model, because the Qlik Sense gives a better performance when the tables are denormalized.

Common challenges of Data modeling

When you start data model for your Qlik Sense application which involves linking tables together, you may come across common challenges which may make your data model behave unexpectedly.

Let us have a look at some of the challenges which you may come across.

Synthetic Keys

Qlik Sense developers are aware that whenever you have common field names in two or more tables, Qlik Sense links them together automatically. When you have one field which is common, then you don't have a problem; it is a clean linking between them. However, when you have two or more fields that are common, Qlik automatically generates the synthetic keys and synthetic table.

> Every time you reload the script, and if it contains the linking of a table with two or more common fields, Qlik Sense gives you a warning about the script containing synthetic keys. This clearly implies that you need to review your data model. Having synthetic keys may not create initial performance issues, but it's highly recommended that you avoid their usage.

Let us assume that you have the following tables:

Sales Table	Budget Table
Region	Period
Period	Product
Product	Salesman
Salesman	BudgetAmt
SalesAmt	

If you try to load this table in Qlik Sense, you will get the following data model:

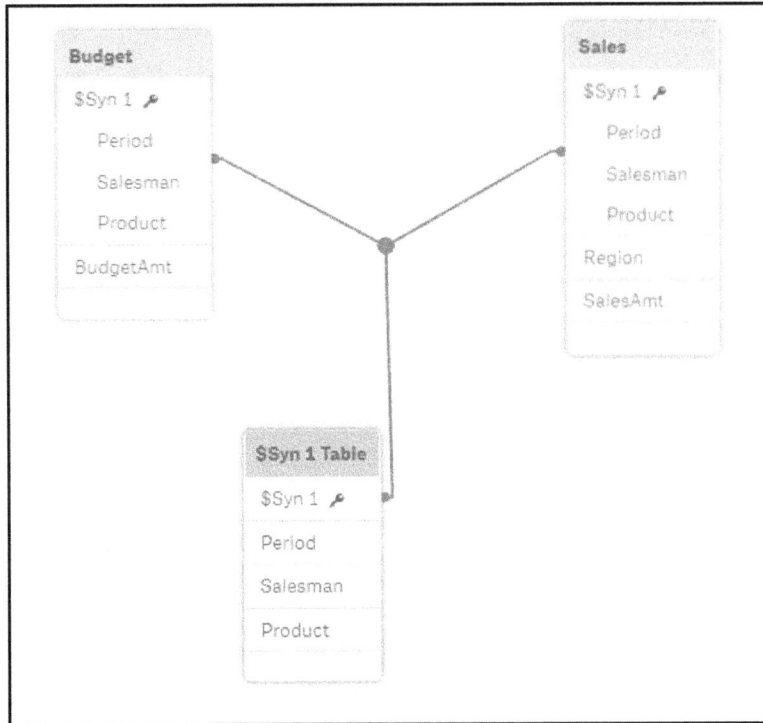

As you can see in the preceding data model, there is one more table that is being created, apart from the sales and budget **$Syn 1**. This table contains the common fields of the tables.

There are four ways you can remove this synthetic table from your data model.

Removing the Fields

In this method, the fields from one of the tables are removed and it won't be loaded at all. Consider the following case where the sales table and the product table are linked together thus generating the synthetic key, as shown in the following image:

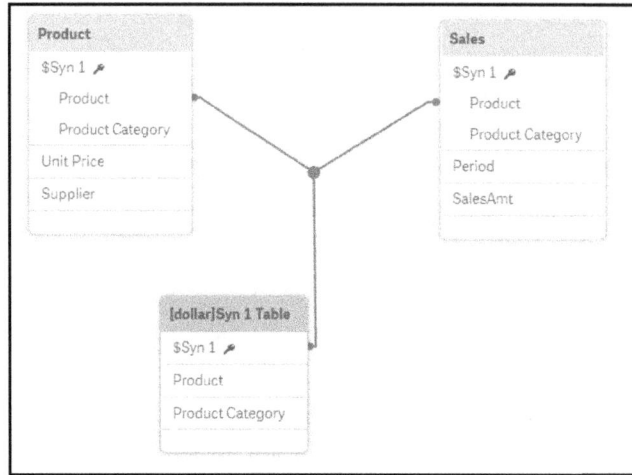

As you can see, there are two fields that are common across both the tables. They are **product** and **product category**. Looking at the data, we can remove the field product category from the sales table because the least granularity field product is available in sales table. Hence removing product category from sales table will not have any impact.

The script and the data model, after removing the field, look as follows:

```
Sales:
LOAD
    Period,
    Product,
    //"Product Category",
    SalesAmt
FROM [lib://Chapter 6/SyntheticData.xlsx]
(ooxml, embedded labels, table is Sheet1);

Product:
LOAD
    Product,
    "Product Category",
    "Unit Price",
    Supplier
FROM [lib://Chapter 6/SyntheticData.xlsx]
(ooxml, embedded labels, table is Sheet2);
```

Renaming the Fields

At times, removing a field does not work, because though the names of the fields are same, they contain different data. They are different fields that have the same name, so it is important to keep both the fields in the data model. In such a case, renaming of such fields helps remove unnecessary joining of table.

Let's see an example:

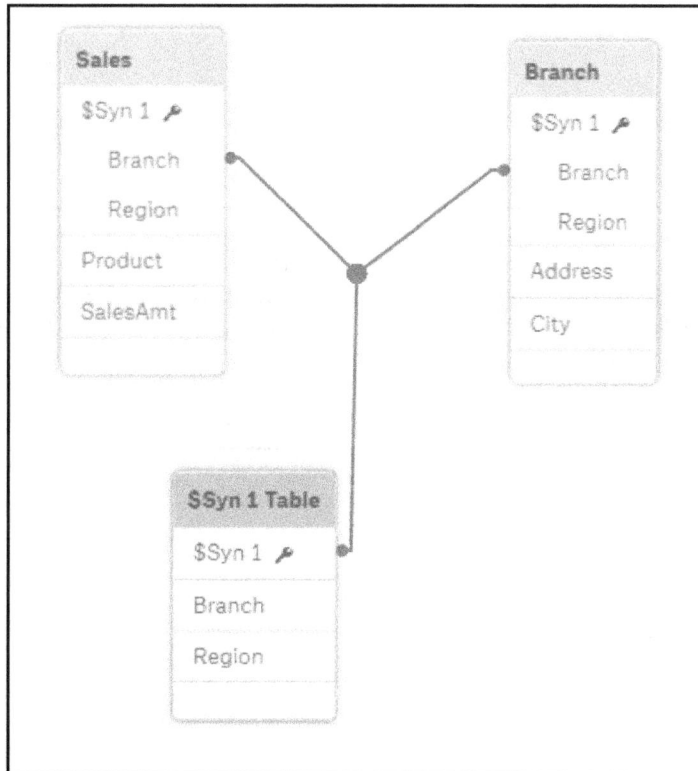

In the preceding example, we can see that both tables sales and branch contain the region field, which is common; however, the region field in the sales table corresponds to the sales region, whereas the region field in the branch table corresponds to the branch region.

After renaming the fields, the script and data model look like the following image:

```
Sales:
LOAD
    Branch,
    Region as SalesRegion,
    Product,
    SalesAmt
FROM [lib://Chapter 6/SyntheticData.xlsx]
(ooxml, embedded labels, table is Sale);

Branch:
LOAD
    Branch,
    Region as BranchRegion,
    Address,
    City
FROM [lib://Chapter 6/SyntheticData.xlsx]
(ooxml, embedded labels, table is Branch);
```

Sales		Branch	
Branch 🔑		Branch 🔑	
SalesRegion		BranchRegion	
Product		Address	
SalesAmt		City	

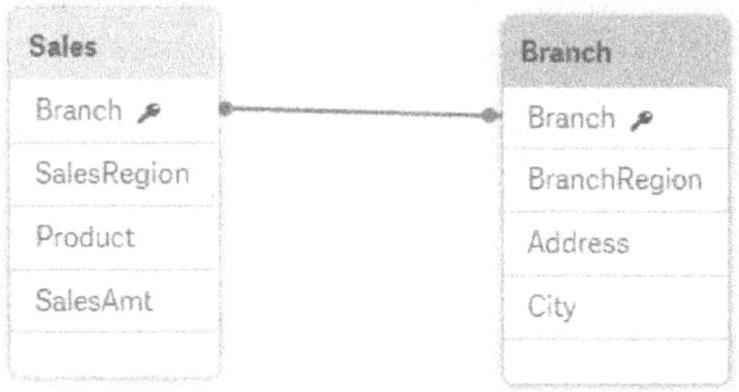

In the preceding example, the **as** keyword has been used to rename the field, but you can also use the **Qualify** keyword. The only difference is that the **Qualify** keyword automatically renames the field to **Tablename.FieldName** (in our case branchregion becomes branch.branchregion) The script and data model shown next has used the **Qualify** keyword:

```
Qualify *;
Unqualify Branch;

Sales:
LOAD
    Branch,
    Region ,
    Product,
    SalesAmt
FROM [lib://Chapter 6/SyntheticData.xlsx]
(ooxml, embedded labels, table is Sale);

Branch:
LOAD
    Branch,
    Region as BranchRegion,
    Address,
    City
FROM [lib://Chapter 6/SyntheticData.xlsx]
(ooxml, embedded labels, table is Branch);
```

Sales		Branch	
Branch 🔑		Branch 🔑	
Sales.Region		Branch.BranchRegion	
Sales.Product		Branch.Address	
Sales.SalesAmt		Branch.City	

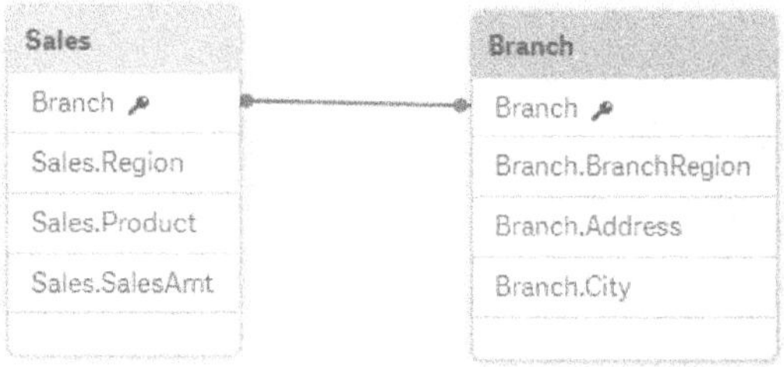

Concatenate

There will be cases where neither removing the field nor renaming the fields will help in removing the synthetic keys, due to the nature of the data contained in those fields. In such cases, it is required to include all those common fields to get the proper analysis of the data.

Consider the following case where both the sales table and the budget table have common fields with same names, that is product, period, and salesman. In such case, you can use the concatenation of both the tables to remove the synthetic keys. (The data model with synthetic table is shown at the start of the topic).

Following image shows the script and the data model view of the concatenate option:

```
Data:
LOAD
    Region,
    Period,
    Salesman,
    Product,
    SalesAmt
FROM [lib://Chapter 6/SyntheticData.xlsx]
(ooxml, embedded labels, table is Sales);

Concatenate (Data)

LOAD
    Period,
    Salesman,
    Product,
    BudgetAmt
FROM [lib://Chapter 6/SyntheticData.xlsx]
(ooxml, embedded labels, table is Budget);
```

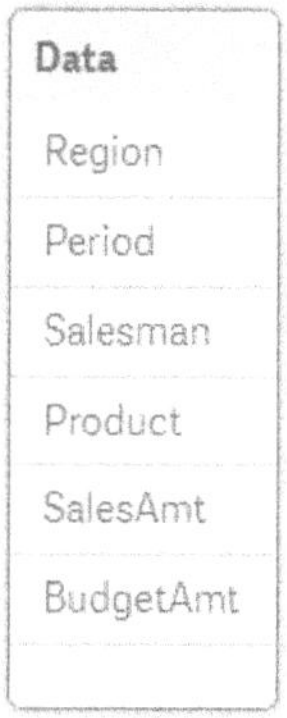

Data
Region
Period
Salesman
Product
SalesAmt
BudgetAmt

Link Table

The problem with the concatenate option is that it works well when the granularity of two tables are same, but when the granularity of the tables is not same, it is not suitable. So in such cases, the link table option is used to remove the synthetic keys.

In this method, we create a logical table also called as link table. The link table contains keys which will link the fact tables and the common fields from the fact tables.

Let us see an example. We take the following image:

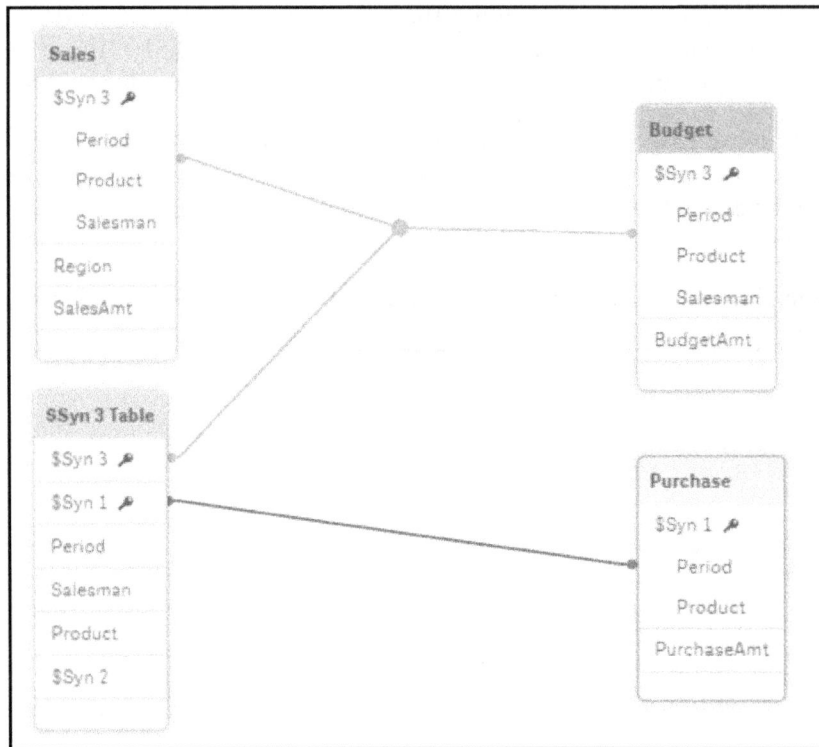

As you can see in the previous screenshot, there are three tables, that is, sales, budget, and purchase. The granularity of all three tables is different, so concatenating them doesn't make sense, and thus a link table approach should be used to remove the synthetic keys.

The logic to create a link table is as follows:

1. Create a unique composite key in each table and comment the common field.
2. Create a link table which contains the similar composite key and common fields from each table and then concatenate them.
3. Remove the fields from the table (if you have used resident load in step 2).

The script is as shown in the following image:

```
Step 1:                                            Step 2:

Sales:
LOAD                                               LinkTable:
    Region,                                        Load Distinct %Key,
    Period,                                            Period,
    Period&'-'&Salesman&'-'&Product as %Key,           Product,
    Salesman,                                          Salesman
    Product,                                       Resident Sales;
    SalesAmt
FROM [lib://Chapter 6/SyntheticData.xlsx]          Concatenate
(ooxml, embedded labels, table is Sales);
                                                   Load Distinct %Key,
Budget:                                                Period,
LOAD                                                   Product,
    Period,                                            Salesman
    Period&'-'&Salesman&'-'&Product as %Key,       Resident Budget;
    Salesman,
    Product,                                       Concatenate
    BudgetAmt
FROM [lib://Chapter 6/SyntheticData.xlsx]          Load Distinct %Key,
(ooxml, embedded labels, table is Budget);             Period,
                                                       Product
Purchase:                                          Resident Purchase;
LOAD
    Period,
    Period&'-'&Product as %Key,                    Step 3:
    Product,
    PurchaseAmt                                    Drop fields Period,Product,Salesman from Sales;
FROM [lib://Chapter 6/SyntheticData.xlsx]          Drop fields Period,Product,Salesman from Budget;
(ooxml, embedded labels, table is Purchase);       Drop fields Period,Product from Purchase;
```

The data model is as shown in the following image:

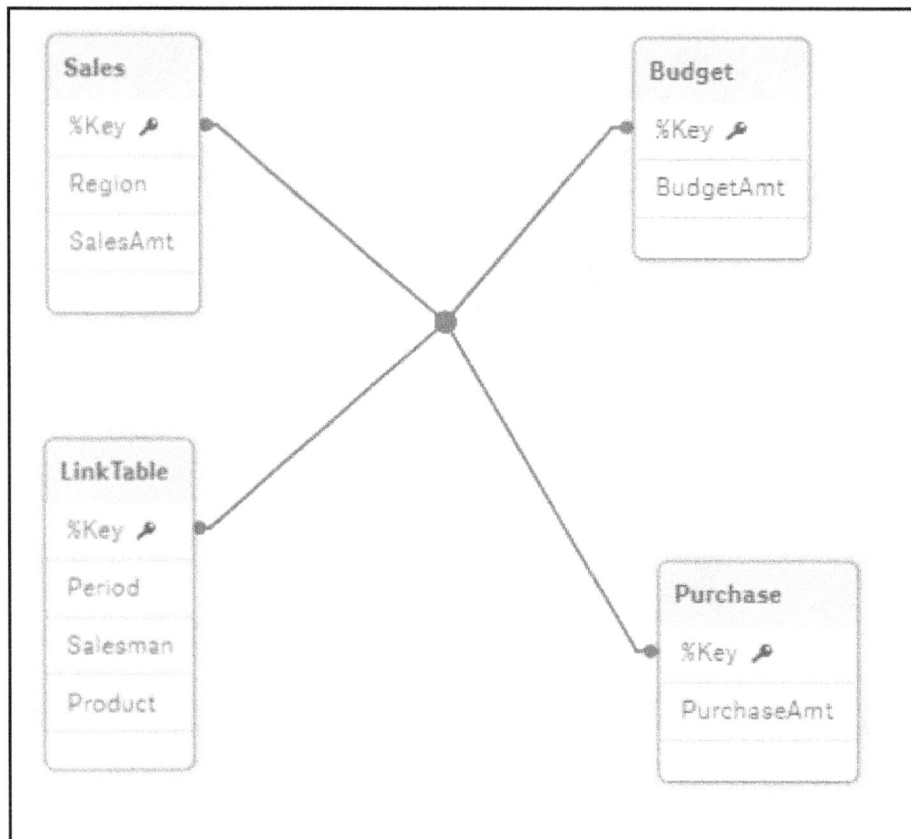

Circular Reference

Circular reference is nothing but the loop which is formed in a data model due to the way the tables are linked with each other, which creates one or more paths of association between two fields of a table.

When such loops are created in a data model, the result set given by the association is always ambiguous and incorrect, and thus it becomes important to remove the circular loops from the data model.

Following image shows an example of the circular reference formed in the data model:

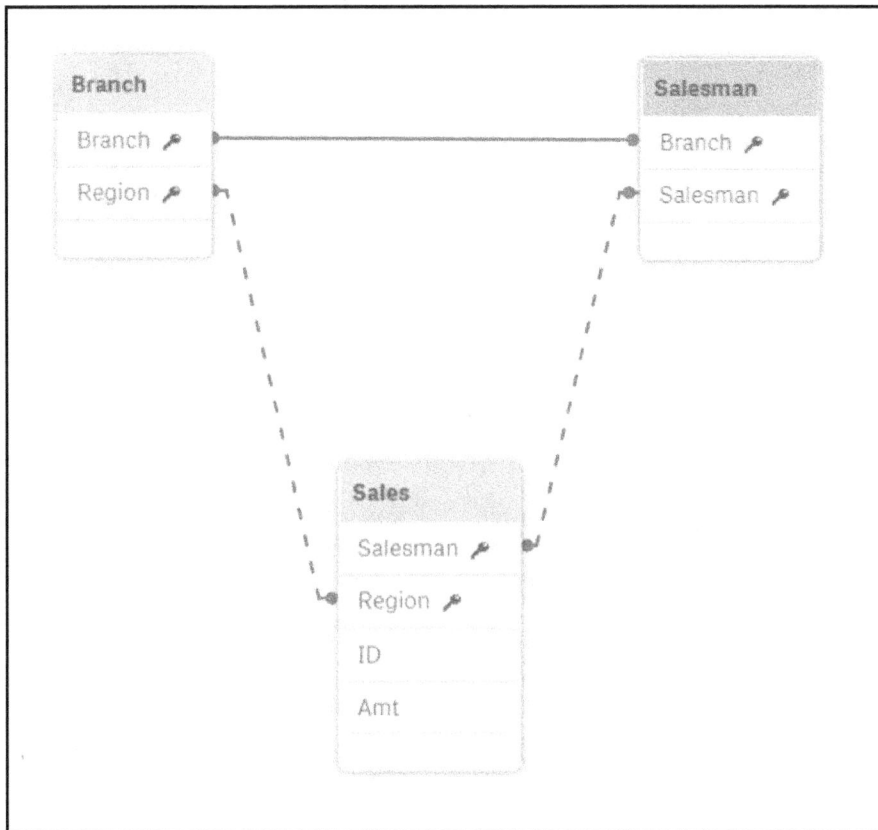

As you can see in the preceding image, whenever there is a loop in the data model, Qlik Sense shows it as a dotted line.

By default, Qlik Sense tries to break the loop by defining one of the tables as loosely coupled table, which means that the association from that table will not work. Qlik Sense generally defines the longest table in the loop as the loosely coupled table.

You can remove the loops using the following ways:

- Removing the field: If a field, which is a part of the loop, is not required for any kind of analysis, then it is better to remove that field and break the loop, as shown in the following image:

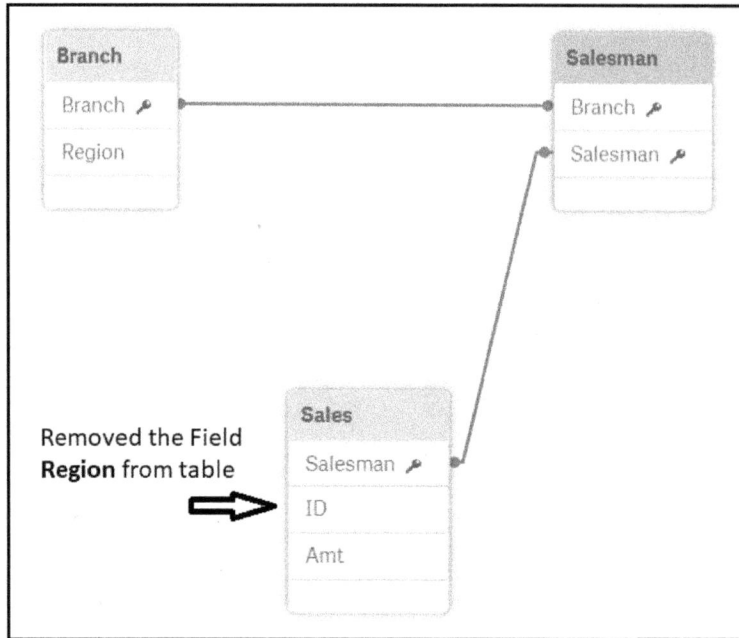

- Renaming the field: If a field is necessary for analysis, then you can rename the relevant field as per the nature of the data it contains and remove the loop from the data model.

It is as shown in the following screenshot:

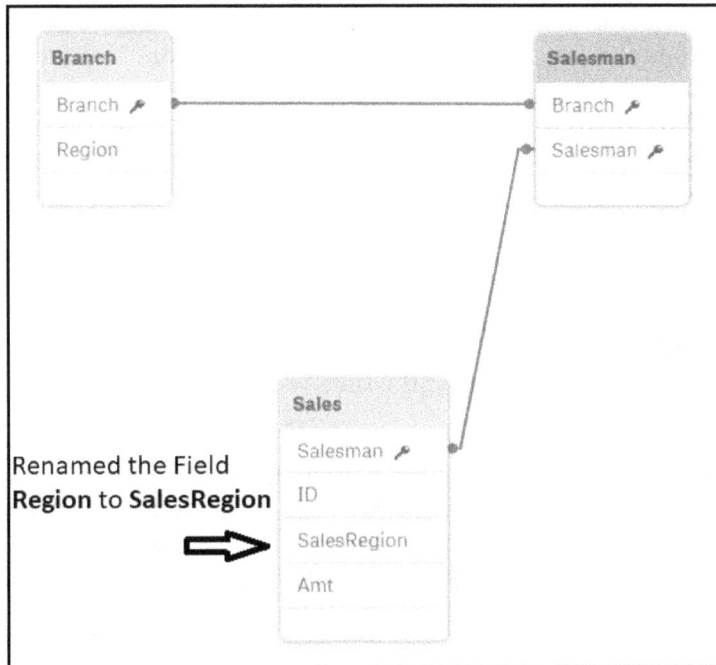

Multiple Fact tables with different Granularity

In real-world scenarios, it is not always possible to have only one fact table in the data model; there will be cases when you need to include multiple fact tables. The immediate solution which we can think of is that we concatenate both the fact tables, but this approach works well only when the granularity of the facts is similar. When the granularity of the tables is different, it is little complicated to use the concatenation of tables.

Let us understand the problem using the following example, where two fact tables need to be linked with each other:

Sales Table	Budget Table
SalesID	Product Category
Product	Salesman
Salesman	Month
SalesDate	BudgetAmt
SalesAmt	

You can see that every record of the Sales table contains the sales details for each product sold, such as sales amount, date, and salesman who sold it. On the other hand, the budget table contains the budget amount for each product category, salesman, and month. So you can see that these two tables have different levels of information. If you concatenate these tables, you will not be able to get the SalesAmt and BugdetAmt comparison, because there are no product and date fields in the budget table, and similarly, no product category and month fields in the Sales table.

So how do we link them together? Before we look at the example and the possible ways to solve this scenario, it is important that we understand the concept of granularity of data.

Granularity of Data: Granularity of data is nothing but the level of details captured in the fact or dimension table. In other words, you can say that granularity of the table is at the data which is represented by the single row in the fact table.

For example, for the fact table shown earlier, namely the sales table, the granularity is at the salesman, product, and salesdate level, because these fields define what level of data has been stored in the fact table. Similarly, for a dimension table like an employee table, the least level of detail can be an employee name, and for a product table, it can be product name with product variant.

Granularity plays an important role in dimensional modeling. If the granularity is defined properly for the fact tables, it becomes easier to get the proper analysis of the data. For a Qlik Sense consultant, it is very important to find the granularity of the data before starting actual data modeling. This helps to find the right associations amongst the data and provide a valuable insight to business.

Now that you have a fair idea about data granularity, let us have a look at the example of multiple fact table with different granularities. There are multiple ways you can link them together, but we will see the basic two ways of handling these kind of scenarios.

Match the granularity

In this method, we try to add or create fields which can match the granularity of the fact tables. We add fields in the fact table which has the least granularity of the data. The reason why we do it in the fact table which has the least level of data is because by using the least level of data you can easily arrive at the upper level of data, namely upper hierarchy. However, it is not possible to get the least level of data from upper hierarchy.

For example, you can get the product category from product field, but you cannot do vice versa, because if you do that, the data sanctity may get lost and you may create duplicate records in the fact table. New fields in the fact table can be added by joining the dimension table, which can get you the higher level of hierarchy or you can derive that field from existing field in the fact table.

If you refer to the earlier example of the sales and budget table, you can see that the budget table is at higher granularity, namely at product category and month level, whereas the sales table is at lower granularity, that is at product and salesdate level. So to match the granularity of tables, we will add new fields, like product category and month in sales table, which has the lowest granularity.

> Product category can be added by linking the product master, and the month field can be derived using the month function on SalesDate field.

Let us see how to code this method. Following is the script for the same:

```
Sales:
LOAD
    SalesID,
    SalesDate,
    Month(SalesDate) as Month, //This field is derived to match with Month field of Budget Table
    Salesman,
    Product,
    SalesAmt
FROM [lib://Chapter 6/Multi Granularity.xlsx]
(ooxml, embedded labels, table is Sales);

Left join (Sales) // We used the join keyword to get the Product Category Field to match with Budget Table
LOAD
    Product,
    "Product Category"
FROM [lib://Chapter 6/Multi Granularity.xlsx]
(ooxml, embedded labels, table is Product);

Budget:
LOAD
    "Month",
    Salesman,
    "Product Category",
    BudgetAmt
FROM [lib://Chapter 6/Multi Granularity.xlsx]
(ooxml, embedded labels, table is Budget);
```

As you can see in the preceding script, we have created two fields, that is the Product Category and Month fields, in the Sales table to match the granularity of the Budget table. After making this change, the data model looks as follows:

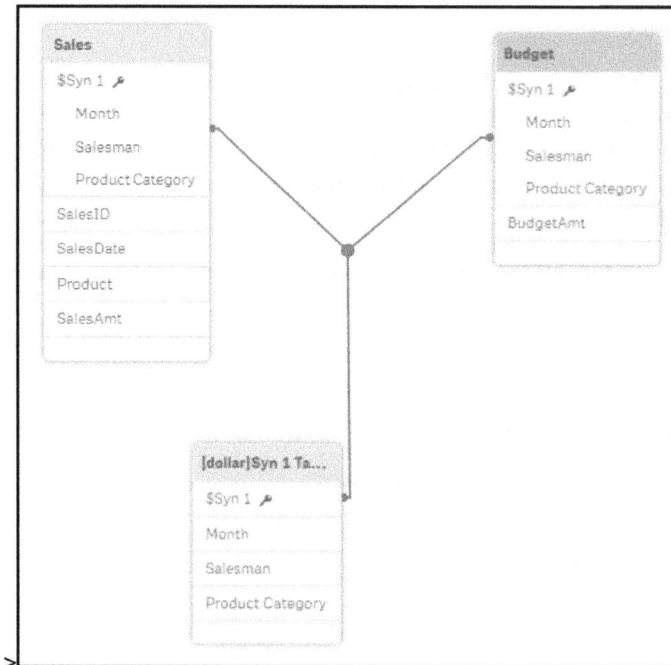

After matching the granularity, we can see that it has created synthetic tables in the data model. Nothing to worry about there, because we know how to solve this using the method learnt in the previous section, that is by concatenating tables or by creating link table.

Generic Keys

The second method to solve the problem is creating the link table using generic keys.

Generic keys are nothing but the combination of primary keys and a symbolic key, which represents several or all values of the field. Generic keys are different from composite keys; you should not get confused between these two. Composite key is just the concatenation of two or more fields and each link value represents one to one relationship of the values, whereas the generic key contains primary key along with the symbolic key, which represents one to many relationships amongst the values of the field.

For example, the generic keys look as follows:

Product_ID &'_'&'<Any>' as %ProductKey

Null() &'_'&Customer_ID as %CustomerKey

Let us try to solve the problem of linking the Sales table with the Budget table discussed in the previous section. Let us start with loading the fact tables. Following is the script for fact tables:

Now let us see the script for the intermediate table which will link the fact table with

```
1    FactTable:
2    LOAD
3        SalesID,
4        //SalesDate,
5        Salesman,
6        //Product,
7        SalesAmt,
8        Product&'-'&'<Any>' as %ProductIDKey,
9        SalesDate&'-'&'<Any>' as %SalesDateKey,
10       'Actual' as Source
11   FROM [lib://Chapter 6/Multi Granularity.xlsx]
12   (ooxml, embedded labels, table is Sales);
13
14   Concatenate
15
16   LOAD
17       //"Month",
18       Salesman,
19       //"Product Category",
20       BudgetAmt,
21       '<Any>'&'-'&"Product Category" as %ProductIDKey,
22       '<Any>'&'-'&"Month" as %SalesDateKey,
23       'Budget' as Source
24   FROM [lib://Chapter 6/Multi Granularity.xlsx]
25   (ooxml, embedded labels, table is Budget);
```

As you can see in the preceding script, we have created two key fields, one for product master linking and other for calendar linking in both the tables.

The keys are formed in such a way that one is the linking field and the other is the symbolic value, both are concatenated and a generic key is created. If you see *%ProductIDKey*, you can observe that in *sales table* we have symbolic value to represent the Product category and in *Budget table* we have used symbolic value to represent the Product. In a similar way, *%SalesDateKey* is created.

You can also note that we have created an additional field called *Source*. It will help us to identify the source of the data after both the tables are concatenated. This will be useful in case any debugging is required. One more thing to note in the previous script is that we have commented those fields which are used in the link; this is because they will be used from the dimension tables.

Now let us see the script for the intermediate table which will link the fact table with dimension table:

```
27    ProductLinkTable:
28    LOAD
29        Product&'-'&'<Any>' as %ProductIDKey,
30        Product
31    FROM [lib://Chapter 6/Multi Granularity.xlsx]
32    (ooxml, embedded labels, table is Product);
33
34    Concatenate
35
36    LOAD
37        '<Any>'&'-'&"Product Category" as %ProductIDKey,
38        Product
39    FROM [lib://Chapter 6/Multi Granularity.xlsx]
40    (ooxml, embedded labels, table is Product);
41
42    DateLinkTable:
43    LOAD
44        '<Any>'&'-'&"Month"as %SalesDateKey,
45        Date
46    FROM [lib://Chapter 6/Multi Granularity.xlsx]
47    (ooxml, embedded labels, table is Calendar);
48
49    Concatenate
50
51    LOAD
52        Date&'-'&'<Any>' as %SalesDateKey,
53        Date
54    FROM [lib://Chapter 6/Multi Granularity.xlsx]
55    (ooxml, embedded labels, table is Calendar);
```

From the preceding script, you can note that we have used the product table and the calendar table to create the intermediate table, which has the same composition of the generic key as we had created in fact table. These two tables are loaded twice because the generic key of both the table has a different sequence of symbolic value. The first load will have the same composition as used in **Sales Table** so that it can link to the values of **Sales Table (with Product)**, whereas second load will have the same composition as **Budget Table**to link with the **Budget Table (with product category)**.

Let us now see the script for loading the dimension tables:

```
58    ProductTable:
59    LOAD
60        Product,
61        "Product Category"
62    FROM [lib://Chapter 6/Multi Granularity.xlsx]
63    (ooxml, embedded labels, table is Product);
64
65    Calendar:
66    LOAD
67        "Date",
68        "Month",
69        "Year"
70    FROM [lib://Chapter 6/Multi Granularity.xlsx]
71    (ooxml, embedded labels, table is Calendar);
```

This is pretty straight, as the field which will be used to link them with the intermediate table is a normal primary key, so no additional scripting is required. Once we reload the entire script, we get the following data model:

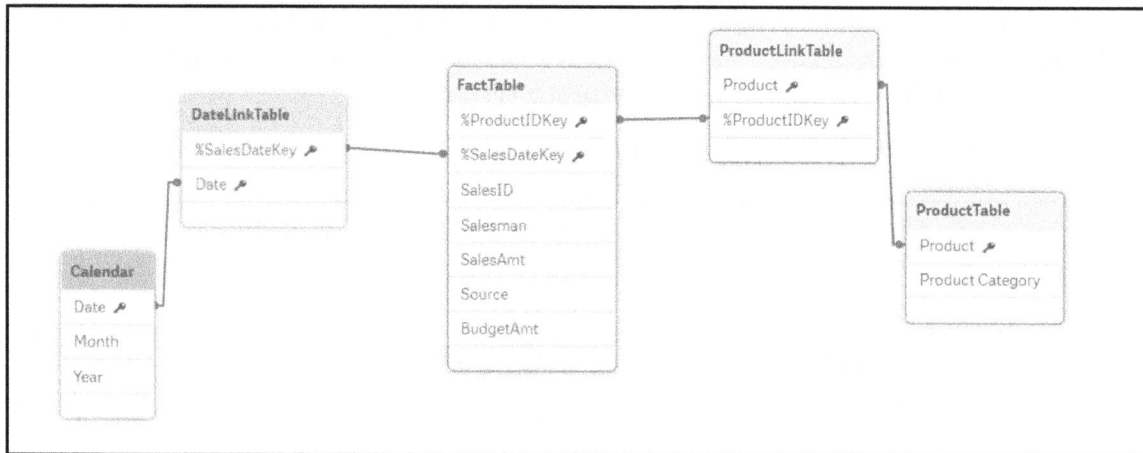

Now let us understand how the data will be navigated when you select one value from a product category field.

Following table shows data from product link table and product:

%ProductIDKey	Product	Product Category	Source
<Any>-ABC	A	ABC	Budget
A-<Any>	A	ABC	Actual
<Any>-ABC	B	ABC	Budget
B-<Any>	B	ABC	Actual
<Any>-PQR	C	PQR	Budget
C-<Any>	C	PQR	Actual
<Any>-PQR	D	PQR	Budget
D-<Any>	D	PQR	Actual

Now when you select the product category **ABC**, it will select all the four values from top, which link to both the tables through %**ProductIDKey** and get us the **SalesAmt** and **BudgetAmt**. The **Source** field shows the name of the table which we had inserted in scripting to identify the source of data.

Similarly, the **Month** field selection will also get us data from both the tables with **%SalesDateKey**.

Script Management

Often it happens with us that whenever we start writing code, we just keep on writing without focusing on the maintenance of the script. This may happen because we are in a hurry to complete the project. But eventually, any haphazard code is difficult to maintain and the code written by one developer would be difficult to manage for another developer.

For example, when you do the coding yourself, you may think that you have done a great job by delivering everything on time, but when you revisit your code after six months to do some modification, it often happens that you forget what you had written and what logic had been applied.

So being a good developer, your focus should not only be on the delivery of value added analysis to your end user, but also on maintenance of the script. Unless you handle your script well, you cannot truly call yourself a good developer.

Good maintenance of the script will help you in the following ways:

- It will save the developers time to debug the code
- It will help you to understand the business logic applied in the script
- Correction and addition of new code to existing code will become easier and faster

Let us see ways through which you can handle your script properly.

Separate Code

Instead of writing a full code on a single page, you should always divide it into number of smaller codes and place them in separate tabs. This will make your script neat and clean, and will help you to debug easily when you need to test.

For example, if your code needs connecting to one fact table and multiple dimension tables, then you should create a separate tab for each table. Or when you have multiple data sets to be linked in your data model, you can separate code as per the data it links. Just like it is seen in the following screenshot:

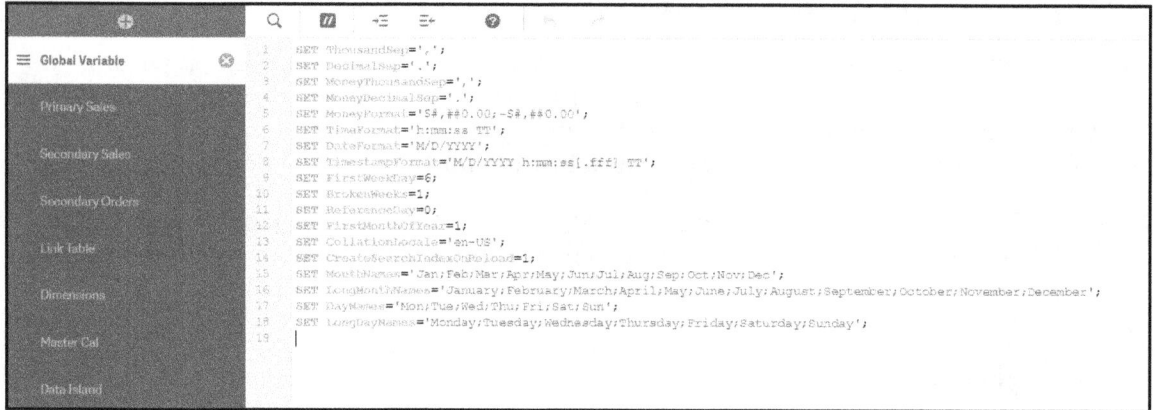

You can see from the previous image that different data sets are separated into different tabs to make it more readable. It is very easy in Qlik Sense to add, remove, and rename the tabs.

To add a new tab, you can click on the + sign given at the center of the tab. See the following image:

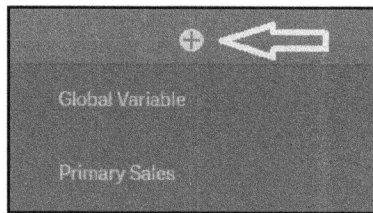

To rename the tab, you can double click on the name of the tab, just as shown in the following image:

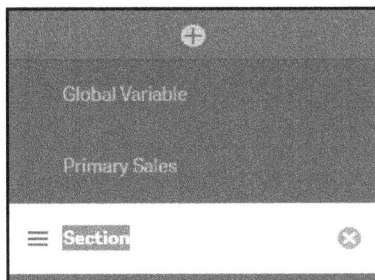

To remove the tabs, you can just click on the cross sign **X** shown at the end of the tab name. The following image shows you how:

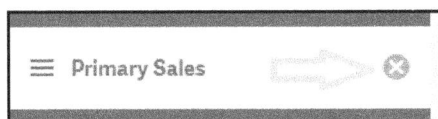

Comments

It is very important that while coding the script, you write the comments along with it. Normally, this is little time consuming, because a coder has to write some extra keywords which describe the code and the logic.

If possible, the comments should be written in simple English, so that it can be easily read and understood by other people. These comments will help you in documenting the entire code and the logic after finishing the scripting.

Comments can be used mainly for two reasons. They are listed as follows:

- To describe the logic written in the code
- To disable a code without deleting it, while doing the R&D

In Qlik Sense, there are three ways in which you can write comments in the code:

- **Single line comment**: To comment a single line of the code, the double slash //is used. Any code which has the preceding double slash will be considered as comment by Qlik Sense. It is used to comment a single line. In case you want to comment multi lines using this method, every line should be preceded by the double slash. For example:

  // This is a single line comment.

Mostly, it is used to comment the fields used in the load script, so that you dont need to remove it from the script. This helps in adding those fields as and when required, just by un-commenting it.

- **Multi line comment**: Multi line comments should start with a single slash and star, that is /*, and end with a star and single slash, that is */. Any code between these symbols will be considered as comment.

This type of commenting is used when a large chunk of code needs to be commented.

For example:

/ This is a multiline comment */*

- **Comment using keyword**: In addition to the previously listed ways, Qlik also has one more way of commenting the code, namely, using the keyword **REM**. Any sentence preceded by the REM keyword will be considered as comment, but it should be ended using the semi-colon.

For example:

REM This is another type of comment;
One thing to note is that whichever way you use for commenting, the color of the text becomes gray.

Tracing: Debugging the script is one of the important parts of scripting. While writing complex business logic in Qlik Sense script, at times it becomes difficult to find the issue in the script. In such cases, we can debug the script using the debugger, or through the **Trace** statement.

Trace statement is used to write strings to script the execution process window which pops up when you reload the script. So it helps by indicating which part of the script is being reloaded.

Trace command is very helpful to debug the code when it contains loops or when you want to find how many records were updated when you used the join statements in the script. So by using the trace command, you can easily write to the script execution window and check the status of your code. This statement not only writes on the execution window but it also write backs to the script execution logs. This makes it more useful to find any issue in the script.

Trace statement can be used to write static text and to print the variable values using the $ sign expansion.

Following is an example of a trace statement:

Trace "Script loading started";

Trace "The Max Value is 1000" ;

Following is the screenshot of the script execution window:

Data load progress

Data load is complete.

Elapsed time   00:00:00

 Started loading data

 "Script loading started"

 MaxDate << Employee Master
 Lines fetched: 1
 "The Max Value is 42967"

 Employee Master << Sheet1
 Lines fetched: 0

Trace
Statements

Naming Conventions

As part of script maintenance, it is important that you follow some standardization in the naming conventions in the script. It will help you to understand the code very easily. That is, just by looking at the code, one will be able to find the purpose of the code, if it is standardized.

- Field names: The field name should be defined such that it can be easily readable by the end users. Most of the times, the table from which the data is pulled in Qlik Sense contains the technical names of the fields, but when using those fields in Qlik Sense scripting, it is important that you change them into more readable form. The name to the field should be given as per the data it contains. For example, if you have the **Prod_code** field in the **Product Table** which contains the product code, then you should rename it as **Product Code**.
- Key field names: The fields which are used to link two or more tables, either a composite key or a normal key, should be preceded by the symbol like %. It becomes easier to find the linking fields by just looking at the % symbol. For example, the linking field for the sales and budget table can be named as **%Sales_Budget_Key.**
- Flag field names: At times you may create some flag fields in the script, depending on the complexity of the code or as needed. These flag fields should also be named such that they can be easily identified. You can use symbol like _before the flag field name. For example, the flag field name can be **_Employee active flag.**
- Temporary field names: You must be creating some temporary fields in the script for various calculations. These fields should be identified easily to understand the logic in the code. You can use the **tmp** or **temp** keywords at the end of the field name to tag them as temporary fields. For example, **Product Category_Temp.**
- Variable names: We all use variables quite frequently in Qlik Sense for various purposes. Though they contains data just like normal fields, they should be named differently so that they can be identified when used at various locations. Generally, the variable names are preceded with a small **v**. For example, vCount, vMaxDate, and so on.

Best Practices in Data Modeling

In the previous sections, we saw what are the common challenges or pain points in data modeling and how to tackle them. With this knowledge set, you can easily start building the data models for Qlik Sense. But there are couple of things which you should know in order to develop the best data model for a Qlik Sense project, which is effective, robust, and flexible in nature.

To do this, there are few points which you should be aware of:

- **modeling schema**: In data modeling, we had seen that the Star schema is the best suited schema modeling for Qlik Sense projects. Following image shows the comparison of the schemas from Qlik Sense project perspective:

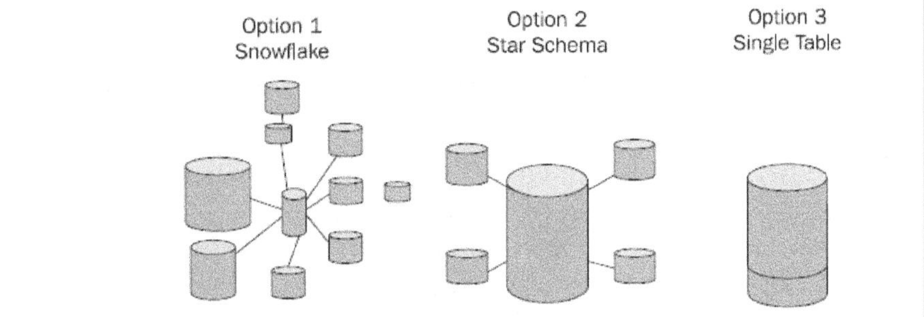

	Option 1 Snowflake	Option 2 Star Schema	Option 3 Single Table
Response Time	Satisfactory	Good	Excellent
RAM consumption	Good	Good	Bad
Script run time	Good	Excellent	Bad
Flexibility Model	Poor	Excellent	Excellent
Complexity Script	Poor	Excellent	Excellent

- **Avoid joins**: At times, there are cases when we need to get fields from different tables into a single table to achieve some calculations or business logic. To do this, the first option which comes to mind is to join those tables and make a single table. Though join is one of the options, but there are few points which should be kept in mind while using it:
  - When performed on large tables, joins are CPU intensive
  - When performed on non-numeric fields, it is CPU intensive
  - When joining field is not unique, it may create duplicate records in the final table
  - When joined on wrong field, it may create cartesian product and increase records exponentially
  - Maintenance of the code becomes tough

> **TIP**
>
> Keeping the preceding points in mind, you can use **join** in your code, but it is recommended to use a different approach to get fields in single table, like mapping functions. Another function which can be used is **Lookup**, but that is slower than mapping functions.

- **Use Mapping functions**: One of the alternatives to the joins are mapping functions (Applymap and Map Using). Mapping functions are the ones which help in mapping one field with another field from another table. It is like joining one table with another table, but mapping function does it differently, allowing you to do many different things which may require complex coding. Mapping functions have two parts, one where the table is loaded with the Mapping as a prefix, second the mapping functions to refer mapping table to map the fields. It is required to declare the table as mapping table before using it.

  When a table is loaded as a mapping table, it is stored in RAM during the execution of the script; once the script finishes, the table gets dropped automatically.

  The table which is to be used as a mapping table must have only two fields: the first field is the one which will be used as a key and the second field will be used as the value which needs to be mapped.

  The mapping functions will map the first value from the mapping table, and thus the sorting order of the mapping table matters when there are duplicate records in mapping table. If no value is mapped, the key value will be used as it is. The function also allows to use a customized value when no value is mapped.

Let us see the syntax of the mapping functions:

Mapping load: To declare a table as a mapping table, the *mapping* keyword is prefixed to the load statement, as shown in the following image:

```
1    Map1:
2    Mapping Load * inline [
3    x,y
4    1, one
5    2, two
6    3, three
7    ];
```

Applymap: This function is used to refer mapping table to map the values. This function must be used within the load statement.

Syntax:

Applymap('Mapping Table Name',Mapping Field Name,['Default Expression]);

- Mapping table name: This is allies name of the table which is declared as the mapping table. This name should be declared in single quotes.
- Mapping field name: This is the field name which will be used as a key to lookup in the mapping table.
- Default expression: This is the expression which should be used when no values are mapped. If you use text, then it should be enclosed in single quotes.

Example:

```
1    Table:
2    Load *, ApplyMap('Map1', MyVal, 'x') as ApplyMapField;
3    Load * inline [
4    MyVal
5    1,
6    2,
7    3,
8    4,
9    5
10   ];
```

In the preceding example, **X** is used when there is no mapping. The output of the previous script is shown next, and will give you a clear idea about it:

MyVal	ApplyMapField
1	one
3	three
2	two
4	x
5	x

You can see in the preceding output that the values 4 and 5 were not there in the mapping table, and thus as per the function used in the script, it gave default expression, that is **X**.

- **Map Using**: The Applymap function can be used only to map one field at a time, so when you want to map multiple fields using the same mapping function, you need to use multiple Applymap functions. To overcome this and to make scripting easy, Map Using is used. One thing to note here is that the mapping is not done every time a field name is encountered in the script, rather it is done once the values are stored in the field in the internal table of Qlik Sense.

Syntax:

*Map *FieldList Using Mapname;*

Fieldlist: It is the list of fields which need to be mapped. The fields should be separated by commas.

Mapname: It is the name of the mapping table.

Example:

```
1    Map MyVal using Map1;
2
3    Table:
4    Load * inline [
5    ID,MyVal
6    A,1
7    B,2
8    C,3
9    D,4
10   E,5
11   ];
```

ID	MyVal	
A	one	
B	two	
C	three	
D		4
E		5

- **Use Optimized QVD load**: Optimized load is one of the ways in which QVD data is read. The load is said to be optimized when there is no transformation logic applied while loading the fields from the QVD. Optimized QVD load is up to 100 times faster than non-optimized load. It is because the compression techniques used while storing the data in QVD is similar to storing the data in RAM. And thus, moving data from QVD to RAM becomes much faster, as no transformation is done.

There are few things which allows optimized load, like:

- Renaming a field
- **Exists()** function with one parameter
- Omitting a field

> It is a best practice to use optimized load whenever possible, because it increases the speed of the script execution. This becomes important when an application needs to be refreshed frequently during the day.

- **Reduce the memory requirement**: We know that Qlik Sense gives better performance when there are less unique values in the application, but at times we increase the uniqueness of the data by using the composite keys in the data model to link multiple tables.

-

So as a best practice in the data model, we should try to reduce as much memory as possible. There are few cases which help us to reduce the memory requirement:

- **Autonumber function**: The **Autonumber()** function helps in converting the string value into numeric value. The function allocates a number value for each distinct string value encountered during the script execution. Because string value takes more memory space than numeric value, the **Autonumber()** function helps to reduce the memory.
- **Remove unwanted and unused fields**: At times, we load all the fields available in the table, irrespective of whether they are currently required or not. The data held by these unwanted fields gets loaded into RAM even when they are not required, which unnecessarily makes the application heavier and reduces the performance of the application. Thus, it is recommended to comment or remove such unwanted and unused fields from data model.
- **Remove the timestamp from date fields**: Another expected unique field is timestamp. It is important to convert them in such a manner that they become non-unique fields. To do this, we can either remove the timestamp (that is, time) from the field by using the *Floor* function, or we can separate the date and time into multiple fields.

- **Hide the Key fields**: Key fields are nothing but the fields which we use to connect two or more tables with each other. It can be a normal primary key, a composite key, or a generic key.

Mostly, the purpose of these key fields is to only make the association possible between the tables; they are never used in frontend for any calculations. We know that all fields of data model are exposed to end users and they can add remove them as and when required in any kind of objects so if an end user uses these key fields in any object, knowingly or unknowingly, it may consume more resources of the server as these fields are unique in nature, and it may result in slower performance of the application.

Thus, it is recommended to hide these fields using the HidePrefix variable. Once you hide them, they won't be available to the end users, but they will be used in background for associations amongst the linked tables.

- **Use aggregated data**: One of the key features of the Qlik Sense dashboard is that it does all the aggregations and calculations on the data set at runtime. It means that whenever a user makes a selection in the data field, all chart expressions get calculated and results are displayed accordingly. Having this feature doesn't mean that we load all the available transactional data and do the aggregation on the fly. Since doing aggregation on the fly needs high amount of resources, so more the transactional data is loaded, more the resources will be required, and if resources are limited, it may give performance issues.

  Thus, as best practice, it is always recommended that whenever possible use the aggregated data instead of transactional data. This will reduce the data volume drastically, and eventually reduce the memory requirement and result in better performance.

  For example, the dashboard developed for higher management may not require the transactional data, but instead they would be interested in aggregated data. So it doesn't make sense to use transactional data and aggregate them on the fly. Instead preaggregation in data model will help to increase the performance.

- **Move logic to data model**: It is always a good practice to calculate the possible business logic at data modeling stage than doing it on the frontend on the fly. Let us understand the reason for the same. Consider a case when you are loading millions of records and you want to apply a simple logic to change the gender codes M, F, and O to male, female, and other respectively. For this, you may use the **If** statement or the **Peek** statement, or any other statement which suits the requirement in charts. However, this calculation will be done every time a user makes any selection in any field, which may increase the load on resources due to the huge data volume. Instead, if the same logic is pre-calculated in data modeling stage, it will take less amount of resources.

Thus, to improve the performance of the application and for optimum resource utilization, we should move all possible business logic to data modeling.

Data modeling Validation

Data validation is one of the critical and important points which is neglected by most of the developers. We will look at this point in detail in the next chapter, but I want to discuss briefly about validation of the data model. While developing the data model with best practices, we sometimes mess with the code and make small mistakes, which may not be wrong syntactically but may be wrong from data perspective.

Thus, it becomes important to do a preliminary validation of the data model to make sure that after doing all the calculations and linkage between the tables, the data gets populated correctly, which further helps in avoiding data related queries after entire development is done.

There are couple of things which you should do for data modeling validation. Let us have a look at them.

Row Count

This is a common way of finding if the data loaded in Qlik Sense matches with the source data or not. It is very simple to find the numbers of records loaded after Qlik Sense script is finished.

You can use this method of validation in two cases: one, when you load the data directly from the source data base to Qlik Sense, and second, after doing any transformation on data, such as, joining the tables, concatenating the table, implementing the incremental script, and so on.

Let us see how we can check the row count.

After the script is finished, you just need to follow these steps:

1. Go to *Data Model Viewer*.
2. Click on the table for which you want to find the record count.
3. Click on preview at the bottom of the screen, or you can click on the button given on right hand top side.
4. Left side window will show you the record count for that table. Actually, it is the meta data of the table.

To validate the record count of the table loaded in to Qlik Sense, you should have record count from the source table. If your source is database, you can simply fire a select query using any query tool or you can use Qlik Sense to do the same. Sample query is shown as follows:

```
Select count(*) from SchemaName.Tablename
```

If both the counts match, then you can simply say that the extraction has happened correctly and data loaded in Qlik Sense is correct.

You might wonder that if we load the data directly from the source system in Qlik Sense, then why would we like to validate the same. This is because at times the driver used to connect to the data source from Qlik Sense is corrupted or is not supported, or any special character may have caused an issue.

To validate the row count after any transformation on a table, you should note the row count of the table before the transformation, so that it can be compared with the row count generated after the transformation is finished.

This is very important because at times the transformation steps, such as left join, right join, and join, may create an issue. They may generate a duplicate value, depending on the values in the joining table, if the values are duplicate in joining table it will sure create duplicate values in resulting table.

If this validation is neglected and if it has created duplicate values, it will generate a wrong result when aggregation is performed on those tables.

Field Meta Data

When you do a concatenation of tables which have non-identical fields, then it creates null values in those fields. These null values at times create lots of problems in visualization, especially in set analysis expression. Thus, null values should be handled properly.

The field meta data available in *Data Model Viewer* helps in identifying null values in the field, as well as the duplicate values, if any.

Following are the various field level meta information available:

%UniverseKey	
Density	100%
Subset ratio	63.3%
Has duplicates	true
Total distinct values	200373
Present distinct values	126856
Non-null values	704696
Tags	$key $ascii $text

Let us understand each of the shown meta information:

- **Density**: It is nothing but the ratio of the total record count of table and the total non-null values in the field. It helps to identify the percentage of null values present in the field.
- **Subset ratio**: This is the ratio of the total distinct values available in the field from different tables versus the present distinct values in this table. This will help you to understand how many records are not available in this table which are otherwise available in the other table.
- **Has duplicates**: It shows if the field has duplicate values or not.
- **Total distinct values**: It shows the total distinct values of the field from all tables (In case it is a Key field).
- **Present distinct values**: This tells how many distinct values are available in this field.
- **Non-Null values**: It shows count of the not-null values from the field.
- **Tags**: This is metadata information about the field, like the data type, key field, geomap field.

Using all this meta information of the field, one can get an idea about the duplicate values and the null values in the field.

Security Strategy

Now that we have connected various data sources and developed the data model, it is time to think about the security.

Qlik Sense provides a solid security mechanism which helps to restrict access to the Qlik Sense at various levels. Qlik Sense provides the security mainly at four levels:

- **Network security**: Provides a secure communication channel between the user and server
- **Server security** by providing access to Qlik resources only to authorized users through QMC
- **Process security** by providing role based access to make sure proper testing is done for development
- **App security** by providing the row and column level data reduction through section access

Let us understand the server security and how Qlik does authentication:

Authentication: Qlik Sense server uses inbuilt proxy and virtual proxy as a gate keeper to allow only the authenticated user to enter Qlik Sense and access the Qlik resources. This gate keeper can be configured as per the requirement to authenticate the users by using various methods like:

- Ticketing
- Sessions
- HTTP headers
- SAML
- Anonymous

Now lets see authorization part of Qlik Sense.

Authorizations: Once the authenticated user gets entry to Qlik Sense, then depending on his authorizations defined, he gets access to the resources of Qlik Sense. This is done using a powerful functionality, that is security rules. Security rules are so powerful that you can build any kind of security. It can be configured at a granular level to provide access to bookmarks and sheet objects.

It can also provide the security using **Attribute Bases Access Control (ABAC)**. So, depending on the user attributes, like group, department and email the security can be provided. Qlik Sense also allows a role based security model, using which the development can be authorized by the concerned person.

The data level security is also possible in Qlik Sense, which is achieved using the concept of section access. Qlik Sense sends the authentication and authorization information to the section access within the application, and depending upon that, Qlik Sense allocates the access to the data.

Following image shows the process through which the security is given:

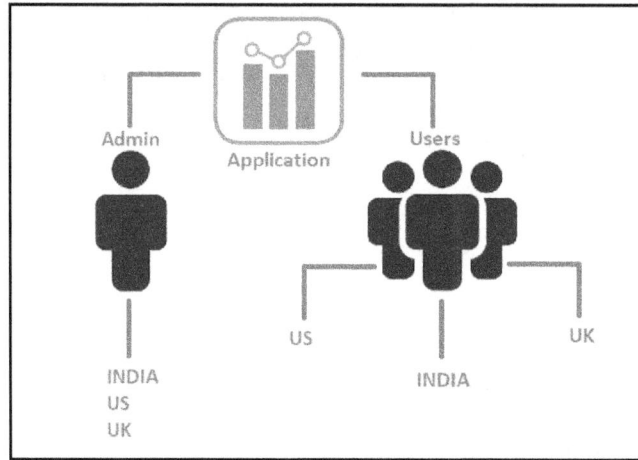

If an Admin logs in, he will see all the data, whereas when other users login, they will see their respective region data. This security consists of two sections, one is section access and other is section application.

Section access: This is the security initialization statement. It should be followed by the access table which gives the data access information. Lets see the components of the Section access table.

Access: It defines the kind of access the user should have. There can be only two level of access, either admin or user. The user with admin access gets access to all the data in the app, unless specific restriction is defined in the access table. The users with user access get access to only specific data set for which they are authorized. It is a mandatory field.

USERID: It is the username which can be compared with the loginID of the user. It should be in domain\username format.

GROUP: It is the name of the user group. It should match with the user group name fetched using the User directory connection in Qlik Sense. It is used when group level access is needed.

OMIT: This parameter is used to define the column level access to the user. It should contain the name of the field for which the access is restricted to user.

REDUCTION FIELD NAME: This parameter defines criteria for data restriction. This field should match with the actual data field loaded in the data model.

Following screenshot shows a sample script for Section access:

```
1    Section Access;
2    |
3    Load * inline [
4    ACCESS,USERID,REGION,OMIT
5    ADMIN,KAUSHIKPC\ADMIN,,
6    USER,KAUSHIKPC\USER1,INDIA,SalesID
7    USER,KAUSHIKPC\USER2,US,Product
8    USER,KAUSHIKPC\USER3,UK,
9    ];
10
11   Section Application;
12
13   Sales:
14   LOAD
15       Region as REGION,
16       SalesID,
17       Product,
18       SalesAmt,
19       LastModifiedDate
20   FROM [lib://Chapter 6/Sales.qvd]
21   (qvd);
22
```

As you can see in the preceding script, we have given access restriction on the region field. Along with that, we have restricted access to couple of columns for some of the users. So when the Admin logs in, he would see all the data available in the application, whereas if user1 logs in, he will see only INDIA region data, as the field SalesID will be hidden for him and he won't be able to see the field SalesID in the application.

Following are few things to remember when using the Section Access in Qlik Sense application:

- The field name for the filed on which reduction is given should be in upper case and the data should also be in upper case
- It is recommended to not apply OMIT restriction on key fields
- The snapshots are stored as per the data restriction of user who takes the snapshot and can be used by other user in story. When the other user moves from story to the application the data seen is based on rights of that user.
- When restriction is given only at group level, then it is mandatory to give internal USERID, that is INTERNAL\SA_SCHEDULER, to enable reload of the script from management console

- INTERNAL\SA_SCHEDULER user with ADMIN access should be there in section access table to enable reload of the script from management console

Apart from this security, there are couple of more security options available in Qlik Sense:

Securing the connection string: Qlik Sense allows you to restrict the access to the connection strings using the standard mode. By default, standard mode is enabled; which makes it compulsory for you to use create the library connections first and then use them when connection is needed to data sources.

Securing the script: Qlik Sense also allows you to import the script from file. This lets you provide the security to your script. You can write the script in text file and then import that text file in Qlik Sense, and Qlik Sense will treat the text of that file as Qlik Sense script and execute the script while reoloading. To allow this, there are two variables used, **Include** and **Must_Include**.

Include and **Must_Include** are the variables which contain the file name that needs to be treated as script. The syntax is as follows:

```
$(Include = Script.txt);
$(Include=LIB://MyScript/Script.txt);
$(Must_Include= Script.txt);
$(Must_Include=LIB://MyScript/Script.txt);
```

When no path is defined, it is assumed to be the current Qlik Sense working directory. You can specify the absolute path or the LIB:// folder path.

The only difference between `Include` and `Must_Include` is that the **Include** statement will not generate an error if the file is not found (it will fail silently), but the **Must_Include** variable will generate the error if the file is not found.

There are two things to remember when using these variables:

- They support only folder data connection in standard mode.
- The syntax is that variable should be within parentheses preceded by dollar sign . You cannot set them as normal variable like Set Include = filename.

[204]

Visualization Strategy

The next step in the project is visualization. Now that we are ready with data, we can start developing the visualization through which data can be analyzed by the end users. End users, except the super user, might not have visibility of how data has been prepared; they will be more interested in analyzing the data and finding the facts from the data.

Let us start understanding the importance of visualization, but before that, let's look at some influencing quotes:

> *Numbers have an important story to tell. They rely on you to give them a clear and convincing voice.—Stephen Few*

> *The purpose of visualization is insight, not pictures.—Ben Shneiderman*

> *The goal is to turn data into information, and information into insight.—Carly Fiorina*

All the preceding quotes try to tell us that we should present our data in such a way that they tell stories. As a consultant, you should know how to turn the data into an insight which can be consumed by the end users to make important decisions.

The purpose of visualization is to give quick and meaningful insights of the data. It should be developed in such a way that users get to know what they should know, instead of providing them with too much of information.

When it comes to creating the analytical visualization, it is a good practice to follow the DAR (Dashboard, Analysis, and Reporting) methodology. It follows the way humans perceive information. It helps your data to speak up and shows you to the least level of information to take corrective actions.

Let us look at the what a dashboard should contain.

Dashboard: Dashboard is the starting point of analysis. It shows the overall picture of the business or a functional area. It helps users to get updates on day to day basis, by giving them high-level information. The key focus of the dashboard are the KPIs (Key Performance Indicators). These are the indicators which can easily tell you the health of the business. For example, percentage of sales achievement helps you to understand if you overall sales goal are on track or not. KPIs like these help to get immediate attention of business users to find anomalies in the business operations.

This is useful for the senior management of the company to get an overall picture, as they are hard pressed for time. This does not imply that the other data points do not matter, but they may not wish to spend time looking at things which are working smoothly. Instead, they would be interested in finding the areas which need attention. The KPIs on the dashboard can easily show them this.

Following is the dashboard screenshot from the demo application Consumer Sales (*from* `https://demo.qlik.com`):

You can see from the dashboard how KPIs can help in getting a snapshot of the business operations. Following are the points which a dashboard should have:

- Aggregated information
- KPIs not more than 10 in number
- Less filters on screen
- Color codes to highlight the outliers

Let us now understand what analysis sheets should contain.

Analysis: These are the sheets which help business users to investigate the problems found using the dashboard KPIs. These sheets are the most interactive sheets. They have detailed charts and graphs which show the breakup of the KPIs by various dimensions, and a wide list of filters which allow for the slice and dice of the data. It allows the users to drill down in the data and find the reasons behind the problem. These sheets can be created separately for each area of analysis.

These sheets will be helpful for the users who want to spend time in exploring the data.

Following is one of the screenshots from the demo application **Consumer Sales:**

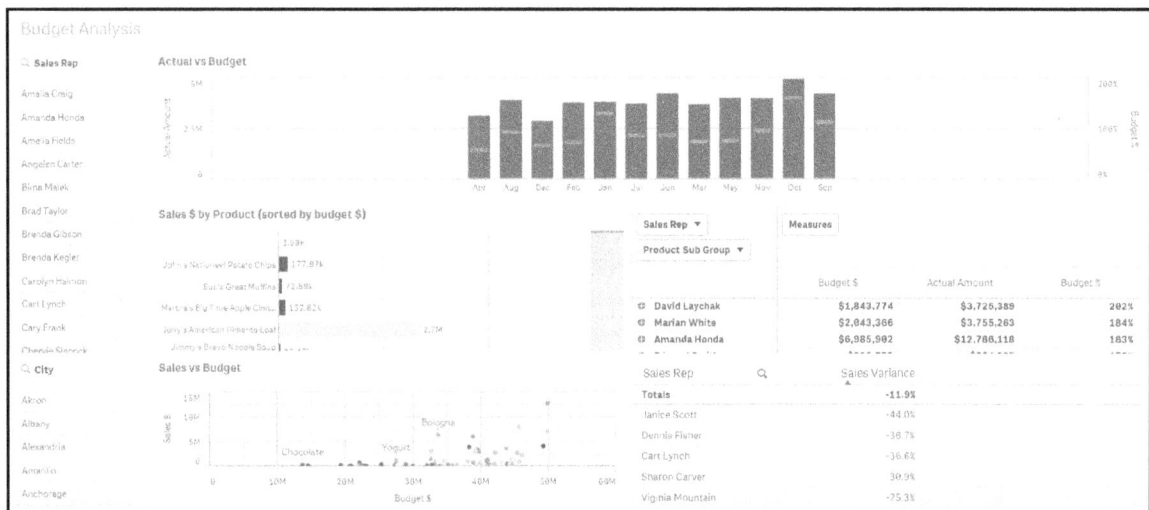

Following are the points which an analysis sheet should have.

- More filters to slice and dice
- Should have information about one area in one sheet, like sales, inventory, procurement, and so on
- Should have graphical representation for easy understanding of data

Let us now look at what should reporting sheets contain.

Reporting: Reporting is a sheet which shows the least level of data, that is, the most granular data set. It contains more of tabular representation than graphical. It helps in taking the required action on the problem. Following is the report sheet from demo application *Sales Discovery*:

Reporting sheet should have the following things:

- Least level of information presented in tabular view
- Should include all the possible data available to find the relevant information to take action

Choices of Objects

One of the important reasons why most of the dashboards and reports fail in getting the users' attention is the wrong choice of objects to represent data. It is not that the business users always look out for jazzy dashboards, but what they look for is useful information helping them to get actionable insights. This is possible only with the help of proper representation of the data, using proper charts and graphs.

Jazzy dashboards do attract users, but if those dashboards fail to provide proper insight into the data, they would not be useful .

Let us have a look at the various objects available in Qlik Sense, along with best suited data for them:

- Bar Chart: One of the widely used graphical representations is bar chart. Bar charts are very easy to understand. They are used when you want to compare values side by side; for example, comparison of sales with budget or comparison of sales of different regions. They can also be used to show additional comparisons using stacked bar charts.

Following are examples of good and bad bar charts:

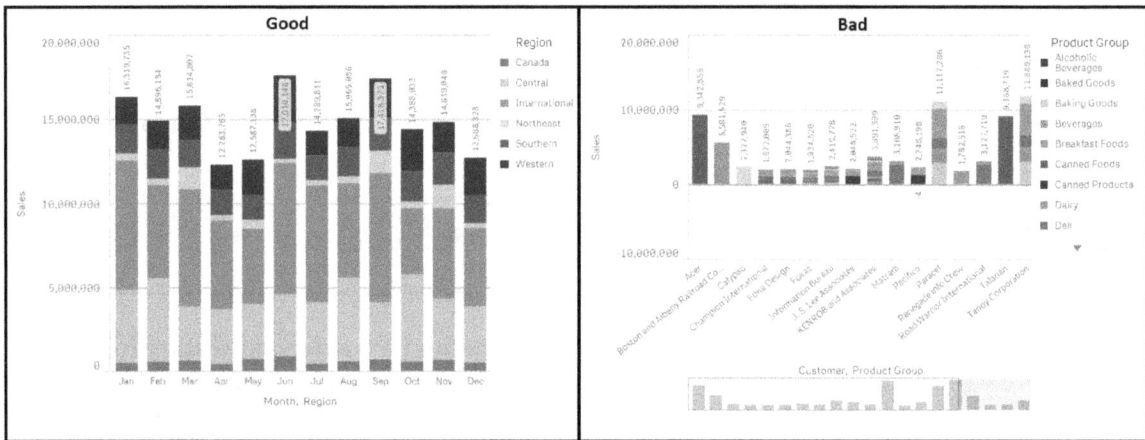

When used as a stacked bar chart, it is important that you choose the second dimension with maximum five to six values, otherwise one cannot do comparison between them, as seen in the bad chart example in the preceding image. There is a limit on the number of dimensions and expressions that can be used in a bar chart. The following table shows the allowed pair of dimensions and expressions:

Dimension	Expression
One	Max 15 expressions
Two	Max one expression

> **TIP**
>
> To get a meaningful analysis out of bar chart, it is recommended that you use max two expressions.

- Line Chart: When you want to represent trend lines, then the best suited graph is line chart. It shows the progression or degradation over a period of time. The dimension used in this chart is always the time dimension, like year, month, day, week, and so on.

A sample line chart is shown in the following screenshot:

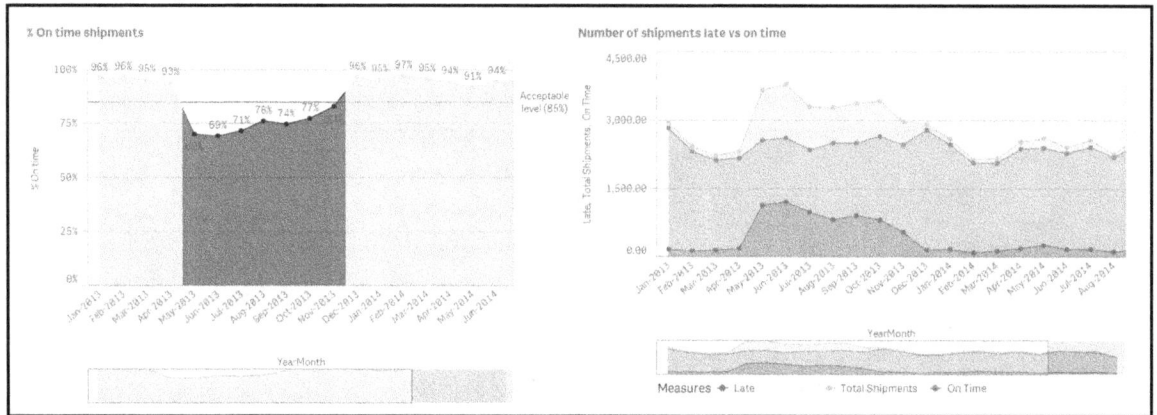

Line charts share the same property as bar charts. They can be used to show the progress of one or more values together, like shown in the preceding figure (refer to chart on the right).

There is a limit on the number of dimensions and expressions used in a line chart. The following table shows the allowed pair of dimensions and expressions:

Dimension	Expression
One	Max 15 expressions
Two	Max one expression

Just like bar charts, line charts are more readable and meaningful when max expression is not more than two.

- Combo chart: This is a combination of bar and line chart. When you want to show comparison of KPIs which have different scales, you can use the combo chart.

For example, the sales amount compared with the margin percentage (both have different scales). If you plot both KPIs on a bar chart, the percentage values will be almost invisible. Instead, you can use the combo chart, which would help you to put sales amount on one axis and margin percentage on the other axis, to make the comparison easier.

Combo chart allows you to use the bar chart along with the line chart, and you can also use symbol instead of bar and line.

Following is a sample combo chart:

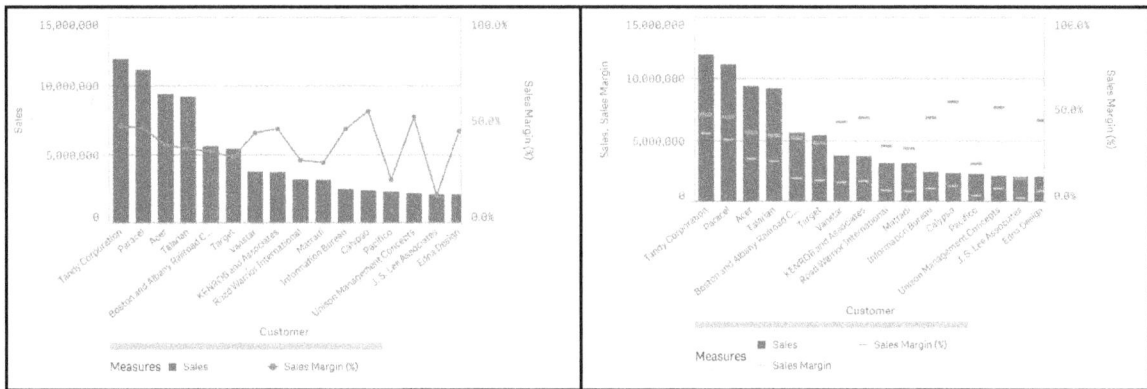

Following table shows the max allowed dimensions and expressions:

Dimension	Expression
One	Max 15 expressions

- **Pie chart**: When you want to show the ratio amongst the dimension values with respect to the overall total, then the best suited graph is the pie chart. Pie chart shows the contribution of a value to the overall total. It shows only positive values.

Following images have sample pie charts of Qlik Sense:

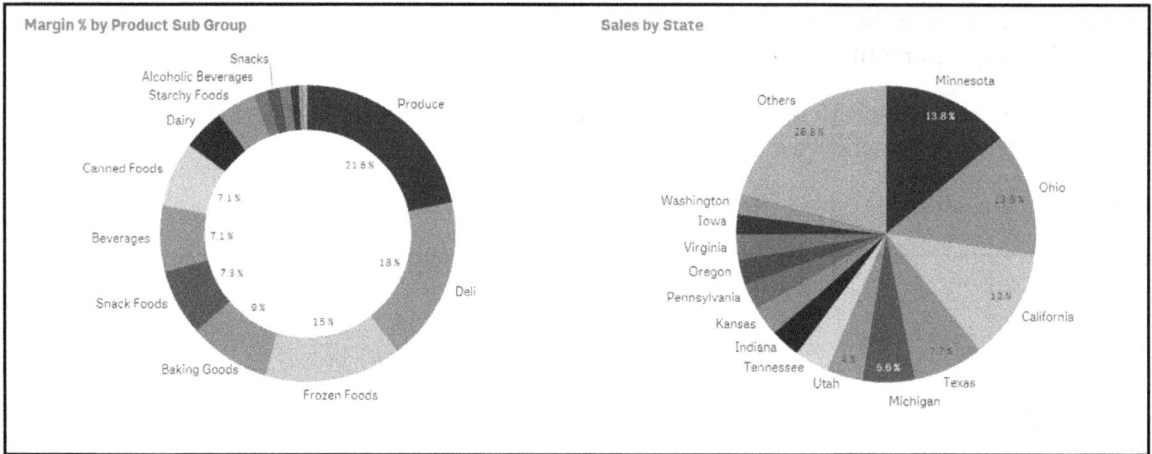

Pie chart only supports one dimension and one expression.

- **Gauge and KPI**: When you want to show the KPI, that is a measure you can use either the gauge or KPI object. Both have the functionality to show the different color combinations as per the values of the expression.

Following are the Gauge and KPI objects:

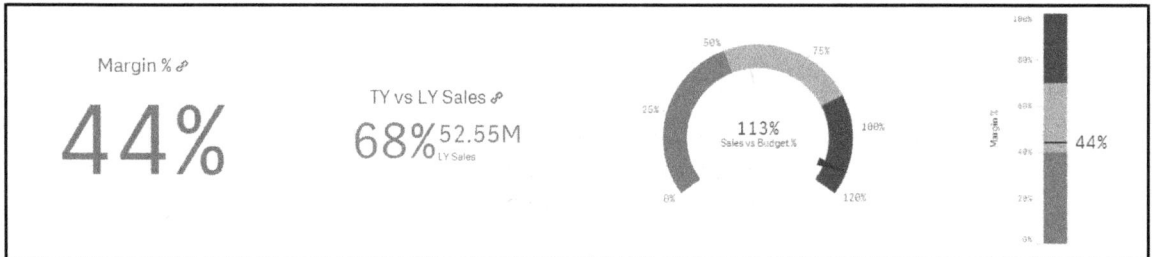

Gauge can show only one expression where as KPI object can have two expressions.

- **Scatter chart**: Scatter charts are used when you want to show correlation between two expressions that share a common dimension. For example, the sales versus margin with respect to customers. Scatter chart allows adding one more expression which is used to indicate the bubble size.
  Scatter charts are very useful to find outliers in the data. For example, when you want to find the customer who only buys less margin products from us or you want to find the customer who buys too many products which have higher margins. This helps in deciding which customer needs what kind of focus and decisions can be taken such that it improves the company's profit.

An example of scatter chart is as follows:

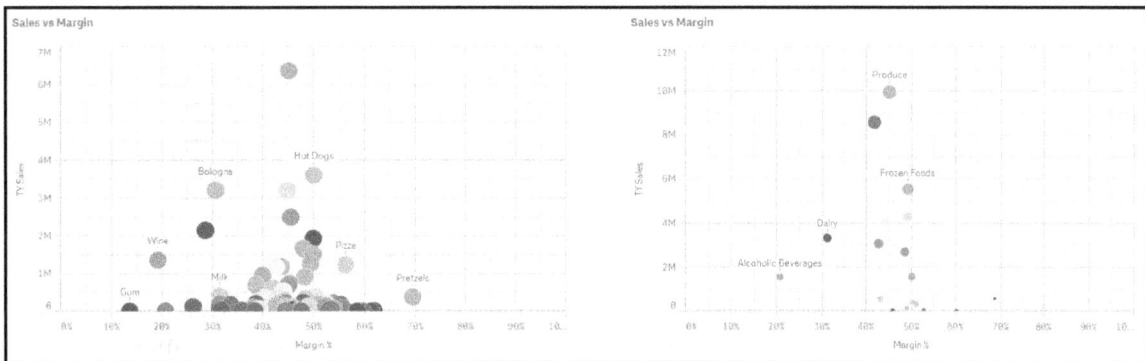

It supports only one dimension and maximum 3 expressions. The third expression is used to indicate bubble size.

For few users, scatter chart becomes difficult to understand due to multiple expressions and their correlations. So depending on the users who are going to consume the dashboard, you should decide whether to use scatter chart or not.

- **Table object**: Table objects are the best objects when you want to show transactional data and show aggregation where dimension values are many. They are also suitable when you want to show multiple dimensions and multiple expressions together. The table objects is best suited to create a report showing transactional data.

Following is a sample table object:

	Invoice Number ▲	Order Number	Customer	Invoice Date	Promised Delivery Date	Sales	Sales Quantity
Totals						$178,200,456.44	3,509,357
	100001	200001	A&B	4/29/2013	4/28/2013	($194.17)	-1
	100002	200002	ActionWorld	4/29/2013	4/29/2013	($990.04)	-17
	100003	200003	ActionWorld	4/29/2013	4/29/2013	($30.00)	-1
	100004	200004	Edia	4/29/2013	4/29/2013	$17.55	1
	100005	200005	Edia	4/29/2013	4/29/2013	($135.87)	-3
	100006	200006	Edia	4/29/2013	4/29/2013	($34.73)	-2
	100007	200007	Edia	4/29/2013	4/29/2013	($3.59)	-1
	100008	200008	Edia	4/29/2013	4/29/2013	($106.92)	-6
	100009	200009	Edia	4/29/2013	4/29/2013	($153.90)	-3
	100010	200010	Edia	4/29/2013	4/29/2013	($138.20)	-4
	100011	200013	Xtreme	4/30/2013	4/30/2013	($222.35)	-2
	100012	200015	Abbott	4/30/2013	4/30/2013	($1,348.13)	-1
	100013	200016	Telus Corporation	4/30/2013	4/30/2013	($94.59)	-1
	100014	200017	Teca-Print	4/30/2013	4/30/2013	($185.06)	2
	100015	200018	Rave Association	4/30/2013	4/30/2013	($10.69)	-1
	100016	200025	Teca-Print	5/1/2013	5/1/2013	$0.00	-1
	100017	200019	Vanstar	5/1/2013	5/1/2013	($509.82)	-4

- **Pivot table**: Pivot table is like the table object, but in addition to that, pivot table allows pivoting of the dimensions to view the data in cross table format. With table object, it is not possible to see summarized data and then drill down data to other dimensions. Pivot table helps you to do that by giving flexibility of expanding and collapsing dimensions. You can further interchange the dimensions from row to column and get the crosstab view of the data.

Following is a sample pivot table:

Region ▼	Measures			
Product... ▼				
	Sales YTD	Sales LY YTD	Sales Variation	Sales Goal
● Canada	$1,408,121	$1,465,848	-3.94%	$2,262,688
Alcoholic Beverages	$18,515	$31,811	-40.30%	$2,208,040
Baked Goods	$15,317	$9,334	64.04%	$2,184,951
Baking Goods	$23,024	$23,433	-1.75%	$2,253,896
Beverages	$48,129	$20,663	132.92%	$2,251,096
Breakfast Foods	$3,157	$3,079	2.53%	$2,187,758
Canned Foods	$131,330	$143,743	-8.64%	$2,262,688
Canned	$1,586	$5,725	-72.29%	$1,495,523

Product... ▼	Region ▼	Measures				
		Canada				Central
	Sales YTD	Sales LY YTD	Sales Variation	Sales Goal	Sales YTD
Alcoholic Beverages	$18,515	$31,811	-40.30%	$2,208,040	$25,220
Baked Goods	$15,312	$9,334	64.04%	$2,184,951	$48,277
Baking Goods	$23,024	$23,433	-1.75%	$2,253,896	$1,585,446
Beverages	$48,129	$20,663	132.92%	$2,251,896	$1,093,400
Breakfast Foods	$3,157	$3,079	2.53%	$2,187,758	$178,010
Canned Foods	$131,230	$143,743	-8.64%	$2,262,688	$374,887
Canned Products	$1,586	$5,725	-72.29%	$1,495,523	$3,236
Dairy	$139,506	$110,346	26.43%	$2,254,177	$286,164
Deli	$404,074	$182,595	121.30%	$2,261,521	$1,484,470
Eggs	$2,649	$2,753	-3.78%	$1,473,217	$10,624
Frozen Foods	$327,709	$265,176	23.58%	$2,281,802	$935,759
Meat	$833	$1,459	-42.91%	$1,144,487	$892

- **Treemap**: Treemap charts are used when you want to show the hierarchy data; for example, when you want to see the product group and its breakup by product subgroup. It shows the data as a tree. Each dimension value represents the branches of the tree. It allows to drill down to the last level of the branch and analyse the data.

Following is an example of a Treemap chart:

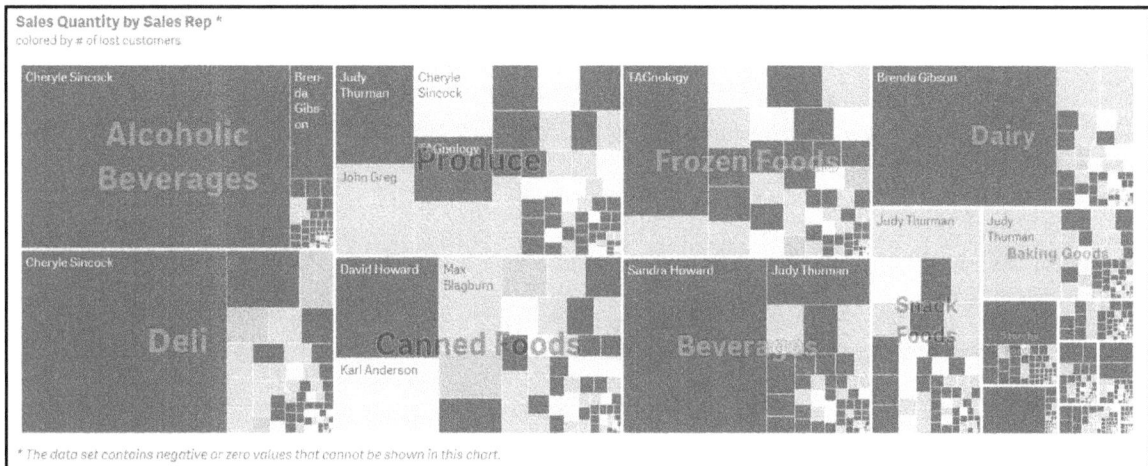

Following table shows the maximum dimensions and expressions allowed in treemap:

Dimension	Expression
Maximum 15	Only one

Though treemap allows maximum 15 dimensions, it is recommended that you don't use more than 3 dimensions in this chart, otherwise it becomes unmanageable and unreadable.

Use of Extensions

Extensions, as the name suggests, allow you to extend the power of Qlik Sense by creating your own charts and graphs using the Qlik Sense APIs. Assume that you want to show some analysis to your business users but it cannot be shown using the available visualization library. In such cases, Qlik Sense allows you to create your own charts and use them in Qlik Sense application.

Qlik Sense has exposed several APIs to extend the capabilities of Qlik Sense. One of such APIs is visualization API. These are the same APIs that are used by Qlik Sense to create its own inbuilt visualizations.

If you are well versed with web technology like HTML and scripting like JavaScript, then you can easily create your own extensions. You can also use third-party APIs and visualization libraries, like D3, Chart.js, Echarts, and so on.

Let us have a look at few extensions which will ease your development and help in making more interactive dashboards:

- **qsVariable**: One of the good extensions is the qsVariable. It helps to set a variable value in four ways, namely as a button, select, field, and slider. Variables are very useful while developing the dashboards and in filtering the data to find the analytics from the data.

The qsvariable extension was developed by *Erik Wetterberg*. The extension can be downloaded from `http://branch.qlik.com/#!/project/56728f52d1e497241ae697f8`.

A screen shot of application using the extension is as follows.

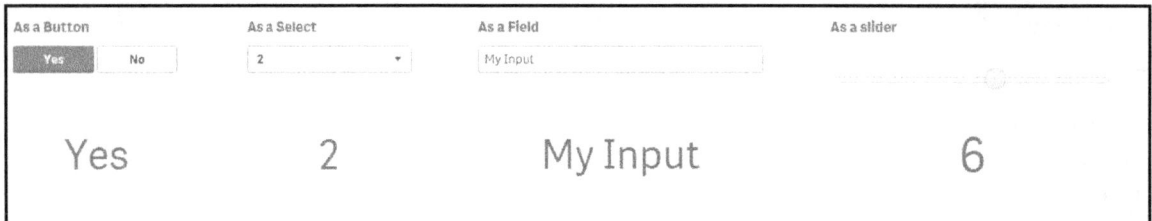

Example of qsvariable extension

- **Trellis chart**: One of the wonderful visualizations, which I feel is missing in Qlik Sense, is trellis chart. Trellis chart helps to look at the same chart with different dimension values. It creates mirror of the charts with different values of the defined dimension. That eventually makes it easier to compare the KPIs. Trellis chart extension was developed by *Michael Laenen*. The trellis chart can be download from `http://branch.qlik.com/#!/project/5718fb1d80955830cdd6e7fb`.

It can create trellis for various chart types, such as bar charts, line charts, pie charts, area charts, lollipop charts, and step charts.

Following are some trellis chart extension screenshots:

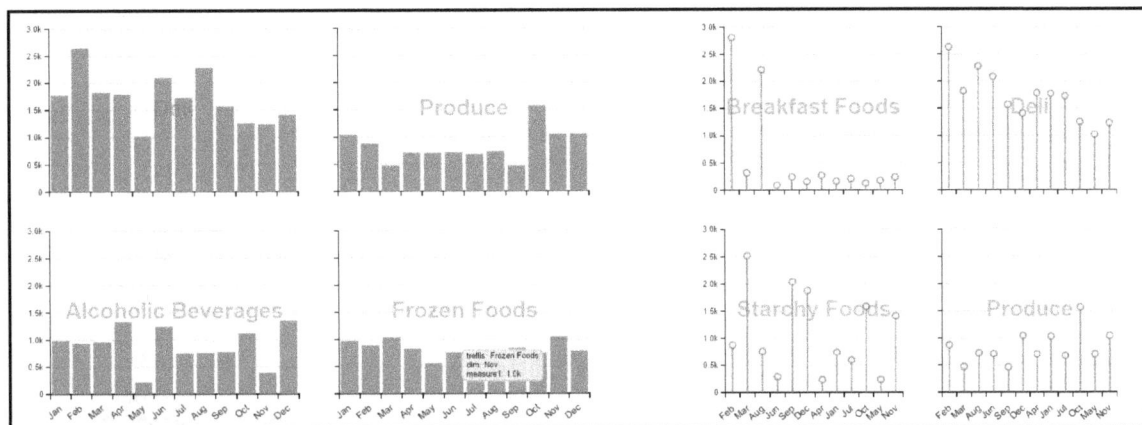

- **Tabbed container extension:** One of the best ways to utilize the canvas to show a number of charts is the container object. This extension can be compared to the container object of QlikView. It allows you to create a different tab for different charts.

It is limited to only five tabs and it takes the visualization from the master library. So to add any visualization in a tab in this extension, you will have to first create a visualization in master library.

This extension is available to download from `http://branch.qlik.com/?_ga=1.118094281.1597184826.1442399999#!/project/5925830c89eaeeb085775473`.

Following is a sample screenshot of this extension:

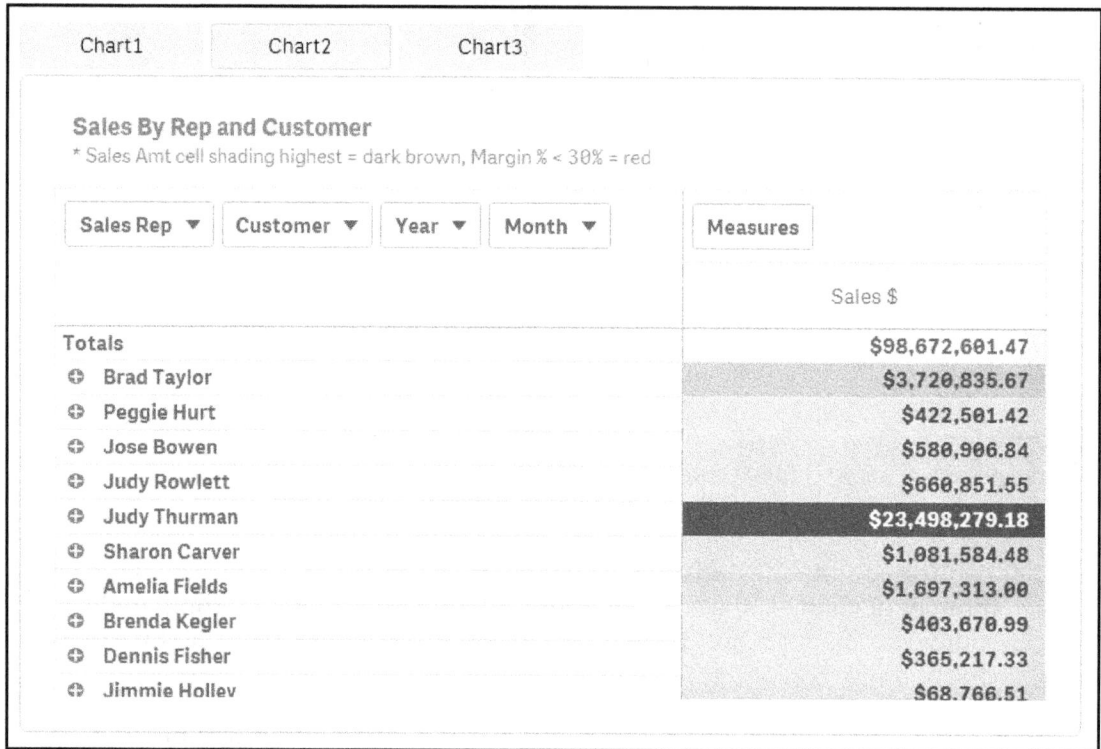

- **Interactive Timeline:** One of the missing charts, which should have been included as a default chart, is Gantt chart. Gantt charts are very useful when you want to show the progress of projects over a time. This extension helps in achieving the same.

This extension was developed by *Ralf Becher*. It is available for download from http://branch.qlik.com/#!/project/56728f52d1e497241ae6989d.

Following is a screenshot of interactive timeline chart:

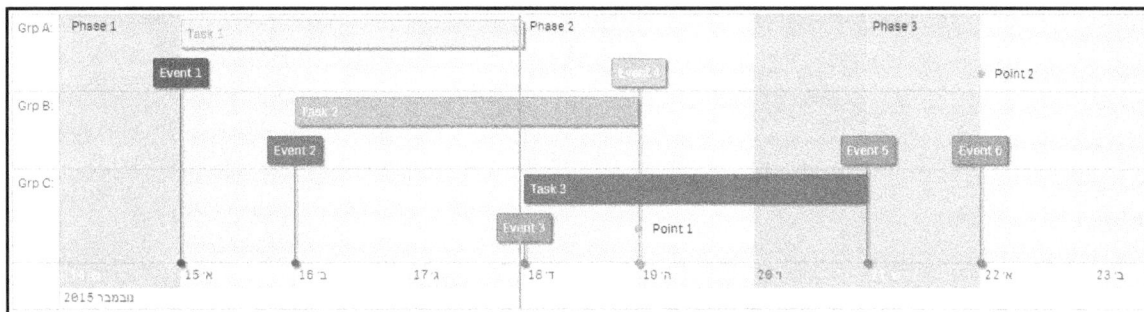

- **Sheet Navigation + Actions for Qlik Sense**: This is a very useful extension, which helps in easy navigation along with the actions. This extension can perform many actions which you may require on every dashboard, such as making a selection, applying bookmarks, clearing the sections, and so on. This extension was developed by *Stefen Walther*. It can be downloaded from `http://branch.qlik.com/#!/project/56728f52d1e497241ae698a0h`

Following is a screenshot of the extension:

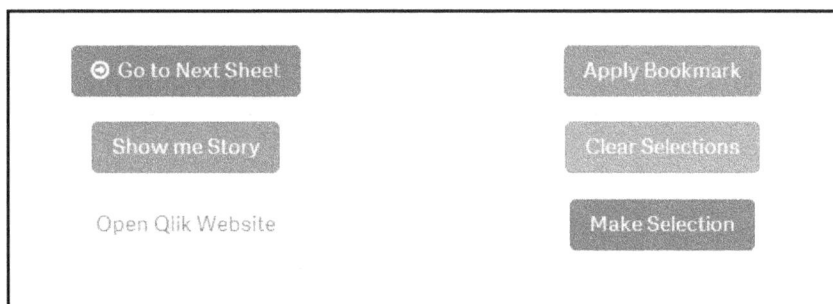

- **SimpleKPI**: If you want to show the KPIs on the dashboard, I would suggest you to go for this extension. It allows you to arrange your KPIs in the best way. You can also include symbolic indication along with your KPI. It can also show the trends of the KPI. One of the good parts of this extension is that it can repeat the icon multiple times to represent the value of the KPI.

It was developed by Alex Nerush. It is available for download from `http://branch.qlik.com/#!/project/5677d80b7f70718900987bff`.

Following is a sample SimpleKPI image:

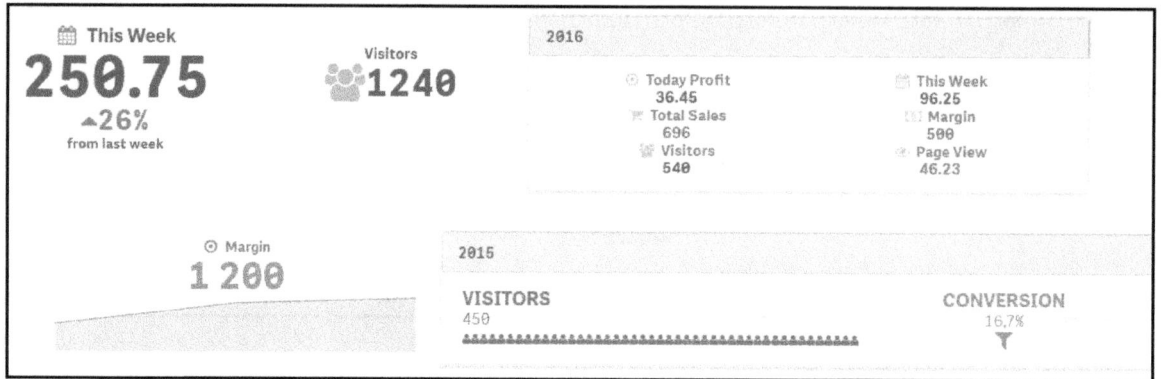

- **BarsPlus:** The default bar charts do not have much formatting options. So if you are looking for a bar with more formatting options, then one of the extensions I would suggest is BarsPlus. Apart from the formatting options, the bars can also be visualized in a better way.

It is developed by *Larry Woodside*. It can be downloaded from `http://branch.qlik.com/ #!project/5858f900c0568806cf368930`

Following is a sample screenshot of the extension:

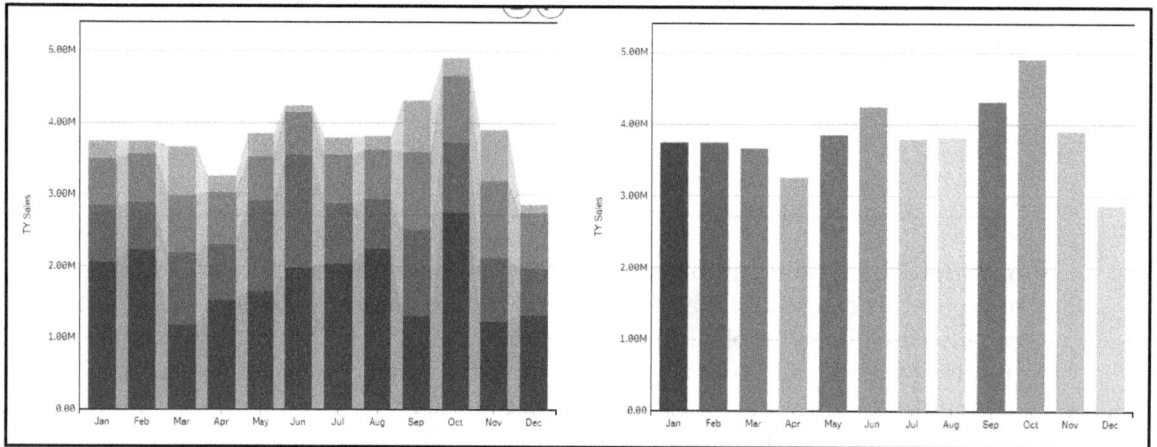

Visualization best practices

We learned in previous section that visualization is the actual output which end users will be seeing. Considering that visualization helps users get insights into their data it becomes important to build more intuitive visualizations considering the best practices.

Let us have a look at few of the good practices

- Understand the data: It is not possible to present data with meaningful insight if you don't understand the data. You should be to make the business user get the best possible information from dashboard especially when there are multiple datasources. You should also know the nature of the data, like whether it is a historical data, a nominal data, or a ratio data. This will help you to understand the best visualization to choose and this enables business quick insights. Thus, it is always important to understand your data before transferring it to dashboards and reports.

- Use KPIs properly: We have seen that KPIs provides important information which gives users a quick insight into their data. If you use a single expression in KPI objects, they show you the values. This KPI objects are not suited for situations where the need is to compare values with a benchmark and find out whether business is going in right direction or not.

  Thus, it is important that along primary value, you also provide secondary information. This helps users compare and decide if it calls for attention or not. You can also use the color code indication along with the KPI. For example, if you are showing a KPI like target achievement, then you can use color codes in the following way: if the value of the KPI is below range then show it in red color, if it is within the range then show it in amber color, or else it should be in green color. . This is because colors can easily get our attention.

  We have seen one of the extensions namely, Simple *KPI* which can be used to show multiple values for comparision.

- Choose color wisely: Colors are very powerful indicators; they can add value to the visualizations. Colors can easily draw our attention to important information and tie our thought process with other elements. For example, the bright colors can be used to get immediate attention.

- Colors also communicate the feelings. For example, red color means that something needs immediate attention, whereas the green color gives a positive feeling, that everything is going well.

  You should always limit the number of colors that can be used in your graphs. Instead of using 10 different colors, you can choose 5 best colors and use the different shades of those colors if required.

  While coloring graphs like table or pivot, make sure that you use colors only to show the outliers, rather than coloring all values of the chart. This will make it more readable and help in finding the anomalies in data.

  Use the light colors wherever possible. You may also ask your client about their corporate colors. This will make it easier for them to accept the dashboards more quickly as they will be comfortable with their own colors combinations.

- Less is more: Most of the developers make the mistake of developing many charts and graphs on a single screen. They feel like giving all the information to the users on single screen. But this approach may not work because too much information will make the users lose interest.

You should use minimum charts on a single screen and make your screen look cleaner. At max, you should draw four to five graphs on a single screen. This will help you to keep the users' focus on the most important chart and its information.

You can leverage the functionality of **Alternative dimension** available in couple of charts to change your dimensions from one to other. This will help you to reduce the number of charts required. For example, if you want to show the sales amount by various dimensions, like region, product group, sales person, and so on, you can put them as alternate dimension and change the chart dimension as required on the fly.

Let's take a look at an example of bad visualization and good visualization. Following image shows the bad visualization:

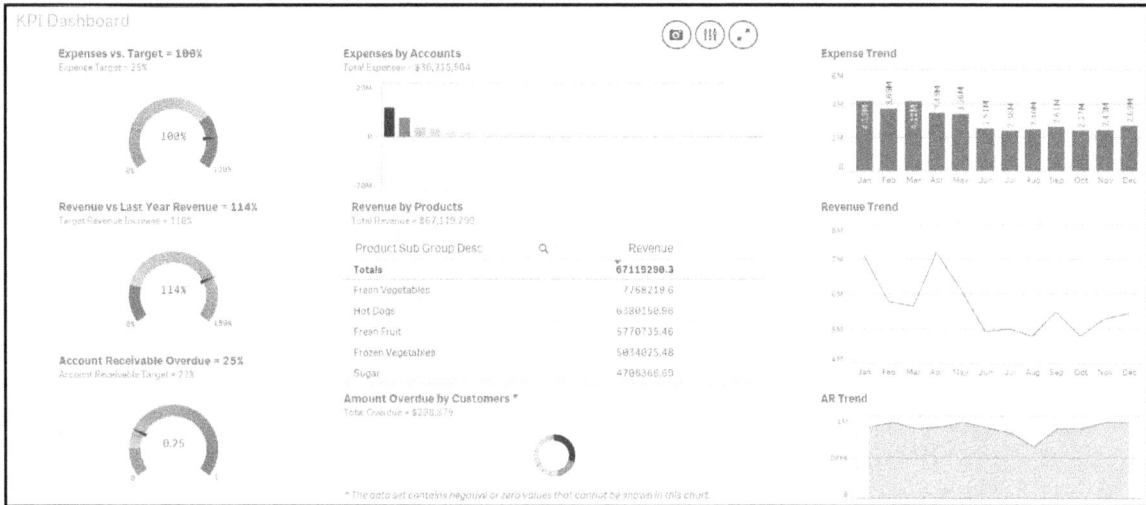

You can see in the preceding dashboard that though the KPIs which are selected are best for the dashboard, the presentation is not good. Proper chart types have not been used to show correct information, and also the size of the chart is wrong; for example, the pie chart is totally impossible to be understood.

Now the same KPIs can be converted into a good dashboard, as shown in the following image:

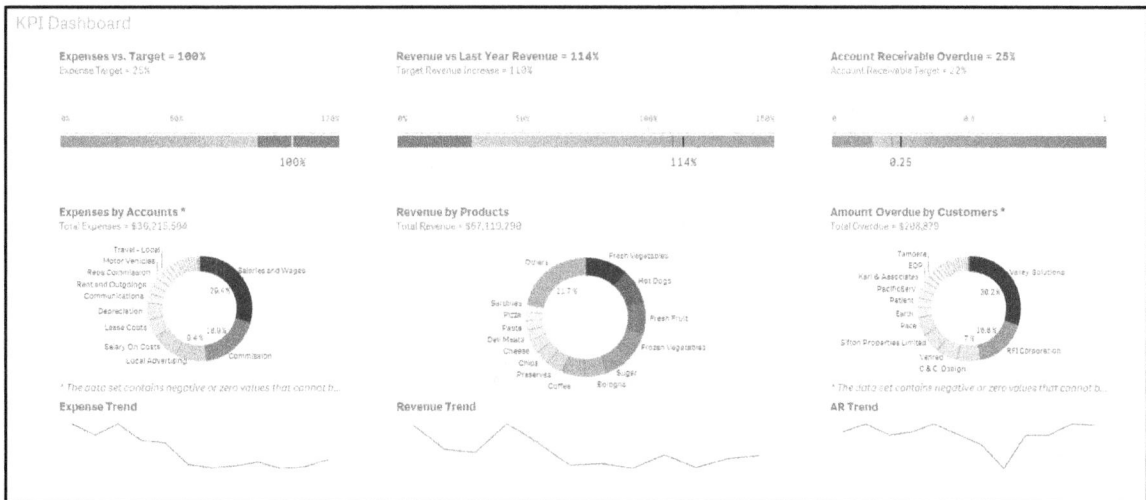

As you can see, it is much clearer than the earlier dashboard. It presents correct information to the end user, starting from showing the overall KPI, then its breakup, and then the trends to give additional information.

Story Telling

Traditionally, the data which is required by the senior management is prepared by someone who knows how the management expects the data. This data is presented to the management in meetings and through presentations.

The objective of such meetings is to analyze the data and find the answers to business problems. However, the objective is hardly met in the same meeting, because when the questions starts arising, after looking at the data, no one has answers to them because the actual data resides in excel.

To overcome such problems and make meetings more interactive, Qlik Sense has introduced a powerful feature called story telling. Story telling allows you to share the insights found from the dashboards to other people in similar way as a power-point presentation, but the advantage is it is always connected with the actual data. In other words, you can say story telling allows you to do collaboration.

The idea of story telling is to showcase the insights derived from your data and emphasize the actions needed. These insights are supported with annotations and various charts which make for a good presentation to the stakeholders.

Story telling uses the snapshots captured from the dashboard and analysis sheets, and adds the narrative parts of those screenshots to explain the findings. When any questions are asked during the presentation of the story, the user can easily switch from presentation mode to analysis mode by taking the audience to the source of the screenshots.

Let us understand how to create a story from the Qlik Sense application. There are few steps which you should follow to create a story:

Finding the insights for the story

It is important to first find the insights from the data which can be presented in the form of story to the management. To find the insights from the data, you must start analyzing your data by asking a series of questions.

You can simply take the screenshots of the charts which answers your question. These screenshots are later used in the story telling to showcase the findings.

You can take the screenshots of the chart using the camera button which gets populated when you take your cursor on the chart, as shown in the following image:

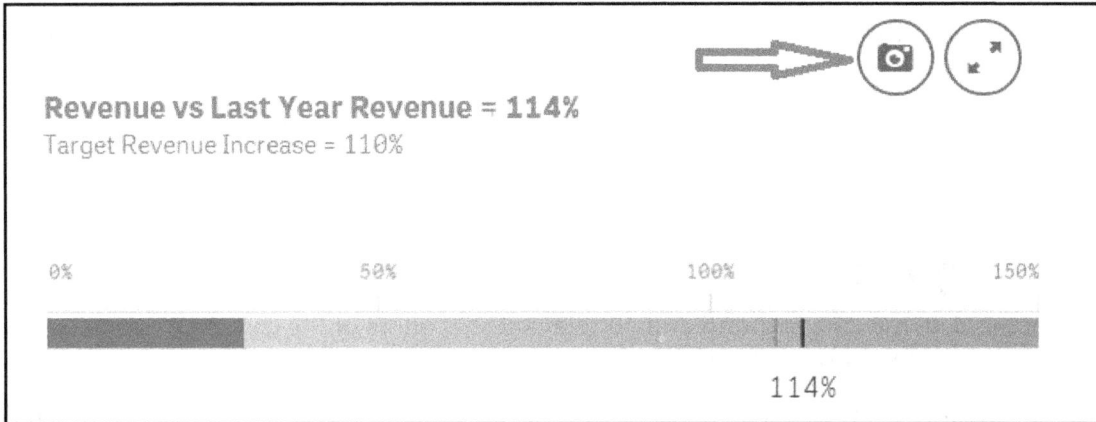

Once you click on the camera button, the snapshot of the chart will be taken and it will ask you to enter the annotation for the chart:

This annotation will be shown when you look for this screenshot in the library while creating the story.

In a similar way, you can take as many snapshots as you need for the story building.

One thing to note about the snapshots is that the data shown in the snapshot will not change even after the application is reloaded with new data. Every time you need to retake the snapshots.

When you look at the library of the snapshots, you will find the date and time when that snapshot was taken. This will help you to find the latest snapshot and use it in the story.

Creating the story

Once the story in the data is found and all relevant snapshots of the charts are taken, you are ready to build your own story board.

To do this, you will have to click on the Stories icon found on the App Overview tab, which is shown next:

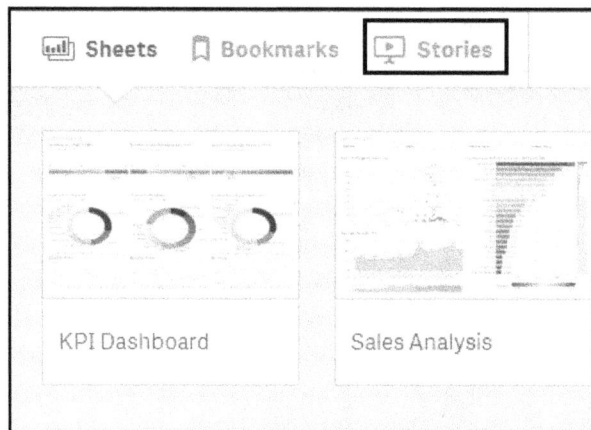

If you are on the sheet, you can click on the icon shown on top right side:

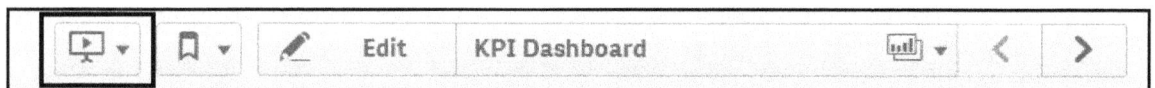

Once you click on these buttons, you will be taken to a new window which will show you the already created stories. Using the same window, you can create a story by clicking on the *Create New Story* thumbnail

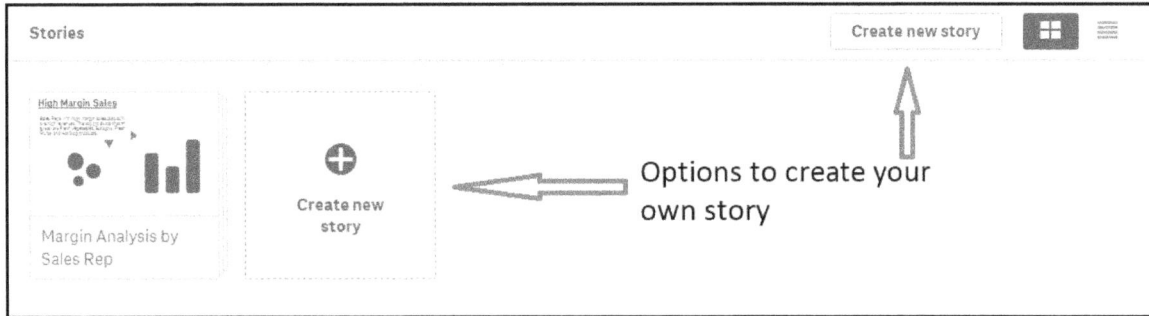

Once you click on the "Create new Story", you will be asked to give a name and description to the story:

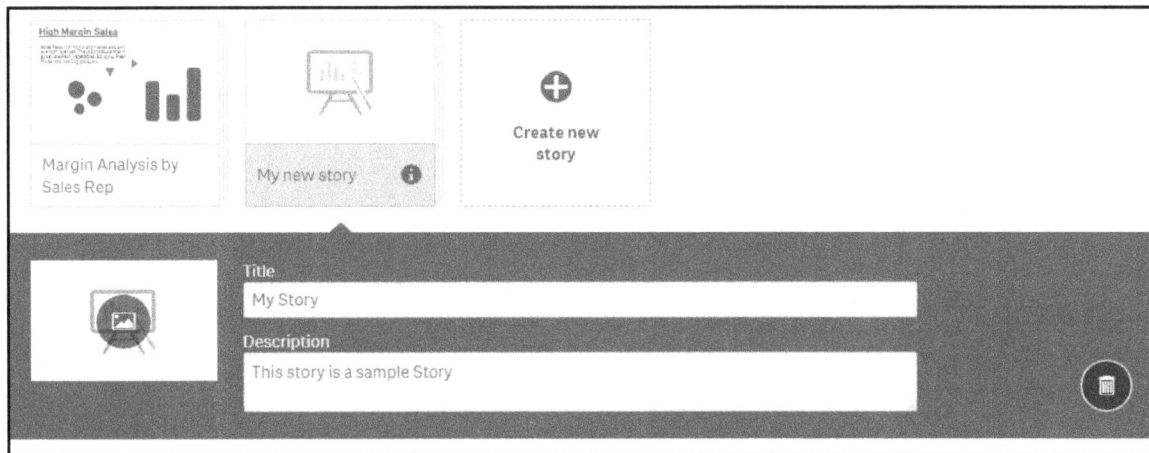

After entering the name and the description, you can click on the story to open the story designing window.

The new window shows a similar layout to what you may see when you create a presentation. It will show you a blank slide which can be used to place the snapshots taken in the first step and add narratives.

You will see couple of icons on the right-hand side of the screen, which are the designing options available along with the snapshot library.

First click on the camera button which is the first icon. Once you click on that, you will see the snapshot library which will show you the list of snapshots taken so far. It will show you the snapshots in the descending order of the date on which they were saved:

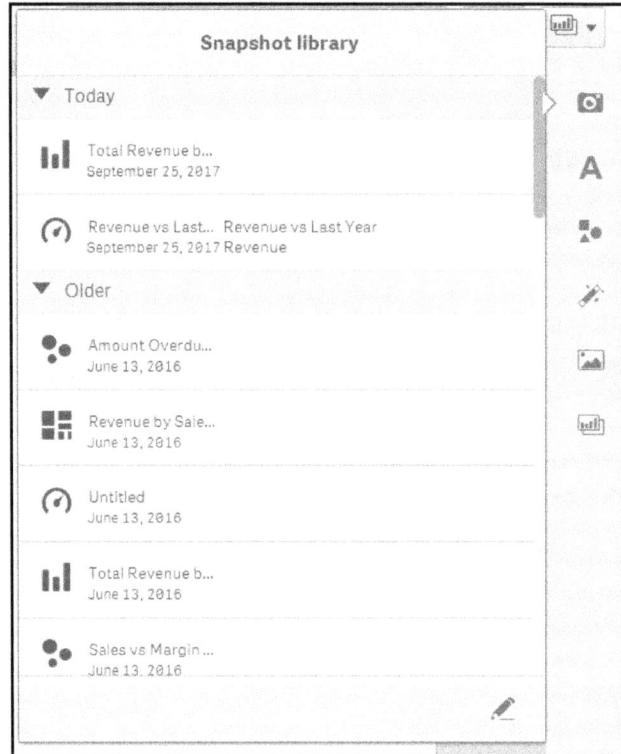

Adding the Screenshots

You can drag and drop the screenshot from the library on the slide. Once you do that, you will see an image of the chart. On top of chart on the right hand side are 3 icons. The first icon helps you to replace the snapshot, the second to edit the object properties and the third to unlock(once unlocked you can resize the screenshot)

An sample screen shot is as follows.

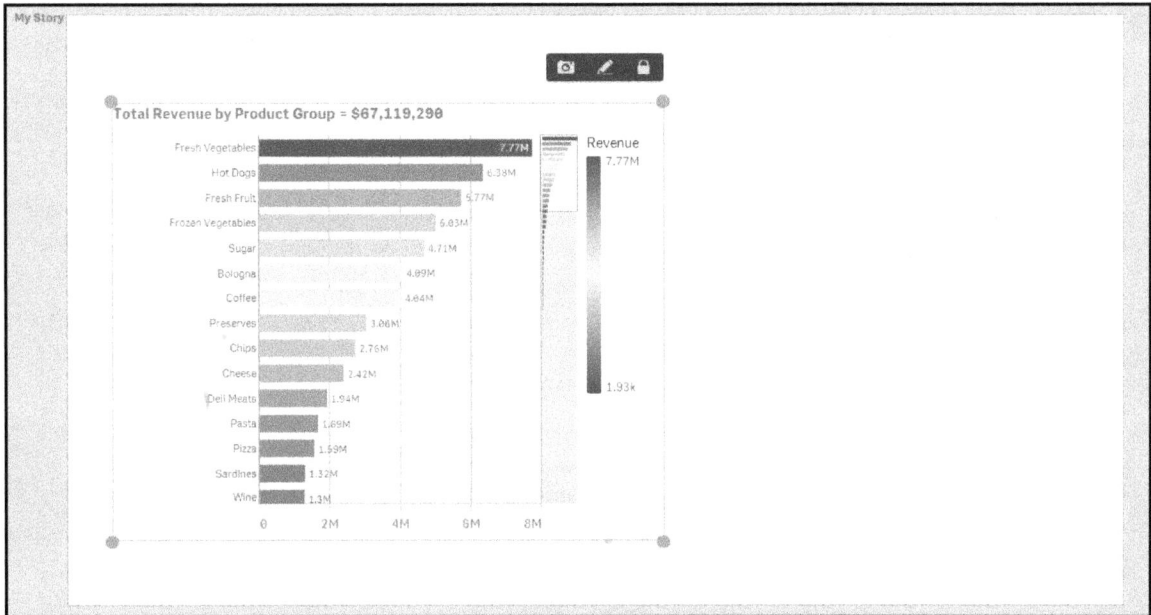

Let us see what are the options available when you click on the edit icon on the screenshot. Following image shows the same:

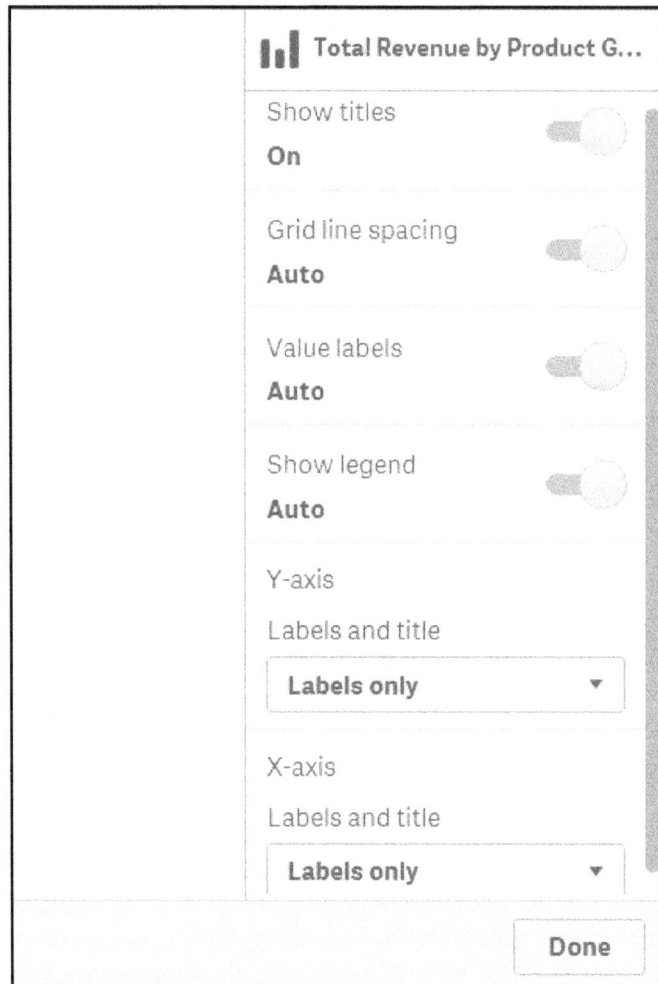

Shown here are the options for a bar chart; every chart will have its own editing options.

Adding Text

There are two ways you can add text on the slides: one is by using the *Title* option and the other is by using the paragraph option:

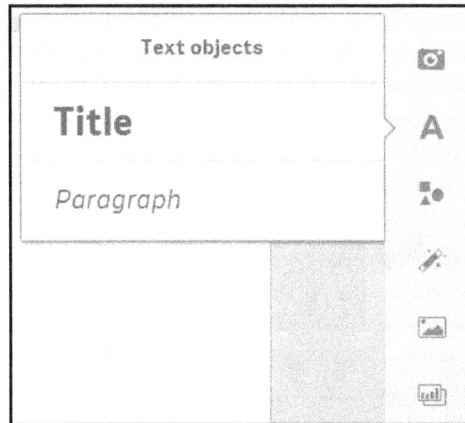

Title will help you to add a title to the slide. The fonts of the object will be bigger as compared to the paragraph option. Similarly, the paragraph object will help you to add the narrative text to your slide.

Once you drag and drop the relevant object, you will need to double click on the text shown on the object to add your own text. These objects will also allow you editing functions:

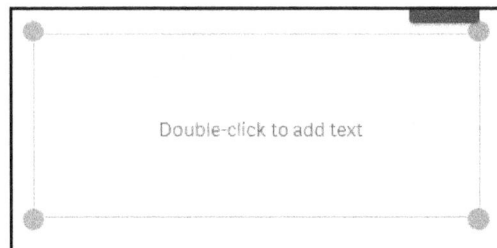

Editing options are as shown in the following image:

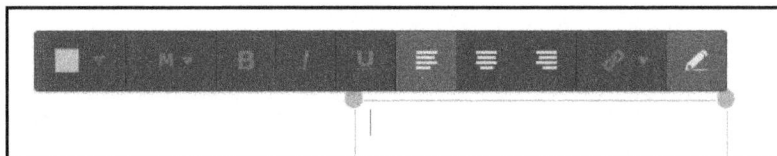

Add shapes

At times, you may like to add some indicator which can indicate the anomalies found on the chart or you may want to take the user's attention on a value of the data point; in such cases, you can use the shapes. The shapes can be dragged and dropped from the shape library available on right-hand side options. Depending on the need, you can choose any one or more shapes and place them on slide. Have a look at the following image to understand the context:

The sample use case is shown in the following image:

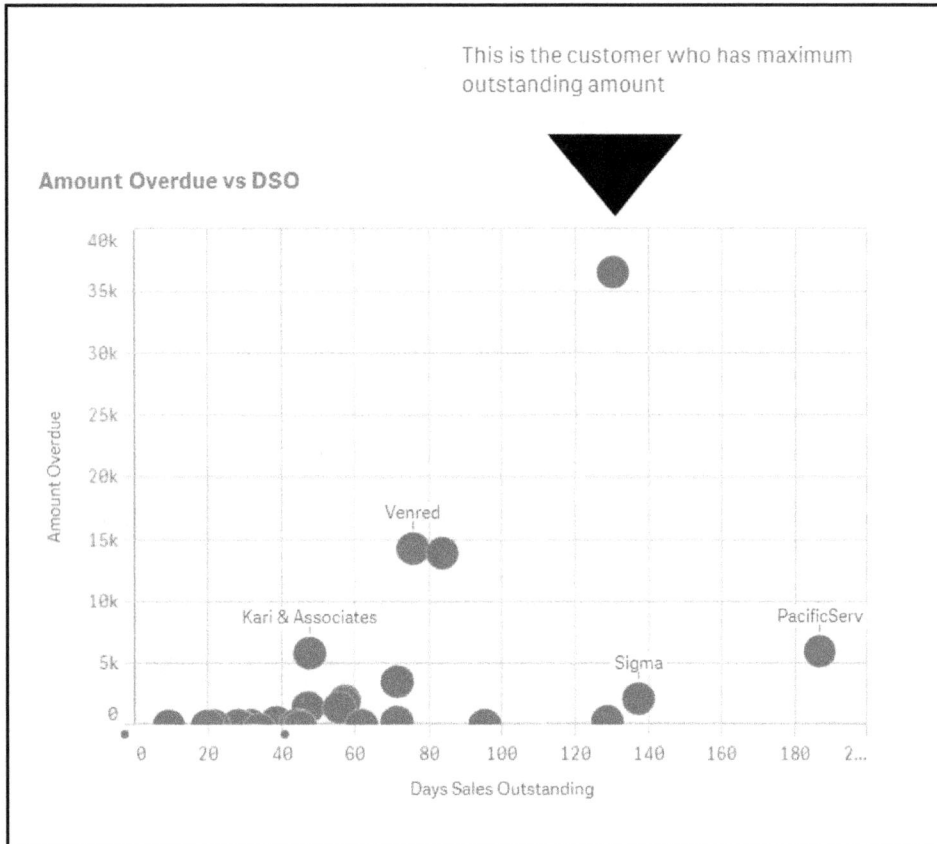

Add effect library

Effect library is used to highlight the highest value, lowest value, or any other value. Once you place this object on the snapshot, it will highlight a particular value and the other values will be grayed out. You can use effect library only with bar chart, line chart, and pie chart.

Following image shows the available options under effect library:

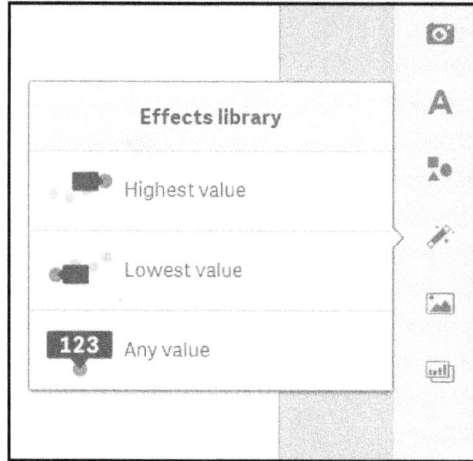

Once you apply the effect library on a bar chart snapshot, it displays the chart as shown next:

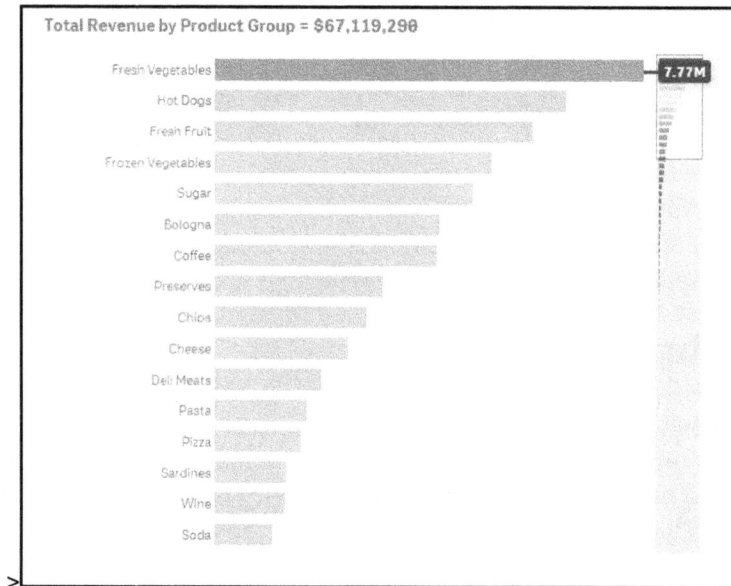

Add images

You can also add images to your presentation by using the image option available on right-hand side. The images which are available in the media library will be allowed to be added on the slides.

Add sheets

Story telling also allows you to embed an entire sheet into the slide. So if you want to present all the objects of a sheet, the better option is to embed it. This option also allows you to make the selections on the charts of the sheet from within the story, you need not go back to the application.

The finished story looks as shown in the following images.

As seen from following figure, we highlight pointers on high margin sales:

High Margin Sales

Sales Reps with high margin sales also achieve high revenues. The top products that they sell are Fresh Vegetables, Bologna, Fresh Fruits, and Hot Dog products.

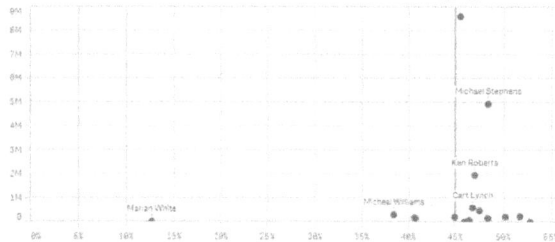

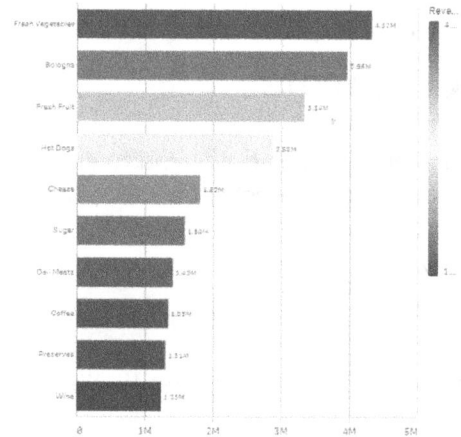

In the next figure, we look at the causes of low margin sales:

Low Margin Sales

Although Sales Reps with low margin sales have more higher revenue products, they still could not achieve the same margin %. As it is displayed on the revenue bar chart, the top product that is being sold by these sales reps is Hot Dogs. We should consider increasing the margin % on this product.

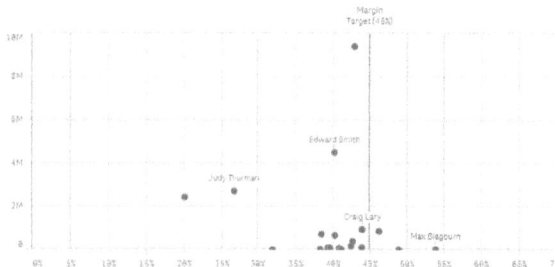

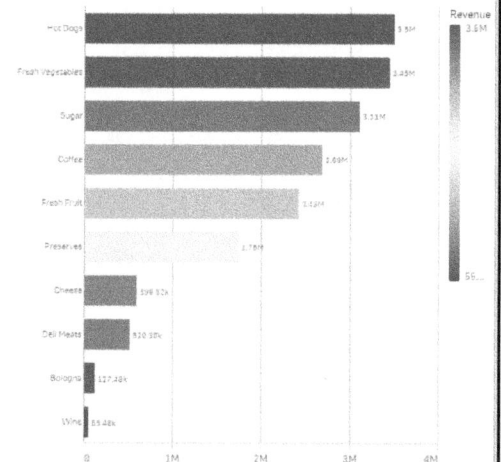

The story telling can be be made more rich by embedding an entire sheet of Qlik Sense app:

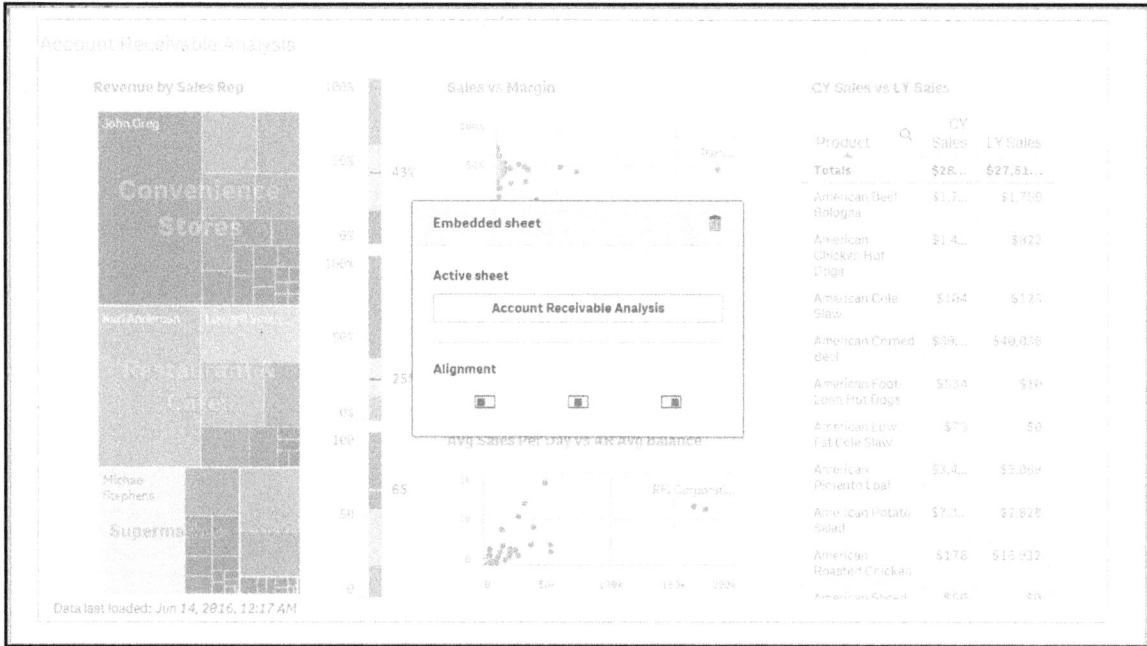

Story presentation

Once you finish creating the story, you are ready for the presentation of your story. To start the presentation of the story, you can click on the play button available in left panel, just like shown in the following image:

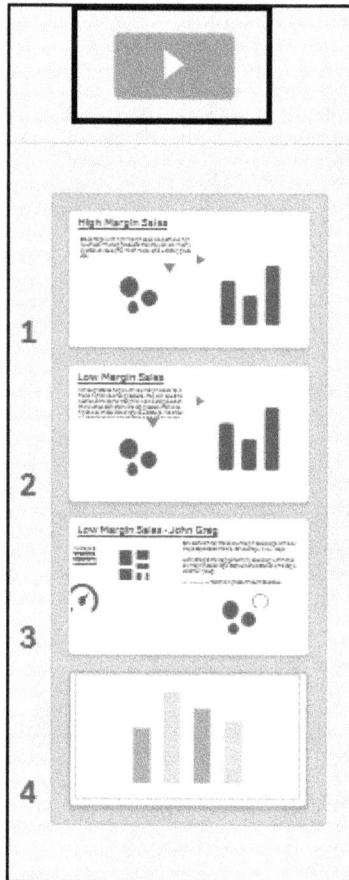

Once you click on the play button, your presentation starts. You can move to the next slides through the buttons available at the bottom of the slide or you can simply press the left and right arrow key from the keyboard of your machine.

Now during the presentation if anyone asks you any question, you can take them back to the application by right clicking on the chart and clicking the *Go to Source* button:

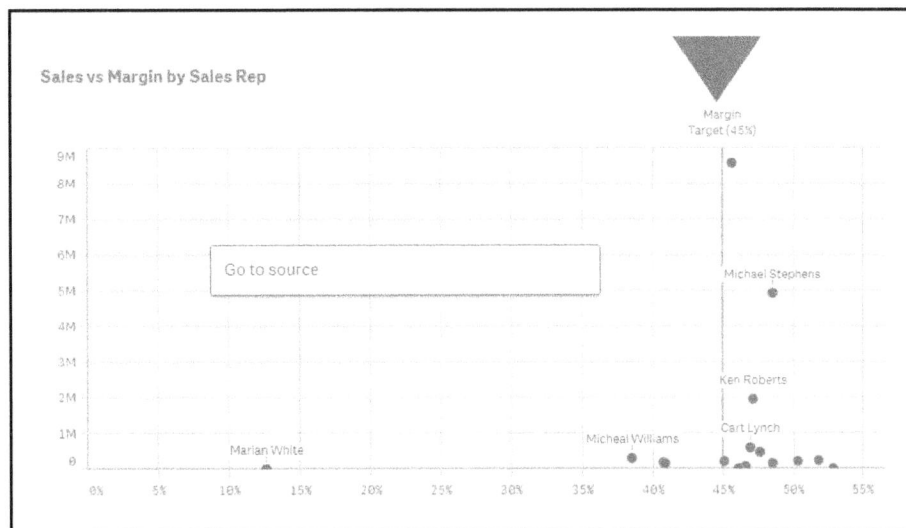

Once you click on the *Go to Source* button, you will be taken to the application where you can slice and dice the information and give proper reasoning to the question asked. You can then return to the presentation by clicking on the Return button

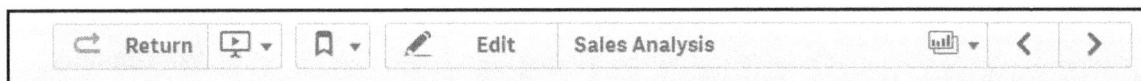

One good part of story is that when you move to the source, the same selections get applied which were applied while taking the screenshot.

Sharing the story

Qlik Sense also allows you to share your story with other users of Qlik sense application (Online) and even users not part of Qlik Sense (Offline). To share the story online, you need to publish the story so that other users can get access to your story.

To share the story offline, you can export the story in either ppt format or in pdf format.

Summary

At the end of the chapter, let us summarize all things we learnt in this chapter. Being the heart of the book, this chapter tried to teach us many aspects of development, starting from getting the data from the source system to converting it into the data insight visualization for end users to consume it.

We started with understanding the data extraction process, where we learned about ETL (Extract, Transform, and Load). Within the ETL process, we focused mainly on the extraction process, where we learned about full load and incremental load. We saw what kind of data would need what kind of load strategy.

In incremental load, we saw how to handle three main scenarios, namely insert, update, and delete. We also saw the scripting and sample outputs for each one of them.

After the extraction phase, we started with data modeling and learned about dimensional modeling with the basic concepts of fact tables and dimension tables. Moving forward, we saw two schemas of dimensional modeling, that is star schema and snowflake schema.

After understanding the fundamentals of data modeling, we looked at the common challenges of data modeling and the ways to overcome them. Then we learned the script management methodology and its importance.

Progressing forward, we looked at the best practices used in data modeling which have positive impact on the performance of your application. We then saw the data modeling validation methods, that is row count method and field metadata information.

We also touched upon the security aspects and looked at the how to write security script to restrict unauthorized access to data and columns of the application.

Once our data got ready, we started learning the visualization strategy, in which we learned about the concept of dashboard, analysis, and reporting (DAR) in detail. Then we started looking at the various objects available in Qlik Sense and understood in which scenarios they suit best. Next we saw how to add our own objects using extension and the impact of good extensions on your dashboards.

Later we looked at the best practices which should be used in our designing. We also looked at an example of good and bad visualization.

As the last topic of the chapter, we covered the power of storytelling in Qlik Sense.

In the next chapter, we will look at the validation of the application, why it is important, and **user acceptance testing (UAT)** and go live strategy.

7
Validation, UAT and Go-Live

In the previous chapter we looked at the best practices for development, visualization, dashboard designing. The development stage is an intense stage in any business intelligence project and following best practices helps to keep the Qlik Sense application robust. In this chapter we are going to learn the importance of the validation. Along with that we will learn how to validate entire Qlik Sense application and make it ready for UAT (User Acceptance Testing). We will understand aspects of UAT and important points considered for conducting the UAT. Post this we will learn about the Go-Live strategy.

> Before learning what is validation and importance of validation, it is necessary to understand the importance of data.

In todays world, the growth of the companies is mainly depended on the how good they can analyze the various datasets available with them like customer data, vendor data, social media data, human resources and many more. Almost all business decisions are made based on these data available with the company. In other words, you can say that the data drives the business and its decisions. So the management and sanctity of the data becomes very important and critical for business.

According to IBM poor data cost US around $3.1 trillion per year. This statistic is only for US, the figure for the entire world will be much more. This cost not only includes the maintenance of data but also includes the lost opportunities of companies due to poor data quality.

Garner has also conducted a survey in year 2011, which states that 40 percent of the company's new initiatives do not succeed due to the poor data quality. This indicates how important it is to have a clean and meaningful data.

In this chapter we will be covering the following topics:

- Introduction and Importance of Validation
    - Data Validation
    - Script validation
- User Acceptance Testing
- Go-Live Strategy

Introduction and importance

Validation is a process of cross checking, which is carried out to indicate that the output generated by an activity is accurate and acceptable. Validation is done for various activities carried out in a task or a process. For example, in report development, validation indicates that the data used for the reporting is taken from authenticated sources, the logic applied in reports are generating correct outputs and reports are created as per the requirements given. Similarly, in software development, validation indicates whether the software meets the basic requirements and functionalities. It also checks if the software produces the desired output or not.

Poor data (Non-validated data) not only has monetary impact on the business but also have other impacts like discussed in the following list:

Impact on confidence: Most of the CEOs have a dependency on the data to take critical business decisions. If the data is of poor quality then it leads to loss of confidence of senior management and they will start looking for some alternative methods to take decisions. In such case they will start doing the business as it was done in older days i.e depending on the information from few key people. This approach may prove to be counter-productive

Impact on opportunities: Poor data also causes business to lose opportunities. There is a cut-throat competition in the market today, if you delay in making proper decision or make poor decision you may lose the business opportunities, because your competitors will take an advantage of that.

Impact on revenue: It is obvious that if you make a wrong decision it will have a severe impact on the financial position of the business. The impact on revenue may be shake the operations of the company. For example, an incorrect premium amount for a flood prone area will lead to loss of revenue.

Impact on reputation of company: If a company exposes incorrect data to its customers or vendors then it will impact the reputation of the company and it will reduce the confidence of customers. For example, if insurance company shares incorrect data to their agents related to premium renewal dates of customers or incorrect incentives calculations will leave a bad taste for customers and agents.

Validation of the source data is a big topic in itself, for the scope of this book we will limit out discussion to Qlik Sense reporting.

> For Qlik Sense project, validation is done to test the data sanctity of reports. Validation also involves testing if the reports are made according to the requirements decided in scope of the project.

Let us now look at the various are where validation can be performed.

Data validation

In Qlik Sense data flows through various stages, for example data starts flowing from source database to QVD and then from QVD to the Qlik Sense application. In the course of this flow at times data may get changed due to the improper linking or improper use of the functions or due to wrong business logic.

Let us have a look at the points which should be checked in data validation.

Data type

When you load data from multiple sources there are chances that the data type of a field gets changed while storing in Qlik Sense. For example, the field which is more prone to change is date field.

Different data sources stores date field in various formats, so when these are loaded in Qlik Sense it gets interpreted by Qlik Sense in different way. For example, when you load the date field from excel it may get stored as text or in number format. It is important to know that Qlik Sense stores date in julian format.

Looking at above example, it is a good practice to validate the date fields and make sure all of them are set in the required date format. There are two functions which helps to set the format of the date field and to convert the text into the date format. Let us look at them in brief.

`Date` function: Date function helps in setting the format of the date. It takes the number as first parameter and format as a second parameter in which date should be shown. The syntax is shown below. It is a part of the formatting functions.

```
Syntax — Date(Expression,'Format')
```

The various formats for date is as below.

DD	For Day
MM	For month in number
MMM	For month name in short form (Set in global variable i.e. MonthNames)
MMMM	Full form of Month (Set in global variable i.e. LongMonthNames)
YY	For last two digits of year
YYYY	For year

`Date#` function: `Date#` function is used to convert the text into date. It takes two parameters, first the text and second the format of the text. It is a part of the interpretation functions. The output format of this function remains same as the original format.

```
Syntax — Date#(Expression,'Format')
The expression is the Date in text format.
Format is the format of the text date.
Example:
Date#('20/09/2017','DD/MM/YYYY')
```

It is recommended to keep the date format same across application, to make the frontend logic easier and manageable. When date field is used in the set analysis for filtering, search string should be in the same format as it is stored in date field.

Null values

Another area which troubles developers during coding is dealing with the **Null** values. Null in Qlik is nothing but the lack of value, always referred as **Null value**.

Null values occurs due to various reasons:

- Directly through source database
- As a result of forced concatenation of table
- As a result of joining tables

It is important to handle null properly in Qlik Sense, because it may give wrong result when aggregation is used. For example, consider below data.

Country	Salesman	SalesAmt
India	A	100
India	A	200
India	B	150
US	C	300
US	D	400
US	D	100
US	E	250
UK	F	300
UK	G	150
UK	H	100
UK		200

As you can see in the previous table the salesman value is missing in last record. So when you load this data in Qlik Sense it will be treated as null. Now consider that you are creating two visualizations, one for the overall Sales Amount KPI and other is sales amount by salesman. Below shown are the sample visualizations for both the KPIs.

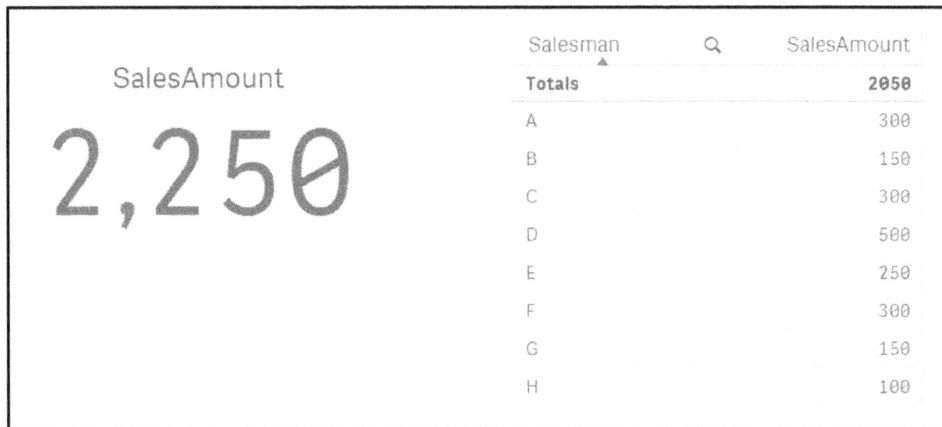

SalesAmount	Salesman	SalesAmount
2,250	Totals	2050
	A	300
	B	150
	C	300
	D	500
	E	250
	F	300
	G	150
	H	100

As you can see in the preceding image, when you aggregate the values at overall level (left side chart), it has aggregated all the values regardless of null, but when you insert that in table chart and show at Salesman level it will not show the SalesAmt for the null value (unless Include Null value option is checked).

In such case this may mislead the users and they may start raising question on sanctity of the data and may stop using Qlik Sense application. Hence handling null values becomes all the more important.

You can handle null values using two global variables i.e. NullAsValue and NullValue.

`NullAsValue` converts the null values into the text value, so that they can easily be identified and handled properly.

Syntax – NullAsValue Fieldlist

Field list is the list of fields for which you want to convert null into text. You can use * to define all fields of the data model.

When you use this variable, you should set the null text using the variable NullValue.

Example:

```
Set NullValue = 'Unknown';
```

Duplicate values

You should be careful about duplicate values as they invariably create a wrong result. They are generated due to below operations.

Joins: We know that joins are used to connect two or more tables, but when the joining table has the duplicate values it creates some duplicate values in the resulting table (for example we have table A and table B and we are creating table C. If table B has duplicate values, table C will have duplicate values). If the resulting table value is used in any aggregation then it may show you the wrong value.

Thus while using the joins between the tables you must make sure that the joining table has the distinct values.

You should perform join operation as shown in following figure:

```
1    Table1:
2    Load Country,
3         Salesman,
4         SalesAmt
5    From [LIB://Validation Data/Duplicate.qvd](Qvd);
6
7    Temp:
8    Load Distinct Salesman,
9         Region
10   From [LIB://Validation Data/SalesMan.qvd](Qvd);
11
12   Left join (Table1)
13   Load Salesman,
14        Region
15   Resident Temp;
16
17   Drop table Temp;
```

One thing to note here that we didn't use the Distinct keyword in joining table, because if we do that Qlik Sense will remove the valid duplicate records from the resulting table.

Script validation

Script validation not only helps to validate the flow of the data but also help in finding the syntactical or variable evaluation errors from the script.

While creating the aggregated layer as per business logic, we sometimes use the variables to do calculations and in complex calculations we may also use the looping functions like for loop or do while loop. In such cases it becomes important to validate the script. Because if the script is not validated you may spend more time in validating the data later and then it becomes difficult to find the problems in scripting.

Qlik Sense provides the debug functionality through which you can run the code line by line and check many things like variable evaluations, record counts of the tables. The debug wizard also allows you to set the breakpoints so that while reloading in debug mode script stops for you to check the values and after your intervention it starts reloading script.

In **Data Load Editor** you will get the option to debug the script on right hand side. Button shown below will start a debug mode of the script.

Debug mode will open 3 tabs at the bottom of the screen those are

- **Output**: This will show you the script execution window
- **Variable**: This will show you variables along with the assigned values
- **Breakpoint**: This will show you the assigned breakpoints in script

Following figure shows the debug options:

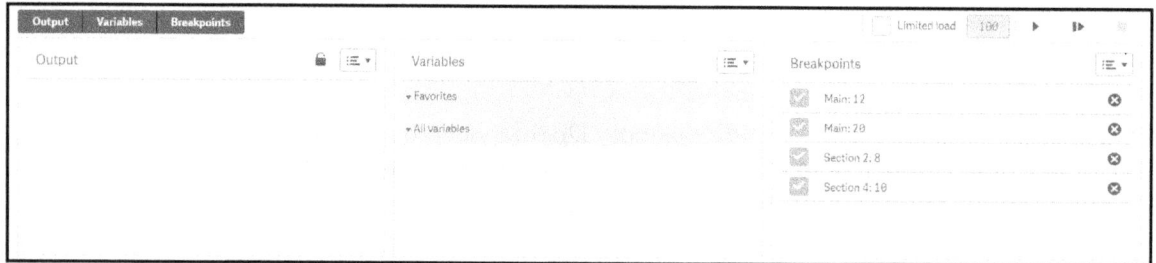

Following figure shows you the options available in debug toolbar:

Limited load 100	This option is used to load only limited numbers of rows and help in reducing the time required for entire script execution.
▶	This option reloads the script automatically till the next breakpoint is reached. On breakpoint it will halt.
▮▶	This option helps in loading the script line by line.
▪	This will end the script execution.

Business logic validation

Let us look at one more aspect of validation which is validation of business logic. Most of the time mismatches in the data are due to the wrong business logic. Business logic may go wrong when consultant misinterprets it or he/she wrongly implemented it. It may happen business users themselves are not sure about the logic. Each one of these reasons may lead to incorrect output of the reports. For example, different users may use different formula to calculate the net profit.

It is always important for a consultant to go through the requirement document created in early stage of the project before starting to code the logic. It may happen that over the course of time the formula changed due to the business policies, in such cases the document should be updated and should get reviewed by the business user and it should be signed off by the user.

To validate the business logic, consultant should divide the logic in smaller parts and start validating each one of them separately. This testing can be done while developing the data model or it can be done after the data model is finished. It is because there will be few logic which will get implemented to generate result at run time.

The method which I use and would recommend to do is that you should load the raw data required by the section of business logic. Once this data is loaded, start putting the required fields on the front end using the filters. Make appropriate filter criteria by selecting relevant values. Use the chart aggregation functions along with KPI object or the best pivot table and see the values and validate the same against the available validation report.

The best visualization which helps in data validation is Pivot table. It is because the calculation written on charts can easily debugged using this chart. If you do not give label to the expression it shows the evaluated values of the search string when dollar sign expression is used. Following screenshot shows you the sample evaluation:

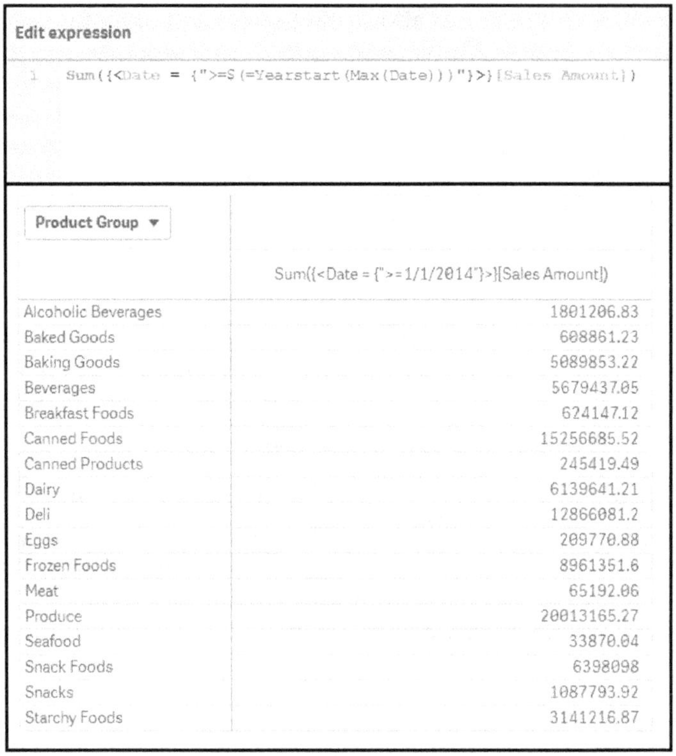

Edit expression	
1 Sum({<Date = {">=$ (=Yearstart (Max(Date)))"}>}[Sales Amount])	

Product Group ▼	Sum({<Date = {">=1/1/2014"}>}[Sales Amount])
Alcoholic Beverages	1801206.83
Baked Goods	608861.23
Baking Goods	5089853.22
Beverages	5679437.05
Breakfast Foods	624147.12
Canned Foods	15256685.52
Canned Products	245419.49
Dairy	6139641.21
Deli	12866081.2
Eggs	209770.88
Frozen Foods	8961351.6
Meat	65192.06
Produce	20013165.27
Seafood	33870.04
Snack Foods	6398098
Snacks	1087793.92
Starchy Foods	3141216.87

You can see that the expression written uses the dollar sign expression to evaluate the year start date for the maximum date. The pivot table shows the evaluated value, which helps to identify the anomalies in the logic applied.

Visualization validation

The dashboard is the area which is directly seen by the end user. Hence we need to ensure that all the values in the front end are correct. We had discussed in earlier chapters about the best practices in visualization, so as a part of the validation process one should check if visualizations suiting the requirements are used.

All other validations are generally performed by the developer to check the sanctity, but the front end validation should be done by a consultant who has the functional knowledge. This is important because this will be as good a validation done by the end user.

Followings are the list of things which should be carried out as a part of the dashboard validation.

Chart type validation

In this type of validation you should check if the chart type used to showcase the KPI is correct or wrong. If there is a chance of improving the visualization suiting the requirement it should be carried out.

For example, you can use the Gauge chart to show the KPI, but to save the space and make it more attractive you can choose different chart like KPI object.

Dimensions and expression validation

This validation is important because sometimes we use dimensions and expressions which are not connected in data model which may create a Cartesian product and may also impact the performance. Say for example when data island tables are used in data model.

You should thoroughly check the dimensions and expression to make sure that logic are properly implemented.

Few other points which are best to be avoided are as follows:

- Use of key fields in count function
- Expression starting with IF conditions.
- Nested IF statements
- IF statement in aggregation function like Sum.
- Custom sorting based on text

Business flow validation

In this type of validation you check if the flow of the dashboard is as per the flow which business expects. The sheets should be arranged such that users get answers to their questions with minimum navigation and clicks. For example, if dashboard is developed for senior management and it contains data for all departments it may not fly. In such cases it is better to create a separate sheet which shows all relevant KPIs. For other users the individual department data can be shown like one for sales, one for supply chain and then human resource.

Performance validation

Performance testing is an important validation as well and should be carried out immediately after the development is done. All aspects pertaining to the performance of dashboard starting from initial load in the memory to the user's selections and exporting data should be performed.

When you click on the thumbnail on Qlik Sense hub, the data for the selected application starts moving to RAM and it shows an opening screen to user. If the application is heavy then it may take little longer to open the application. If it takes more than 10 seconds, user may lose interest and not use the application.

Even after opening the application consultant should check the time taken to refresh the charts and graphs once the values are selected in the filters. If the complex calculations are written on visualization, then it may take time.

Due to these delays user may stop using the application and the adoption of dashboard may get impacted and thus it becomes important to do a preliminary check before UAT stage.

User acceptance testing

Until now whatever testing was conducted, it was done by the implementation team to make sure that they deliver the best project, but it is the business users who have the final say about the project. Their usage will decide the success of the project.

User Acceptance Testing is the kind of testing where the dashboard is released to a select set of users who will spend a good amount of time in testing the dashboard from all aspects. They will look at if the dashboard fulfills the requirements given in early stage of the project, if it produces the correct data, if it gives the analysis which they are looking for etc.

Another aspect of the UAT is to make end users comfortable so that they can easily understand the sheets which are developed. Once the testing is finished, user may and may not ask for changes. If they find a bug and ask for changes then bugs should be corrected by the developers. UAT phase is the key to the adoption of the dashboards.

It is important to conduct the UAT testing because during development though the developers may be familiar with entire process but could become victim of tunnel vision. They may miss out some crucial steps in the development.

It may also happen that they misunderstood the requirement or one of the requirement itself is missing. In such cases UAT testing helps to find such shortcomings in the development.

There are many things which you should consider before starting the UAT. They are listed as follows:

- **Identify right time for UAT**: You must understand one thing that you are going to give the access of the dashboards to the end users. Your dashboard is going to create a first impression on them. If the dashboard is not fully developed or tested internally by the consultant and development team, it may will not excite the user. Thus it is important that a consultant know when the dashboards are fully ready for the UAT stage. Consultant should not hurry to start the UAT.
- **Identify the users**: In an organization you may find many users with different roles and they may have access to their own data. A consultant should identify the key users who understands the given requirements and who has correct access to the data. If a user has access to restricted data they may not be able to complete the entire validation and when it goes into production the results for the data which was not accessible to user could be wrong. The user should be the one who had given the requirements or someone who understands the requirements given and who is well verse with business operations.
- **Train the users**: The users may or may not know how to use the software, thus it becomes important to given them training on how to use the software. They should be trained on frequently needed features such as how to filter the data, how to navigate between sheets and so on. This will increase their confidence on the system and increase their excitement and interest to use the software.

Once the UAT phase starts a consultant should spend time with users to help them. Consultant should take users through the initial requirements given, to avoid unexpected comments from the users.

Go-Live Strategy

This is the stage of the project, where development is complete, validation performed and is accepted by the key users. Till now the project was made accessible to only a small group of users, but to make it available to a large group you need to think about the Go-Live process.

As a part of preparation of the Go Live you need to take of aspects as follows

- **Assign the licenses**: You should make sure that all business users have been allocated licenses. This is because users will ask for the access immediately after the Go-Live. So you should be prepared for this by giving them license and appropriate roles.

- **Train end users**: Users should be aware of the software and how to use it properly before they actually start using the software. Thus for a successful Go-Live you should make sure that end users are given proper training. If they are not trained, they will struggle to use the software and which may lead to decrease in their interest. You should also create some videos which users can refer whenever it is required for them to understand the concepts of the software.

- **Make user manual ready**: You should make a user manual for each of the dashboards which are developed. It is because you may have written complex calculations which end user should be aware of. They should know what are the calculations which are done behind one KPI. This will increase their trust on the dashboard and increase the adoption of the dashboard.

- **Define the escalation matrix**: It is important to define the escalation matrix. This helps users to know whom to approach whenever they encounter problems. The first level escalations can be handled by the IT team and then it can be given to the development team to further investigate in the issue. Most of the time the problems faced by the end users can easily be addressed. Thus they should be well educated to reduce the escalations.

- **Send the communication**: Once the preparation is done, you should send a proper communication to the end users and to the stakeholders about the Go-Live. It becomes important to involve higher management for the Go-live. Whenever the senior management start using the other users too start using and thereby improving the adoption.

- **Prepare the presentation and a small demo**: You should prepare a good presentation for the Go-Live day. The presentation can contain few slides on the scope of the project and the requirements given. A few slides can be devoted to introducing Qlik Sense and its features to create excitement in users. You should also give a short demo of what have you developed and demonstrate how it can help end users to enhance their decision making. Once the users see an actual working of the dashboard an excitement is automatically created and users will be more willing to use the dashboard asap.

Summary

In this chapter we learned about the validation and important aspects of validation. We looked at the reasons why validation is important, how it can impact the business operations.

Moving ahead in chapter we looked importance of different types of validations for a successful project. After validation stage we looked at what is meant by UAT and why it is important. We talked about areas such as identifying right time, right user and training the user which should be taken care before UAT.

Lastly we saw how to prepare for the Go Live day. In that we talked about different areas such as license assignment, training users, user manual preparation, defining escalation matrix and demo presentation.

In the next chapter we will look at the necessary steps needed post Go Live. We will also see why it is important. The excitement initially created should be taken forward and the momentum maintained.

8
Post Go-Live

In the previous chapter, we looked at the importance of data validation. We also looked at visualization validation. Validation is a sensitive topic as the adoption of BI depends largely on it.

We also went through the various ways to do validation. The chapter also looked at the importance of **UAT** (**User Acceptance and Training**) and making users comfortable with dashboard. Taking care of validation will help the consultants to get the business users' confidence and also avoid extensive rework.

In this chapter, we will cover what a consultant should look at from a post go-live perspective The areas covered are:-

- Adoption Strategy
- Maintenance Strategy
- Auditing
- Documentation

Post go-live activities help build user confidence and lead to increase in usage of Qlik Sense.

Adoption strategy

One way to measure success of a BI Project is to see how good the adoption is. We can measure this with a Qlik app. We recommend the use of Qlik Sense Montioring apps to analyze the logs and analyze user adoption. There can be tendency for a consultant to relax after project go-live. Once the project go-live happens, it's very crucial for the consultant to ensure that the adoption is high and there is no loss of momentum.

In this section, let's look at the various factors which contribute toward adoption, such as user training, user manual, demos, and videos.

User training

User training is the most important part in adoption strategy. We must never forget that as a consultant we are very familiar with Qlik Sense, but for the users, it may be a very new subject. The users will be of various types:

- Some users will be very new to Business Intelligence and would have largely used Excel for their reporting requirements. These set of users may be apprehensive as they need to move away from their comfort zone. Extra efforts are needed to make these users comfortable, and they will need initial motivation and hand holding.
- The other set of users will be the ones who are working on traditional tools. They have already migrated from Excel and will be familiar with BI. The traditional tools are largely Information Technology driven projects but these users will be new to the concept of self-service. They may not be aware of other features, such as search, collaboration/story-telling, and mobility. These users are relatively easier to train and will be quite excited to move to Qlik Sense.
- The consultant may encounter some users who are already familiar with the new generation of BI software. These users will be the most easiest to train. They just need to get familiar with the interface of Qlik Sense software. These users can be instrumental in helping the spread of adoption and can help other business users as well.

Mentioned next are some of the points a consultant must consider during end user training.

Train the trainer

Whenever an organization buys BI software like Qlik Sense, it buys it with the intent of using it for a long period of time. During this period, the organization can expect lot of employee churn. It will not be possible for the consultant to keep doing the training as new employees join. Similarly, the organization may be geographically distributed with multiple offices and it may not be feasible for the consultant to do the training at all the places.

To overcome these challenges, the consultant must identify and ensure that there is an internal champion within the organization who can take care of this task on an ongoing basis. This user must be thoroughly trained and should be hands-on with Qlik Sense software. He/she should also be very familiar with all the aspects of Qlik Sense applications from business perspective, and be aware of all Key Performance Indicators (KPI) and functionality of every sheet of the application.

The advantage of having such an internal champion is manifold. They can be leveraged for:

- New trainings and refresher trainings on an ongoing basis
- Assisting business users and initial hand-holding till the user gets comfortable
- Preparing user manuals, documentation, or/and videos for any changes happening in the application or for newer applications which are built
- Monitoring usage and performance

It is advised to do the train the trainer training on one on one basis with the identified person. By end of the training, the person should be confident to use the software, create sheets and visualizations, publish sheets, create appealing stories, use book marks, and explain associative capabilities. The user should also be able to explain and relate the dashboards and sheets with the business requirements. The user should explain to the actual end users how they can analyze with the application and how it can help them take better decisions.

It's recommended that the person be part of initial end users trainings which the consultant undertakes. There should be some trainings where this person does the training and the consultant is present just to assist. This will help in smooth transition of training responsibility to the person and benefit the organization.

Qlik Sense Administration training

Similar to how a consultant should identify an internal user for Qlik Sense product and business training, another user should be identified for managing Qlik Sense administration. This user can be the same user as earlier or can be different.

Qlik Sense Administration is another ongoing activity which needs attention. The ongoing tasks include:

- Assigning licenses to newer users
- Blocking the users who have left the company
- Creating streams
- Publishing applications

- Creating tasks
- Writing security rules
- Managing content libraries
- Checking uptime
- Performing ongoing auditing

The consultant must make the admin user comfortable with all the routine tasks. For larger organizations, it might become difficult for one person to manage everything, and as a best practice, the administration might be delegated. Qlik Sense has few default built-in roles for the Qlik Management Console. The roles are:

- RootAdmin
- ContentAdmin
- DeploymentAdmin
- AuditAdmin
- SecurityAdmin

As explained in the previous section, the users who will manage the QMC (Qlik Management Console) should be trained separately. The admin user should be aware of Qlik Sense deployment options and load balancing, and should be familiar with adding new nodes.

The training should be interactive and the consultant must also explain the architecture of Qlik Sense and its various components. The consultant must explain practical situations which the admin will encounter. The consultant must give sample requirements and ask the admin to create the same. An example situation could be: Assign Qlik Sense token to user Mark. Mark should have access to Sales and Marketing stream and should not have access to Finance stream. Mark should not be able to export data. Mark should not be able to create new applications, but should be able to publish his custom sheets to other users in Sales/Marketing streams.

Training should also cover the following aspects:

- Qlik Sense installation on central nodes and rim nodes
- Qlik Sense up-gradation
- Proxies, virtual proxies, and authentication mechanisms
- Backup and restoration
- User directory connectors

Training Process

The training process can't be generalized and will vary from company to company and situation to situation. There can be various approaches to training and this should be best discussed with the relevant stake holders and decided. The two broad approaches can be summarized as:

A single long training

A single training is a continuous training which may stretch for a period of 2-3 days. This approach may be good in certain conditions. It's usually tough for users to take break from their routine job and spend 2-3 days, but certain occasions, like starting of month/quarter/year, may be less taxing for them and they can spend this time. There can also be occasions when there is a long weekend and the users may be willing to accommodate.

This approach will work well where the users are spread in multiple cities and it's easier to get all of them together for 2-3 days. The single continuous training works well for those users who are already familiar with BI software.

Multiple short trainings

Multiple short trainings are meant to cover the entire training, not in one go but it is spread across sessions. These can be short 2 hours or half day sessions. This approach is good when the business users can't allocate continuous time. This works well for users new to BI software; this approach allows the users enough time to practice. The trainings shouldn't have a long gap between two sessions. Long gap breaks the continuity.

Though this approach is difficult if the users are spread across, there could be workarounds, like using online meetings or video-conferencing.

Training Methodology

Training's work best when they are interactive. The consultant must engage with the users, and the pace of the session can be altered depending on how well the users are receiving the training. The consultant can give examples from other companies in similar domain and the benefits derived with Qlik Sense.

Some of the topics which you can cover as part of end user training are:

- Introduction and need of business analytics (can be skipped if the users are familiar)

- Introduction to Qlik Sense, Qlik Sense Associative Model and its benefits
- Login process and introduction to Qlik Sense Hub
- Qlik Sense application navigation
- Interpreting and working with visualizations (charts, tables, extension, and maps)
- Creating or duplicating sheet
- Getting to know the master items and creating visualizations using the master items.
- Using global smart search
- Using global filters and selections
- Accessing and using Qlik Sense app from a hand-held
- Creating book marks
- Snapshots, annotations, and story telling
- Exporting data

Ensure the following tips while training:

- Record the videos so that the users can revisit at their convenience
- Do not overwhelm the user
- Make sessions interactive and let the users practice in the session
- Study the application and give an example of how the users can analyze (for example, if Sales was down in January, analyze the reason for the same by drilling and comparisons)
- Ensure application shows correct values
- Conduct refresher session

User Manual

User manuals are very useful for the users to get details once the training is over. A user may find the training sessions useful but may not be able to remember everything. A good user manual helps the users to easily find answers to their queries.

The user manual can be broken into:

Technical document

The technical documents cover the relevant documents which are product specific. In short, these are help guides and can be referred to by the users when in doubt. The technical document can be further broken down into:

Administration

The administration manual consists of documents relating to installation, deployments, backups, and restorations. These are documentation from infrastructure perspective.

QMC is another area of administration pertaining to users, applications, streams, tasks, user director connectors, content libraries, security rules, nodes, and proxies.

The consultant can leverage the extensive documentation provided by Qlik on its help website. The consultant can augment the documentation with company specific screen shots.

Product Usage

The product usage manuals are something for the business analysts' and the business users' consumption. These manuals help the users get familiar with Qlik software and cover the points regarding the product features, navigation, self-service, collaboration, and visualizations.

A lot of these can be found on the Qlik help site and the consultant can improve it with customer specific settings, URLs, and screen shots.

Functional document

Functional documents are very specific to the application and map the application with the business process and the relevant Key Performance Indicators (KPIs). The consultant must try to make this as exhaustive as possible. Every sheet should be explained in detail. An example can be seen next.

If we take an example of Human Capital application, a demo of which is available the Qlik website (`https://demo.qlik.com`), the dashboard can be explained as follows:

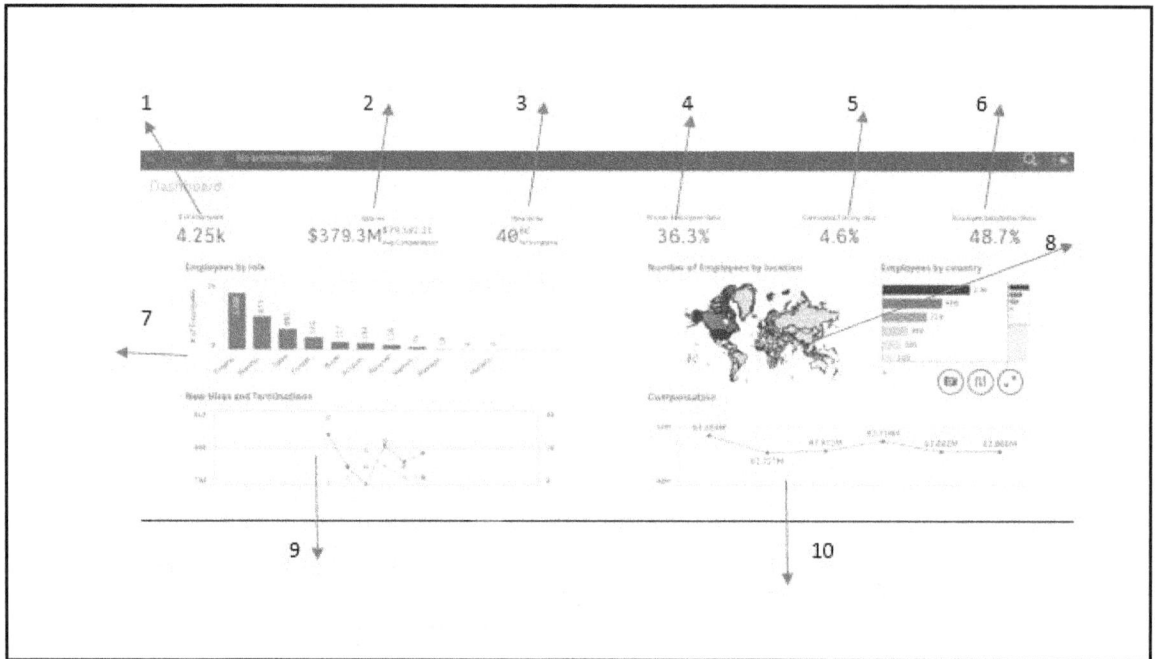

Screen shot of HR application

This Qlik Sense application focuses on Human Capital Management. The focus areas are around employee development, geographic distribution of employees, gender wise employees, and compensation. The application looks at the performance of the employees and it also has reporting on employee details.

The dashboard tracks the number of Key Metrics. The Key Metrics marked in preceding figure (from 1 to 10) are some of the important parameters. They are explained in the following section:

1. The KPI object gives a easy view of Number of employees.
2. The KPI object gives comparison of total compensation and average compensation.
3. The KPI object allows easy comparison of new hires versus termination.
4. The KPI object shows percentage the women employee ratio.
5. The KPI object gives users idea of completed training ratio.
6. The KPI object helps users understand the employee satisfaction ratio.

7. The bar graph helps users to see in a graphical way the number of employees department wise.
8. The map represents the employee distribution by geography. The darker the color, more the concentration of employees in that region.
9. The Line chart shows the hiring and termination trends over the period.
10. Similarly, the line chart at the bottom shows the compensation trend over the period.

What analysis can you do?

All the preceding Key metrics can be then looked at from different aspects. A user can do multiple selections (one or multiple) like:

- Country
- Gender
- Role
- Month-Year

This allows you to look at different aspects and get actionable insights.

FAQs

Frequently asked questions (**FAQs**) is a good to have document, allowing users to easily get answers to questions. The FAQ can be fine tuned based on user feedback and questions. These can be simple questions, such as:

- What is the URL to access Qlik Sense Hub?
- What is the format in which I should enter the username?
- How to export data to CSV?

FAQ makes it easier for the users to refer to a single document.

Top management use

Top management plays a very important role in taking the adoption to newer level in the company. Once this happens, other users in middle and lower management follow suit.

Many organizations where adoption is very high, often have policies where all reviews happen on Qlik Sense software. This automatically sets the stage for everyone to start using Qlik Sense. A carrot and stick approach can be followed by the top management. Users with top usage of Qlik sense software can be awarded.

Videos

Videos are one of the best ways for a user to learn more about the BI software. Smaller videos are more effective than one large video. Like documentation, these videos too can be broken into:

Technical Videos

Technical videos are the ones which are Qlik Sense product specific. They help the users to get familiar with Qlik Sense software. Many of these videos are already available on Qlik websites and they can be made available either as links within the technical document or provided with Qlik Sense software as an additional sheet.

An example can be seen in the following figure:

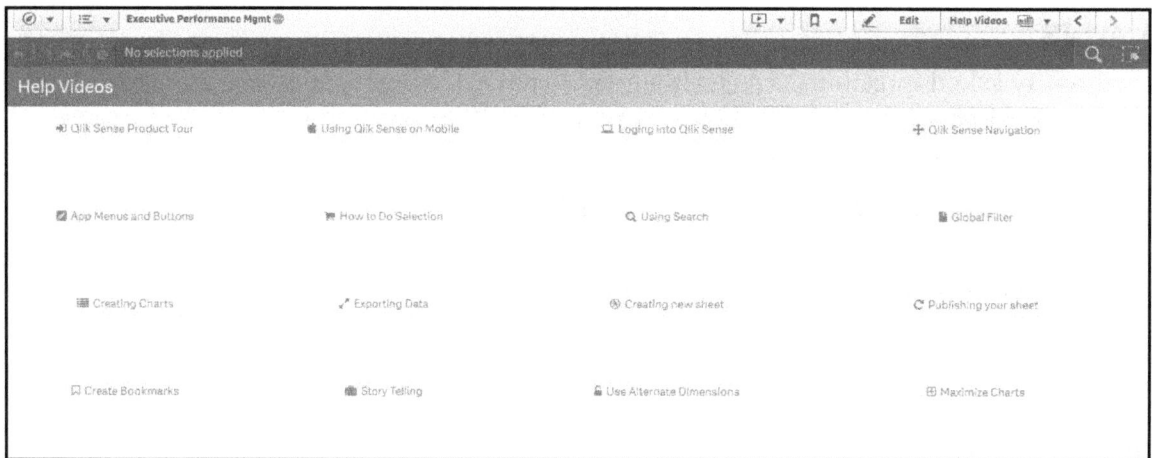

Screenshot for a training sheet

You can create a similar sheets using extension available from Qlik Branch called Sheet Navigation and Action (`http://branch.qlik.com/#!/project/56728f52d1e497241ae698a0`). The extension can be used as button. The following figure shows the properties on right:

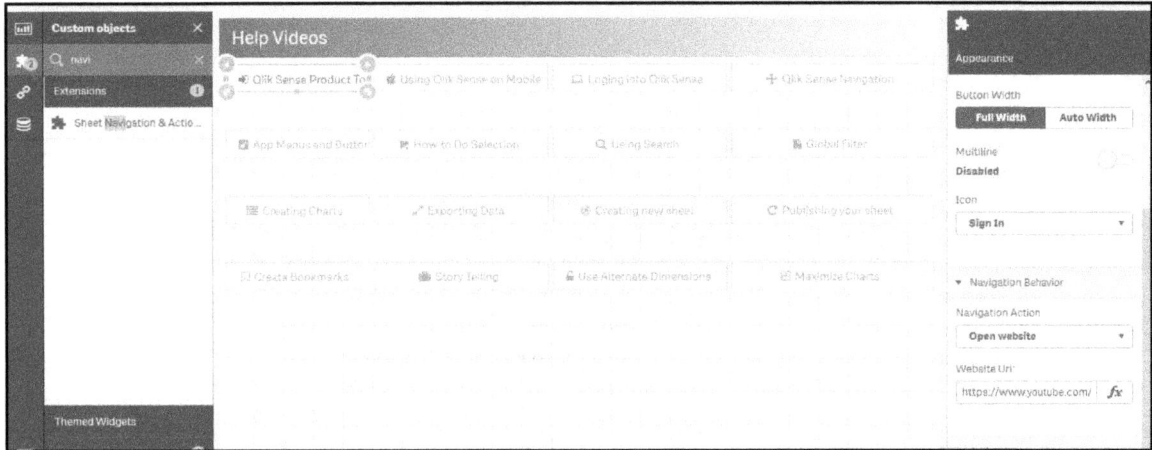

Creating the help sheet

Lot of videos are available on Qlik Help YouTube channel of Qlik and can be easily leveraged.

> A couple of examples from Qlik YouTube channel are mentioned next:
> Qlik Sense product
> tour: `https://www.youtube.com/watch?v=85QHuNNeaCg`
> Qlik Sense mobile tour: `https://www.youtube.com/watch?v=-QSH4r5lgOk`

Some of the videos need to be created by your team, which would be very specific to your organization. For example, How to login into Qlik Sense (this ideally should be can be sent as a part of introductory emails).

An example which shows a user entering the Qlik Sense URL (as shown in the following image the `bi.yourdomain.com` will be replaced with actual name), following by how to enter the credentials (`domainname\username`) will be helpful to user:

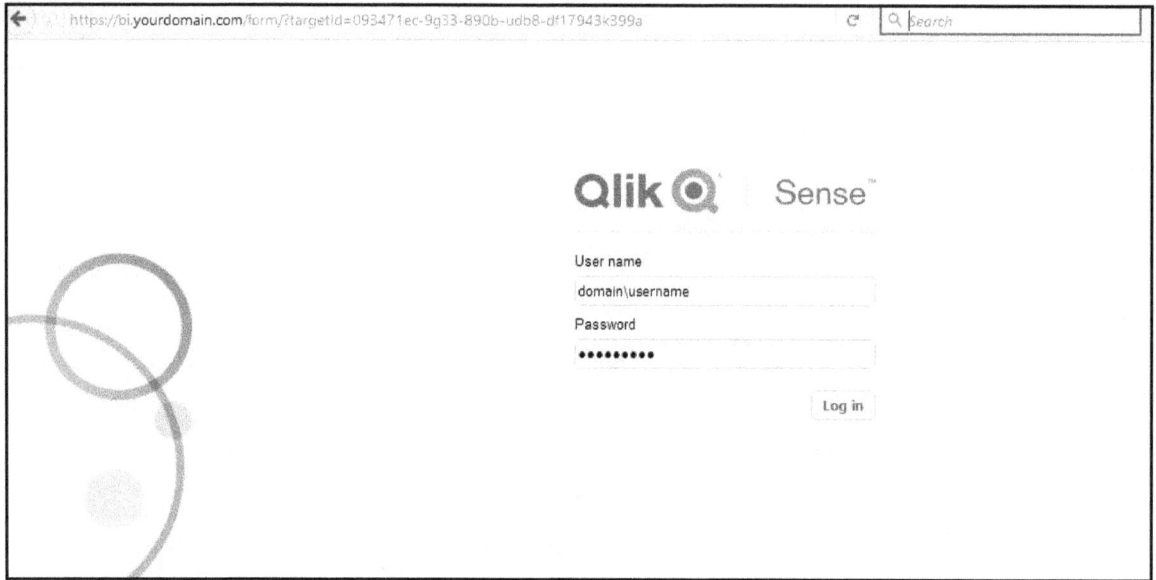

Login screen help

Functional videos

These are application specific videos which help the user become familiar with the Qlik Sense application. For example, if it is a sales application, there can be a short video making the user aware of the different sheets in the application, and explaining what each sheet is meant for and how the user can do their analysis.

Such videos create a lot of value add for the user and build confidence in them to quickly start using the Qlik sense applications.

Maintenance strategy

Maintenance strategy is another important area which is necessary post go-live. What are the different areas a consultant should look at? Some of them are mentioned next.

Application performance

The **unique selling proposition** (**USP**) of Qlik Sense is its in-memory architecture and fast performance. Business users are always short on time, and long wait times for a BI application is recipe for failure.

Over a period of time, the application size increases and the number of users or concurrency of users may also increase, thereby slowing down performance. More applications which consume resources on the Qlik Sense server may also be added .

Qlik Sense provides some in built applications which help you to review the performance. These monitoring applications can help you to immediately see the bottlenecks and take preventive measures. Some of the measures which you can take for improving performance are listed as follows.

Upgrade infrastructure

RAM and CPU are the two parameters which contribute to Qlik Sense application performance. Sizing the server is important to get the best performance from Qlik Sense. Over a period of time, the sizing which was valid initially may no longer hold true. This can happen due to the factors mentioned earlier: increase in data, applications, and concurrency.

Once you find out that the hardware sizing is no longer sufficient, the sizing exercise should be redone and accordingly you can look at couple of options:

- Increase CPU and/or RAM
- Add a rim node and distribute load

If you have a server which has free CPU and Memory slots it becomes easier to increase CPU and/or RAM. If the requirement of RAM/CPU is quite high and in certain scenarios where it becomes more meaningful to add a rim node which is closer in geography to the user the second option works better.

Application optimization

A badly designed application over a period of time becomes slow and has performance impacts. The application should be designed as per best practices, and some of things which can be avoided are:

- Bringing in all the columns of a table. (Get only the columns required for reporting needs. The easy development allows you to add a column at a later date if required.)
- Trying to do calculations in the frontend. Calculations can be managed at the user interface layer or they can be managed at the data modelling layer. Try and do all the calculations in the modelling layer. In other words, calculated columns and similar requirements can be pre-calculated and stored in QVD files. Only the calculations which can't be managed in modelling can be done at the frontend. Calculations performed in the visualizations are CPU intensive and any slice and dice done by user results in spike of CPU as calculation has to be done again for new selections. Having a proper balance is necessary.
- Using synthetic keys. The usage of synthetic keys slows down the Qlik application. Hence it should be avoided.
- Using two tier or three tier data structure. This depends on the business requirements and what approach to take should be carefully chosen.

The following figure shows both the 2 tier and 3 tier structure side by side. Choose the one which best suits the requirement.

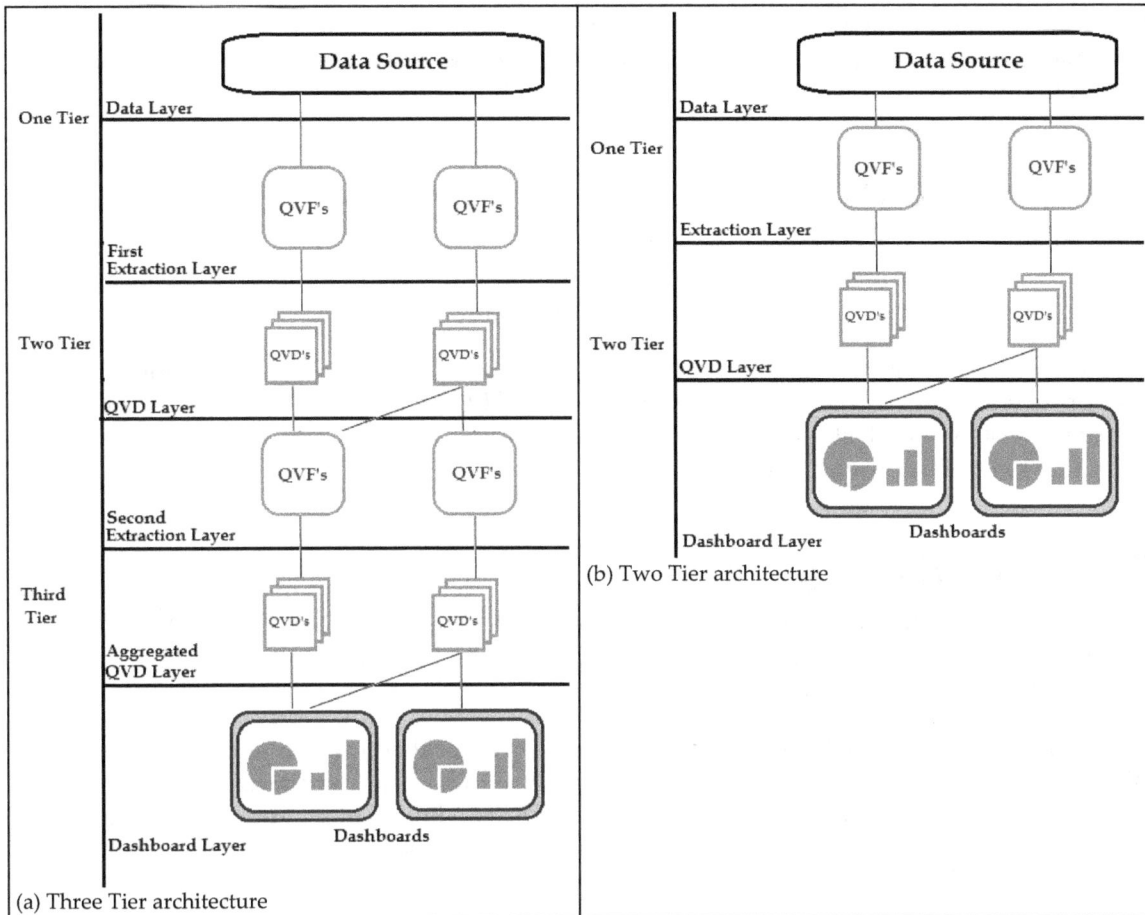

(a) Three Tier architecture

(b) Two Tier architecture

Comparing the architectures

Review visualization

Visualization is another area which needs to be reviewed at regular intervals. A table instead of a chart will be more CPU/RAM intensive. Some business users who are new to BI software will initially prefer having tables instead of charts. This may be a good approach initially for a user to become familiar, but with time many of the tables can be replaced with charts.

Repetition of charts across sheets can also impact performance. It's best to avoid this as much as possible. The users can be made aware of easy navigation which Qlik Sense offers and they can easily move to any sheet from the current sheet.

The users should be encouraged to use global filters. This helps reduce the clutter. User can also take benefit of the global search. Global search makes filters on every sheet redundant. This not only helps in freeing up space on the sheet but also optimizes RAM consumption.

How much data to keep

How much data to keep is a question to which every customer will have different answer. Normally, customers are happy to keep last three years of data in Qlik Sense application, and this is good enough for them to do comparisons and see trends.

In case you haven't taken this into consideration, it's possible that Qlik application is storing data of several years thereby increasing the need of CPU and RAM on the server. If the customer is okay with last few years then the application can be modified, and this will definitely help in improving the performance.

On-demand app generation

There may be situations where customer data sources have huge data. Getting the entire data in a single app can cause severe performance issues. Since the customer wants to analyze all the data, a workaround should be thought of.

With Qlik Sense, we have the option of doing something called on-demand app generation. What this means is that the main Qlik Sense application has the summarized or aggregated data. A user can make relevant selections and he/she can be given an option of seeing the details in another application. This application can take the selection, and based on the selection, the details app shows the details required.

This approach is recommended for large data sources or big data. This approach also gives the user the flexibility of associative analytics, and at the same time, the performance too can be smartly managed.

Data quality check

Data quality is one of the important factors which business users look at. The book has dedicated a chapter to data validation.

The data validation might break sometimes if the business process has changed or the logic for calculation has changed. An incorrect logic used in coding may lead to incorrect data when financial year changes.

Any issue has to be taken on priority and resolved quickly. The user should be made aware, and clear communication should be sent out about the time required to fix the new logic or business process.

New updates and versions

Qlik Sense with launch of its version June 2017, will now be having 5 releases in an year. The updates bring in newer functionalities. This also becomes a reason for conducting a refresher training. The newer releases also bring in capabilities which the users are expecting, but were not available in earlier releases.

The maintenance strategy should consider the roll-out of these newer releases and feature enhancements. The feature enhancements can also throw up newer use cases and create opportunity for driving BI expansion and adoption. It is always a good practice to have the new updates tested on a test environment before updating the prod environment.

Source changes

Change in source can happen when the source application vendor releases patches or newer versions. This can have an impact on the existing Qlik Sense application. The change management for such situations must be taken care of. Again as a best practices the changes should be done on a test environment first.

Newer sources too can get added, such as competition info, which was earlier not available. This information becomes useful to the customer for comparing performance with other competitors. An example would be a pharma company getting information of sales of other pharma company from a third party source. Another example could be a company wanting to bring in data from Facebook page or twitter handle to understand their customers sentiments. Although these additions are referred to as change requests but still they relate to an existing application and hence proper maintenance is required.

Auditing strategy

Auditing is an important aspect of any BI project. Organizations are governed by regulatory rules and non-compliance can have huge damages. Thus, governance has become a key aspect for organizations these days. The organizations can even have full time auditing departments.

Qlik is very good in governance and has a specific audit admin role for the QMC. The Audit admin has to ensure that the auditing requirements are fulfilled. Some of the things an Audit Admin has to look at are mentioned as follows:

- Look at License compliance
- Keep checking for users who have left the company should be disabled and license revoked
- Ensure users have access to relevant streams
- Ensure that applications meant for specific streams are published only in that stream
- Ensure users are allowed correct rights (for example, export rights should be judiciously allocated)
- Keep auditing the security rules on regular basis

Documentation

Documentation is a necessary point to be considered and we have stressed this at multiple places in the book. We won't be covering this in detail again, but it's important to maintain the relevant documentation, such as scope of work, functional documents, project plan, code comments, test cases, deployment document, and architecture document.

People change over time and having good documentation helps the people who weren't part of the project earlier to quickly get hang of the project and cater to newer needs of the business or modification in the existing project.

BI project also involves integration and customization, and these too should be clearly documented. Other documents which should be maintained are the QMC settings.

Summary

The post go-live period is many a times neglected, and this leads to a drop in adoption of the software, thus resulting in poor return on investments for a company. The post go-live phase of a project requires extensive interaction with business users and continuous initial hand holding. This chapter's focus was on ways to make the post go-live phase a success.

We studied the importance of user trainings, maintaining manuals, and FAQs. Videos are often a great way for users to learn, and they should be used extensively. We had a look at other aspects which contribute to good performance like continuous monitoring of application response time and ways to handle a performance degradation. For the business users, what matters most are factors like ease of use, ability of self-service, performance, mobility, and accuracy of data.

Other aspects which we should look at are the monitoring apps of Qlik Sense, allowing us to check usage, performance, and auditing. Lot of possible issues can be addressed before they escalate.

In the next chapter, we will look at common pitfalls which can lead to downfall of the project and undermine all the hard-work done. These are some of the mistakes which even a seasoned professional might make, and hence, the chapter assumes lot of significance. The topics which will be covered are: avoiding of over commitment, importance of documentation, importance of listening, importance of hand-holding in initial stages of post go-live, and avoiding unpleasant surprises.

9
Avoiding Common Pitfalls

The last chapter covered the various aspects a consultant needs to look at once a project goes live. This phase of the project is as important as any other phase. The chapter looked at some of the aspects involved in this phase, such as importance of conducting user-trainings, creating help materials such as user manuals, and creating videos which can be referred to as and when required.

The chapter covered other areas which should also be looked at, such as on-going maintenance, auditing, and documentation.

In our journey so far, we have always tried to highlight the importance of following best practices and point out areas where a consultant has to pay special attention. This chapter will highlight some common aspects where consultants go wrong.

The topics which we will cover in this chapter are as follows:

- Art of listening
- Importance of documentation
- Pitfalls of over-committing
- Preparing for the unexpected
- Avoiding last moment surprises
- Importance of hand holding

The art of listening

You must be wondering what has art of listening got to do with a Business Intelligence project. Trust me, once you read this section, you will appreciate why this is such a crucial part in a consultant's day to day routine.

In the earlier chapters, we had a look at how a consultant in the life cycle of a project has to work with several stake-holders. He/She has to often deal with people with different profiles. These profiles could be technical, functional, or business.

We have often noticed that more often than not, BI developers are more comfortable talking to technical stake holders. Though this is understandable in the initial phases, for him/her to be a wannabe consultant, they need to come out of this comfort zone. The comfort zone arises due to the very fact that developer always considers himself/herself as a technical person and is at ease discussing on technical aspects of the project.

When they have to progress to the role of a consultant, they need to start interactions with functional or business stake-holders. Though technical stake-holders play an important role in a project, we must always remember that the requirements come from business and functional stake-holders. This also paves way for requirement gathering session.

If you recollect, in the earlier chapters we had touched upon the aspect of understanding business process and subsequently, requirement gathering. The meetings with relevant stake-holders will make way for the next steps. An important part of such meetings with these people is having **meaningful** conversations. And the **most important part of a conversation is the art of listening.**

Here are a few notable quotes worth having a look at:

> *If you make listening and observation your occupation, you will gain much more than you can by talk." -Robert Baden-Powell*

> *"When people talk, listen completely. Most people never listen." -Ernest Hemingway*

> *"The art of conversation lies in listening." -Malcom Forbes*

Now that we have the context, let's explore this in more detail. As we have the requirement gathering conversations with the stake-holders, we get to know more about their needs and what they expect. When they speak, a consultant should listen with rapt attention and also make notes.

It has been our experience that a consultant can easily get distracted during the conversation and start thinking about technical feasibility of the business needs. An example can be a business user mentioning the need for an exception report. It's very easy for the consultant to fall in the trap of immediately thinking about technical feasibility of the request; how can this be achieved, would I need specific coding to be done or is it out of the box, and so on. In trying to get answers to the questions, **you lose the connect with the business user.** By the time you stop thinking, the user might have made few more points and you would have missed them. This can cause potential problem areas and be a cause for conflict at a later stage.

Another aspect which often leads to missing out potential important points is best explained by the following quote:

> *"Listen with curiosity. Speak with honesty. Act with integrity. The greatest problem with communication is we don't listen to understand. We listen to reply. When we listen with curiosity, we don't listen with the intent to reply. We listen for what's behind the words."*- *Roy T. Bennet*

As a consultant, this pitfall needs to be avoided for sure. Listen with full attention and always try to understand what the user is saying. An urge to ask a question may keep running in your mind and potentially cause you to miss the message the user is trying to convey. Keep jotting down notes and make them into a proper document post your meetings.

This art of listening will definitely help you in building better relations with you clients. Hence, we urge you to start practicing this valuable art. This will not only help you in your professional life but in personal life as well.

Importance of documentation

In the previous chapters, we have often talked about the importance of documentation and why it's a very crucial part of any project.

People often neglect the documentation aspect. Everyone knows and realizes the importance of documentation, but somehow miss implementing this practice. Often, this leads to project failures. The reasons for not following the practice could be many but the impact of not having documentation can be suicidal. Some of the pitfalls are:

- The stake-holders, the project champion, the consultant, and the developer not being on the same page
- No clarity on final scope and delivery
- Missed KPIs in dashboards
- Significant difference between expected and delivered UI(User Interface)
- Difficulty for a developer to modify code written by another developer
- Havoc created by change management
- Validation issue arising from lack of test cases
- Lack of visibility and transparency
- No clear process

Documentation is often considered a boring work and it is one of the key reasons why people are reluctant to do it. As a best practice, a consultant must ensure that he/she and the team doesn't keep the documentation pending till the last moment. It's always better to reserve some part of working hours towards documentation and keep this as a daily practice.

The consultant must keep emphasizing on the importance of documentation and must lead by example. The team should be explained the benefits documentation brings to them and how it can avoid re-work.

Documentation brings in even more advantages and they can be seen mentioned in the next sections as well.

Avoiding Over-Committing

Projects can go wrong due to multiple reasons. One of the reasons is over commitment from the consultant's end. Setting wrong expectations is bound to leave the client unhappy and dissatisfied.

This is but natural for anyone to be promised one thing and given another. Many of us have faced similar situations. Have you come across a situation when your holiday went bad because you expected one thing and got another?

Imagine planning a holiday at a resort. You visited the website of the resort, saw some great pictures and looked at different facilities available, and decided to book and visit there. Once you reached the resort, suddenly it didn't seem like what you had seen on the website. Facilities which were mentioned on the website were either not there or not working up to the expectation. Wouldn't you feel cheated and short changed?

In contrast, imagine you were given more than what was promised. Imagine getting a complimentary meal or a free spa, which wasn't part of the package. How would you feel in that case? Elated and overjoyed, right!

You client too experiences the same thing. Over-commitments are made by some consultants to please the client and get the project. Over-commitments can be of various natures, such as:

- Infeasible timeline for delivery
- Features which are not currently present and are expected in future

- Quality of people working on the project
- Promised domain expertise
- Infeasible performance

These are some of them. There could be many more. A quote which I particularly like is:

"Underpromise;overdeliver."-- Tom Peters

From the preceding analogy, we can easily relate how delivering more than promised will always help build customer confidence and trust in you. As a consultant, it is your duty to set the expectation right. Be clear with what is possible and what is not. If something is possible via a workaround, explain how it will work.

Give time lines which can be met and keep some buffer for contingencies. If you have committed on a feature which is futuristic, specify clearly in advance with expected time-frame. (Remember, Qlik too in its legal disclaimer mentions that *Road-map information should not be relied on in making a purchasing decision.*)

Preparing for the Unexpected

Though a consultant can prepare for factors which can cause project delay, a lot of situations may be unexpected.

How can you be prepared for the unexpected? To be frank, it's not possible to be 100 percent ready, but following proper process can help to be nearly there.

It's always better to have back-up plans if you expect something might go wrong. If you are doing something for the first time, do some research and study all the available sources. Let's take an example. Suppose you are connecting to a data source which you haven't worked on earlier. Try to get all the information about the same and also look in different forums to see what problem the users have faced. This will help you avoid mistakes which others have done and help you save on re-work.

Another example which may not be anticipated well is migration of source to a newer version can cause changes in the data model. In such a scenario a properly followed data model (snow flake or star schema, depending on the requirement) and a modular approach will cause minimum disruptions.

A consultant should be prepared for other issues occurring, such as unclean data causing data validation issues. Workarounds can be planned in such scenarios (example can be using Excel based mapping). On premise systems getting migrated to cloud based may causes connectivity issues. The consultant should be prepared to overcome such situations by using other ways, like REST, or building custom connectors.

Avoiding last minute surprises

Last minute surprises can often create serious dents in the success of your project. The consultant has to be aware of all the situations which may result in such surprises and must take care of avoiding them.

Let's look at few of them.

Missed timelines

Timelines are often very sacrosanct for businesses. A business may have planned lot of things based on a delivery date, and it should not come as a surprise on the last day about project not being completed. This can leave a very bitter taste and the bad experience may linger for a very long time.

The consultant must realize the importance of this and keep the stake-holders informed about the actual progress, and highlight gaps if any. The gaps, if any, need to be addressed in timely way and should not be kept till the last moment for resolution.

It is always good to have timely reviews with the client, enabling greater transparency. This also brings up possible bottlenecks, and effective solutions can then be planned.

Infrastructure

Infrastructure related surprises can delay the go-live of projects and thereby rob all the initial excitement of the users. Many organizations are process driven, and making any change request is going to be time consuming and will require several approvals.
So a consultant must ensure that he/she has given sufficient notice and provisioned the time required to arrange necessary infrastructure to successfully run the software. Missing the points could result in unbudgeted expenses for the customer, along with delays associated with approvals and procurement. Some of the points which can get missed out are:

- Need of a trusted **SSL (Secured Socket Layer)** certificate

- Need of Fully Qualified Domain Name (FQDN); for example, `qlik.companyname.com`
- Need for necessary ports to be opened on the firewall
- Authentication/Authorization related requirements
- Reverse Proxy may be needed if the client is not willing to have Qlik Sense directly in **Demilitarized zone (DMZ)**
- Proxy related settings

Lot of these can be avoided with proper documentation and checklists to ensure you are truly ready for go-live.

People changing

People are always the assets of an organization. It's always important to have the right mix of people and processes. People following the processes make the organization resilient and the projects have a greater chance of being successful.

Projects often go for a toss when a key person is no longer available. This can happen at the customer's end or can happen at the consultant's end. Thus, the responsibility of minimizing this from occurring lies with both the client and the consultant.

The best way to avoid these kind of pitfalls is to have strong documentation. Business Requirement Document (BRD), Functional Requirement Document (FRD), Requirement Specification (RS), and Scope of Work (SOW) can help mitigate the risk from the client's end.

From the consultant's end, it's important to have technical documentation. Documents such as architecture, UI wire-framing, and design document are important. Practicing coding best practices and having proper comments can minimize this risk.

Whenever a change of person happens, the consultant has to spend time with the new person in charge and ensure both are on the same page. The documents will also help to show what had been agreed on earlier. The change impact of a person leaving needs to be conveyed by the consultant to the stake holders, and at the same time, the consultant must ensure that he/she gives enough confidence to manage this change.

The impact is larger if project champion leaves the organization. This aspect has to be especially taken care of by the consultant. This risk can be mitigated to a certain extent if the consultant establishes rapport with all stake holders and is part of the meetings with the end users.

Data Validation Issues

Data mismatch occurring during go-live stages can happen and cause disruptions. This can happen due to untested cases, such as change of financial years or unexpected negative values in data.

The users tend to get disappointed if the figures they see on the dashboard are not to their expectations, even if you have delivered great looking dashboards. The consultant must plan about avoiding these scenarios by having detailed test cases. The data must be tallied with existing reporting tools or manually generated reports.

The consultant must also have the business users do a detailed data validation before go-live. This helps to get acceptance of the users and also helps in making them familiar with the software.

Hand-holding

Hand-holding is the part of a project area where a consultant makes the end users comfortable using the software. Though you may have created best of documentation and training materials, a user may still need initial guidance and comfort.

An analogy to make this understandable can be of driving a car. Say you haven't driven a car and have decided you want to commute to your office by a car. You decide to buy a car. When you buy a car, the car manufacturer gives you its manual. You can also search internet for learning videos. All of these can help you get over the initial jitters of driving a car. But are these good enough for you to get on the road and drive like an expert. The answer is an obvious NO.

You need initial hand-holding to get over the nuances of driving a car. Firstly, you need to get hang of all the controls. You need to get hang of the judgement of using steering wheel. The same goes with adjusting mirrors for optimum view. Depending on transmission, whether it's manual or automatic, you need to learn and adjust accordingly. Is this knowledge enough ? Frankly speaking, the answer is again NO.

As a driver, you need to get familiar with real life driving conditions. Driving in traffic is different from cruising on a highway. You also need to get parking skills, especially if it's parallel parking. You also need to get familiarized with driving in night, as this is a different ball game compared to driving in day light. Same goes with driving in difficult conditions, such as rain or snow. Driving can also throw different challenges in form of driving on winding roads or steep uphill driving, and many more

Imagine a user who is new to analytics. He/She has now suddenly been given a BI software like Qlik Sense, and is asked to work on it and help his/her organization is finding business insights! The given analogy will now start making sense.

Many people do not enjoy conducting end user training and enabling newbies to analytics requires commendable effort. This is indeed strenuous work and takes lot of bandwidth. Hence, we see in many projects that the consultant takes this part of the project lightly and often asks the users to look at documentation.

A consultant must always remember that there will be different sets of users. The users can range from ones who are completely new to analytics, few who have had elementary exposure to analytics and few of them may have worked on a tool like Business Objects and some on new age tools. The hand-holding process will obviously not be the same for all the users.

A user who finds the software difficult to use will at some point of time stop using the software and may spread negativity, which can be infectious and spread to other people in the organization. Hence, the consultant, once he/she delivers the project, must focus lot of attention in making the users comfortable. This can be achieved by conducting multiple user trainings. A consultant must carefully weigh which approach will give better results-either two or three days of continuous training or breaking the training into small modules spread over a period of time.

The trainings must cover all the aspects which the end user will encounter in day to day usage. Take them through all the areas, including navigation, visual data preparation, self-service, explaining usage of charts, global filters, search, and story telling. This will boost the confidence of the users and enable them to start using the software.

The consultant will be benefited by investing in this stage. The advantages are tremendous; the primary being high adoption in the organization. The users themselves become your champions and can be your references for you to get further projects.

Once the users master the usage of Qlik Sense software, they themselves will come up with more use cases, and thereby bring more work for the consultant.

Summary

This chapter is important for a consultant. Often the consultant puts in lot of efforts and hard work to make his project a success. The intention of the book is to help the consultant achieve this via best practices.

This chapter should be revisited often by a consultant, as during the course of a project, the finer aspects, which are often the pitfalls for a project, get missed out. It helps the consultant to avoid the common mistakes which lead to pitfalls in a project. The chapter covered areas which the consultant may have never known are important, like art of listening. The chapter also touched upon other areas, such as importance of documenting and avoiding over commitments.

In this chapter we looked at one of the aspects which often throws project schedule haywire, the unexpected surprises. Lastly, we looked at the importance of hand holding and enabling the end user to confidently use and best utilize the software. This also holds lot of advantages for the consultant.

The next chapter is aimed to help the consultant gather some information in various domains, such as pharma, retail, and BSFI (banking sector and financial institutes). It will help the consultant to have a better conversation with the business users. The knowledge gathered in the chapter will also help them in understanding the requirements better and suggesting value-adds. The chapter will try to cover the use cases relevant to these domains and help the consultant to relate to business terminologies.

10
Knowledge Sets

In the previous chapter, we looked at pitfalls and how a consultant can avoid falling into those pitfalls. A lot of effort goes into making a project successful, and it's important that a consultant should avoid common mistakes leading to pitfalls.

The chapter covered some of the common mistakes which can be avoided, such as not listening properly, lack of documentation, over committing, and not ensuring enough hand holding of the end user.

In this chapter, we will look at knowledge sets. This chapter is primarily intended to make you aware about some of the industry verticals and become familiar with the way they function. The chapter is also intended to make you familiar with some of the **Key Performance Indicators** (**KPI**) which are looked at by business users. The chapter should be able to help consultants relate to the business requirements more easily.

> This chapter is not meant to make you a domain expert. The consultant should look at specialized courses to master any specific industry vertical.

In this chapter, we will cover the following topics:

- Insurance domain
- Retail domain
- Pharmaceuticals verticals

Getting to know Insurance

Wikipedia defines insurance as a means of protection from financial loss. It is a form of risk management, primarily used to hedge against the risk of a contingent, uncertain loss.

A simple explanation is that all of us face risks in our day to day lives, and we would obviously want protection from those risks. For example, if I own a car, then whenever I drive there is an element of risk there in the form of damage occurring to the car due to accidents. The damage can occur due to other reasons as well, such as natural calamities or car theft. In the occurrence of an accident, the repair costs may run into several thousands. As an individual, I wish to have some protection and mitigate my risk. In other words, I want to *insure* my car.

So what should I do? I go to a company which issues this insurance. These companies are called Insurance companies, and I have to buy a motor insurance from such a company. The company will collect a fee called premium from me, and in return, I would get an "insurance cover" for a specified period. The insurance cover means the maximum amount which the insurance company will pay me in case of damage occurring to my car. The value of premium and the insurance cover will change over period of time as the car gets old. The company would issue me a motor policy. In the policy will be mentioned the details of the insurer, vehicle, and other terms and conditions. Some of the points which would be covered in the policy are:

- Name of insurance company issuing policy: For example, Majestic General Insurance Limited
- Name of insurer: Mr. Mark Brown
- Other details of insurer like address, email, and phone number
- Policy number: This is a unique number assigned by the Insurance company
- Period of insurance: For example, 1st January 2017 00:00:00 to 31st Dec 2017 23:59:59
- Vehicle details: Make of the car (for example, Honda); model of the car (for example, Accord); color (for example, Red); year of manufacturing (for example, 2015)
- Insurance amount: This may also be called IDV (Insurer Declared Value); for example, 19,000 USD
- Premium amount: The amount payable by the insurer; for example, 1,500 USD
- Geography: For example, New Jersey

- Agent name: The agent's name/code through which it was sold (for example, Mr. John Bush)
- Discounts: Any discounts which may have been applied (for example, no-claim bonus)

Before a policy is issued, there are lot of process which insurance companies follow. The details in the policy are some of the important parameters for a company to decide whether they wish to issue a policy and if they decide to issue what is the premium amount which will levied.

The values of premium and insurance cover will vary from one insurance company to another.

In case a damage occurs to my car, what I need to do is to file a *claim* with the insurance company. The claim would be processed by the company. The processing involves several internal processes. There could be a physical inspection done. The claim could be accepted or rejected, depending on circumstances. If the claim is accepted, the insurance company would reimburse my claim. If rejected, the damages would have to be borne by me. The reason for claim rejection could be several. Some examples could be accident caused after drunken driving or self-inflicted damage to the vehicle. The claim could also be rejected if the policy had expired.

Lets us look at the different entities in the insurance domain. The following figure shows the entities and the relations:

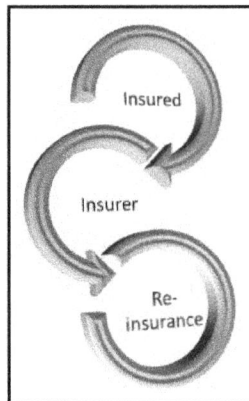

Entities in an insurance industry

Insured

Insured are the beneficiaries of an insurance policy. In short, they are the customers of insurance companies. The insured may be end users or they could be corporates.

Individuals are people like you and me who buy policies for various needs, like health insurance, life insurance, motor insurance, travel insurance, and more.

The corporates can buy the insurance for their employees (for example, medical, life, and travel) or they can buy the insurance for themselves (for example, property insurance, fire insurance, and motor insurance for corporate vehicles).

Insurance Companies

Insurance companies are the ones who issue the policies. The line of business of an insurance company is broadly classified into two areas:

- General Insurance
- Life Insurance

A diagrammatic representation of insurance companies is shown in the following image:

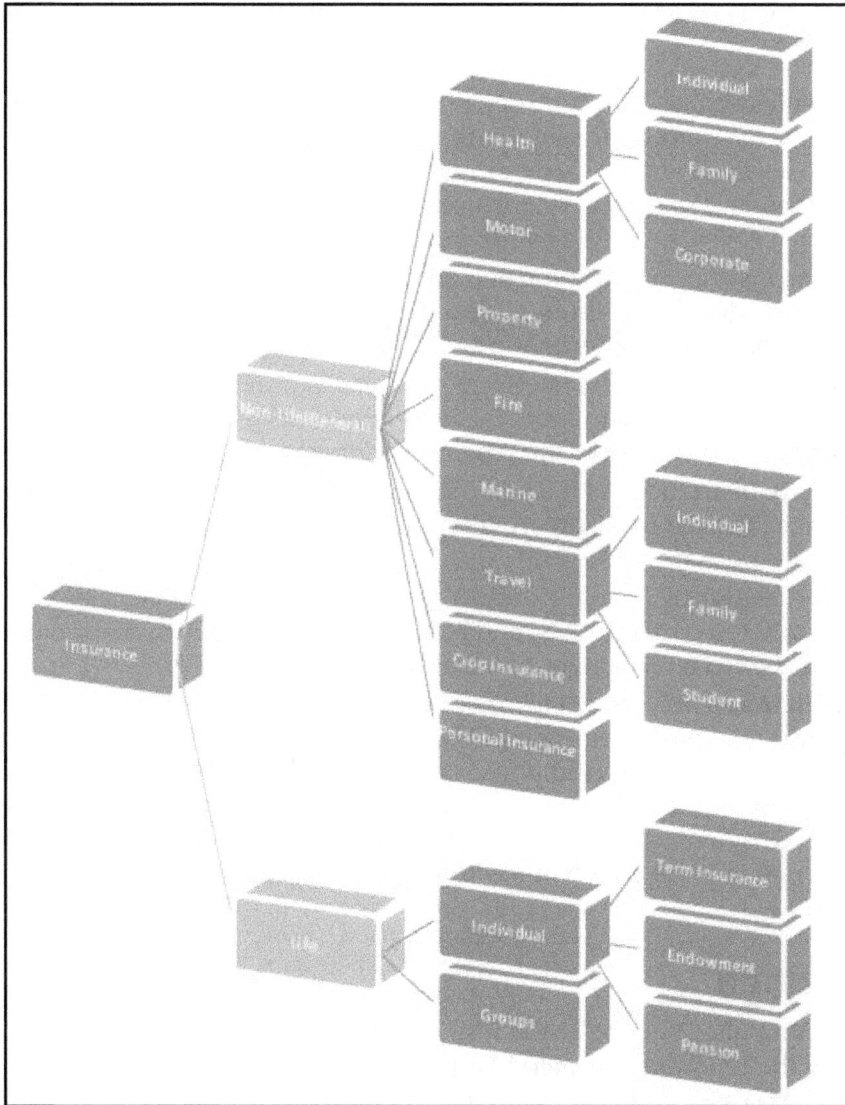

Insurance Line of Business

General Insurance

Any insurance which is not life (non-life) insurance comes under general insurance. Some of the examples are:

- **Travel insurance**: This type of insurance is bought by people who are traveling. This may be domestic or international travel. The insurance will cover any loss which a traveler might face during the travel, such as loss of baggage, medical expenses, and so on. Travel insurance can be sought by an individual for his personal coverage or for covering entire family.

- **Marine insurance**: This type of insurance is mainly bought to protect from loss or accidental damage to ships, cargo. The insurance usually covers this from the point of origin to the destination.

- **Fire insurance**: As the name suggests, this insurance will cover the damages in event of damage due to fire. This is usually purchased in addition to property insurance and will cover the cost of repairs or reconstruction.

- **Property insurance**: As the name suggests, this type of insurance policy covers damage incurred to a property due to natural calamity, like flood, earthquake, or any such mishap.

- **Motor insurance**: Motor insurance is purchased for road vehicles-two wheelers, three-wheelers, cars, trucks, and buses. The insurance is to cover damage due to accidents, collisions, thefts, or natural calamities

- **Health insurance**: Health insurance is purchased by the insured to cover expenses that may occur due to health related issue, hospitalization, and surgery related expenses. The health insurance can be bought by an individual or it can be bought for the entire family. There are health insurance polices available which cover critical illnesses. The health insurance policy can also be bought by a corporate to cover health of its employees.

Life insurance

Life insurance is a policy bought by the insured from the insurer. The policy essentially promises to pay the beneficiary named by the insured in the event of the death of the insured. On some occasions, the life insurance policy may cover critical illness or any major disability.

Life insurance polices can be of various types:

- **Term insurance**: Term insurance is a type of life insurance which covers the insured for a specific time period. An example could be 25 or 30 years. The insured keeps paying an annual premium till the end of the term insurance period. If the insured survives the term insurance period, the insurer does not pay anything.
- **Endowment**: An endowment policy covers the insured for the entire life. It is a mix of insurance and investment. In these types of polices, the insurer pays a lump sum amount at the end of the policy duration.
- **Pension**: The pension type of life insurance is more of an investment policy, allowing the insured to build up corpus post his/her retirement. In event of survival, the insurer will pay a lump sum amount at the end of policy, and thereafter pay a monthly/annual amount till the survival period.

Re-Insurer

Before we jump to reinsurance, let's quickly understand how does an insurance company earn. As mentioned in the previous example, where Mr. Brown purchased a motor insurance by paying a premium of 1,500 USD, so would there be several thousands of people who would buy policies for their vehicles.

For simplicity, let's assume that 1000 people bought policies, each paying premium of 1,500 USD. So, the insurance company has effectively collected 1,500,000 USD (one and half million dollars). Out of 1000, let us assume 50 of them had accident/damage claims. Again, for example sake, if we take that the company paid 5,000 USD for each of these claims, the company spent 250,000 USD to pay for the claims. This means that the company made 1,250,000 USD (for simplicity, we aren't counting the expenses incurred by the insurance company on sales/marketing/operations/employee and other costs). Insurance companies also do investments and increase the profitability.

In the preceding example, all looks well, doesn't it? However, there could be a scenario wherein due to a natural calamity multiple vehicle get damaged. This situation can create chaos and have heavy financial implications for the insurance company. For example, say 200 vehicle engines got damaged due to floods, and if each of them claimed 10,000 USD towards repairs. In such case, the claims would run to 2,000,000 USD. This amount actually exceeds the total premium collected and leaves the insurance company with deficit of 500,000 USD.

This type of risk is detrimental to the fortunes of the insurance company. To mitigate this risk, the insurance companies (referred to a cedent), purchase insurance from a re-insurer. This insurance is termed as reinsurance. The following figure depicts this.

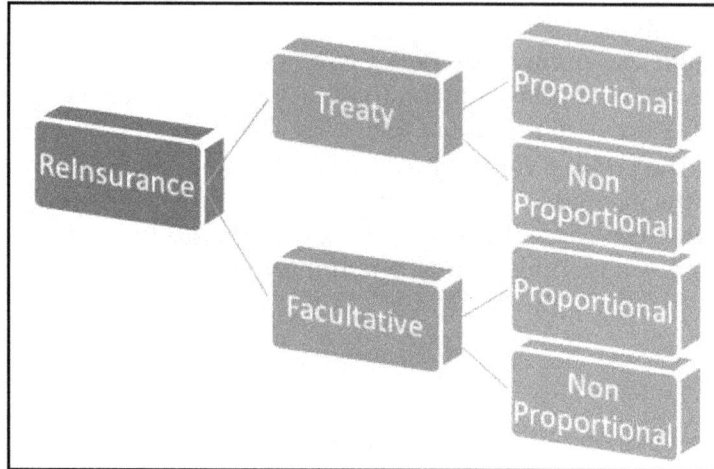

Types of Reinsurance

Let's look at the different types of reinsurance depicted via the previous figure:

- Facultative reinsurance is purchased by the insurance companies (cedent) for risks which are not covered or may not be sufficiently covered. This type of reinsurance covers risk for an individual policy issued or specific risk. The re-insurance company prices the contract depending on the risk they perceive, and this will be separate for each risk/individual.
- Treaty reinsurance means a type of coverage which is for a specified time period. This type of reinsurance does not take into account risk due to individual policy or specific risk. This reinsurance covers entire risk or only portion of risk during the specified period.
- Proportional: In this type of reinsurance, in event of claim the re-insurer receives on a agreed percent a proportional amount of premium earned by insurance companies. When paying claims, the reinsurer bears a proportional amount of the claim cost.
- Non Proportional: In this type of reinsurance, the re-insurer doesn't have a proportion of premium and claims. The reinsurance comes into force only when the insurance companies' losses go beyond a certain limit. The limit again depends on what agreement the re-insurer and the insurance company have in terms of risk covered.

Terms frequently used in insurance

Before we proceed further, let us quickly understand the frequently used terms in insurance industry:

- **Premium**: Premium is a one time or annual payment made by insured to the insurance company for the insurance coverage. The insured can be an individual or an organization. The amount of premium will depend on various factors, the most important being the risk perceived by the insurer.
- **Claims**: Claim is an application made by the insured to the insurance company for getting reimbursement to cover damages incurred. The process of filing a claim is defined in the policy document or provided by insurer as a separate document.
- **Policy**: Policy is the agreement between the insured and the insurer, mentioning the details of insurance coverage. The policy mentions coverage, duration of coverage, the exceptions, the premium amount, and other important details.
- **Agent**: Agents are the sales representatives of the insurance companies who sell the polices to the insured. The agents can be of different types. They can be employees of the insurance company or external third party agents.
- **Underwriter**: Underwriters are people working for the insurance company who evaluate the risk potential of the insured, depending on various factors like region, age, and others. They take the decision whether to issue a policy or not, and if yes, then they decide the coverage and premium price.
- **Actuary**: They are the employees of the insurance company and have expertise in the field of economics and mathematics. They do statistical analysis of risk and effect of insured events happening.
- **Loss ratio**: Loss ratio is the ratio of claims paid versus the premium amount calculated. For example, for every 100 USD collected, if an insurance company pays 35 USD, then the loss ratio is 35 percent. An insurance company ideally looks at keeping the ratio to a minimum value. The loss ratio can differ for every business and will vary across geographies.
- **Beneficiary**: This is a term used in life insurance. The beneficiary is the person nominated by the insured, who gets the insurance amount in event of death of the insured.
- **Commission**: Commission is the amount paid by the insurance company to an agent. The amount of commission varies, depending on the volume done by the agent.
- **Exposure**: Exposure is risk of a possible loss.

- **Incurred but not reported** (**IBNR**): IBNR is the amount which an insurance company has to pay to the insured who has suffered a loss but hasn't reported a claim.

Insurance organization

Insurance companies have various functions which are needed for smooth functioning. The functions can be broadly categorized into front office, back office, distribution, and operations. Let us look at this insurance organization structure in more detail. Though the structure may vary across companies, the following gives an overview:

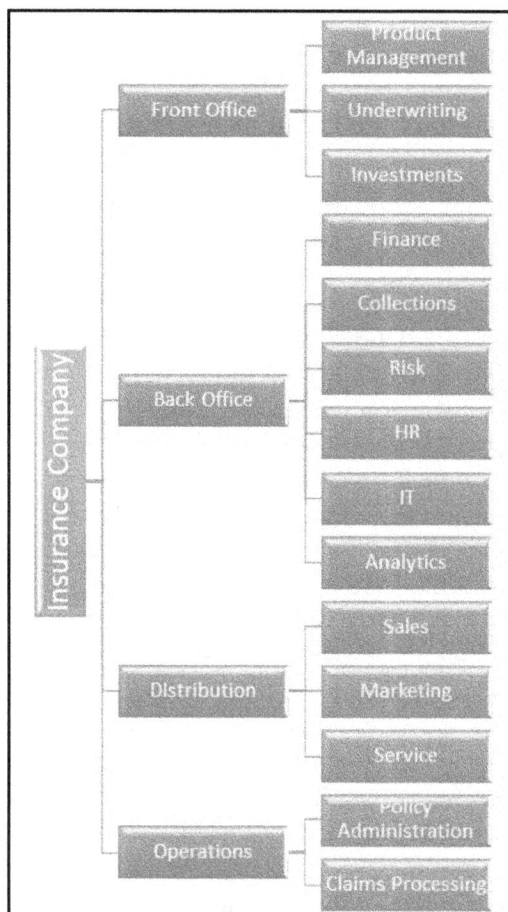

Different functions in Insurance

Let us look at the functioning of these functions.

Distribution

Distribution essentially is a function which interfaces with existing and prospective clients. It is also known as distribution channels. Distribution is largely comprised of Sales, Marketing, and Service. Let us look at them.

Sales

Sales is an important function for an insurance company, as people in sales reach out to potential and existing customers to bring in revenue for the company. Sales for an insurance company happens in two areas:

- New sales: New sales is the sales when a policy is sold for the first time. This sales can happen via various channels. We will look at the different channels in the next section.
- Renewals: Renewals are the sales which happen when a customer renews the policy before it expires. The renewals are not applicable for those policies which have single premium. Renewals are more relevant for term insurances, health, motor, property, fire, marine, and similar type of insurances.

In insurance, sales can happen via various channels. The following figure gives the perspective.

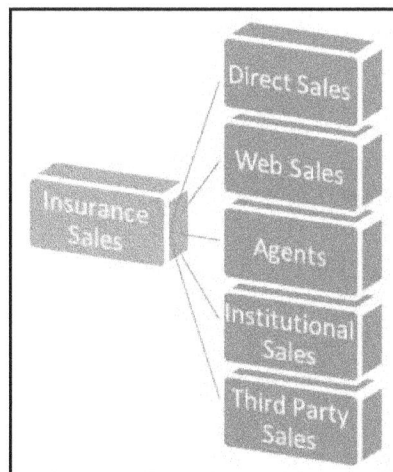

Sales channels in Insurance

The different channels which are shown in the previous figure are explained below.

- **Direct Sales:** Direct Sale is done by the company itself. This is achieved by the network of offices across the geography it operates in. The insurance company has a head office and then multiple zonal offices. Each zonal office has regional offices, and so on. The following figure depicts the hierarchy:

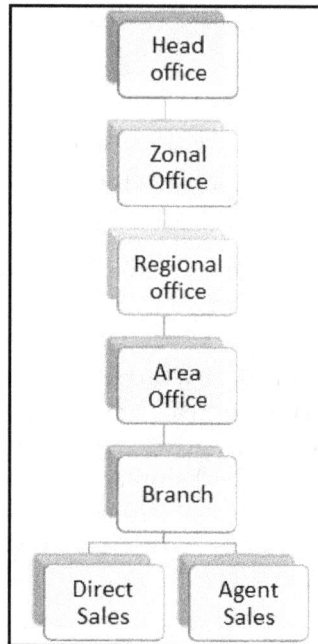

Sales Hierarchy

- **Web Sales:** With the advent of technology, people have become comfortable buying online. The insurance companies use this to their advantage and give the option of buying policies online for the end users. Having a good web sales strategy helps the companies reach out to a wider audience, and at the same time, cut down on cost. The online portals give the option of online chat to the buyers to get their queries resolved and help them choose the policies they need.

- **Agents:** Insurance agents are essentially individuals who are not direct employees of an insurance company. They are usually self-employed and they reach out to their potential customers with the intention of selling them policies. An insurance agent can be dedicated to one insurance company or can carry policies from multiple insurance companies. For every sales that an insurance agent does, he receives a commission. The insurance agents are another way for an insurance company to reach out to a large audience and keep the cost low, as they are not on the payroll of the insurance companies. The insurance agents bring in human element for customers who prefer interacting with a person and getting to know the different policies.

- **Institutional Sales:** As the name indicates, the sales done by institutions are referred to as institutional sales. These institutions can be large financial institutes, banks, or brokerage houses. Normally, they sell to **HNI (High Network Individuals)** customers. These institutions have a field force of their own and help the insurance companies reach out to larger audience. These institutions get a commission for selling the products of an insurance company. They typically carry products from multiple insurance companies. Apart from insurance, these companies may carry other products as well, such as mutual funds, loans, and other investment products.

- **Third Party Sales:** Another way insurance companies sell is via third party sales. An example can be third party websites. Such websites are aggregators and provide a single interface for the buyers to look at products from different insurance companies. The buyers can give input parameters, such as age, insurance amount, duration, and so on, and these websites then contact individual insurance companies and get premium values. The user can then choose the one that best suits him/her and even buy the policy online. These websites earn commission on each policy sold via them.

Marketing

Marketing is an important function in an insurance industry. Marketing team is responsible for building brand of the company and coming out with ways to make existing customers and prospects aware of new product launches. Marketing is always on the lookout for ways and means to have a great strategy to reach out to correct audience. Insurance companies spend a lot on marketing their products, and hence it's important for marketing to understand which channel gives better results.

This helps them to invest more in productive channels. Some of the channels which the insurance companies look at for reaching out to their audience are shown in the following figure:

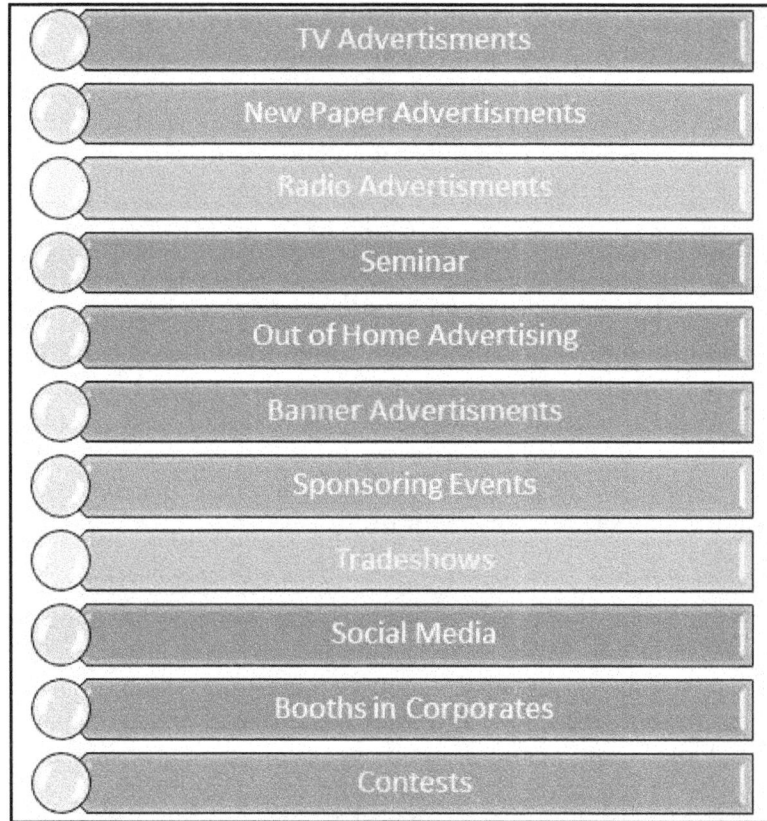

Marketing channels

Marketing is also involved in miscellaneous activities, such as keeping the website updated, updating the blogs, getting involved in business planning, and so on.

Service (Post Sales)

Service function is responsible for serving the customer requests once they purchase a policy. The Service function gets several requests from customers, such as corrections in policy, filing of claims, policy document related questions, and other similar complaints/grievances.

Ensuring customer satisfaction is very important for the service function as this helps build customer confidence and also makes way for better customer retention. With the progress in technology, insurance companies offer various channels to address customer grievances. The following diagram shows the various means insurance companies use to have customers reach out to them:

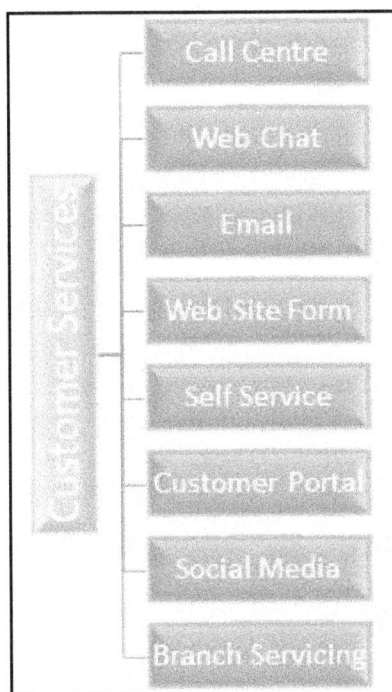

Service channels

Though the figure is self-explanatory, let us quickly summarize it:

- Call Center: Call center is a traditional approach, where customers reach out to insurance companies via telephone. The call center employs service personnel to answer queries. These days it is common for companies to have a toll-free number, allowing customers to reach out without incurring telephone charges.

- Web-Chat: Web chat is a text based chat allowing customers to visit web site of the insurance company and chat with an agent. It is similar to a call center where there are service personnel waiting to respond to chat requests.

- Email: Call centers and web-chat may not be available 24x7, so companies use emails to receive grievances. The companies offer a support email (support@companyname.com), or they may offer multiple email ids, for example, claims@companyname.com, renewals@companyname.com, and so on. On writing an email, a ticket is created automatically and an acknowledgement sent to the customer.

- Web Site form: Web site form is a form usually available under support section of the company's website. The web site form takes inputs such as customer name, email address, contact number, policy number, and reason for compliant; it may give additional fields, such as description box, and may even allow images to be uploaded.

- Self-Service: Self service allows customers to resolve a lot of compliants themselves without going through a support channel.

- Customer Portal: The customer portal is a section of website that is available to the customers once they login. Customer portal allows the users to see all their details with respect to number of policies, premiums, claims, and so on. The customer portal may internally have other channels for support, such as chat, raising a ticket, or emailing the problem. With customer portal, the advantage is that the customers can track the status of their complaints.

- Social Media: Social media has now become a popular way for users to reach out to companies. Companies operate dedicated twitter handles or facebook pages where customers can leave comments/posts/tweets. These channels are continuously monitored by the company and responses are sent from the same channels.

- Branch servicing: Branches offer the comfort of face to face interaction for the customers. Some customers (especially senior citizens) are still used to this traditional approach and do not mind traveling to their nearest branch.

Front Office

The front office comprises of various functions, such as product management, underwriting, and investment. We look at them briefly.

Product Management

Product management function in insurance is responsible for coming out with different products. As mentioned earlier, an insurance company operates in various areas, such as life insurance, motor insurance, property insurance, and health insurance.

Having just one product for each of these doesn't help. Insurance companies want to reach out to the maximum audience and hence the need to have multiple products in one line of business. If we take example of life insurance, we see insurance companies having multiple products in life insurance, such as:

- Term insurance plans
- Endowment plans
- ULIP (Unit linked insurance plans)
- Life Insurance with saving plans
- Pension/Retirement plans
- Group insurance plans

Insurance companies can make these plans based on customer feedback, or in some cases, if competitor insurance company launches a plan. Once the new plans are taken over by marketing, it's important for the insurance company to keep monitoring the performance of these plans. Considering the cost involved in marketing efforts, plans which do not perform well may be discontinued.

Underwriting

Underwriting is mainly responsible for risks before issuing policy to a customer. They look at exposures before deciding on coverage they can offer to a customer. In case the perceived risk is high, the insurance company may decide not to issue a policy. In some cases, if the underwriter feels that the risk is high, he/she may charge more premium for a coverage. Let's look at some examples:

- Life insurance premium for a smoker will be more than one for a non-smoker. Similarly, premium for stuntman will be much more than a regular office goer.
- Motor insurance for a car model which is prone to accidents will be more than for a similarly priced model which has lower accident probability.
- Property insurance for a house located in earthquake prone area will be more than for a similar house in area which is not in seismic zone.

There could be cases where the underwriter issues a policy where risk is significant, but he/she may put in some exclusion causes there. Underwriting is critical for insurance companies business as they have to manage trade-off in either being aggressive or being conservative.

Underwriters are highly specialized in risk assessment. Analytics plays an important role for an underwriter, as historical data helps to arrive at risk assessment.

Investments

In the earlier section of this chapter, we mentioned how insurance companies make their money. Just to summarize, if 1000 people buy policies by paying 1500 USD each as insurance premium, then the insurance company gets 1,500,000 USD. There could be cases where some of this amount goes towards paying claims. Insurance companies also take reinsurance to mitigate the risk of claim amount exceeding premium amount. The amount an insurance company makes is typically the difference of amount earned via premium and amount spent due to claim payouts and expenses.

Insurance companies look at increasing the profitability by investing this amount. They invest the amount into financial instruments like bonds, derivatives, stock market, and so on. The amount which an insurance company can invest may be governed by a regulatory body.

These investments help the insurance company keep the right amount of working capital and at the same time make surplus funds earn.

Operations

Operations takes care of important functions like **Policy Administration** and **Claims processing**. Let us look at these functions.

Policy Administration

Policy administration function, as the name suggests, relates to managing the policies. The policy administration is involved in various functions, such as:

- Maintaining records
- Policy issuance
- Policy changes/correction
- Policy renewals

- Maintaining claims information
- Policy cancellations

The policy administration has to follow approval process, has to follow underwriting rules before policy can be issued/changed/cancelled.

Claims Processing

Claims processing is a complex function in insurance. This function has to deal with the entire life-cycle, from the filing of claims by a customer to acceptance or rejection of the claims.

As explained in an earlier section of the chapter, a claim is when an insured reaches out to the insurance company in event of a damage. For example, suppose my car met with an accident, then I would have to incur its repair costs. However, if I have a motor insurance policy which is active (not expired), then these costs can be claimed from the insurance company. The process of asking for this money is called a claim.

Every insurance company has a process for the claim. An example process is shown in the following diagram:

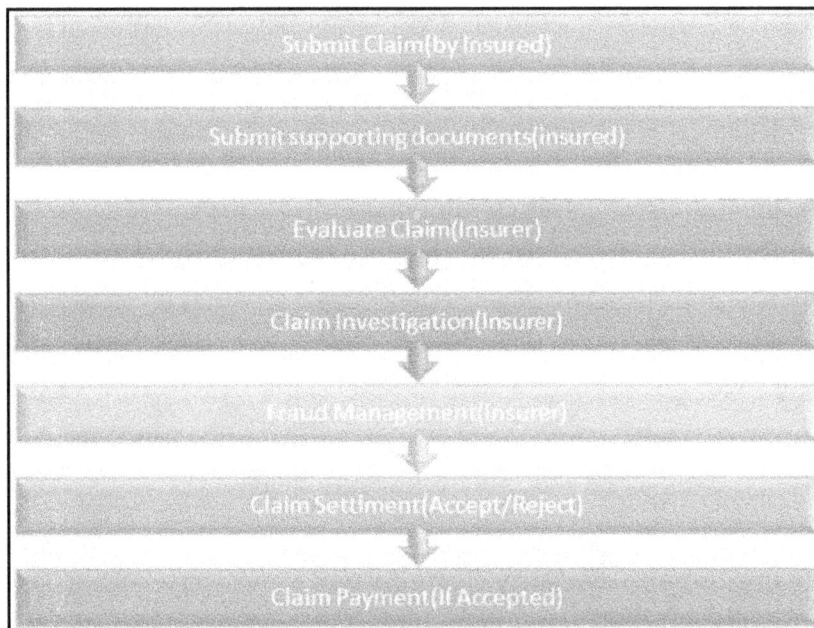

Submit Claim(by Insured)

Submit supporting documents(insured)

Evaluate Claim(Insurer)

Claim Investigation(Insurer)

Fraud Management(Insurer)

Claim Settlement(Accept/Reject)

Claim Payment(If Accepted)

Claim processing flow

The process is as shown in diagram and starts when an insured submits a claim(the process will vary from company to company. It can be done via any of means which was explained in section where we looked at the ways an insurance company provides service and was depicted Claims process flow diagram. The supporting documents need to be added. The next step is taken by the insurance company, which is to evaluate the claim (it goes through various checks, such as validity of policy, exclusion checks, and other policy terms). If the claim passes these checks then the company may do a claim investigation. This may involve physical visit by an insurance company representative to check the damage or validate bills, or any similar activity depending on the type of insurance.

Fraud checks can also be carried out if the company is not convinced about the claim. After all these steps, the claim will either be accepted or rejected. If accepted, the claim payout is done by the insurance company. There could be cases wherein on claim rejection the insured may take legal option to pursue the rejection.

Back office

The back office consists of functions such as Finance, Collections, Risk, HR, IT, and Analytics. Let's have a look at these functions.

Finance

Finance function is another important function for any insurance company. It is responsible for all financial operations. Some of the roles which the finance function needs to oversee are:

- Maintaining financial health of the company
- Planning
- Budgeting
- Reducing expenses and operational costs
- Managing working capital and requisite cash
- Managing financial risk
- Financial reporting
- Managing compliance and rgulatory requirements

Analytics plays a critical role for finance department. Good analytical tool can help them to reduce expenses and improve efficiency. Financial and statutory reporting is another area where analytics plays a key role.

Collections

Collections is responsible for billing and collections (payments due from the customers). Collections are important for insurance companies to manage working capitals. The collection department needs to work with several entities, such as customers, agents, institutional companies, and corporates.

Risk

As the name suggests, risk function manages risk and critical function for insurance companies. The profitability of a company can get severely affected by risks, and a good risk department helps an insurance company immensely. When we talk of risks, an insurance company has to manage several risks. Some of them are mentioned next:

- Risk of fraudulent claims
- Risk from underwriting
- Cyber-security related risk
- Risk occurring from investments (for example, stock market collapse)
- Risk from competition
- Risk due to non-compliance and other regulatory mandates
- Strategic risks
- Operational risks

HR

Human Resource (HR) function takes care of various functions. Some of the functions which HR is involved in are:

- Employee training
- Employee performance management
- Managing payroll and compensation
- Employee recruitment
- Succession planning
- Employee retention and reducing Attrition

IT

Information Technology (IT) provides necessary infrastructure to run critical business applications. IT also plays an important role in maintaining governance and security. It also enables connectivity to the data sources and helps other departments to run analytics.

Insurance industry runs several critical business applications. Some of these are core policy management applications for life and general insurance, productivity applications, and collaboration applications. IT also takes care of running portals for customers and agents.

Analytics

Analytics is an important function in insurance industry. It helps various functions in the insurance company by assisting them in analyzing data and helping them improve their decision making. It's often referred to as MIS (Management Information System).

Analytics prepares various dashboards and is responsible for making changes like adding new source or adding/editing KPI. Let us look at some of the KPIs in the next section.

KPIs which are used in Insurance

Now that we have a fair idea on insurance domain, as a consultant we now need to look at what are the KPI which matter to the business users. These KPI will now be easy for you to understand after you have understood the insurance business.

Finance KPI

The finance KPI enables the finance department to look at various aspects related to finance. These KPIs allows finance controllers to monitor financial health of the company. Some of them are mentioned next:

- Revenue analysis-Actual versus Budget (are our revenue as per planned targets)
- Revenue trend (month on month, quarter on quarter, and year on year (YoY)) (are we growing compared to previous periods)
- Revenue trend (current month versus last year same month, current quarter versus last Year same quarter) (how are we performing when compared to same period of last year)
- Portfolio analysis of various funds and customers (are we making right investments)
- Company reserves and solvency margin (do we have enough working capital)
- Cost analysis by each expenditure head
- Cost expenditure by each cost center
- P&L(Profit and loss) account for each branch as separate cost center (understand which branch needs attention and should a poor performing branch be closed down?)

- EBITDA (Earnings Before Interest, Taxes, Depreciation and Amortization) and profit after Tax (Profit analysis)
- Ratio Analysis (Liquidity Ratio, Asset Ratio, Profitability and debt Ratio)

Underwriting KPI

Underwriting is an important function and they need to look at trends involving claims, loss ratio and few more parameters . This allows them to improve profitability of the insurance company.

Lets now look at the KPI which underwriting looks at.

- Profitability indicator (loss ratio, risk cost per policy)
- Product section analysis (under profitability and liability section)
- Rate monitoring (helps pricing polices for property insurance)
- Client level reporting (analyze profitability at client level)
- Underwriting decision (measuring risk and pricing policies)
- Claim detection on the basis of Underwriting decisions (improves underwriting process)
- Integrating underwriting and claims (helps improve decision making)
- Loss ratio analysis (understand claims versus premium)
- Policy portfolio analysis (helps to work out average premium rates)
- Optimizing approval process (find delays and work on improvements)

Acturial KPI

Actuary looks at the risks involved and some KPIs help them to assess the risks. Let us look at some of them:

- Experience analysis(helps understanding profitable products,channels, investments)
- Surrender rate (understand cancellations of existing polices)
- Persistency rate(understand retention ratio)
- Withdrawal rate (understand factors influencing withdrawal rate)
- Mortality rate (understand probability of death and risk associated)
- Morbidity rate(risks due to occurrences of diseases)
- Loss ratio (ratio of claims versus premium)
- Repayment rate

- Claim triangulation (helps analyze claims over period of time and plan reserves)
- Product profit analysis (product performance analysis)
- Claim cost analysis (helps analyze cost of claims including processing cost and look for areas of improvement)
- Profiling of risky segment (helps looks at risks and plan mitigation strategies)
- Solvency ratio (measurement of risk which company cannot absorb)
- Asset and liability (understand impact of assets and liability)

Premium KPI

Premium is the revenue stream for a company and one of the most important aspects. The premium details are closely monitored by various functions in insurance and there are lot of KPIs which are specific to premium. Some of them are mentioned as follows:

- Comparison of premium at various levels-current year versus corresponding period last year; Year till date and Budget (at company, line of business, channel, and branch level)(360 degree analysis of premium)
- Analysis of new businesses, renewals, cancellations and endorsements, make model type (motor insurance) (understand new customer acquisitions, loss of existing customers)
- Branch wise list of proposals pending to be issued, along with status (understand efficiency and find areas of improvement)
- High premium policy; premium per policy above a threshold value (helps understand high revenue customers and also understand risk)
- LOB wise average ticket size (understand performance of LOB)
- Commission, agent name, and premium (agent payout analysis)
- Policy with coverage period of more than one year (helps understand probability of repeat business)
- Premium retention ratio(analyze successful customer retention)
- Premium analysis - sum insured report, reinsurance, and net premium
- Premium received in advance (all policies where the start date is from next month), along with commission (helps understand good customer and focus on policies which are no renewed)
- Clients with policies more than a certain premium amount (understand high focus customers and plan retention strategy)

Claims KPI

Like premium, claims too matter a lot for an insurance company. The more the claims, the more reduction in profit for an insurance company. Claims help the underwriting and actuary to look at the risks associated. The commonly used KPIs are mentioned as follows:

- Average cost per claim and comparison over time (understand if average claim costs are increasing and important input for underwriters)
- Claim settlement ratio (ratio of rejected claims versus passes claims. Client prefer companies having higher claim settlement ratio)
- Claim settlement time (time required to settle a claim. Clients prefer companies who settle claims quickly)
- Loss ratio (ratio of claims paid versus premium earned and key input for underwriters. The ratio should be less for increased profitability)
- Claim processing costs and comparison over time (help to look for areas of optimization to reduce processing costs)
- Daily high gross claims (example, 1 million) and net claims (example, above 0.5 million) for each policy (understand claims crossing defined thresholds)
- Comparison of operational reserve, total claims paid, and closing claim reserve - old claims (gross and reinsurance) (parameters effecting profitability)
- Comparison of operational reserve, total claims paid, and closing claim reserve - new claims (gross & reinsurance) (parameters effecting profitability)

Ratio Analysis

Ratio analysis helps insurance companies to quickly analyze the health of the company. Loss ratio, for example, should be very less. These are looked at from various dimensions, such as channels and agents. Let's look at some of them:

- LOB wise Net loss ratio - Net incurred claims/Net earned premium
- Channel wise Net loss ratio - Net incurred claims/Net earned premium
- For high premium policy - net loss ratio (outstanding UPR (unearned premium reserve) gross and RI for such policies separately)
- Agent wise loss ratio and commission (helps cutting down on agent responsible for high loss ratio and reward agents with lesser ratio)
- Location level drill down (helps understand profitable and loss making locations)

Expense Analysis

Expense analysis helps the companies to look at all areas where the company is spending. Ideally, the companies look at reducing the expenditure (as the saying goes-every penny saved is a penny earned). The list can be exhaustive, but let's look at areas which are closely monitored:

- Department wise expenses (analyze expenses across departments)
- Channel wise expenses (analyze expenses across channels)
- Expense incurred which are more than a certain value (for example, 5 million) (easily understand high ticket expenses)
- Month on month expense trend of major expense heads (for example salaries, advertisements) (understand areas to focus on for cost optimization)
- Comparison of expenses with last period (analyze if expenses are increasing over time and plan future budgets and look for areas of optimization)

Use cases in insurance

It is good for the consultant to know the different areas in which business users use analytics. Let us look at some of the areas.

Sales performance

Declining revenue is one of the main business challenges in insurance industry. With ever increasing competition, the companies struggle to improve profitability and increase revenues. With insurance companies going omni-channel, the customer has multiple options of buying.

It's important for the insurance companies to make effective use of their prospects and customer list. Enabling agents and other channels to sell more products at a good profit is one of the effective ways to improve revenue. Agents need to be made aware of the products to ensure the right product is sold to t he right audience. Mis-selling to customer can cause regulatory and compliance issues.

Another way of improving profitability is by reducing operating cost and curtailing unnecessary expenses.

Insurance companies look at better sales forecasting, tracking of opportunities, better management of pipeline and focus on increased lead conversions.

Some of the solution areas which companies look at for sales function are:

- Omni channel analytics
- Agent performance analysis
- Product analysis
- Persistency analysis

Marketing Performance

With increased competition, the insurance companies try to out do each other with aggressive marketing. One of the important things that marketing function looks at is hitting the sweet spot in the right customer segment. It is important to identify the right segment and focus on penetrating the segment, yielding maximum profits. Since marketing efforts require lot of expenditure, every campaign or promotion needs to be used effectively to get the maximum ROI.

Some of the solution areas which marketing looks at are:

- Campaign analysis and ROI analysis
- Up-sell and cross-sell to existing and new prospects
- Identifying best and worst performing products
- Customer segmentation analysis and targeting
- Profitability analysis

Investments

As mentioned earlier, the insurance company invests the amount earned via premiums. This is to increase profitability, and to mitigate risks as well in the event of excessive payouts due to claims. As a consultant, you can help customer analyze their investments. This is an important area which the insurance company needs help. Some of the solutions which an insurance company looks at:

- Assets under management (AUM) and their growth rate
- Revenue contribution of investment and ROI
- Investment portfolio analysis and management.

Risk

Risk in insurance industry needs to be closely looked at. Risks can wipe off the insurance company's profit. Risk arise from various factors like natural disasters, frauds, regulatory non-compliance and bad investments. The insurance company has several use cases in areas of risk:

- Meeting regulatory compliance
- Market/Portfolio Risk
- Fraudulent claims management (may need predictive analytics)

Underwriting and Claims

Increase in number of claims reduce the profitability of the insurance company. Its important for an insurance company, the underwriters have the visibility of these claims. This helps the underwriters to better understand risks. This data also helps them to better classify the risks and proactively discover risk concentrations. The solutions areas could be:

- Understanding fraudulent claims
- Analysis of loss ratio
- Analysis of claim settlements
- Analysis of policy portfolio

BI/IT/Reporting

Insurance companies need critical information and need in depth analysis to uncover newer areas of profitability, reduce operating costs, mitigate risks, and improve efficiency. BI(busines intelligence) helps them to get all critical information about various functions, enabling them to take smart business decisions. Some of the solution areas are:

- IT audit and compliance
- Regulatory compliance
- Profit and loss analysis across different business units
- Financial reporting/Regulatory reporting
- Operational and financial control
- Expense management

Knowing Pharmaceuticals and Life-sciences

In today's fast paced life, which is full of stress and anxiety, and with many leading sedentary life styles, the average person tends to fall sick. Most of us have fallen sick at one point or another. Some fall sick more often and some a little less frequently. The number of diseases which were earlier unknown have started surfacing (for example, H1N1). For known diseases, the virus/bacteria are getting drug resistant.

Whenever we fall sick, we go to a doctor. The doctor prescribes medicines/drugs and helps us to get better. We go to the pharmacy and after showing the prescription get the medicines. We hardly think about how this medicine is manufactured and what efforts it takes to make one.

Pharmaceuticals and life-sciences companies are the ones who manufacture the medicines. These are commercial organizations and require license from regulatory body before they can sell the medicines. An example of regulatory body is US Food and Drug Administration (FDA). Every country, where the pharmaceutical company sells, will have such a body and the pharmaceutical companies needs to adhere to all guidelines and compliance.

Once they get the licenses, these companies can mass manufacture and sell their medicines/drugs in the market. These companies also invest substantially in research and development and keep developing newer drugs or improving existing ones. Apart from humans, the companies may also manufacture medicines for animals and livestocks.

Let's look at different entities in the pharmaceutical industry. The following figure shows the different entities. Let's look at each of them briefly.

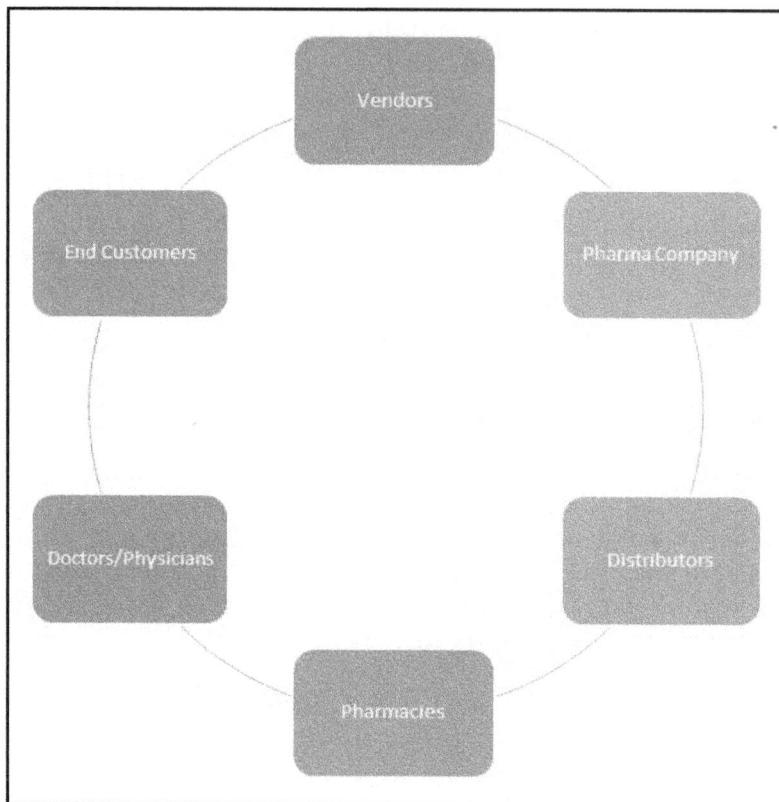

Entities in Pharmaceuticals

Vendors

Any finished product requires raw materials. Pharmaceutical companies usually depend on other companies which make these raw materials, and the vendor plays an important role in supplying the perfect raw materials. Pharmaceutical companies need precision in the raw materials and they perform stringent quality and control before they accept them. This is important, simply because the quality of the raw material affects the final outcome of medicine.

The quality of the raw material affects the formulation. Certain components are known to cause side effects to patients, and if percentage of these components change,s it could be fatal. FDA keeps a close watch and deviations may lead to cancellation of licenses.

The raw materials can be classified into:

- Raw material for excipient: These are raw materials which are needed to carry the drug and meant for stabilization. These may be further classified into multiple categories, such as coatings, binders, colors, flavors, and preservatives.
- Raw material for API: Active Pharmaceutical Ingredient or API is the part of medicine which is responsible for the action of the drug (for example, anti inflammatory). The raw material for this is very critical, and as mentioned earlier, can lead to severe repercussions in event of deviations.

There are other vendors who are responsible for packaging the product. The medicine may be packaged in plastics, glass bottles, or foils, or have paper packaging.

Pharmaceutical company

Pharmaceutical (pharma) companies are the companies involved in manufacturing of drugs/medicines. Pharma companies may manufacturer either brand or generic, or both of them. Similarly, pharma companies may deal in both prescription or otc (over the counter) types of drugs.

As there are newer outbreak of diseases, pharma companies try to understand the diseases and how they can be controlled at molecular level. Drug companies have to spend a lot of money and effort in new drug production. The pharma companies are regulated by regulators (for example, FDA). They have to manage the entire ecosystem of doctors/physicians, key opinion leaders, competition, vendors, and distributors.

Pharma companies try to be profitable by producing and patenting newer drugs and entering newer geographies and new therapeutic areas. Pharma companies incur a lot of expenses during drug discovery and clinical trials. The marketing, promotion, and associated activities incur lot of expenses.

The pricing decided by the pharma companies have to be precise and enable the companies to sustain, increase profits, and at same time, stay ahead of competition.

Distributors

Pharmaceutical companies have geographically distributed end users (patients). End users buy their medicines from the pharmacy/retail stores. It is virtually impossible for any pharma company to directly sell to the pharmacies. The sheer volume of logistics involved makes it difficult to have such a kind of model.

This is where distributors bridge the gap. Distribution can be a simple or a complex hierarchy, depending on the geography and volumes which any pharma company handles. A distribution example can be summarized as per the following figure:

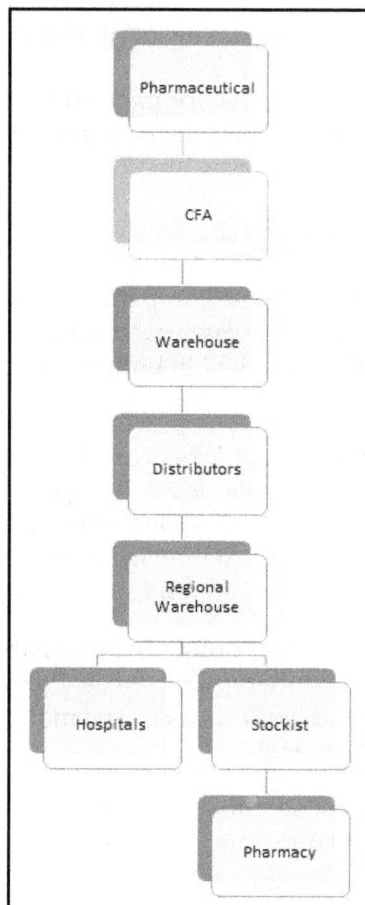

Pharma distribution mechanism

Let's briefly understand the roles of each of them briefly:

- **CFA**: CFA or Clearing and Forwarding Agents are the ones responsible to maintain stock of the pharma company. On request, a CFA supplies the drugs/medicines to the distributors (they are also known as super stockists). The number of CFAs may be one or more, depending on the geography and penetration of the pharma company in a particular market.
- **Warehouse**: It is the area where actual inventory (or stock of medicine/drug) is stored. The warehouse could be owned by the company or it could be rented. The warehouse can either be a central warehouse or a regional warehouse. Regional warehouse keep the stock in a particular region and this enables faster delivery to a stockist/pharmacy
- **Distributors**: Distributors or super stockists are the ones to whom pharma company does billing with, or in other words, the distributors place an order on the pharma company. This is commonly referred to as **Primary sales.** Having distributors makes it easy for the pharma company to have better logistics. The distributors manages several stockists and hospitals.
- **Stockists:** Stockists or sub-stockists are the ones who supply the drugs/medicines to the pharmacies. They may also supply to smaller hospitals. The stockists place their orders with the distributors. This is commonly referred to as **Secondary sales**. Stockists are associated with a distributor and they in turn manage several pharmacies/smaller hospitals.
- **Hospitals:** Hospitals often perform surgeries and cater to patients post surgery. They require medicines/drugs in significant quantities. The hospitals, depending on their size and requirement, may buy directly from a distributor/super-stockist or may buy from stockist.
- **Pharmacy:** Pharmacies are the outlets from where patients buy medicines. We will look at this in next section.

Pharmacy

Pharmacies or retail stores are the ones who supply the medicines/drugs to the end customers. The pharmacies place their order with stockists/sub-stockists. This is commonly referred to as **Tertiary sales.** Medicines may be classified as prescription based and over the counter (OTC) ones. Prescription based medicines require a doctor's prescription before a patient can buy them. OTC are the ones which can be sold by even retails stores (examples can be cough tablet, band-aid, and so on).

Online pharmacies

The information technology advancements have made online shopping very popular with the end users, and this has led to mushrooming of online eCommerce websites.

This concept has now caught up with medical industry as well and many companies are now offering eCommerce sites as an option to the customers. The customers can visit the websites, login, upload prescriptions, and get home delivery of the medicines.

These online pharmacies depending on the volume and geography to which they sell may purchase the medicines from distributor or a stockist.

Doctors/Physicians

Doctors and Physicians are the critical people for any pharmaceutical company. The doctors are the ones who actually prescribe a drug for the patient. A particular drug may be manufactured by several pharma companies and it's largely up-to the doctor to prescribe a drug from a particular pharma company.

Hence, pharma companies take lot of efforts to catch attention of doctors. The doctors are frequently visited by representatives of the pharma companies, often referred to as Medical Representatives (MR). The MRs provide free samples of medicines to the doctors. The doctors are many times even sponsored by the pharma companies to attend important conferences, seminars, and events.

End consumer (patient)

The end consumers or the patients are the ones who consume the medicines. They buy them from local pharmacy or retail store (only OTC). These days there are options available for consumers to buy medicines online as well. This actual end consumer is usually difficult for a pharma company to track. They may have to depend on third party survey companies to get those details.

Terms frequently used in pharmaceutical industry

Whenever a consultant interacts with business, there are lot of jargons which the users use. Knowing these jargons or pharma terms helps the consultant to instantly relate with business users' requirements.

API

Active Pharmaceutical Ingredient is defined by WHO as:

A substance used in a finished pharmaceutical product (FPP), intended to furnish pharmacological activity or to otherwise have direct effect in the diagnosis, cure, mitigation, treatment or prevention of disease, or to have direct effect in restoring, correcting or modifying physiological functions in human beings.

In short, this is the actual medicine.

Batch Processing

Manufacturing method used by pharma companies where product is manufacturing process is spread over several steps. There could be time gaps between the steps. Tight quality needs to be maintained as there could be contamination between the steps.

Brand Name

Any pharma product usually has three names. Chemical name is the scientific name based on the chemical structure and molecular formula. Brand name is the patent which was applied by the pharma company when it first created the drug. The patent has validity. Once the validity expires, other pharma companies can manufacture the same drug and sell the same. This is called Generic name. The core composition of active ingredients must be same.

Continuous Processing

In continuous processing, raw materials are sent via non stop process till the final product is produced. The quality issues are relatively lower in this method.

Expiry

Expiry refers to the date that every drug must carry, beyond which it should not be consumed by the patient. The expiry of the drug depends on composition and can have wide range, from few days to few years.

Expiry is an important parameter which all pharma companies want to track. Excessive production of a drug will increase inventory of the drug, and if it is not sold withing the stipulated time, the drug will expire and cause losses to the manufacturing company.

FDA

Every industry, be it insurance, banking, or pharmaceutical, has a regulatory body which frames the governance and rules, and monitors the individual players. The regulatory body protects the consumers from unfair practices and gives level playing field to all the players.

Food and Drug Administration (FDA) is the governing body in pharmaceutical industry. It is responsible to protect the health of patients by ensuring the quality and safety of drugs manufactured by pharma companies. It also helps speed innovation, which can make medicines more effective, safe, and affordable.

Generics

Generics are the drugs which are manufactured by pharma companies once the patent (brand name) held by the original pharma manufacturer expires. Generics should be equivalent to the brand medicine in terms of API, intended dosage strength, and way it is administered. Generics too come under the regulatory bodies. They help to bring down the prices of the drug (reason being multiple pharma companies manufacturing the same drug).

KOL

Key Opinion Leaders (KOL) are very important for any pharma company. KOLs are usually physicians or doctors of high repute and they are keenly followed by other physicians and doctors. The KOLs are influential people and are often involved in research activities. They are mostly key speakers in international forums and are also involved in writing articles.

Pharma companies have management of KOLs as one of their important KRAs (Key Result Areas). They engage the KOL while developing new drugs and get critical feedback from them. They may also be consulted for clinical trials.

Since KOLs are considered thought leaders, they are followed by peers, and it's important for pharma companies that KOLs prescribe their medicines. Like CRM (Customer Relation Management), there is a term called KRM (KOL Relation Management).

New Drug Application

New Drug Application (NDA) is the process by which a pharma company approaches the regulatory body to sell and market a new drug.

There is a significant amount of documentation which the pharma company needs to submit in an NDA. The following are the important aspects which should be part of NDA:

- Detailed test of clinical trials conducted
- Ingredients and composition of the drug
- Any side-effects noticed during animal studies, and whether the risks outweigh the benefits of the drug
- Manufacturing, processing, and packaging processes

New drug manufacturing requires huge amount of research in their laboratories. There is a lot of to and fro before the exact formulation is reached. This process may require involvement of experts and KOLs. Thereafter, extensive tests are carried out on animals to discover side effects. Once this stage is cleared, the drug is tested on humans to test safety and effectiveness.

OTC

Over the counter (OTC) drugs are the drugs that can be sold by pharmacies without the need of a doctor's prescription. The regulatory body decides which are the drugs that are safe and can be consumed by patients without doctors' prescriptions.

The strategy of a pharma company is different for OTC than for the prescription drugs. For OTC, the pharma company directly reaches out to the patients via various channels, such as advertisements, news papers articles, hoardings, social media, and other channels.

Primary Sales

Primary sales is sales done by a pharma company to the distributor or super stockist, and this happens via CFA (Clearing and Forwarding Agent).

Secondary Sales

Secondary sales is sales done by the distributor to the stockists, online pharma companies, or hospitals.

Tertiary Sales

Tertiary sales is sales done by stockist to a pharmacy or retail store. This is facilitated by MR (Medical Representatives) or pharma companies' representatives.

Therapeutic Areas

Therapeutic Areas or TA are the various areas of diseases and therapy. Some of examples are oncology, urology, cardio vascular, ophthalmology, neurology, rheumatology, and orthopedics. A pharma company may have products for all the TA or some of them.

For future growth and expansion, a pharma company should look at getting into newer TA.

Pharma organization

A pharma organization has various divisions, summarized by the following diagram:

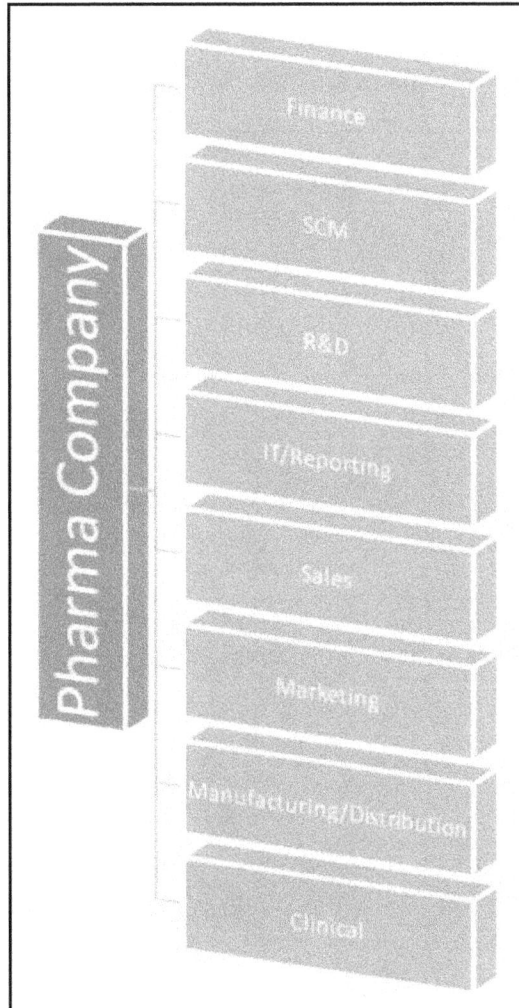

Division in Pharmaceutical company

Sales

Sales is the revenue stream for any pharma company and comprises of various distribution channels, such as distributor sales, stockist sales, pharmacy sales, hospital and clinic sales, online sales, and field sales.

A typical Sales hierarchy for pharma can be seen in the following diagram:

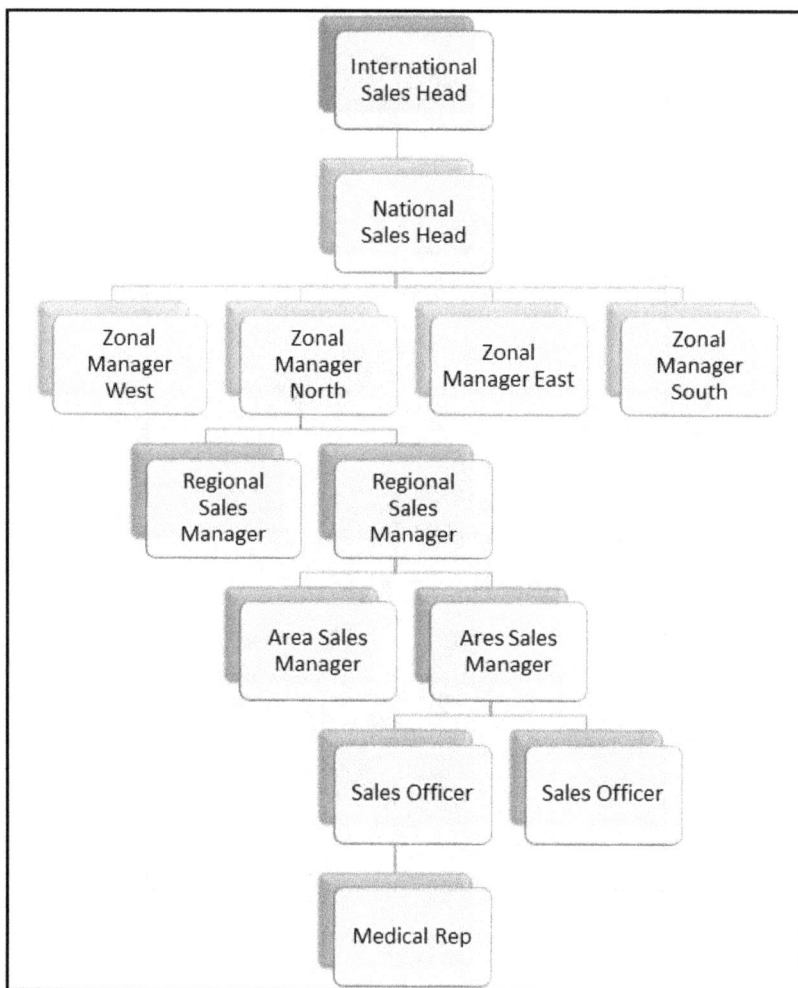

Sales hierarchy in pharma

The international sales or global sales is taken care of by international sales head, who reports to the global CEO. Depending on the size and geographical operations, every country may have its national sales head. The national sales head would report to the country head and global sales head.

For every country, the sales hierarchy can have several zonal sales head. The number of such zonal sales heads would depend on the size of the country. The number is typically in the range of 4 to 10. Zonal heads have regional sales heads reporting to them. Each region is further divided into areas and each area has an area sales head. An area sales head has several sales officers working for him/her. At the end of hierarchy, there are medical representatives (MR).

The senior sales team engages in preparing strategical plans and focuses on executing them. They are the ones who allocate the sales quotas to the people below in hierarchy. They have to work closely with the marketing team and align with them.

MRs are important links in the pharma sales and they are the ones who can bring lot of feedback to the think tank of pharma companies. MR are the ones who are out on the field, visiting stockists, pharmacies, and doctors. They keep visiting doctors and updating them about the latest happenings with respect to the latest drugs or improvements in existing ones. They do their best to influence the doctors to prescribe drugs of their company. They usually carry samples along with them during their visits to the doctors/physicians. They collect valuable feedback from the doctors on effectiveness of their medicines. They also try to find out any new requirements which the doctors may have.

MRs have their task cut out as doctors can either be general physicians or they may be specialized (example Ear and Throat, MD-Cardiac). They have to keep themselves updated with the product portfolios. If the doctor is a KOL, the MR has to be very precise and manage the relation very carefully.

The MRs also visit the distribution channels, like stockists and pharmacy stores. Apart from the objective of getting these channels to place orders, a lot of feedback is also collected from them. The MRs can also get important information as to which doctors are prescribing their medicines and which are not. This allows them to map the doctors/physicians better. The more they map the distribution channel, the better they can forecast future orders. This can help the company to plan the production and decide on the inventory levels to be maintained.

The visits are planned along with their reporting heads, and at the end of the day, the MRs have to update the system with details of their visits.

Marketing

Marketing function in pharmaceutical industry is responsible for promoting the medicines and drugs manufactured. The marketing function may use various mechanisms to do promotions. Some of them are:

- Advertisements
- Sponsoring pharma events
- Social media messaging
- Collaborating with KOLs to talk in relevant forums
- Articles in pharma journals
- Free samples to doctors/physicians and hospitals/clinics

For a large size pharma company, there could be global and regional marketing groups. The promotions and campaigns have to carry the global messaging and regional teams can add some local flavor. The marketing teams need to segment their markets and, on an ongoing basis, identify the profitable markets and make all efforts to maximize them.

Understanding demographics with respect to physicians and patients can help them to plan better campaigns and get the best ROI. They have to keep getting feedback from the ground to understand how the market is responding, and thereby adjust the marketing strategy and create greater impact.

Finance

Finance in pharmaceutical takes care of financial strategy, planning, and budgeting. The overall responsibility of managing financial risks and adhering to regulatory compliance lies with the finance.

The roles of finance include:

- Managing cash flow and working capital
- Tracking profit and losses incurred
- Reducing cost and improving operational efficiency
- Managing corporate governance
- Managing financial and operation risk
- Managing regulatory compliance
- Managing merger and acquisitions

SCM

Supply Chain Management (**SCM**) covers all the aspects of manufacturing: procurement of raw materials, manufacturing, packaging, and distribution. In short, it covers planning, sourcing, manufacturing, and distribution. The process flow is as shown in the following figure:

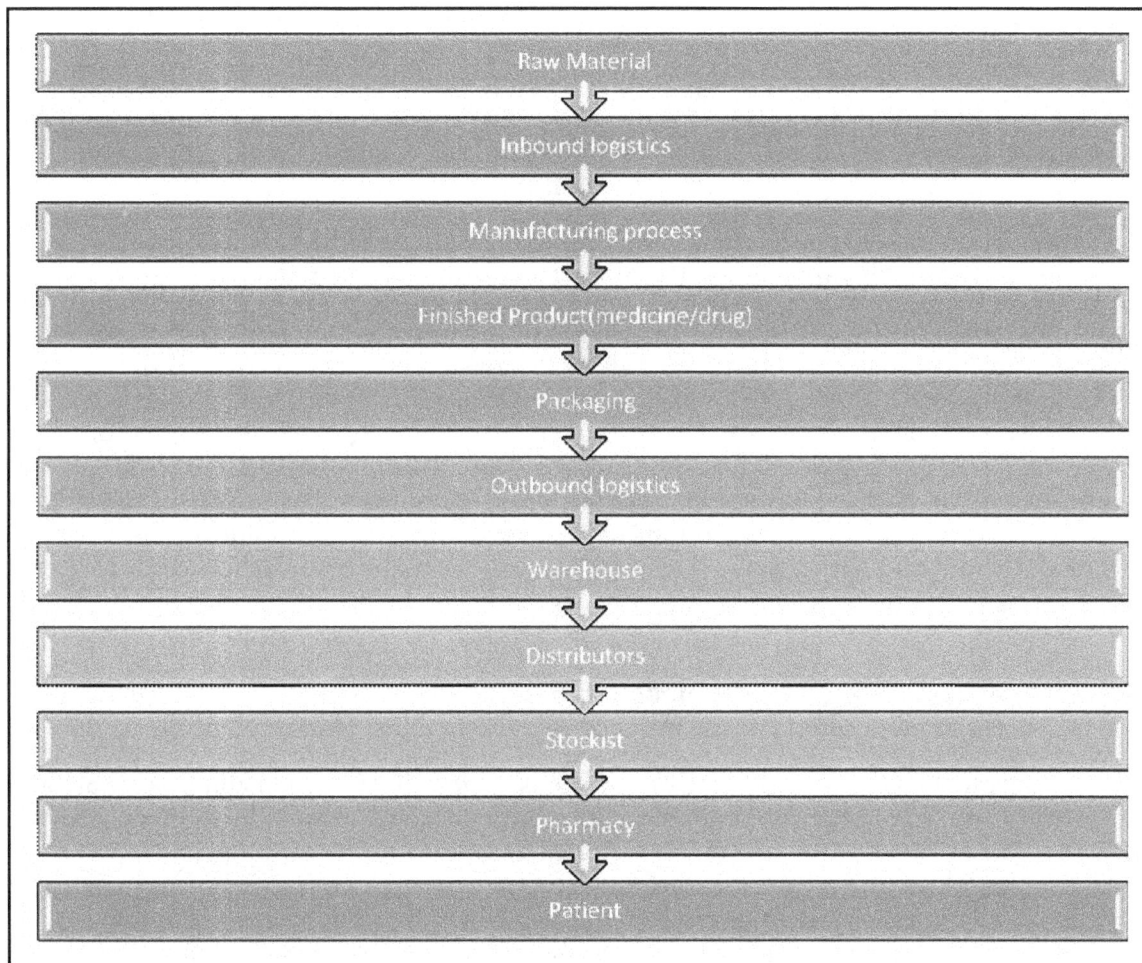

Supply Chain in Pharma

The supply chain must ensure maintaining relationships with vendors/suppliers and distribution partners. SCM has to do lot of analysis on procurement, note any quality issues, and ensure quality raw materials and in time delivery of them.

SCM has to keep analyzing performance of various suppliers and ensure proper purchasing decisions. Procurement is a part of SCM. The procurement must keep improving on negotiations and save costs. They should also look out for new vendors and partners. Analyzing logistics is an important area as well and can help in cost reduction and improved efficiencies.

Research and development

The process of discovering new drugs and enhancing/improving the existing ones is an ongoing process. Research and Development (R&D) is an important area for any pharmaceutical company. It can help pharma companies increase revenue with new drugs. It can also help expand pharma companies' footprints in various TAs.

R&D is one of the major spends any pharma company undertakes. Many a times, the efforts in developing new drugs are met with failures. The costs involved also vary, depending on the drug being created. If it's based on existing molecule, the cost will be less. A totally new drug will have huge expenses.

Production of new drug involves lot of research and consultation with field experts. The virus and bacteria causing diseases need to be studied in depth. The virus/bacteria can mutate and make the task more difficult. Once the drug is developed, it has to undergo rigorous testing. The drug has to be extensively tested on animals. The tests have to be performed in different conditions, and the observations with respect to side effects need to be noted. Any adverse effects may require the formulation to be fine tuned and the testing process repeated. Once this stage is over then tests needs to be done on humans.

A comprehensive documentation of the previous aspects needs to be noted and then new drug application process needs to be undertaken with the regulatory body. Patents can be filed and the brand registered to stay ahead of other competing pharma companies.

Risk management has to be taken care of at various stages. The sword of compliance always hangs over the head of pharma companies, right from approval process till ongoing audits. R&D should be given feedback on competitive landscape and all other information which helps them to bridge any product shortcomings.

IT/Reporting

Information technology (IT) and Reporting/Analytics is another important function. IT takes care of providing mission critical business applications, such as enterprise resource planning (ERP), customer relation management (CRM), dealer management system, learning management systems(LMS), lab information management systems (LIMS), and human resources management systems (HRMS). They take care of other applications needed by R&D, clinical, quality analysis, and control.

Analytics/Reporting provides all of the departments with flexible analytical capabilities. Considering pharma is a dynamic industry, optimization and new development is done on an ongoing basis. Analytics also has to bring data together from multiple data sources/applications and provide informative dashboards to the business users.

Manufacturing/Distribution

Though this may seem to be overlapping SCM, the manufacturing and distribution function is involved in the actual intricacies of manufacturing and distribution.

The intricacies involve receiving the raw materials and doing quality checks on the raw materials. If the threshold is not met, the raw materials will not be accepted and returned to the vendor. Maintaining stringent quality standards is an important area. There can be contamination between steps of manufacturing and that can be very counter-productive.

Once manufacturing is done, it again undergoes quality analysis and quality control tests. Subsequently, the packaging and labeling is very important aspect. Incorrect packaging and labeling are sure to cause problems and may get noticed by regulatory bodies.

There is need to compare batches results and do detailed reporting. Manufacturing plants run round the clock, and hence it's important to maintain up-time performance and do planned downtime for upgrades and maintenance.

Since the plants run round the clock, people work in shifts. The shift performance and employee performance need to be monitored. It is important to comply with governance through the entire process.

HR/Training

Human Resource (HR) is responsible for people management and, like in any industry, responsible for recruitment, attrition management, employee compensation, employee performance management, payroll, and succession planning. The HR works with every department to manage their people's requirements.

Lot of companies in pharma have a specialized training department. Training in pharma is very critical. The pharma industry is very dynamic, and with outbreak of newer diseases and continuous product development and improvements, it's imperative that the sales team be made aware of all these developments.

Training department conducts various training programs to keep the sales team updated. These may be classroom trainings or online trainings. The training function has to keep evolving with the training program and keep tracking the effectiveness of the program. They have to work with the sales team to understand feedback and find innovative ways to make the training easy and intuitive to the sales team.

Clinical

Clinical in pharmaceutical plays an important role during clinical trials. They take responsibility for evaluating drug performance during clinical trials and noting any drug reaction or side effect. Clinical also is involved in submitting all data, such as trial data and procedures, to the regulatory bodies.

Some parts of trials may also be given to partner organizations, commonly referred to as **Clinical Research Organizations** (**CRO**). The human trials are crucial and clinical function has to identify shortcomings and manage patient tracking and reporting.

Clinical also works toward reducing trial costs, mitigating risks, and taking preemptive measures. Let us look at some of the KPIs which business users look at in pharma.

KPIs which are looked at by Pharma industry

Sales KPI

Sales is an important revenue source for a company. Sales in pharma is usually very aggressive and the KPIs help them quickly look at the areas of improvement. The KPIs also let them know what is working and what is not working. The other KPIs which are looked at are as follows:

- Analysis of physician segmentation with respect to specialization, geography, number of prescription, KOL mapping (helps to do right messaging)
- Budget versus target and over time (month on month, quarter on quarter, year on year, current month versus last year same month, current quarter versus same quarter last year)
- Revenue performance breakup with respect to country, zone, region, and area (understand performance across multiple geographic dimensions)

- Product/brand performance breakup with respect to country,zone, region, and area (helps plan product strategies)
- Margin analysis across time/geography/brand/therapeutic area(understand profitable and unprofitable products and invest more in successful areas)
- Market share analysis and competition analysis (analyze competition and plan action for areas needing improvement)
- Primary sales versus secondary sales and over time (help prevent dumping of stocks and check for a healthy ratio)
- Secondary sales versus tertiary sales and over time (helps understand actual sales)
- Top and bottom performing distributors/stockists
- Top and Bottom performing MRs
- Call/visit analysis of MRs, call effectiveness analysis, comparison of number of existing prescription and new prescriptions (360 analysis of MR)
- Total calls versus productive calls (helps plan future visits)
- Percentage of coverage by MR (understand if need of more or fewer MRs)
- Number of prescriptions versus competition (understand competition and plan right messaging to physicians)
- Number of new prescriptions over a period of time (helps increase market share)
- Discount Analysis and what-if analysis (improve profitability)

Marketing KPI

Marketing has budgets allocated and they need to spend the money wisely for various campaigns and promotions. Considering the diverse channels for marketing, the marketing function is often an avid user of BI. KPI for Marketing department which matter are:

- KOL mapping and activity ROI (understand if sufficient efforts are taken to map key influences)
- Physician loyalty analysis (helps focus on loyal physicians and plan marketing strategy)
- Social media feedback (Sentiment analysis)
- Campaign expenditure analysis (details analysis on campaign spends)
- Campaign ROI percentage across channel/time/geography (helps invest in successful campaign in future)
- Patient demographic analysis (understand patients better and plan specific campaign for demographies)
- Performance after new product launch (analyze success of new launch)

- Percentage of doctor awareness versus unawareness (about the drug of the company)
- Competition analysis (understand market standing with respect to competition and plan strategies in weaker areas)

Supply Chain KPI

Supply chain is an important function that manages the procurement, logistics, and production. For supply chain the KPIs which are important are as follows:

- Cost variation of raw materials across vendors/geography/time (understand buying pattern across dimensions and improve buying decisions)
- Vendor wise QA analysis (vendor analysis helps buying decisions)
- Vendor wise spends (understand spends better)
- Inventory trends across products/time/geographies (important to plan production and plan promotions in case of excess inventory)
- Inventory turns (understand over or under stocking)
- Logistical cost analysis across vendor/channel/time/geography (analyze logistics costs across parameters)
- Labeling and compliance reporting (direct statutory impact)
- What-if and forecasting (helps plan pricing strategy and plan future)
- Contract compliance reports (helps compliance with respect to contracting)

Plant Operations

Companies do not look at using BI in plant operations early on. The plant operations is involved in actual production activities and they can contribute to the profitability by improving efficiency and reducing wastage. For them, they may look at various KPIs, such as:

- Analysis of machine efficiency (understand effective utilization and helps planning jobs)
- Actual run times versus standard run time comparison (another parameter to help understand utilization)
- Analysis of machine audit (helps to monitor health of machines)
- Analysis of production across shifts (understand shift utilization and plan production better)
- Staff performance across shifts (plan workforce across shifts)
- Analysis of downtime (understand impact of downtime and factors causing downtime)

- Analysis of open versus completed work orders (helps to plan future orders and impact on current orders)
- Scrap analysis in percentage (wastage analysis and cost impact)
- Work in progress cost reports (helps understand cost better for job in progress)

Finance KPI

Finance needs KPIs which tell them the overall financial health of the company. Some of the KPIs they may want to look at are as follows:

- Account payable analysis over time/vendor/geography (understand outstanding payments across parameters)
- Account receivables analysis over time/distributor/geography (understand expected payments across multiple parameters)
- Profit and loss analysis over division/time/geography/products/business division/therapeutic area (helps understand profitable and unprofitable business areas)
- Expenses analysis, GL wise (analyze expenses across general ledgers)
- Trial balance (understand balances gl wise)
- Working capital reports (understand financial health of company)
- Asset deprecation (important parameter effecting balance sheet)

R&D KPI

Research and Development is a function which helps pharma companies to expand their foot print in market. Like marketing, R&D too has budgets allocated and they need to monitor some of the key KPIs such as:

- R&D cost allocation analysis (helps to understand cost allocation across drugs)
- Budget versus actual expenditure over time (understand expenditure and variance with budgeted values)
- Expenses per drug (helps in pricing the drug)
- Product life-cycle development reports (helps understand 360 view of drug development)
- Expenses as percentage of sales (helps to understand profitability and plan pricing)
- Percentage of success versus failures (helps to plan future investments and focus on areas of success)

- Drugs comparison with respect to therapeutic areas and competition(understand position in market with respect to competition and plan strategies for deeper market penetration)
- Drugs in various phases of development (helps plan go to market)

Clinical KPI

Clinical functions do trials before drugs can be launched and they too have to manage several KPIs. Let's look at some of them:

- Compliance reporting (analyze compliance readiness across parameters)
- Regulatory reporting (analyze regulatory requirements)
- Trial comparisons (compare trials and understand various aspects for success)
- Serious flags (understand items needing immediate attention)
- Proportional reporting ratio (understand side effects across various parameters)
- Drug safety reports (understand safety)
- Gap analysis (understand gaps between actual and desired values)

Information Technology KPI

Information technology is a supporting function to all the other business functions. BI is one such support which IT gives to the other functions. They are technology enablers and the KPIs which matter to them are:

- SLA (Service level agreements) management report (understand quality 0f service provided)
- Cases analysis (open, pending, and priority)
- (KPI helps to understand support performance and important criteria as it impacts customer satisfaction)
- IT audit and compliance reports (understand compliance from various aspects and readiness for audits)
- Analytics usage reports (Monitor adoption and usage of application)
- Project performance analysis (analyze projects across multiple dimensions)
- TCO analysis across projects (How much is spend to own and maintain projects)
- ROI analysis across projects (How much returns do i get from my investments on projects)
- IT expenses; budget versus actual (Monitor expenditure and compare with budgets)

Human Resources

Human resources (HR) looks at KPIs which enable them to analyze optimum recruitment, employee costs, attrition and several others. Some of them are mentioned as follows:

- Attrition rate analysis (analyze how many people are leaving and helps plan strategies if attrition rates are high)
- Training effectiveness report (understand which training are useful and which arent. Helps to plan future trainings)
- Training ROI (are the investments in training yielding good results?)
- Ratio analysis of lower/middle/senior management (helps maintain proper balance and plan succession)
- Employee composition by age, gender, and tenure (understand if company is having right mix of people)
- Cost per employee analysis (understand expenditures on workforce)
- Time to recruit analysis(how soon is a recruitment request getting satisfied)

Use Cases in Pharma

Use cases help the consultant to understand how the different departments use analytics for their day to day analysis. We will cover some of the use cases.

Sales and marketing

Sales managers have their tasks cut out in managing sales across geographies. They have to deal with multiple products across therapeutic areas. MRs need proper information to target right doctors, do perfect territory planning, and plan visits.
Some of the use cases for sales and marketing are:

- Physician analysis and perfect targeting
- Territory management and planning
- Revenue analysis
- Brand management
- Product management

Executive management

The executive or top management looks for a comprehensive view of the health of business, and at the same time, they want to be sure of complying with regulations. They are short of time and want to see important KPIs in a nutshell. The use cases are:

- Performance across company, division, product performance, and geographies
- Cost, revenue, spend, and profitability management
- Regulatory and compliance management
- Forecasting and budget management

Supply Chain Management

Supply chain management manages the life cycle of production and there are lot of use cases in this area:

- Sourcing cost and supplier performance management
- Contract compliance and management
- Compliance and regulatory management
- Reducing operation costs and improving efficiency
- Inventory management

Finance

Finance function usually has the following use cases:

- Expense management
- Profitability management
- Working capital management
- Governance, compliance, and risk management

Human resources

Human resources function has various use cases:

- Workforce management
- Rewards management
- Payroll management

- Recruitment and attrition management
- Succession planning

Knowing Retail

Retail industry is a **B2C** (**Business to Consumer**) industry. Retailers directly sell to the end customers. Retailers buy from manufacturers and sell to end customers for a profit. The way they sell varies and happens across various channels, such as:

- Physical stores
- E-commerce portals
- Telephonic channel
- Online/Offline hybrid
- Social media

The various channels allow retailers to reach wider set of audience. The approach of selling across various channels is called **omni-channel sales**.

The physical stores are the traditional brick and mortar stores. This channel still continues to be popular for certain products. The physical stores give the customers the advantage of seeing, feeling, and trying the product before they purchase. The sales representatives at the store offer personalized touch and can provide valuable advice to the customers. The physical stores, though convenient for the customers, cause additional expenses for the retailer as there are additional costs of owning/leasing the store, employing staff, and other maintenance charges. However, the instances of product returns are very less as customers get to see the product before purchase.

E-commerce channel is the online channel and is getting very popular with technology and popularity of smart phones. E-commerce is made available these days as online portal and even as mobile app, giving convenient option to the customers. The customers get to know about the products via images on the portal/app and accompanying description. Though the customer loses on seeing and feeling the product, there are other advantages like shopping from place of convenience and at their preferred time. For the retailer, the cost of running online channel is cheaper and is accessible 24 hours. The drawbacks are maintaining loyalty of the customers, any downtime with portal, and higher instances of product returns. The product returns add to the logistics costs and reduce profitability.

Telephonic/Call center channel is another way retailers allow customers to buy. The products may be advertised over television/radio/magazine with the product details. The advertisement usually has a toll-free number where customers can call and place the order. The retailer may give the option of cash on delivery. This channel is quite similar to the e-commerce channel. The costs incurred are less but chances of returns are higher.

The online/offline hybrid model is a relatively recent phenomenon. In this model, the customers go to the online portal/mobile app and shortlist the product they want to buy. The retailer gives them the option of seeing/trying the product in a nearby retail outlet. The customer after visiting the store can place the order. The customer gets best of both the worlds (online/store).

Retail organization

The retail organization has various functions, which can be summarized with the following figure:

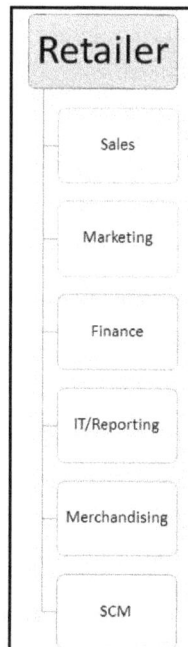

Functions in Retail

Sales

Sales in retail today is omni-channel and it's important for retailers to focus on all of them, as customers' preferences vary and some time the same customer may buy via different channels. Retailers today focus on providing seamless experience to the customers, irrespective of channels.

For offline or retail stores, the aim is to improve efficiency and reduce operating costs. To provide good experience, the stores have got to have polite and efficient staff, and stores layout have to be attractive. The retailer wants to improve sales productivity across channels and across sales representatives. The stores need to be planned in perfect locations and should be easily accessible to the customers.

Online sales is very competitive and it's very easy to lose a customer to competitor. Providing easy and fast experience, coupled with quick delivery and flexible payment options, is important to keep the customer interested and make him/her return again. Some of the KPIs and the use cases which the sales looks at are mentioned as follows:

KPIs

- Sales versus budget across time, channel, product, and geography (measure sales performance across multiple dimensions)
- Labor costs as a percentage of sales (helps understand costs and plan pricing)
- Footfall versus average sales per transaction (understand customer behavior and plan strategy to increase average sales per transaction)
- Return analysis across product, channel, time, and geography (understand reason of product returns across multiple dimensions)
- Returns as percentage of sales (understand if returns are high compared to sales)
- Sales margin analysis across product, channel, time, and geography (profitability analysis across dimensions)
- Inventory analysis (helps plan promotions and pricing)
- Shift analysis (understand and plan number of people in shift)
- Customer service feedback analysis (helps understand feedback and strategise on areas of improvement)
- Target versus actual delivery times (analyze deliveries and how it impacts customer satisfaction)

Use Cases

- Omni-channel analytics
- Revenue and profitability management

- Sales productivity management
- Budgeting, planning, and forecasting

Marketing

Marketing function is very important in retail due to fact that it's a B2C business. Retailers reach out to the audience via various mechanisms, such as:

- Television advertisements
- Newspaper/Magazine/Radio advertisements
- Social media and internet advertisements
- Sponsoring events
- Participating in consumer events
- Partnering with other institutions, such as banks and running credit card offers

Marketing has to be very innovative and keep customers interested. For marketing to effectively run promotions and campaign, the customer segmentation has to be spot on to make the promotion/campaign effective and get a good ROI. Marketing has to identify the profitable segment to increase their bottom lines. Marketing runs customer loyalty programs to ensure customers come back and keep purchasing.

Brand management is another key area for marketing. People recall good and popular brands, and usually stick to their favorite brands. This is an ongoing activity and needs to be optimally performed. Some of the KPIs and the use cases which matter to marketing are as follows:

KPIs

- Customer profiling based on purchase history, spend capacity, spend frequency, and visits (360 understanding of customer, helps targeting, up-sell and cross-sell)

- Campaign performance across channels(understand which channels give good leads and improve brand visibility)

- Campaign spends and ROI trends (understand which campaigns give good results)

- Social media sentiment analysis (helps plan future strategies and do action for any negative sentiments)

- Customer survey analysis (helps understand customer needs better and plan products)

- Footfall analysis and co-relation with sales (understand customer experience and monitor conversion of footfall into actual sales)

Use Cases

- Customer buying patterns and profiling

- Campaign performance management

- Market basket analysis

- Loyalty program analysis

Finance

Finance function in retail is similar to other industries and largely responsible for planning budgets and managing working capitals.

Finance also looks at reducing costs and improving efficiency. Governance and compliance are other aspects which fall under preview of finance. Finance also needs to manage operational risks and do the financial reporting.

Let us look at some of the KPIs and use cases:

KPIs

- Profit and loss analysis across channels, products, geography, and time (understand profitability across various parameters)

- Expense trends across channels, stores, and time (understand how expenses are happening across multiple dimensions)

- Account payable across merchants (understand the outstanding dues to merchants)

- Working capital report (key parameter to measure financial health of company)

- Risk, governance, and compliance reports (understand if organization is compliant in all aspects)

Use Cases

- Expense management/spend analytics

- Profitability management

- Budgeting and performance

- Forecasting and what-if analysis

- Risk management and compliance reports

- Working capital and cash flow management

IT/HR/Analytics

IT function in retail is similar to IT in other industry and largely responsible for running mission critical applications, such as ERP, CRM, point of sales, e-commerce portal, merchandising, and other related applications.

HR of retail too is similar to HR in other industry and looks after employee recruitment, payroll, workforce management, and training.

Analytics provides key insights to various departments and helps them to improve in decision making. Retail industry is dynamic and the analytics team needs to keep improving on the dashboards.

The KPIs and use cases which are looked at by IT/HR/reporting are:

KPIs

- SLA management report (Monitor service level agreements)

- Case analysis (open, pending, and priority) (KPI helps to understand support performance and important criteria as it impacts customer satisfaction)

- IT audit and compliance reports (understand compliance from various aspects)

- Analytics usage reports (Monitor adoption and usage of application)

- TCO analysis across projects (How much is spend to own and maintain projects)

- ROI analysis across projects (How much returns do i get from my investments on projects)

- IT expenses; budget versus actual (Monitor expenditure and compare with budgets)

- Workforce, payroll, and benefits analysis (important KPI for human resources)

- Attrition rate analysis (analyze the percentage of people leaving company)

- Training ROI (how useful are the trainings)

- Employee composition by age, gender, and tenure (helps to understand if balance is perfect)

- Cost per employee analysis (helps to understand manpower costs)

- Time to recruit analysis (how soon is a recruitment request getting satisfied)

Use Cases

- Workforce management

- Rewards management

- Payroll management

- IT governance, compliance, and audit mnagement

- SLA management

Merchandising

Sourcing, sometimes also referred to as merchandising and buying, is an area which encompasses buying products from vendor/supplier/manufacturer and then selling. Merchandising also includes displaying of products in an effective way, making it attractive for the customers and promoting buying.

The sourcing strategy is an important area. How much to buy and when to buy are some of the factors which influence the negotiations. The customers' interests and demands also influence the sourcing in a big way.

The aim of merchandising is to improve margins, thereby increasing profitability. Product pricing across channels is another area which needs to be looked at. Let us look at some of the KPIs and use cases:

KPIs

- Merchant/Vendor performance (Understanding how each vendor is performing. Useful to rate vendor and negotiate rate contracts)
- Historical buying trends
- SKU (Stock keeping unit)wise performance analysis (which products are doing well and which arent)
- Revenue analysis over time/brand/channel (performance analysis across various dimensions)
- Forecasting and what-if analysis (Understand impact of price revisions via what-if and forecasting helps keep stake holders updated on future performance estimates)

Use Cases

- SKU detail analysis
- Merchandising buying effectiveness
- Discount analysis
- Vendor/Manufacturer performance
- Margin across products/brands
- Assortment planning
- Category analysis
- Increasing shopping basket size

Supply Chain Management

Supply chain management (SCM) is about buying the products from the merchant/vendor and making it available across the different channels, thereby enabling customers to buy.

The aim is at improving the efficiency of supply chain. Logistics and transportation also have costs associated and SCM looks at ways and means to reduce this cost.

Inventory is an important area in supply chain. How much inventory to keep can be tricky. Having less inventory may make the product unavailable in event of large purchases. Excess inventory can lead to losses if the product has limited shelf life or if it becomes out of fashion. Some of the KPIs and use cases which matter are mentioned as follows:

KPIs

- Procurement trends across time, geography, and vendors (how does our procurement look like, are we buying the same item at same or different prices. How does procurement vary across vendors)

- Discount trends across categories, vendors, and time (Discount analysis can help to come out with good pricing strategy)

- Vendor performance analysis (can be used to segment vendors and arrive at preferred vendor list)

- Inventory turns and analysis (analyze are we overstocking or understocking)

- Forecasting and demand planning (important KPI to plan for future manufacturing)

- Variance in Forecast versus actual sales (helps to understand and plan better forecasts)

- Logistical analysis (all analysis with respect to logistics)

- Returns across categories/vendors (helps to understand why customers are returning products and is it across all categories or does buying from a vendor causing more returns)

- Delivery time analysis (important as it impact customer satisfaction)

Use Cases

- Inventory management

- Procurement management

- Vendor performance management

- Forecasting and demand planning

- Warranty and returns management

- Logistical expense management

- Product availability across stores/channels

Summary

This chapter is intended to make readers aware of few domains. The intention is not to make the reader domain expert but enable him/her to converse easily with the business users and understand terminologies and KPIs which are needed by specific industries.

In this chapter, we looked at how the insurance industry works and different entities which insurance works with. We looked at frequently used terms in the insurance industry and also went through the different functions/departments the insurance industry has. We also looked at the KPIs and few use cases.

Like insurance industry, we looked at the pharmaceutical industry. The chapter took you through entities, frequently used terminologies, and the functioning of the various departments, along with KPIs and use cases. A similar exercise was performed for the retail industry as well.

In the next chapter, which will be the last chapter, we will look at implementing the concepts learned in this book. The chapter will simulate a real world example and take you through the approach, and you will also learn how to build a Qlik Sense application for the use case.

11
A Real Life Case-Study

In the previous chapter, we got familiar with certain industry domains. We had a look at insurance, pharmaceuticals, and retail domains. The chapter took us through the business processes and the terminologies used by business users, and we looked at the KPIs used by these domains.

This is the final chapter of the book; we will look at a real life scenario and try to implement the learnings from the preceding chapters. The chapter will look at a manufacturing company and its business scenario. We will look at the expectations of the business users and the KPIs which matter to them.

The chapter will then proceed to go through the actual process of how to implement the requirements, including data modelling, development, and visualizations. We will also look at validation, UAT, and go-live.

The chapter will cover the following topics:

- Introduction to Adventure Works Cycles
- Preparation
- Understanding the existing system and landscape
- Understanding the business challenges
- Defining approach and solution
- Execution
- Post Go-live steps

Let's get started!

Introduction to Adventure Works

Let us now see how we can put our learning in the previous chapters to use. For this, we need to look at a real life scenario. Let us look at a fictitious organization called **Adventure Works Cycles**, henceforth referred to to as **AWC**.

AWC has chosen Qlik Sense as their enterprise analytical platform. It is looking to implement Qlik Sense across its various departments. The different functions which want to take benefit from Qlik Sense are:

- Sales
- Finance
- Manufacturing
- Human resources

They want to implement Qlik Sense in phases and want to roll it out initially to the sales function and thereafter to the other functions.

AWC has awarded the implementation work to Jim, a Qlik Sense Consultant.

With this background, let us understand how Jim goes about the job of implementing Qlik Sense. Jim will be putting to use the concepts he learnt in the book.

> **Disclaimer:** The AWC is based on sample database provided by Microsoft and is freely available on the Microsoft site.

Preparation

At the start of the book, we studied the advantages of preparing for a project and trying to harness information whic

Studying AWC Website

Websites of companies have good amount of information, helping us understand their objectives, missions, goals, products, and services. Jim visited the website of AWC, and after studying the website, he made the following observations.

AWC is a large multi-national company, headquartered in United States of America. The company manufactures and sells metal and composite bicycles. The company has sales operations in multiple regions, as seen in the following figure:

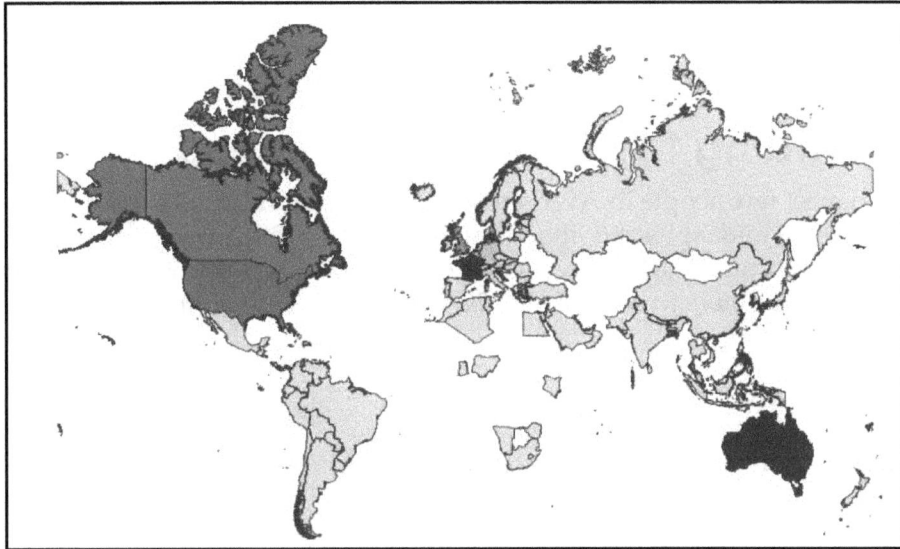

Sales region for Adventure Works Cycles

As seen in the previous figure, AWC has presence in the following countries:

- Australia
- Canada
- France
- Germany
- UK
- USA

AWC has the following offerings to cater to its market:

- Accessories
- Bikes
- Clothing
- Components

Jim also read various articles and interviews of senior management of AWC. He read the interview of CEO Mr. Ken Sanchez and got to know that AWC is planning to expand to lot of new countries. They have invested in technology knowing that technology is a big enabler for business.

Understanding the Business Process

Jim decided to meet few people in AWC and understand more about their business. Considering that the initial phase is about implementing BI (business intelligence) for sales, Jim decided to focus on sales operations. Jim got to know that AWC is both business to business (B2B) and business to consumer (B2C) organization. In simple terms, it sells to:

- Retails stores
- Directly to individuals

The customers or individuals can buy the products of AWC by:

- Visiting the retail stores
- Directly buying online via e-commerce portal

Though bulk of the orders come from retail stores, the company is looking at increasing the sales from online and e-commerce portal. His understanding after reading Mr. Ken Sanchez's interview got confirmed after speaking to few people of AWC about their expansion plans.

Getting to know Organization Hierarchy

Jim understands that for him to be successful, one of the things he must do is understand the people in the organization. During the meetings when he explored the business process, he spent time in knowing the organization. He could then prepare a chart, as follows:

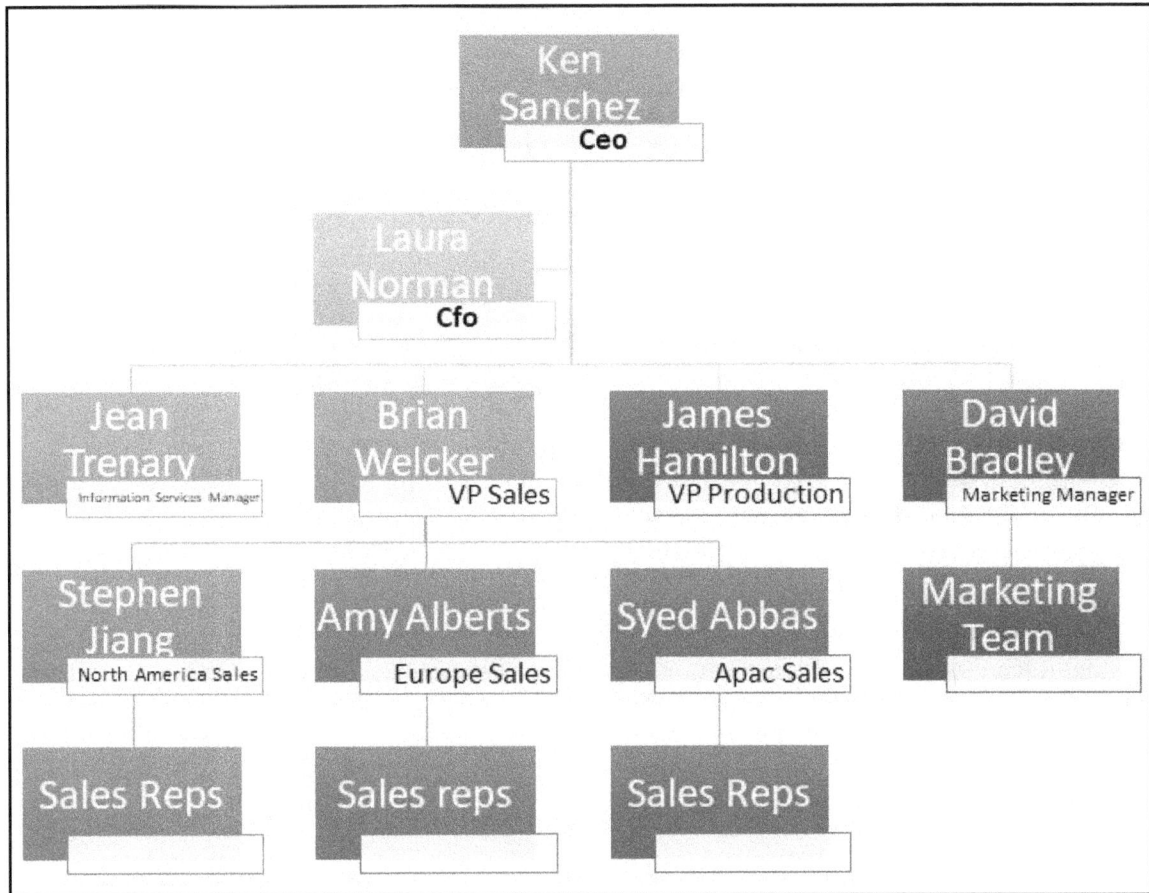

AWC organization hierarchy

As seen in the previous diagram, the executive team consists of CEO and CFO. The VP sales and the marketing manager report to the CEO.

The VP of sales, Mr. Brian Welcker, has three sales managers reporting to him. The three sales managers manage:

- North America (USA and Canada)

- Europe (France, Germany, UK)

- Pacific (Australia)

The three sales managers have several sales representatives reporting to them.

Identifying Business Champion

Jim has to figure out who would be the business champion for him in the initial phase. There are several people in the sales function. AWC is headquarterd in United States and Jim got to know that North America is the biggest market for AWC. All the senior management is based out of North America.

Jim got to know that VP of sales, Mr. Brian Welcker, had been a key person in the buying decision of Qlik Sense. Brian is an avid technology user and is looking at analytics to make strategic business decisions. Jim also understands that a project champion plays a crucial part in driving adoption, and if Brian is happy with Qlik Sense dashboard, he will spread the word in AWC and other departments will be more willing to adopt Qlik Sense. Jim now knows that Brian is the person who would be his business champion.

Jim needs someone from technology side to get all the information about the existing systems. He also needs to plan infrastructure needed to run Qlik Sense and other system requirements with technology stake-holder. Jean Trenary is the information services manager. Jean looks after all applications and IT infrastructure, and Jim would work closely with him.

Understanding the existing system and landscape

Before starting the project, Jim has to know the data sources on which he needs to work. He needs to know the existing landscape and what kind of analytics is being used. Jill sets up a meeting with Jean to understand the details. Based on the discussions with Jean, Jill makes the following observations.

AWC, as mentioned earlier, is both a B2B and a B2C company. It gets orders from retail stores or via the e-commerce portal. To cater to this scenario, AWC has good systems in place. The landscape can be seen in the following figure:

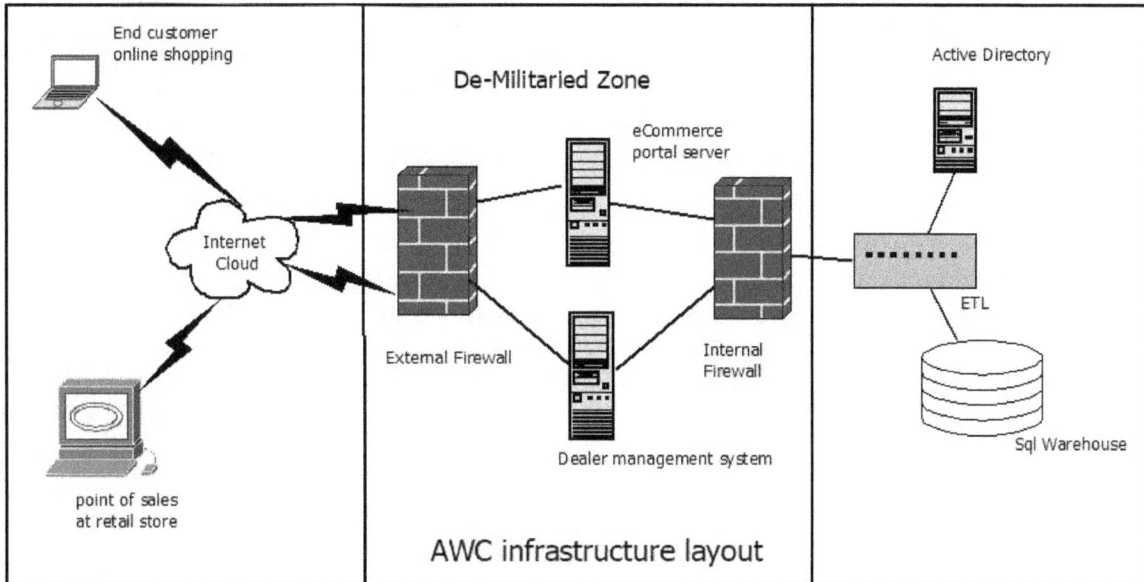

End customer
online shopping

De-Militaried Zone

eCommerce
portal server

Active Directory

Internet
Cloud

External Firewall

Internal
Firewall

ETL

Dealer management system

Sql Warehouse

point of sales
at retail store

AWC infrastructure layout

AWC Infrastructure network

As seen in the previous figure, AWC has Microsoft SQL as the centralized data warehouse to store the data. Present in the de-militarized zone are two applications, namely, the e-commerce website and the dealer management system.

The end customer can directly buy by visiting the e-commerce portal. The order placed will finally flow into the SQL server database after the ETL process. If customer visits a retail store and buys, the sales is captured via point of sales. The dealer management system allows retail stores to place bulk orders on AWC. The data from POS and DMS will finally flow into the SQL server database after the ETL process.

AWC does not use any BI software. The reporting is done via Excel. Jean has a team of two people, who on a periodic basis take export from the applications and thereafter prepare these reports manually. A lot of time is spent in getting these reports. Jean gets lot of ad-hoc report requirements from the users and he is very keen to have Qlik Sense implemented, as this will reduce the burden on his team.

Jim also discusses with Jean about tech savviness of the business users. He gets to know that there are different categories of users. Brian is good at technology, and in his earlier company was using analytical tool. CEO and CFO are traditional users and have been consuming Excel. They however love to use iPads and would be happy if they get Qlik Sense on their hand-helds. This information is useful to Jim for when he plans UAT with the business users. He needs to cater to all types of audience.

Understanding Business Challenges

Now that Jim has understood the way AWC operates, the next logical step is to understand the business challenges. Jim will be focusing on sales related challenges. The readers, as an exercise, can work on other areas, such as manufacturing or human resources.

Jim set up a meeting with the CEO to get an overview of the business challenges and the expectations from the BI system. The readers can refer to the conversation in *Chapter 2 (Preparing for the project)* on how to get the answers from stake-holders. Jim, based on his discussion with the CEO, makes the following observations.

The business users of AWC currently get few reports which come from the e-commerce portal and dealer management systems. They are unable to get a single consolidated view. To get that, there is lot of manual intervention needed, where few MIS (management information system) personnel extract data from both systems in Excel and manually prepare the reports.

The challenges faced by the business users are numerous; few of them are mentioned as follows:

- No real time visibility to the data (manual reports take two to three weeks)
- Manually created reports do not show clear trends
- There is no easy way to slice and dice data
- There is no flexibility to analyze events (for example, why did sales decline in the month of May)
- Sales heads wants easy way to find out opportunities to up-sell and cross-sell
- It's difficult to compare quota versus actual at different dimensions
- It's difficult to find top N customers, product categories, product sub-categories, regions, stores, and sales person

The CEO advised Jim to get the detailed business requirements from Brian.

Gathering Business Requirements

Jim now needs to get the actual business requirements, which will help him develop the Qlik Sense application. Since Brian heads the sales and also happens to be the champion, Jim needs to meet Brian and get all the business requirements from him. For the meeting, Brian gets along his colleagues heading sales of North America, Europe, and Apac.

Based on the earlier findings, Jim knows that lot of business users are traditional and haven't been exposed to the BI system. Jim proposes showing a quick demo to the business users. The demo can help them know the capabilities of Qlik Sense and make them aware of what are the different possibilities with Qlik Sense. A demo application relating to their industry will help Jim to get requirements in a crisp manner. Jim shows the demo app from Qlik website (`https://demos.qlik.com/qliksense/ConsumerGoodsSales`). A screenshot is shown next:

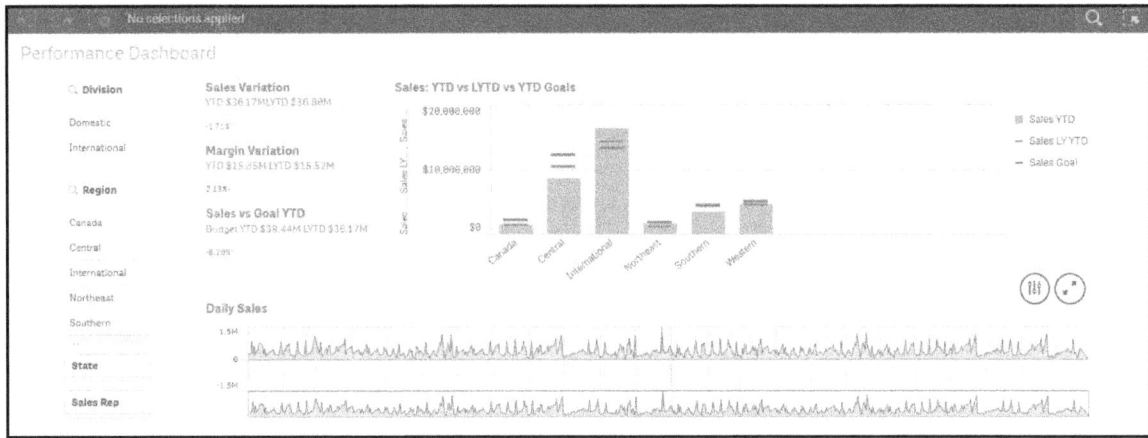

Sales performance application

The demo can encompass the useful KPIs, the way users can do their analysis, do slice and dice of data and how they use qlik to make better business decisions. Based on the discussions with Brian, Jim gets to know the need for the following KPIs:

- Omni-channel dashboard with sales comparison
- Comparison of quota achievements for different time periods (month, quarter, and year)
- Comparison of revenue with the previous year's, for the same period (current month versus same month previous year, current quarter versus same quarter previous year, and current year versus last year)
- Month on month sales trends
- Year on year sales trends
- Ability to monitor all the preceding KPIs with multiple parameters, such as country, product, product category, salesrep, and reseller
- Salesrep performance over time

- Identification of top and bottom performing products, resellers, and salesreps
- Ability to identify cross-sell and up-sell opportunities

Following are some other requirements that came out from the discussion:

- Application should be accessible over internet
- Every morning, the users should see fresh data
- Application should have data level security and allow the users to see only their and their sub-ordinate's data
- Mobility is an important requirement, considering frequent travel of sales people
- Governance should be maintained for self-service

Jim also wanted to understand the success criteria from Brian. Based on the inputs from him, Jim knows he has to take care of the following points:

- Fast performance
- Ability to see performance of both channels in a single view
- Data should be correct till two decimals
- Ease of use and ability for the end users to create their own visualizations
- Ability to get actionable insights
- Timely delivery of the application
- Good adoption amongst the users

Jim suggested some value-adds, which were accepted by Brian, but most of them were to be done in a subsequent phase. The value-adds were as follows:

- Bringing in demographic and economic data, which would help AWC to plan setting up operations in newer regions
- Bringing in data from social media to understand customer sentiments
- Usage of advanced maps to get deeper insights
- Extending analytics to resellers
- Reseller categorization into categories like platinum, gold, and silver
- Analyzing the impact of training on salesrep and replicating successful trainings
- Adding market potential as factor to analyze performance

Jim is all set to start his work now. However, before jumping to development, he has to look at what approach and architecture to follow.

Defining approach and solution architecture

For Jim to define the solution and the data architecture, he needs access to the database system. He approaches Jean Trenary for getting access to the data warehouse and gets the access.

Once Jim gets the access to the system, he starts exploring every table related to sales available in the warehouse. This helps him to understand the nature of the data stored in the table and how it is linked to other tables in the warehouse.

He lists the dimensions and fact tables in the data warehouse which he would need to cater to all the sales related requirements.

Dimension tables are as follows:

Table Name	Description
DimCustomer	This table stores all customer related data. The customer data is captured only for the online channel. It stores the demographic information, like FirstName, MiddleName, LastName, Birthdate, and Gender. The primary key in this table is *CustomerKey*.
DimDate	This table stores calendar data. It stores the date, month, year, week, fiscal year, fiscal quarter, fiscal semester, and so on. The primary key in this table is *DateKey*.
DimDepartmentGroup	This table contains the name of the department. The primary key in this table is *DepartmentGroupKey*.
DimEmployee	This table stores employee data. It stores the employees' demographic information, like FirstName, LastName, Birthdate, and Gender. Along with that, it also stores the employees' leave count, department name, territoryid, and so on. The employee is responsible for taking orders from the reseller. The primary key in this table is *EmployeeKey*.
DimReseller	Reseller data is captured in this table. The table contains details like Name, BusinessType, Address, Yearopened, numbers of employee they have, and so on. The primary key in this table is *ResellerKey*.

DimGeography	This table contains geographical information, like city, region, state province, and country. The primary key in this table is *GeographyKey*. It also has a foreign key, that is *SalesTerritoryKey*.
DimProduct	This table contains product related information, like name, color, size, class, style, model name, weight, list price, and dealer price. The primary key in this table is *ProductKey*. The foreign key in this table is *ProductSubCategoryKey*.
DimProductCategory	This table contains name of the product category. The primary key in this table is *ProductCategoryKey*.
DimProductSubCategory	This table contains a product's sub-category name. The primary key in this table is *ProductSubCategoryKey*. The foreign key in this table is *ProductCategoryKey*.
DimSalesTerritory	This table contains sales territory data, like region, country, and group. The primary key in this table is *SalesTerritoryKey*.

Fact tables are as follows:

Table Name	Description
FactSalesQuota	This table contains sales quota. The sales quota is available at month and employee level. It is available only for the Reseller Channel. The primary key in this table is *SalesQuotaKey*. The foreign keys in this table are *EmployeeKey* and *DateKey*.
FactResellerSales	This table stores transactional data. It stores the sales from the reseller channel. It stores information to link to different dimension table. Along with that, it also contains unit price, order quantity, sales amount, tax amount, freight, order date, ship date, and due date. It doesn't have a primary key, but has the following foreign keys: ProductKey, OrderDateKey, DueDateKey, ShipDateKey, ResellerKey, EmployeeKey, and SalesTerritoryKey.

FactInternetSales	This table stores transactional data. It stores the sales from the online channel. It stores necessary information to link to different dimension table. Along with that, it also contains unit price, order quantity, sales amount, tax amount, freight, order date, ship date, and due date. It doesn't have a primary key, but has the following foreign keys: ProductKey, OrderDateKey, DueDateKey, ShipDateKey, and SalesTerritoryKey.

As per the understanding of data structure, Jim prepares the following data architecture for sales application:

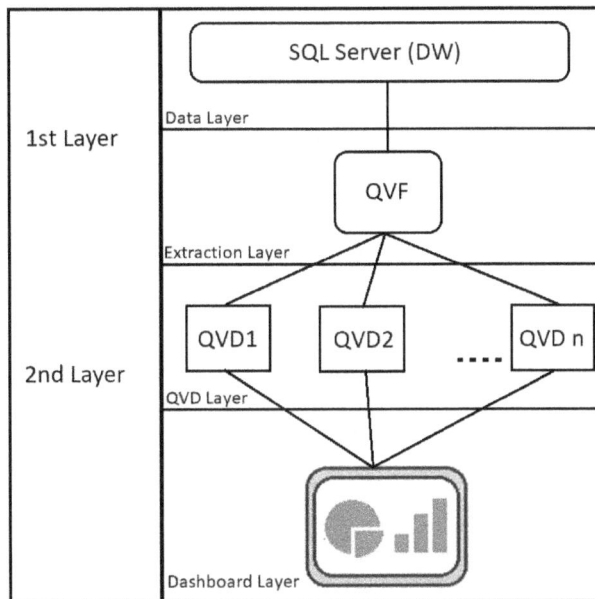

For Jim, the approach is to create a single application for extraction and transformation. This approach works well as it is easy to manage than creating multiple extraction applications to fetch the data. This approach has another advantage in such scenario where data is limited and the data refresh requirements are not frequent.

The need initially is for one application. The application should also have transactional detail. In this scenario, it is not necessary to have an aggregation layer and hence 2-layer data architecture is more suitable.

Jim now works on a good data model, and following best practices, he creates a data model based on star schema for better performance. The model is shown diagrammatically as follows:

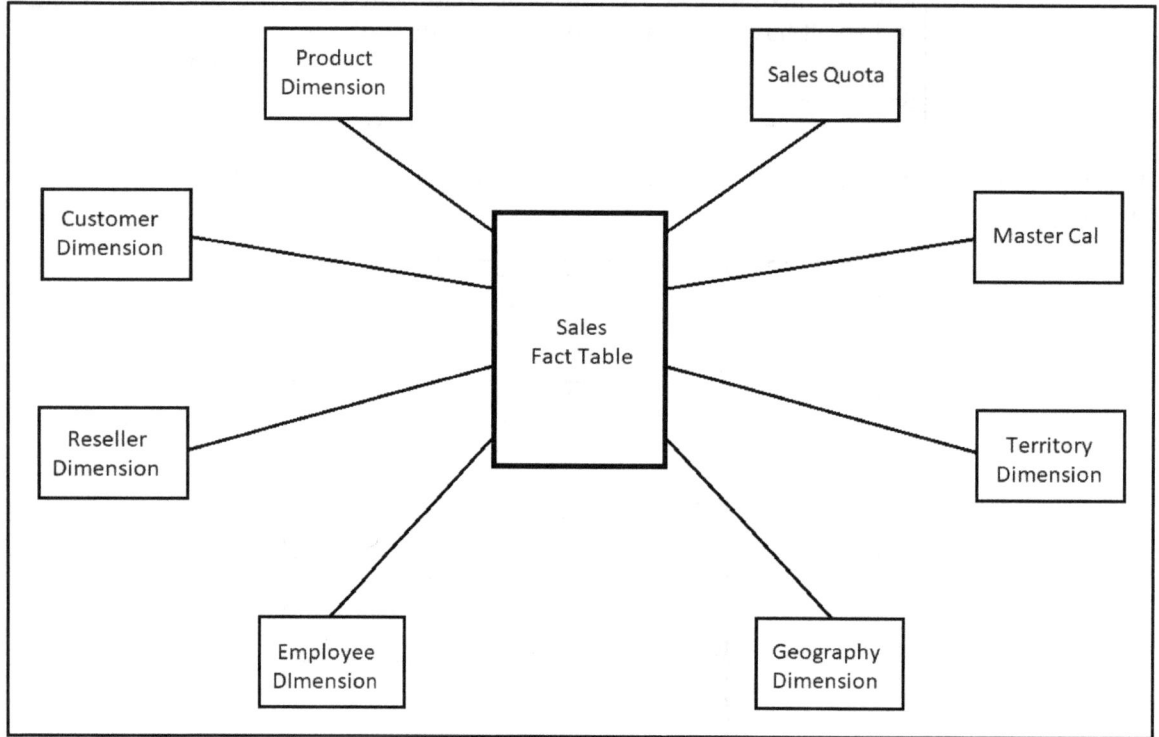

Star schema data model

Execution of project

Now that Jim has frozen the data architecture and best fit data model, he can start the development work. He decides to start with the extraction process. (For this example, we will fetch the data from data warehouse available in Microsoft Access database.)

Extraction

First thing that Jim needs to do is to create a connection to the database. Microsoft Access database can be accessible to Qlik Sense via an ODBC driver, so he will have to create an ODBC connection to connect to the Access database.

Let us see the steps used by Jim to create an ODBC connection to the data source:

1. Open the ODBC data source wizard.

You need to go to Control Panel | Administrative Tools | ODBC Data Source (32 Bit).

Once you click on that, the following window will open:

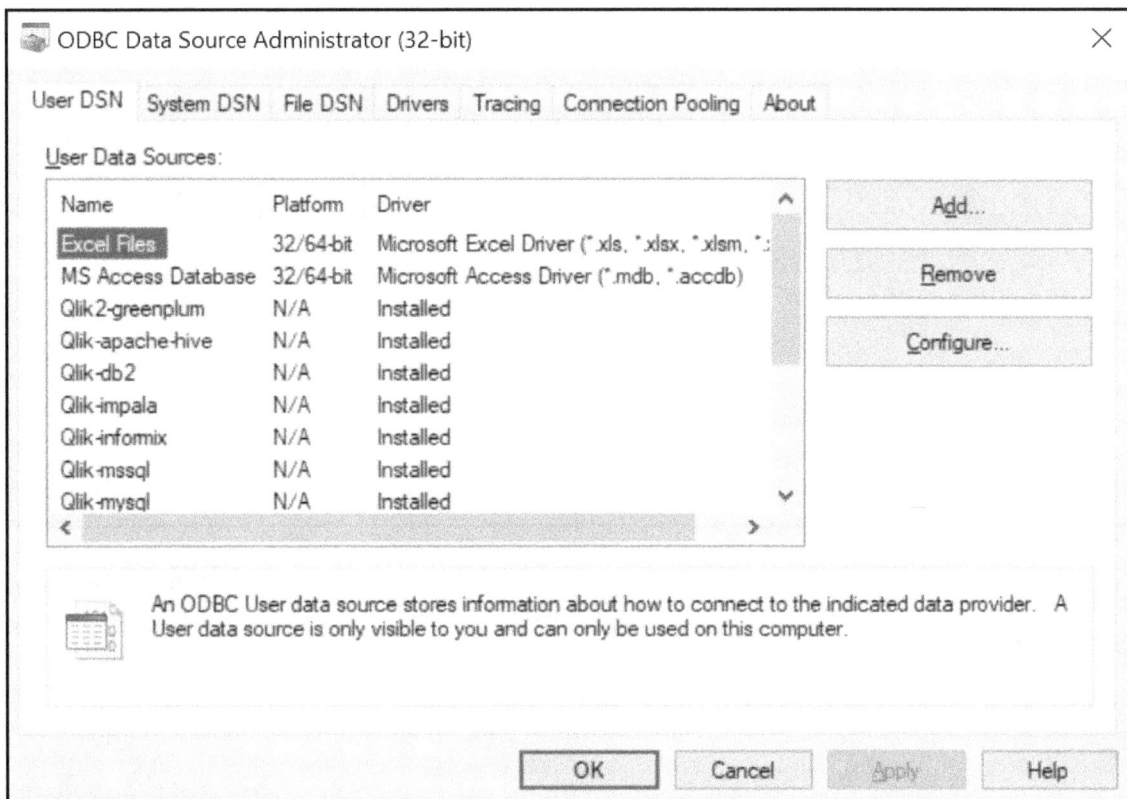

2. Click on **Add** to create a new DSN (Deep Space Name). Once you do that, the following window will open:

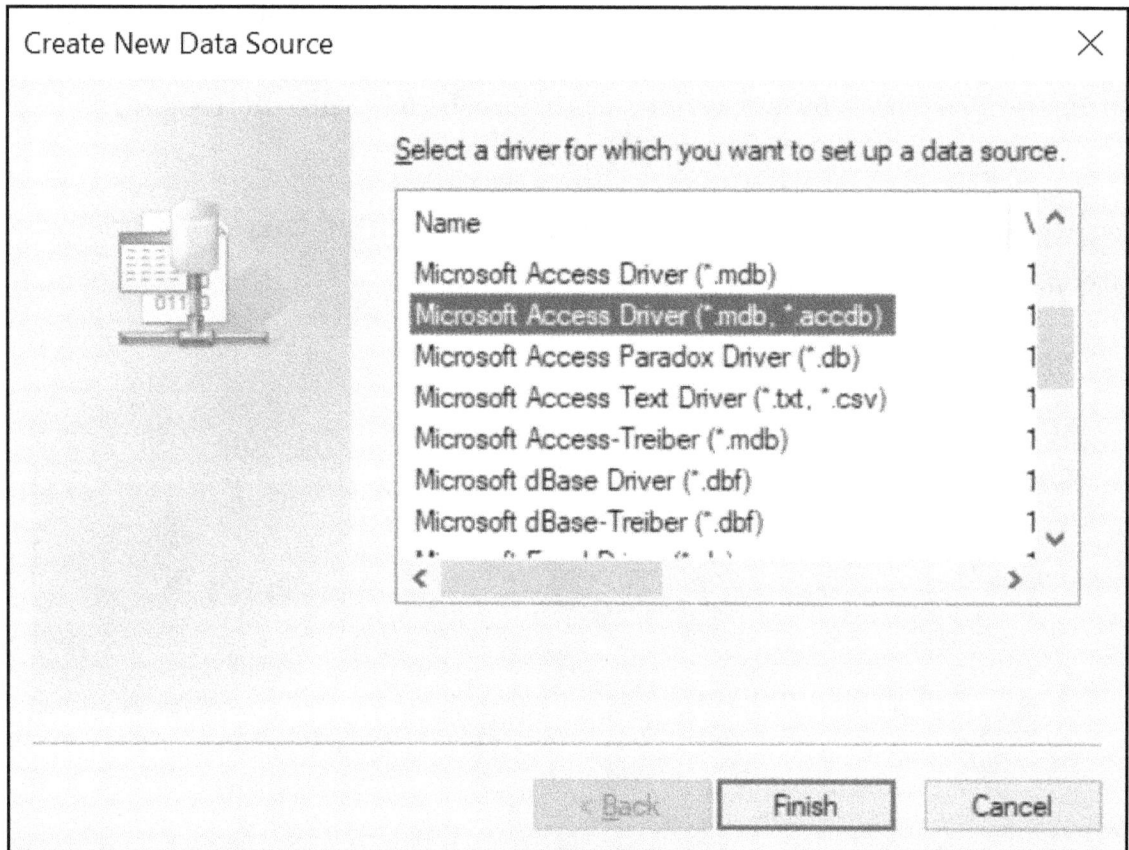

You will be asked to choose the driver which you want to use to connect to your database. In our case, we choose the drive which is **Microsoft Access Driver (*.mdb, *.accdb)** , as shown in the previous screenshot.

3. Once you select the driver and click on **Finish**, a new window, **ODBC Microsoft Access Setup**, will open. Here you need to give a name to your connection. We have given the name as **AdventureWorks**. You can also give the description of your data source. Then you need to select the Access file. To do this, you need to click on the **Select** option, as shown in the following screenshot:

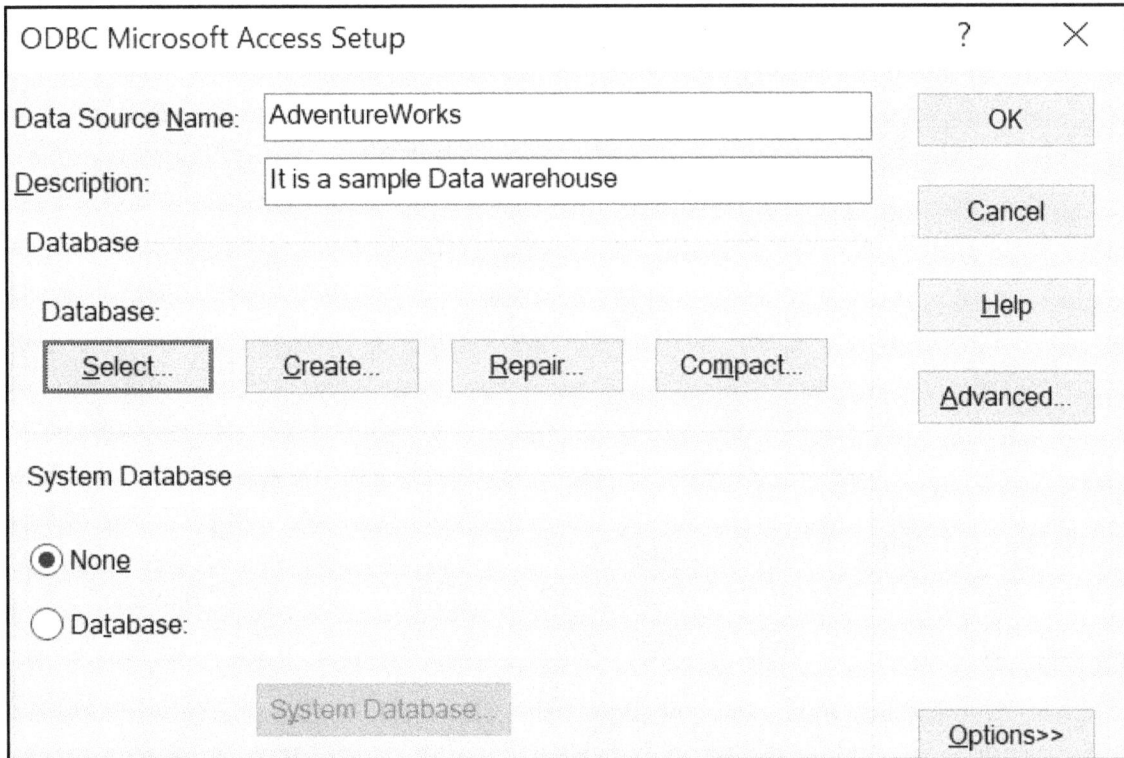

4. After clicking on the Select button, you will be taken to a window where you will have to locate the Access file stored on your machine. Following image shows you the same, where we have located the Access file from `C:/Qlik Sense/Chapter 11`:

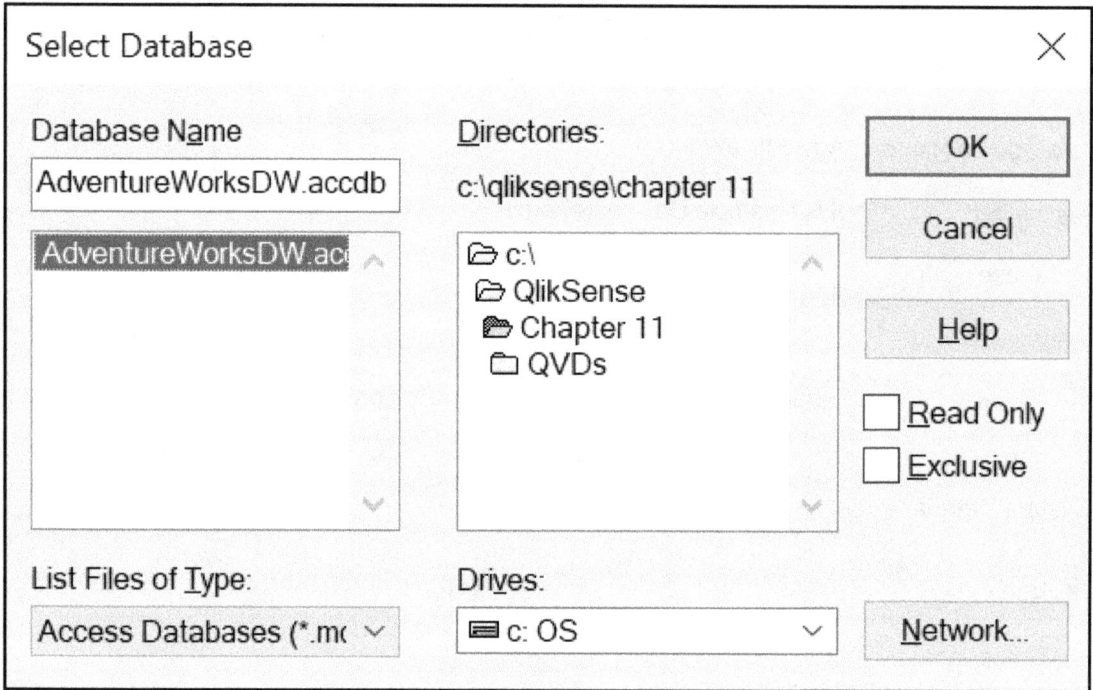

5. After locating the file, you need to click on the **Ok** button to select the database.
6. Then click on the **Ok** button to create a new connection. Once the data source is created, you will see a new entry under **User DSN**, as shown in the following image:

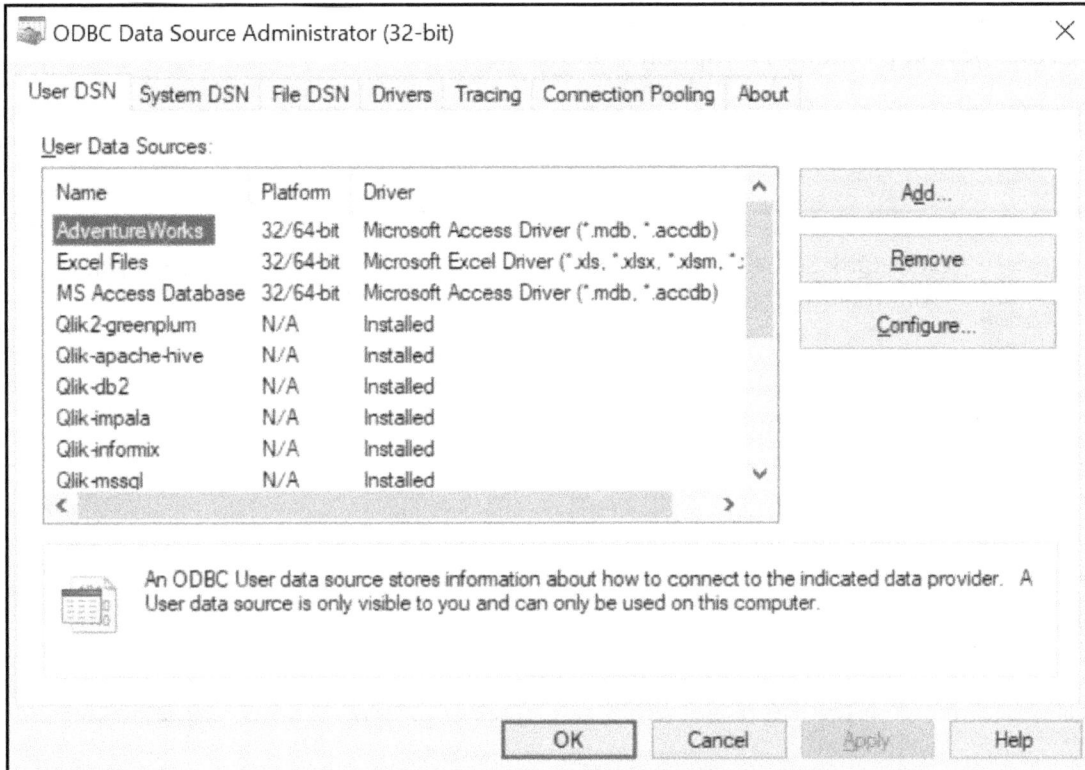

If you do not have Microsoft Access installed, or if you are unable to see the Microsoft Access driver, the same can be downloaded from `https://www.microsoft.com/en-us/download/details.aspx?id=54920`.

Extraction in our example

Now that Jim is ready with the database connection, he can start with the extraction process.

To extract the data tables from the data source, we will start creating the new Qlik Sense application. For this, you need to open **Qlik Sense Desktop**.

The example will work best with Qlik Sense June 2017 or above.

Once Qlik Sense Desktop is open, you can create a new application by clicking on the **Create new app** button. The option is shown next:

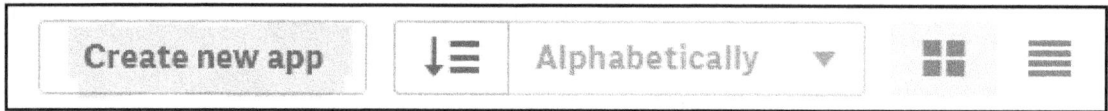

Once Qlik Sense Desktop has opened, you can also access all the options from the browser through `http://localhost:4848/hub`

We can see how Qlik Sense hub can be opened from the following screen shot.

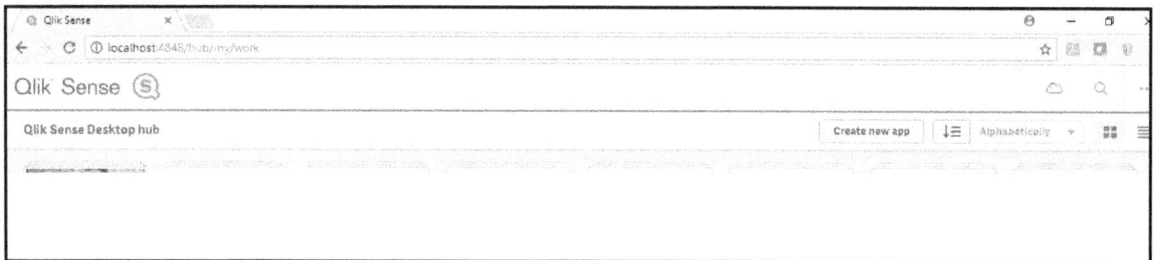

Accessing Qlik Sense Desktop from browser

Give a name to your application and click on the **Create** button. The new application will be created, which can be seen in the hub.

Then click on **Open app** to open the application. You will be given two opens: one, **Add data from files and other sources-**this option will allow you to load data using the drag and drop options, and second, **Script Editor**, namely using manual scripting.

Click on **Script Editor** to open the script window to start writing the script.

First thing to do is to connect to the data source using the ODBC connection created in the previous section. To do this, click on **Create new connection**:

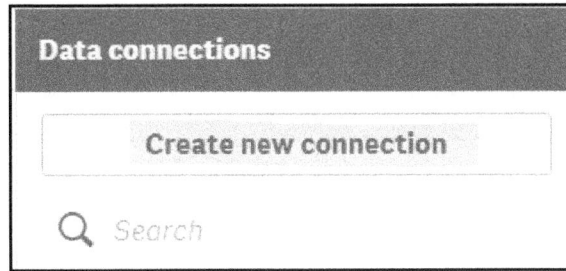

Once you click on **Create new connection**, you will be asked to select the driver using which you want to create the new connection:

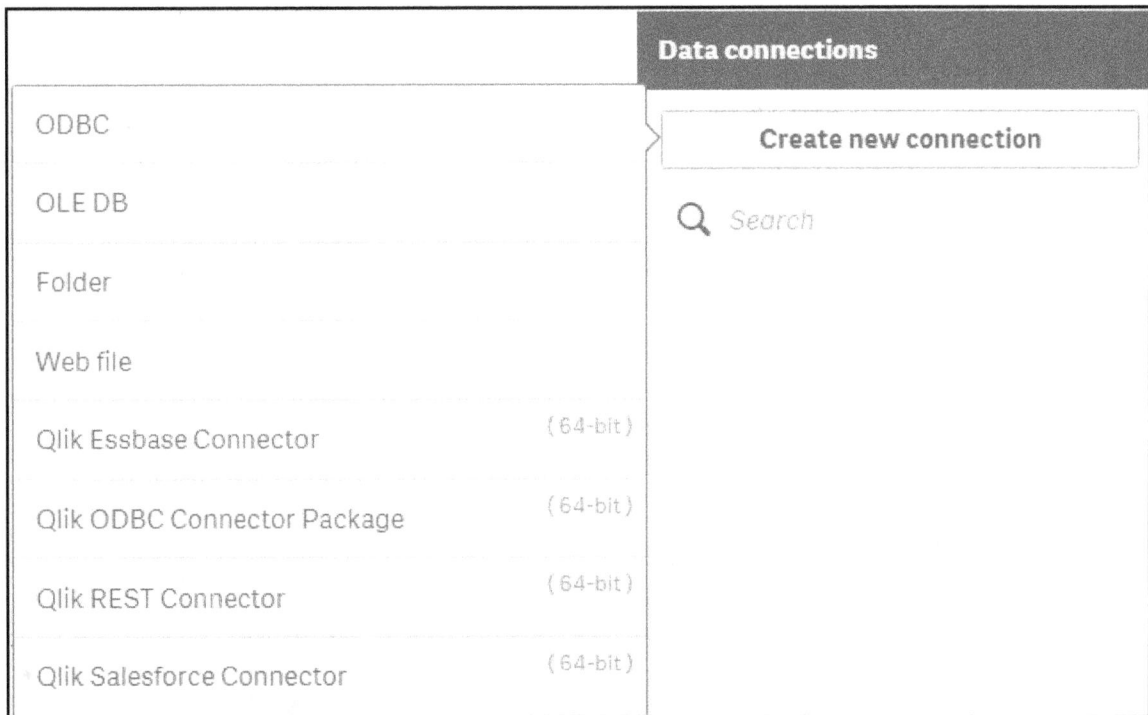

	Data connections
ODBC	Create new connection
OLE DB	Q Search
Folder	
Web file	
Qlik Essbase Connector (64-bit)	
Qlik ODBC Connector Package (64-bit)	
Qlik REST Connector (64-bit)	
Qlik Salesforce Connector (64-bit)	

In our example, we are going to use ODBC, so you need to click on **ODBC**. Once you do that, it will open a window where you will be shown the available DSN connections, as shown in the following screenshot:

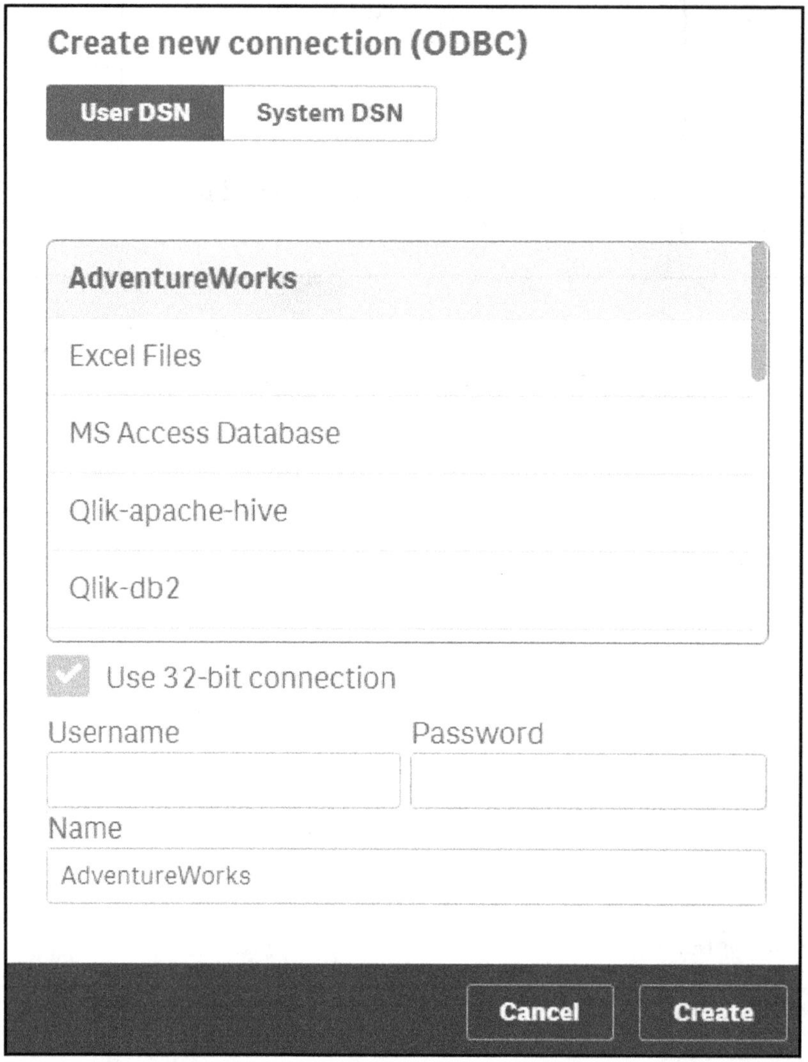

Create new connection (ODBC)

| **User DSN** | **System DSN** |

AdventureWorks

Excel Files

MS Access Database

Qlik-apache-hive

Qlik-db2

☑ Use 32-bit connection

Username

Password

Name

AdventureWorks

Cancel   Create

In the previous section, we had created **User DSN**, thus we will click on **User DSN**. Once you click on that, you will see the **AdventureWorks** DSN that we had created. Click on **AdventureWorks** and check the box **Use 32-bit connection**; this is because we had created DSN using 32-bit configuration. Give a name to the connection and click on the **Create** button.

> We are not giving any username and password, because our data source doesn't require that. However, when you connect to other data sources, like Oracle, MySQL, SQL Server, and so on, you need to enter a user name and password to create a successful connection.

Once the connection is created, you will see it under **Data Connection** on the right hand side, as shown in the following screenshot:

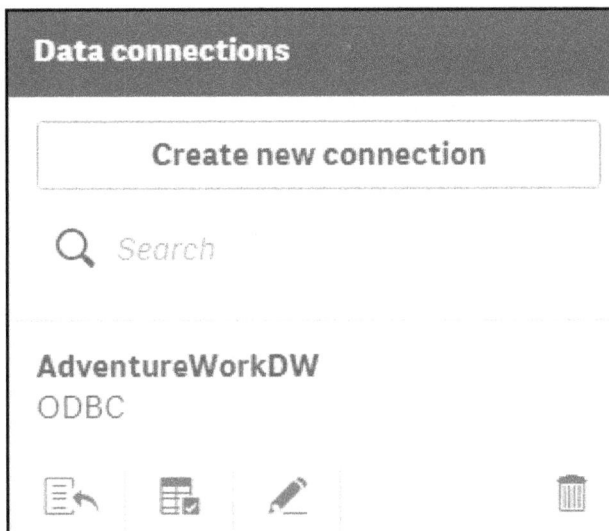

This connection was to connect to the data source, but we would need one more connection to connect to folder for storing the QVD files.

To do this, you again click on **Create new connection** and then click on the **Folder** option. It will ask you to give the path of the folder where you want to create a connection and a name to the connection. You should give such a name that you can easily identify the use of that connection. Let's assume we give a name to the connection called **QVDs**.

Now that we are ready with every connection, let us start writing the code.

We will start by entering the connection string of the data source which we had just created, namely, **AdventureWorkDW**. To do this, click on the first option, **Insert Connection String available**, under the connection name on the right hand panel, as shown in the following screenshot:

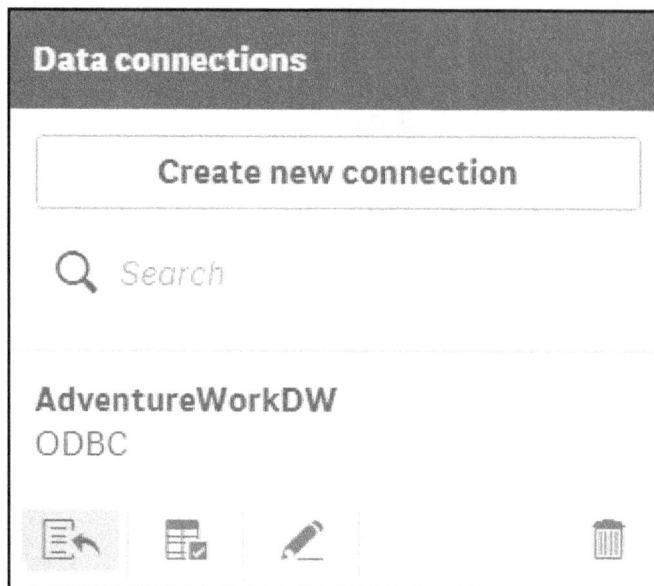

Once you click on that, you will see the following auto generated script line on the scripting window:

```
LIB CONNECT TO 'AdventureWorkDW'
```

Now there are couple of ways through which you can fetch the data: one is using separate script for each of the tables, and second is using **For Loop** to extract all the tables. In our example, we will use the second option to load the tables in one go; we will use **For Loop**.

To run **For Loop**, you need to know the number of tables that need to be extracted from the data source. For this, we will create a temporary table which will have the list of the tables which need to be extracted.

We will start by creating a separate tab to write this code and we will name this tab **Load Table List**. The script is shown in the following image:

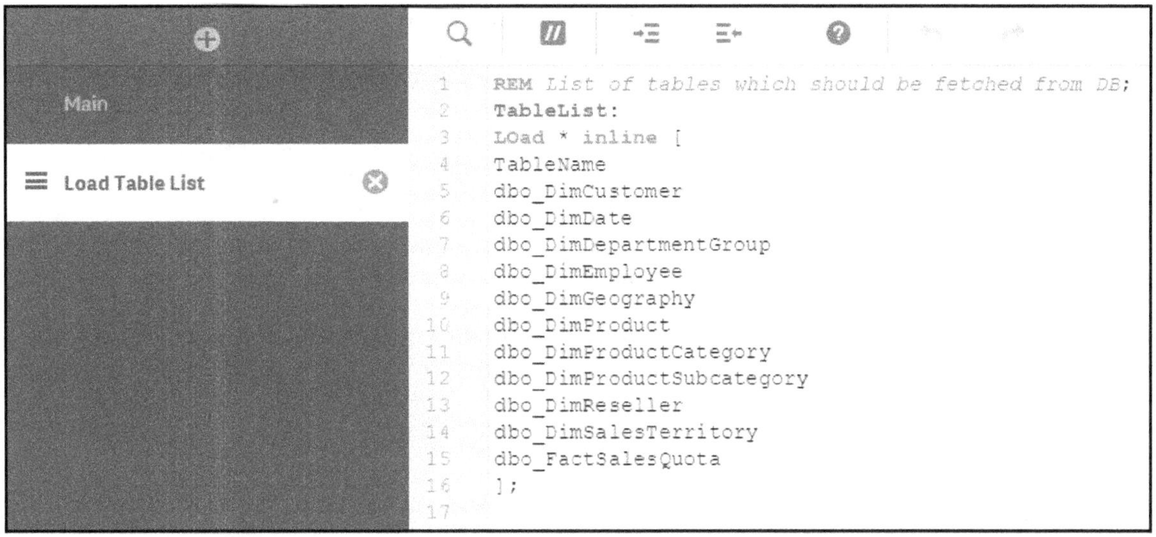

```
1    REM List of tables which should be fetched from DB;
2    TableList:
3    LOad * inline [
4    TableName
5    dbo_DimCustomer
6    dbo_DimDate
7    dbo_DimDepartmentGroup
8    dbo_DimEmployee
9    dbo_DimGeography
10   dbo_DimProduct
11   dbo_DimProductCategory
12   dbo_DimProductSubcategory
13   dbo_DimReseller
14   dbo_DimSalesTerritory
15   dbo_FactSalesQuota
16   ];
17
```

You can see in the preceding script that we have created an inline table that has the list of tables which need to be extracted. One thing to note here is that we have not listed the transaction table names, that is, fact tables, because those tables should be loaded using the incremental load, which we will see later.

The script to load this table is shown in the following image:

```
1    Let vCount = NoOfRows('TableList'); //Find the numbers of tables
2
3    For i=0 to $(vCount)-1  // For loop to load each table
4
5    Let vTableName = peek('TableName',$(i),'TableList');  // Peek each table name from the TableList table
6                                                          // and store in variable
7
8    $(vTableName):
9
10   Sql Select * from $(vTableName);
11
12   Store $(vTableName) into [LIB://QVDs/Layer 1/$(vTableName).qvd];
13
14   Drop table $(vTableName);
15
16   Next
17
18
```

You can see in the preceding image that we started with finding the number of tables that need to be extracted from the data source using the NoOfRows() function and stored that value in a variable, so that we can use that in for loop.

Then we started with `For Loop`, one thing to note here is that we started loop from 0 to minus 1. This is because the table stores the data from index 0, so when we fetch individual table name using the `peek` function, we can refer to the correct value of the table.

Then within for loop, we used the SQL command to extract the table, and then used the `Store` statement to store the extracted table in the QVD.

Later, we dropped the table, because the purpose of this application is to extract the data and store in QVD and not to keep the extracted data in this application.

Now let us see the script for incremental load. In our example, we have used two fact tables, namely `FactInternetSales` and `FactResellerSales`.

Following image shows the first part of the incremental script:

You can see in preceding screenshot that we started with listing the required fact tables in temporary table and used `for` loop to run the script for each table.

Here, we will first find if the QVD is created or not; if it is not created, then full data should be extracted for the table, else incremental load logic should be applied. For this, we have used the function `QvdCreateTime()`, to know the created datetime of the QVD. If it doesn't exist, then it will return Null() value. Using the `IF` statement, we define which scripts to run when QVD exists and when it does not.

If you look at the script, we have created `%SalesKey` in the preceding load. This is to make a primary key in the table so that we can use it in incremental load.

Following screenshot shows the second part of the script, which takes care of incremental load:

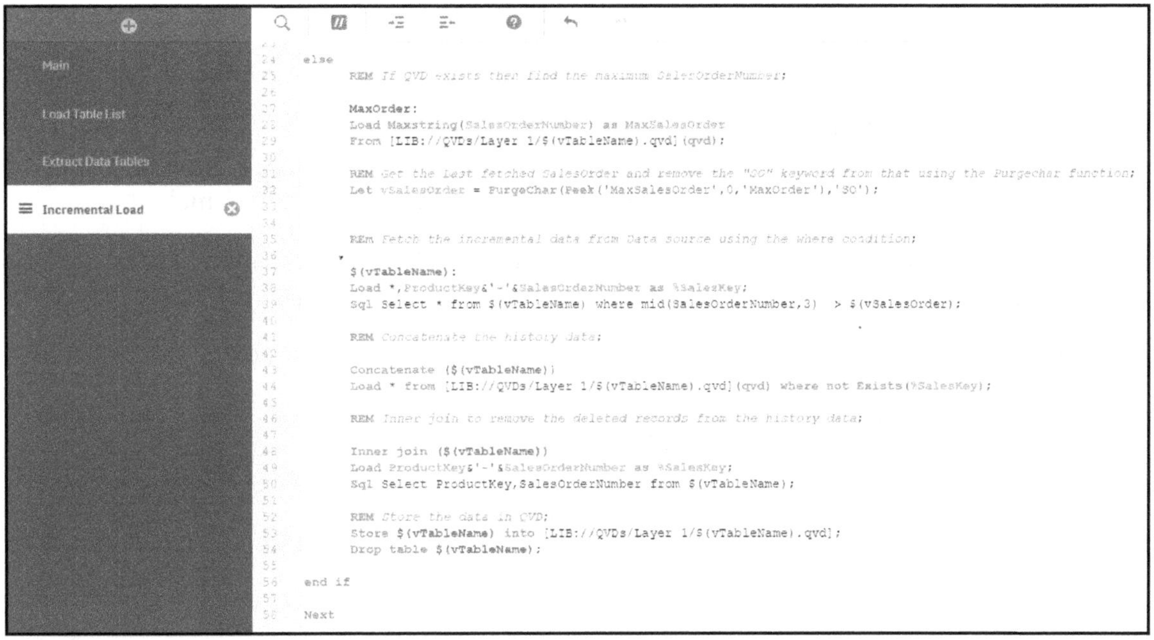

The script in the preceding screenshot shows incremental load in the else part of the IF statement.

If you look at the script, we started by finding the last fetched sales order from the QVD data and stored the same in variable. While storing in the variable, we removed the text part of the sales order by using the `purgechar()` function.

Then we fetched the incremental data from the table using the where condition in the SQL script and concatenated the same with the existing QVD with the `Exists()` function. This would take care of the insert and update of the data in the QVD. To remove the deleted data from QVD, we used the inner join condition, as shown in the preceding image.

At the end, we stored the data in the QVD and dropped the table.

This ends the extraction of all the required tables from the data source. Now we will see how to create a data model using this QVD and creating a dashboard on top of it.

Data modeling

To do this, we will create another Qlik Sense application in the same way we created application for data extraction. Let us say we name it `AdventureWorkDashboard`.

Once the application is created, open `Data Load Editor` to start scripting.

Because we are using desktop version for this example, we will have to create a new folder connection to connect to the QVD folder created in the previous section. Follow the same steps we discussed. You may also give the same name to the connection, namely `QVDs`.

Let us start with adding script to fetch data from each QVD that was created in the extraction process.

Click on the `Select Data` button from `Data Connection`, as shown next:

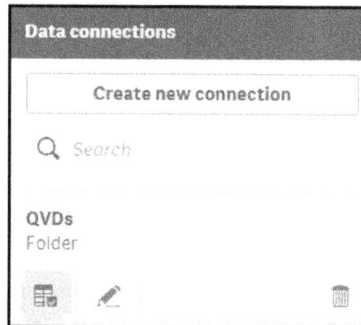

Let us start with adding all the dimension tables, and then we will add the fact tables. To start with, let us add `Customer Table`, as shown in the following screenshot:

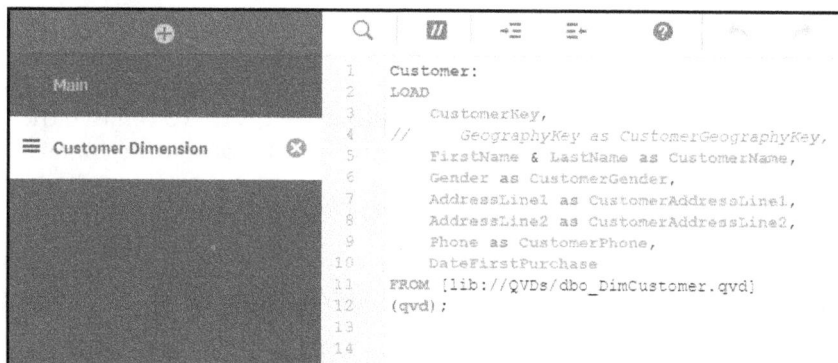

You can see that we have loaded all the fields except `GeographyKey`. This is because we don't want to show the geographical information of the customer.

Similarly, we add another table, `Reseller Table`, as shown in the following screenshot:

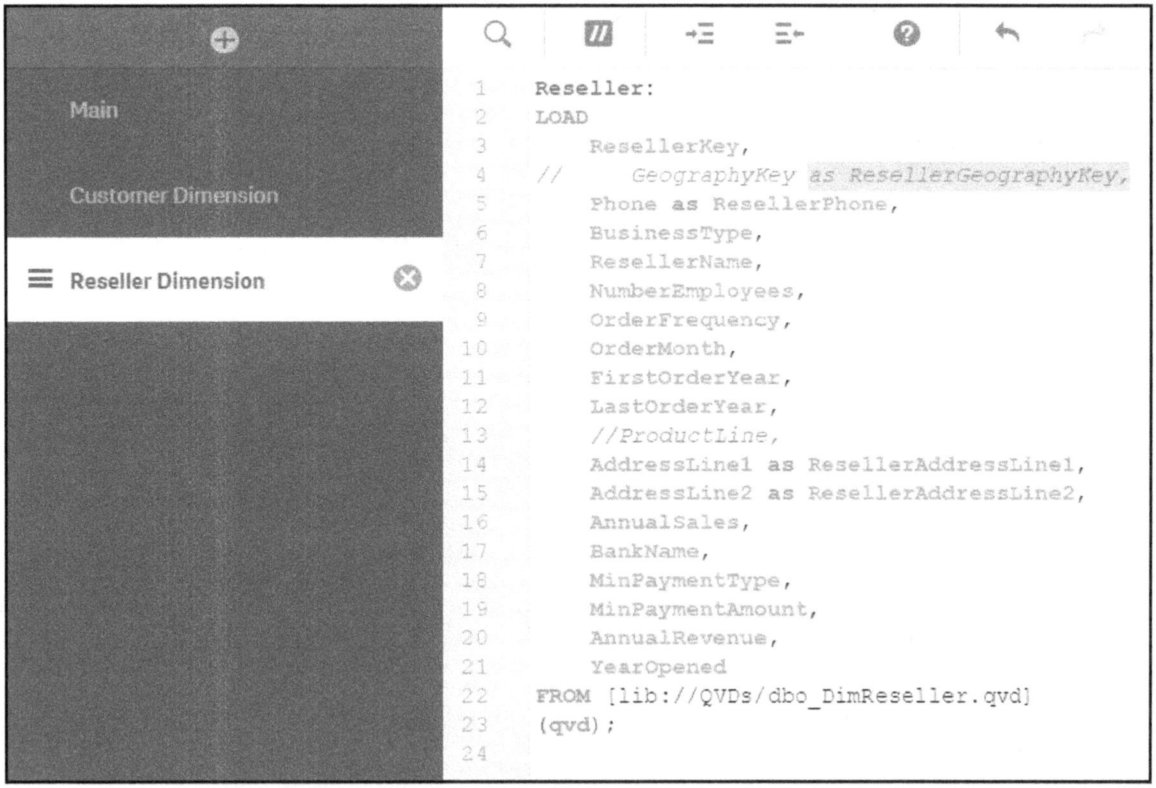

```
 1   Reseller:
 2   LOAD
 3       ResellerKey,
 4   //      GeographyKey as ResellerGeographyKey,
 5       Phone as ResellerPhone,
 6       BusinessType,
 7       ResellerName,
 8       NumberEmployees,
 9       OrderFrequency,
10       OrderMonth,
11       FirstOrderYear,
12       LastOrderYear,
13       //ProductLine,
14       AddressLine1 as ResellerAddressLine1,
15       AddressLine2 as ResellerAddressLine2,
16       AnnualSales,
17       BankName,
18       MinPaymentType,
19       MinPaymentAmount,
20       AnnualRevenue,
21       YearOpened
22   FROM [lib://QVDs/dbo_DimReseller.qvd]
23   (qvd) ;
24
```

In Reseller table also, we have commented the `GeographyKey` field.

Now we will load `Employee Table`. The script is as follows:

```
1   Employee:
2   LOAD
3       EmployeeKey,
4       ParentEmployeeKey,
5       EmployeeNationalIDAlternateKey,
6       ParentEmployeeNationalIDAlternateKey,
7       //SalesTerritoryKey,
8       FirstName&' '&LastName as EmployeeName,
9       MiddleName,
10      NameStyle,
11      Title,
12      HireDate,
13      BirthDate,
14      LoginID,
15      EmailAddress,
16      Phone,
17      MaritalStatus,
18      EmergencyContactName,
19      EmergencyContactPhone,
20      SalariedFlag,
21      Gender,
22      PayFrequency,
23      BaseRate,
24      VacationHours,
25      SickLeaveHours,
26      CurrentFlag,
27      SalesPersonFlag,
28      DepartmentName,
29      Status as EmployeeStatus,
30      EmployeePhoto
31  FROM [lib://QVDs/dbo_DimEmployee.qvd]
32  (qvd) where DepartmentName = 'Sales';
33
34
```

While loading the `Employee` dimension, we have concatenated two fields, namely `FirstName` and `LastName`, to make the full name of the employee. We have used the `where` condition to fetch only Sales employees, because we only need sales employees' information and not the entire company's employee information.

Now we will load the `Territory` table, as shown in the following screenshot:

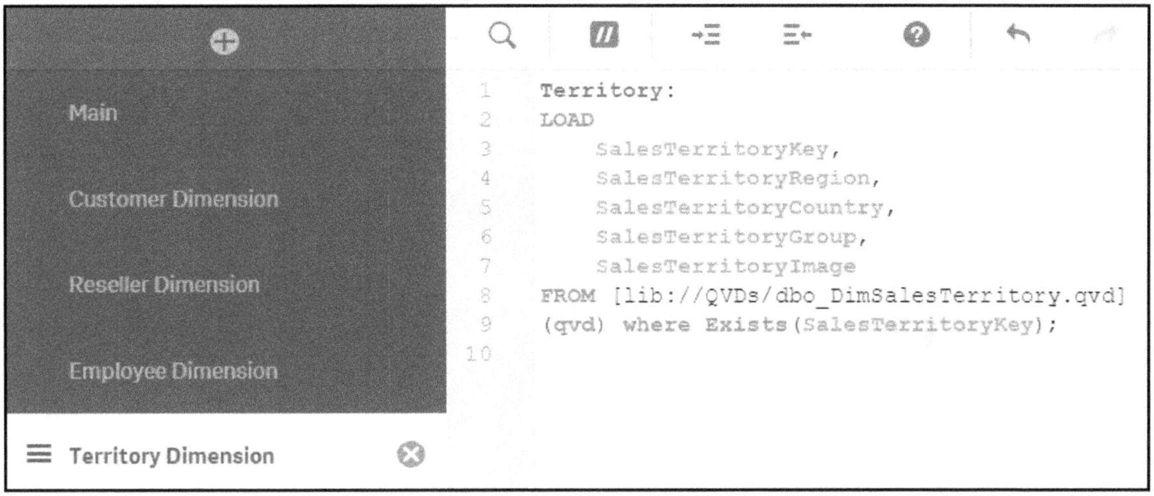

```
1    Territory:
2    LOAD
3        SalesTerritoryKey,
4        SalesTerritoryRegion,
5        SalesTerritoryCountry,
6        SalesTerritoryGroup,
7        SalesTerritoryImage
8    FROM [lib://QVDs/dbo_DimSalesTerritory.qvd]
9    (qvd) where Exists(SalesTerritoryKey);
10
```

In the preceding script, you can see that we have used the where exists condition to load only those territories where actual transactions have happened.

Before we load the table `Product`, we will look at the two tables that need to be linked with it. They are `ProductCategory` and `ProductSubCategory`. The `ProductSubCategory` table has a direct linking with the `Product` table using the foreign key `ProductSubCategoryKey`, whereas `ProductCategory` doesn't link to the `Product` table directly-it is linked to `ProductSubCategory` using `ProductCategoryKey`.

Because the dimensions tables have only names, it is best suggested to use the Applymap function to link them to the product table.

To use the `Applymap` function, we will have to load the mapping table first. The script for the mapping table is as follows:

```
  1  ProductCategory:
  2  Mapping LOAD
  3      ProductCategoryKey,
  4      EnglishProductCategoryName
  5  FROM [lib://QVDs/dbo_DimProductCategory.qvd]
  6  (qvd);
  7
  8  ProductSubCategory:
  9  Mapping LOAD
 10      ProductSubcategoryKey,
 11      EnglishProductSubcategoryName
 12  FROM [lib://QVDs/dbo_DimProductSubcategory.qvd]
 13  (qvd);
 14
 15  ProductSubCategorytoCategory:
 16  Mapping LOAD
 17      ProductSubcategoryKey,
 18      ProductCategoryKey
 19  FROM [lib://QVDs/dbo_DimProductSubcategory.qvd]
 20  (qvd);
 21
 22
```

Menu items on the left panel: Main, Customer Dimension, Reseller Dimension, Employee Dimension, Territory Dimension, Mapping Table

There are three tables loaded as mapping tables: one for getting product sub category name, one for getting product category key, and last for getting product category name.

Now we can load the `Product` table and use the Applymap function to get the name of the category and sub category. The script is as follows:

We have used the where exists condition to load only those products that have transaction associated with them.

Next, we will load the `SalesQuota` table. The data available in `SalesQuota` is at quarter level. To show month on month comparison between the actual sales amount and the sales quota, we will convert the quota amount to month level by dividing the numbers by three.

Following is the script to load the `SalesQuota` table:

You can see in the preceding script that we have loaded the same data three times, but every time with a changed date. The dates are changed using the `Addmonths()` function.

Now we will load the fact tables. There are two fact tables, one for internet sales and the other for reseller sales. Both of them have common fields and one or two different fields. Applying best practice, we will concatenate them to make a single fact table.

Following screenshot shows part one of the script:

```
 1    Sales:
 2    LOAD
 3        ProductKey,
 4        OrderDateKey,
 5        DueDateKey,
 6        ShipDateKey,
 7        CustomerKey,
 8        PromotionKey,
 9        CurrencyKey,
10        SalesTerritoryKey,
11        SalesOrderNumber,
12        SalesOrderLineNumber,
13        RevisionNumber,
14        OrderQuantity,
15        UnitPrice,
16        ExtendedAmount,
17        UnitPriceDiscountPct,
18        DiscountAmount,
19        ProductStandardCost,
20        TotalProductCost,
21        SalesAmount,
22        TaxAmt,
23        Freight,
24        CarrierTrackingNumber,
25        CustomerPONumber,
26        OrderDate,
27        Date(Floor(OrderDate)) as Date,
28        DueDate,
29        ShipDate,
30        'Online'as Channel
31
32    FROM [lib://QVDs/dbo_FactInternetSales.qvd]
33    (qvd) where OrderDate <= MakeDate(2013,11,30);
34
35    Concatenate
```

Menu items: Main, Customer Dimension, Reseller Dimension, Employee Dimension, Territory Dimension, Mapping Table, Product Dimension, Sales Quota, Sales

In the preceding script, you can see that we have loaded the internet sales data. While loading, we have converted the OrderDate field into a date field and added one more field, namely Channel, to identify the channel of sales. Additionally, we have removed the unwanted data using the where condition.

The second part of the script is as shown in the following screenshot:

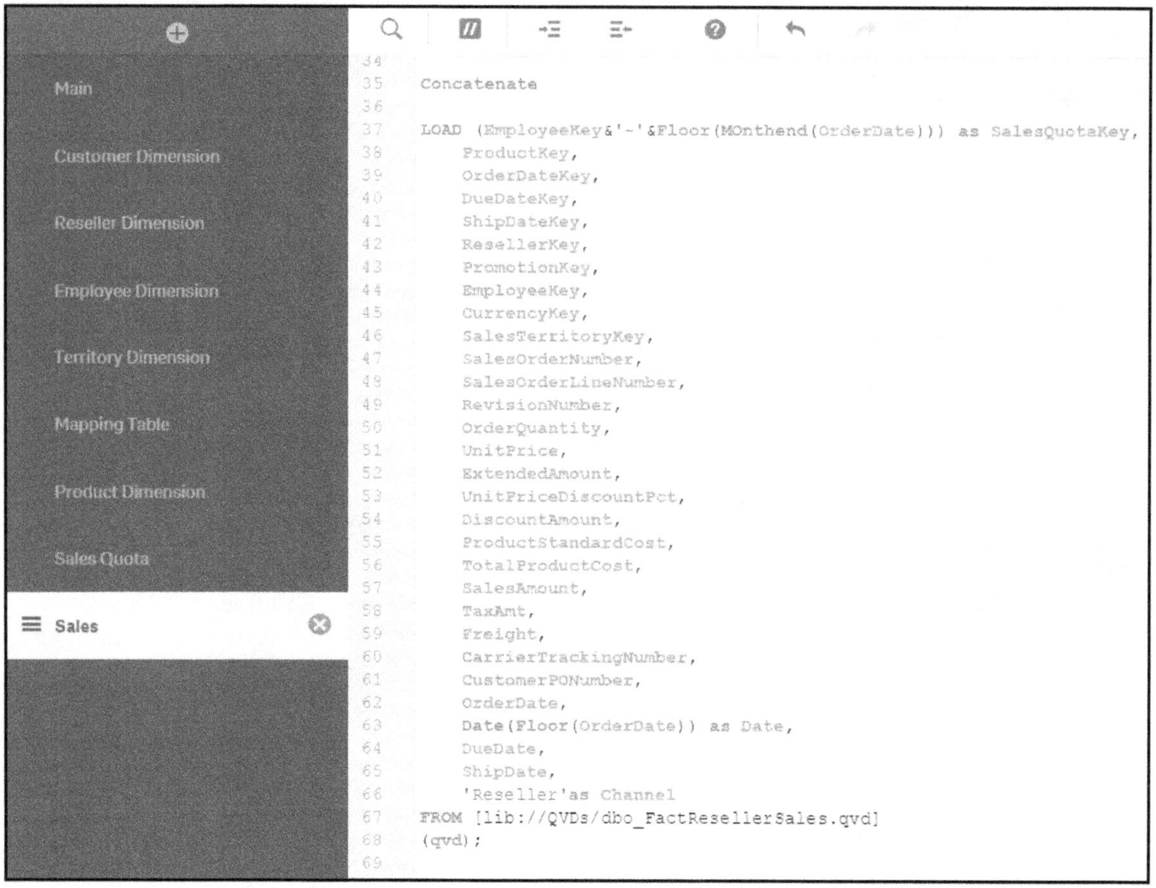

In the preceding script, you can see that we have done the same thing as we did with the internet sales table, that is, added a new field and converted the date field. We have also created a new field to connect to the `SalesQuota` table, because quota is available only for reseller sales.

Next is to load the `Master Calendar` table. This table is created using the date field available in the fact table loaded in the previous script. The script for `Master Calendar` is as follows:

```
1    REM FInd the Minimum and Maximum Date from the table;
2    FindMinMaxDate:
3    LOad Min(OrderDate) as MinDate,
4        Max(OrderDate) as MaxDate
5    Resident Sales;
6
7    Let vMinDate = num(Peek('MinDate',0,'FindMinMaxDate'));
8    Let vMaxDate = num(Floor(Monthend(Peek('MaxDate',0,'FindMinMaxDate'))));
9
10   Temp:
11   Load Date($(vMinDate) + RowNo() -1) as TempDate
12   AutoGenerate 1
13   While Date($(vMinDate) + RowNo() -1) <Date($(vMaxDate));Add
14
15   MasterCal:
16   Load Date(TempDate) as Date,
17       Day(TempDate)  as Day,
18       Month(TempDate)  as Month,
19       MonthName(TempDate)  as MonthYear,
20       'Q'&Ceil(Num(Month(TempDate))/3) as Quarter,
21       Year(TempDate)  as Year,
22       Week(TempDate) as Week,
23       WeekDay(TempDate) as WeekDay
24   Resident Temp;
25
26   Drop table Temp;
27   Drop table FindMinMaxDate;
28
29
30
```

As you can see in the preceding script, we have taken the minimum and maximum date from the fact table and used them to create a master calendar.

Finally, we will load the `Geography` table. The Geography table contains the name of the country which can be used to show sales amount for that country on map. For this, we can use the default functionality of Qlik Sense, where it automatically finds the fields which can be used for creating map fields. But to do this the data needs to be loaded using the data manager.

Once you add the geography table using the data manager, an automated script will be generated, which will have some mapping tables to get the Geo information from inbuilt Geo QVDs. Full script can be found in the code bundle. Following screenshot shows some part of the script:

The scripting for data modeling is done and now we are ready to reload the script. The option to reload the script is available at the right-hand side corner, with label `Load Data`.

Once the script loading finishes, you can go to **Data Model Viewer** to see the data model view of the script. You can open the **Data Model Viewer window** from the navigation button available on the left-hand side corner. The data model will look like the following screenshot:

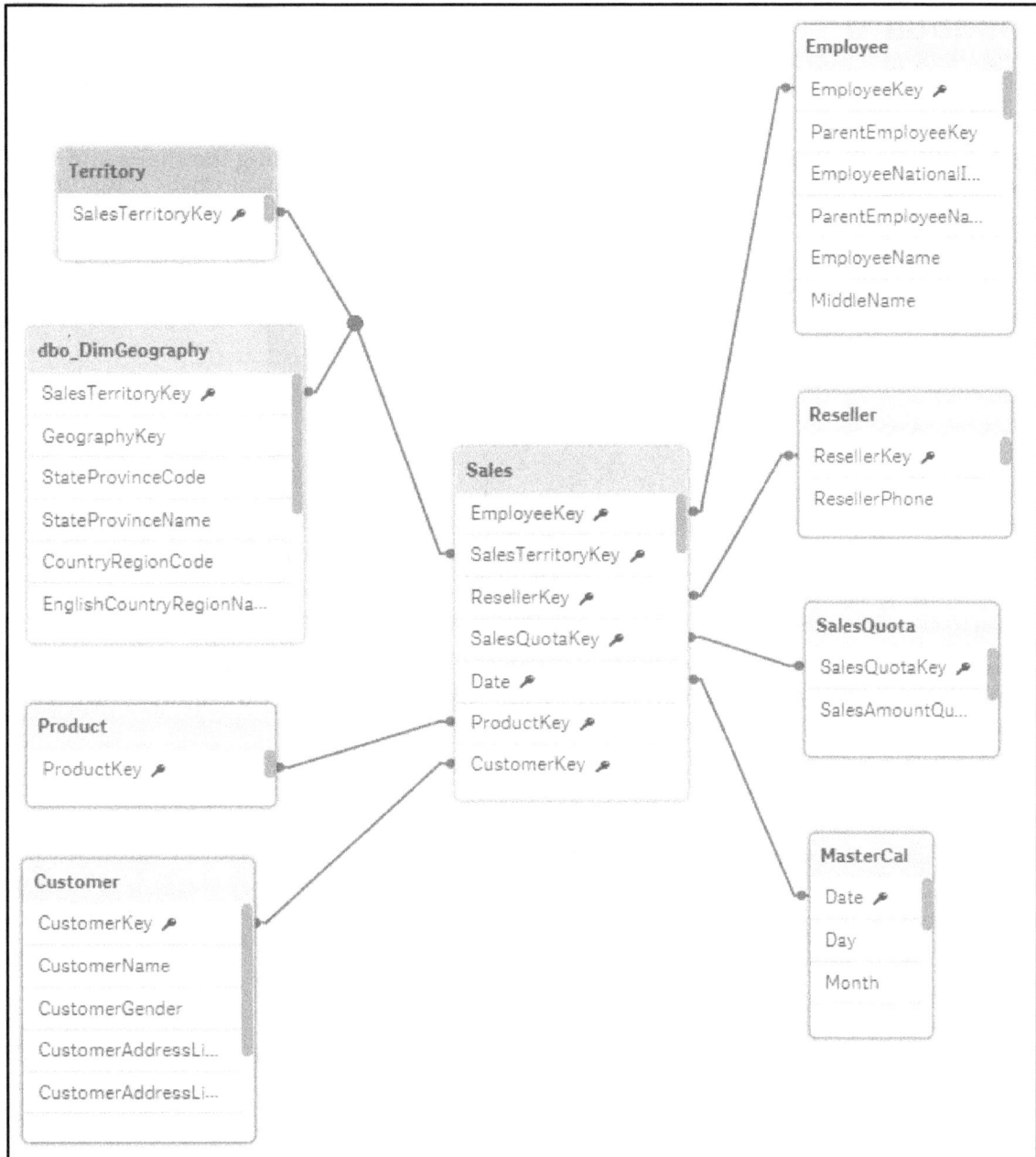

You can see that the data model looks similar to what Jim had designed on paper. It follows the star schema model which is best suited and will give better performance.

Dashboard

We finished the major part of the application by completing data modeling. Now it is time to start visualization.

We will start with creating **Master Items** and then we will be designing the charts and graphs. To begin, we will define **Dimensions** in the list. For this, we will click on the **Master Items** button available on the left hand side and click on **Dimensions**, as shown in the following screenshot:

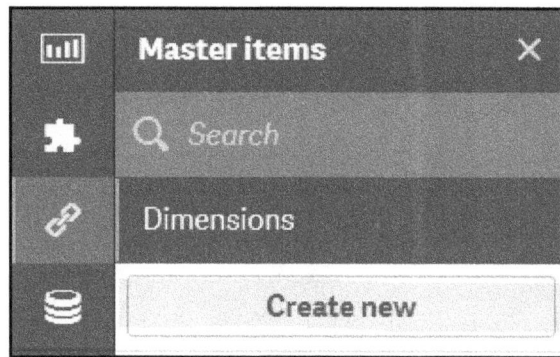

Once you click on the **Create New** button, a new window will open which will allow you to define a field as dimension from all the available fields in data model, as shown in the following screenshot:

Create new dimensions

Single   Drill-down

Filter by table   Field:

All tables   ▼   EmployeeName   ✕ *fx*

🔍 Empl   ✕   Name:

EmployeeKey   EmployeeName

EmployeeName   Label Expression

EmployeeNationalIDAlternate...   *fx*

EmployeePhoto   Description:

EmployeeStatus

NumberEmployees   Dimension color

ParentEmployeeKey   ▢ ▼

ParentEmployeeNationalIDAI...   Tags:

                                                                          ⊕

                                         Add dimension

                                                          Done

As shown in the preceding screenshot, you get two options: one is to define a single field as dimension or create a drill down dimension. Once you select any one option, you can select the field from the list and give a name to that field. You can also define the label expression, if you want to change the label dynamically. You can assign color to your dimension if you want.

Once all the settings are done, you can simply click on **Add Dimension** to create a new dimension in the master list. In previous example, we have chosen **EmployeeName** as the dimension. Similarly, you can add as many dimensions as you need.

Now you can select the **Measures** option and click on **Create New** to create a measure. Once you click on it, the following window will open:

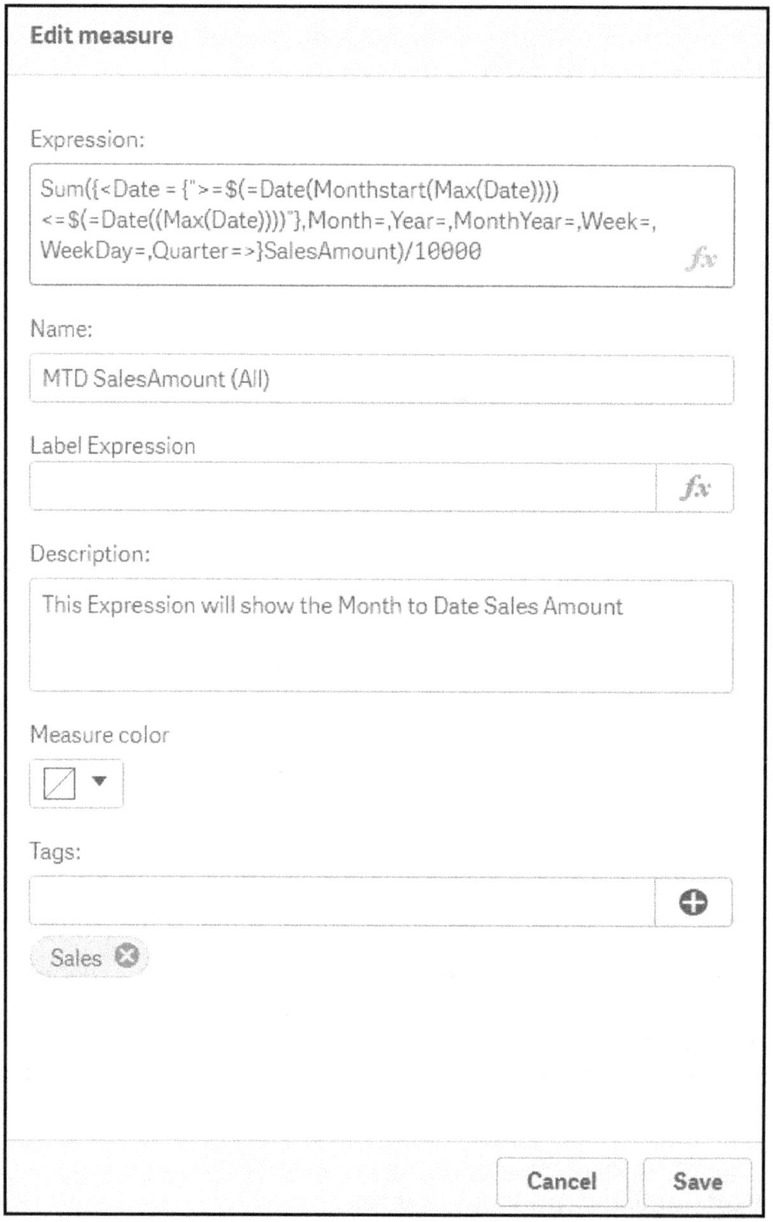

Edit measure

Expression:

Sum({<Date = {">=$(=Date(Monthstart(Max(Date))))
<=$(=Date((Max(Date))))"},Month=,Year=,MonthYear=,Week=,
WeekDay=,Quarter=>}SalesAmount)/10000   *fx*

Name:

MTD SalesAmount (All)

Label Expression

                                                                        fx

Description:

This Expression will show the Month to Date Sales Amount

Measure color

▢ ▼

Tags:

                                                                        ⊕

Sales ✕

Cancel   Save

As you can see in the preceding window, you can define the desired calculation in the **Expression** box. Give a proper name to your expression and **Description** if required. You can give a small description about the expression, like the working of the expression or the output generated by the expression. The option to give a specific color to the measure is also available. You can also give a tag to your expression, so that it can be easily searched.

The previous screenshot shows the sample expression to calculate the **Month Till Date** sales amount. Similarly, you can create as many measures as you need.

Following is the list of expressions which you can create:

Expression Name	Calculation
MTD Growth percentage (All)	(Sum({<Date = {">=$(=Date(Monthstart(Max(Date)))) <=$(=Date((Max(Date))))"}, Month=,Year=,MonthYear=,Week=, WeekDay=,Quarter=>}SalesAmount)/ Sum({<Date = {">=$(=Date(Monthstart(Max(Date)),-12))) <=$(=Date(Addmonths(Max(Date),-12)))"}, Month=,Year=,MonthYear=,Week=,WeekDay=, Quarter=>}SalesAmount))-1
MTD Sales Quota Achievement percentage	Sum({<Date = {">=$(=Date(Monthstart(Max(Date)))) <=$(=Date((Max(Date))))"},Channel ={"Reseller"}, Month=, Year=,MonthYear=,Week=,WeekDay=, Quarter=>}SalesAmount) / Sum({<Date = {">=$(=Date(Monthstart(Max(Date)))) <=$(=Date((Max(Date))))"},Channel ={"Reseller"}, Month=,Year=,MonthYear=,Week=,WeekDay=, Quarter=>}SalesAmountQuota)
PMTD SalesAmount (All)	Sum({<Date = {">=$(=Date(Monthstart(Max(Date)),-1))) <=$(=Date(Addmonths(Max(Date),-1)))"},Month=, Year=,MonthYear=,Week=,WeekDay=, Quarter=>}SalesAmount)/10000
PQTD SalesAmount (All)	Sum({<Date = {">=$(=Date(QuarterStart (Max(Date)),-1)))<=$(=Date(Addmonths(Max(Date),-3)))"}, Month=,Year=,MonthYear=,Week=,WeekDay=,Quarter= >}SalesAmount)/10000
PY MTD SalesAmount (All)	Sum({<Date = {">=$(=Date(Monthstart(Max(Date)),-12))) <=$(=Date(Addmonths(Max(Date),-12)))"}, Month=,Year=,MonthYear=,Week=,WeekDay=, Quarter=>}SalesAmount)/10000

PY QTD SalesAmount (All)	Sum({<Date = {">=$(=Date(QuarterStart(Max(Date),-4))) <=$(=Date(Addmonths(Max(Date),-12)))"},Month=,Year=, MonthYear=,Week=,WeekDay=,Quarter=>}SalesAmount)/10000
PY YTD SalesAmount (All)	Sum({<Date = {">=$(=Date(YearStart(Max(Date),-1))) <=$(=Date(addmonths(Max(Date),-12)))"},Month=, Year=,MonthYear=,Week=,WeekDay=, Quarter=>}SalesAmount)/10000
QTD Growth percentage (All)	(Sum({<Date = {">=$(=Date(QuarterStart(Max(Date)))) <=$(=Date((Max(Date))))"},Month=,Year=, MonthYear=,Week=,WeekDay=,Quarter=>}SalesAmount)/ Sum({<Date = {">=$(=Date(QuarterStart(Max(Date),-4))) <=$(=Date(Addmonths(Max(Date),-12)))"},Month=, Year=,MonthYear=,Week=,WeekDay=, Quarter=>}SalesAmount))-1
Rolling 12 Months Sales Amount (All)	Sum({<Date = {">=$(=Date(Monthstart(Addmonths(Max(Date), -12))))<=$(=Date((Max(Date))))"},Month=, Year=,MonthYear=,Week=,WeekDay=, Quarter=>}SalesAmount)/10000
YTD Growth % (All)	(Sum({<Date = {">=$(=Date(YearStart(Max(Date)))) <=$(=Date((Max(Date))))"},Month=,Year=, MonthYear=,Week=,WeekDay=>}SalesAmount)/ Sum({<Date = {">=$(=Date(YearStart(Max(Date),-1)) <=$(=Date(addmonths(Max(Date),-12)))"}, Month=,Year=,MonthYear=,Week=,WeekDay=, Quarter=>}SalesAmount))-1

Given here are some KPI calculations out of the entire list; for exhaustive list, you can refer to the code bundle.

Now that we have created all the KPI calculations in the master list, we are ready to start with the designing of the dashboard.

It is good practice to include an introduction page in your application. The introduction page gives information about the application and the users know exactly what to expect from the it. A good introduction page should give an overview of the application, including what data it contains and what kind of analysis is available in it. The sample introduction page created for Adventure Work Sales application is shown in the following screenshot:

Let us see **OmniChannel Sales Dashboard:**

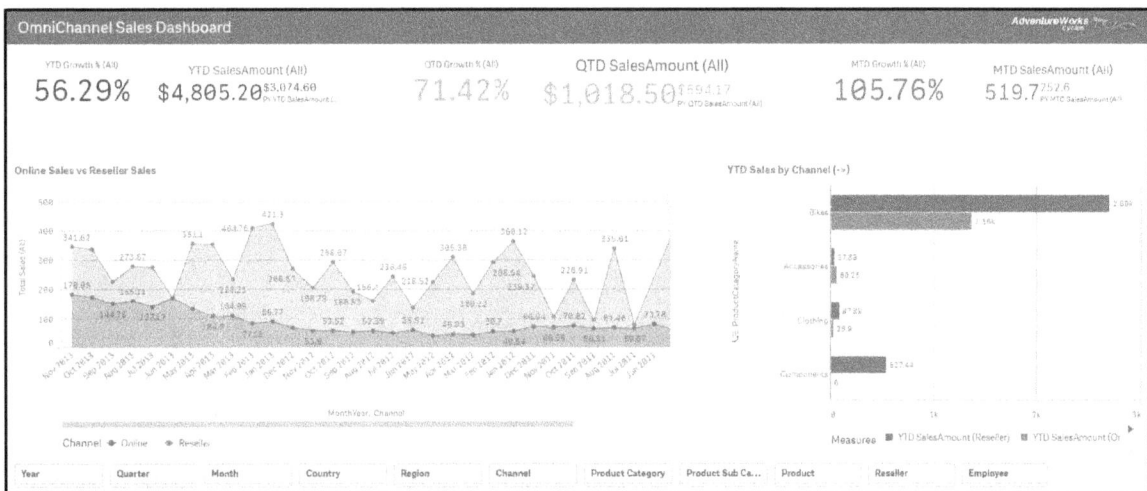

You can see in the preceding screenshot that it gives the following insights into the data.

- YTD (year till date) growth percentage: This KPI helps the users to compare the business of this year versus last year
- QTD (quarter till date) growth percentage: This KPI helps in finding the QTD growth as compared to the same quarter last year
- MTD (month till date) growth percentage: This KPI helps compare the current month business with that of last year same month

- Trend: This trend gives a clear bifurcation about the sales between two channels and shows which channel is performing well over a period of time
- Bar chart: It shows the channel wise sales by product category, to understand which channel is performing well in what product category

> Symbol -> denotes that the chart has drill down functionality and symbol @ shows that the chart has alternate dimensions.

Let us have a look at the Reseller Dashboard:

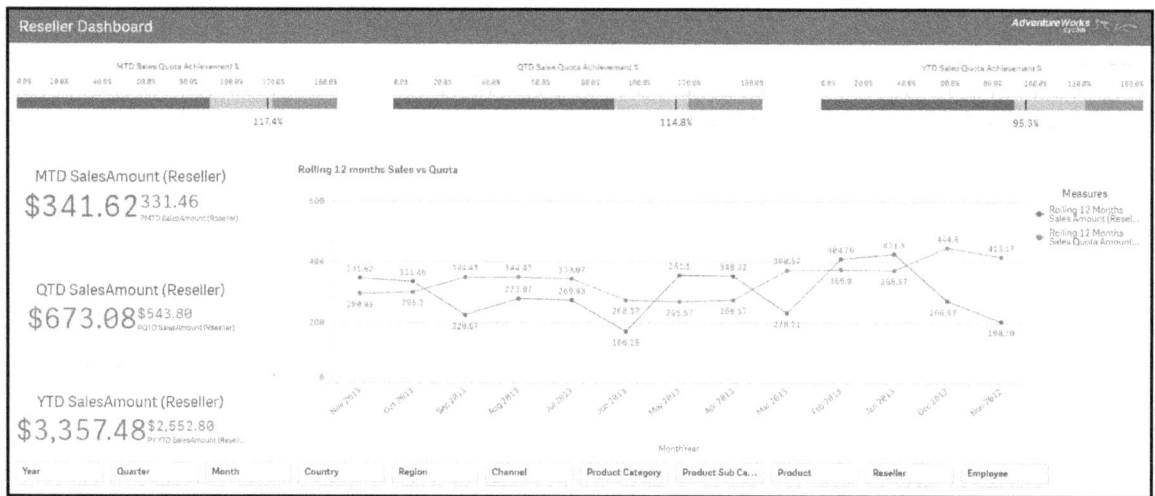

This dashboard shows the sales analysis for the reseller channel. It gives the following insight into data:

- MTD sales quota achievement percent: This KPI shows how much quota has been achieved for the month
- QTD sales quota achievement percent: It tells how much quota has been achieved for the quarter
- YTD sales quota achievement percent: It shows how much quota has been achieved for the year

All the preceding KPIs also had color coding, which gives a clear indication if the percentage achievement is within the expected range or not.

Some of the other KPIs as as follows:-

- MTD sales amount: This KPI shows the current month and the previous month sales amount
- QTD sales amount: This KPI shows the current quarter and the previous quarter sales amount
- YTD sales amount: This KPI shows the current year and the previous year sales amount
- Trend: This trend is for rolling 12 months and it shows the sales versus quota

Now let us see the Sales Analysis sheet:

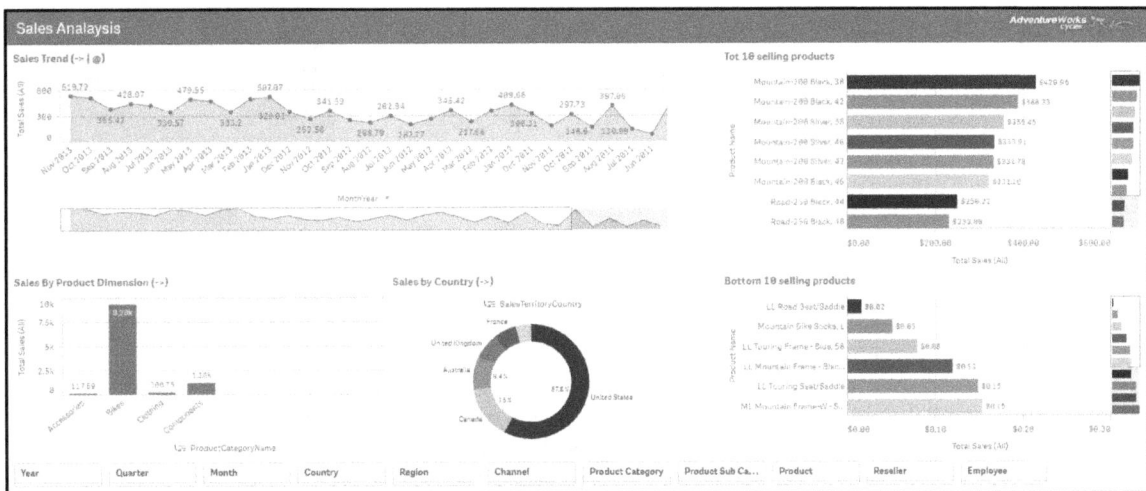

This visualization shows the following analysis:

- Sales trend: It shows the total sales over a period. This helps to find the sales trend for any dimension value which can be selected from the filters given at the bottom of the visualization. This chart can be drilled down to week and further to day level.

- Sales by product dimension: It gives a drill down from product category to product sub category to individual product. This chart helps in finding which product category is doing good business.

- Sales by country: This chart shows the contribution of each country toward total sales. It also gives insights about which country has maximum sales by looking at donut chart
- Top 10 selling products: It shows the best performing products.
- Bottom 10 selling products: It shows the worst performing products. Looking at this chart, the users can decide whether to continue this product in future or not.

Let us have a look at the Employee Performance sheet:

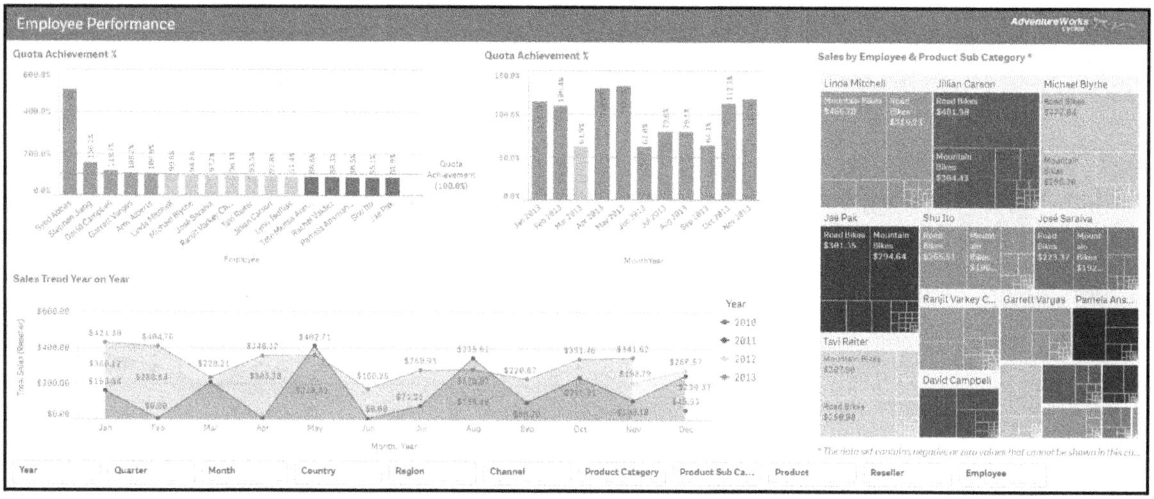

This visualization helps the users to know the following things:

- Quota achievement percent: This chart shows the quota achieved by all the employees and finds which employee is working hard. It also gives insight that there is something wrong with one of the employees, namely Syed Abbas. It seems his quota has not been assigned properly and that needs attention.
- Trend: This chart shows the year on year monthly sales. So if a user wants to know about the performance over time of any one or a group of employees, this chart can give a good picture.
- Quota trend: This chart shows quota achievement over time.
- Treemap: This chart shows which employee has sold which product sub category most.

Now let us see Product Analysis sheet:

Product Analysis AdventureWorks

List of Product not Sold in United Kingdom

Sales by Sub Category and Region

Product Sub Cat... ▼	Region ▼					
	Australia	Canada	Central	France	Germany	Northeast	Northwest
Bib-Shorts		$4.08	$1.41	$1.08		$1.74	$1.52
Bike Racks	$1.77	$4.34	$1.42	$2.39	$1.74	$1.56	$2.35
Bike Stands	$0.82	$0.43		$0.30	$0.32		$0.56
Bottles and Cages	$1.64	$0.79	$0.06	$0.56	$0.56	$0.07	$0.62
Bottom Brackets	$0.44	$0.81	$0.21	$0.46	$0.26	$0.33	$1.04
Brakes	$0.56	$1.07	$0.38	$0.76	$0.29	$0.51	$1.17
Caps	$0.44	$0.85	$0.30	$0.36	$0.35	$0.27	$0.52
Chains	$0.09	$0.11	$0.05	$0.12	$0.05	$0.06	$0.17
Cleaners	$0.20	$0.31	$0.08	$0.14	$0.14	$0.11	$0.23
Cranksets	$1.68	$3.07	$0.79	$2.46	$1.16	$1.58	$4.05
Derailleurs	$0.73	$1.12	$0.24	$0.86	$0.33	$0.40	$1.21
Fenders	$0.61	$0.77	$0.60	$0.19	$0.29		$0.90
Forks		$1.64	$0.41	$0.42		$0.58	$1.26
Gloves	$0.57	$4.91	$1.72	$1.57	$0.75	$7.11	$3.11
Handlebars	$0.28	$3.06	$1.45	$0.97	$0.44	$1.63	$2.86
Headsets		$1.42	$0.33	$0.29		$0.38	$1.23
Helmets	$4.58	$8.10	$2.30	$3.69	$3.13	$2.35	$6.32
Hydration Packs	$1.28	$1.79	$0.47	$0.86	$0.88	$0.61	$1.06
Jerseys	$8.47	$13.77	$5.83	$5.59	$5.64	$5.31	$7.58
Locks		$0.42	$0.16	$0.11		$0.15	$0.16
Mountain Bikes	$284.34	$530.16	$268.96	$192.83	$109.73	$157.36	$712.12
Mountain Frames	$3.55	$89.03	$44.15	$31.04	$5.77	$32.24	$93.49

Filters: Year | Quarter | Month | Country | Region | Channel | Product Category | Product Sub Ca... | Product | Reseller | Employee

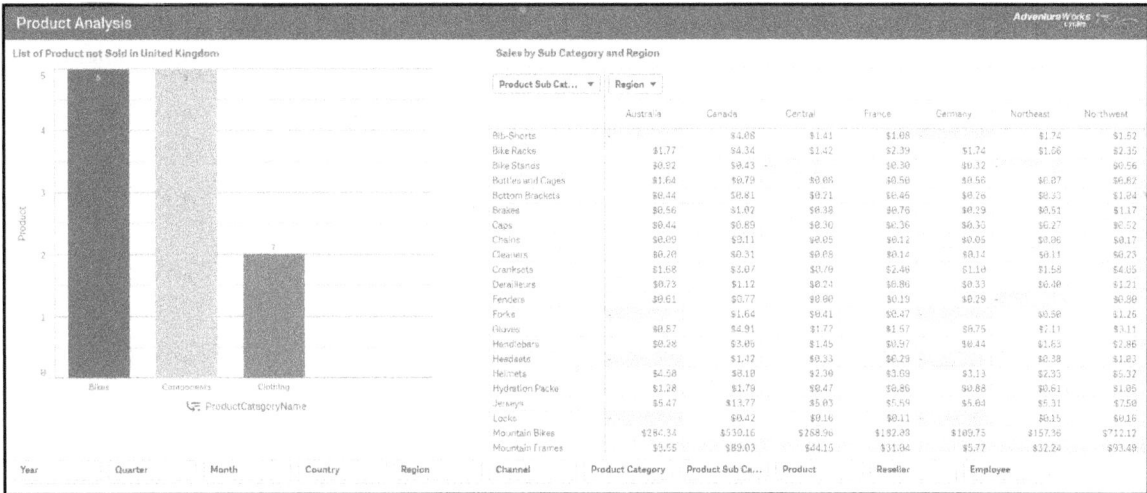

This visualization on the sheets help us with following analysis:

- Bar chart: This chart shows the number of products that are not sold in one of the regions. By default, the selection is for United Kingdom, but it can be changed to other regions using filters at the bottom of the sheet. This gives an insight about which product should be focused on in which region.
- Pivot chart: It gives a clear idea about sales of each product sub category in each region.

Let us see what will be included in Reporting sheet:

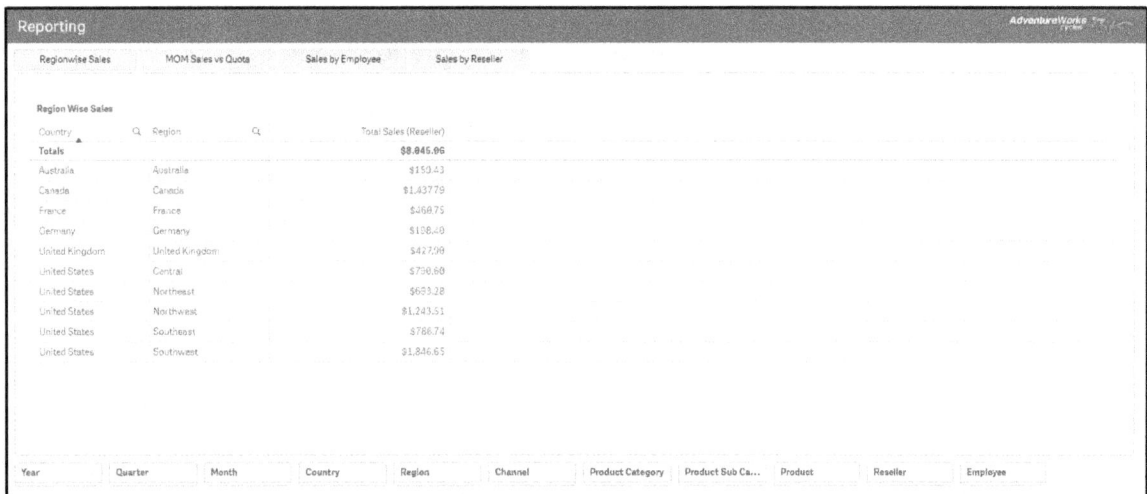

Reporting AdventureWorks

Regionwise Sales | MOM Sales vs Quota | Sales by Employee | Sales by Reseller

Region Wise Sales

Country	Region	Total Sales (Reseller)
Totals		$8,845.96
Australia	Australia	$150.43
Canada	Canada	$1,437.79
France	France	$468.75
Germany	Germany	$198.40
United Kingdom	United Kingdom	$427.99
United States	Central	$790.60
United States	Northeast	$693.28
United States	Northwest	$1,243.51
United States	Southeast	$788.74
United States	Southwest	$1,846.65

Filters: Year | Quarter | Month | Country | Region | Channel | Product Category | Product Sub Ca... | Product | Reseller | Employee

Reporting shows the transaction data at various dimension levels. Like in the preceding screenshot, we have region wise sales, month on month sales, and employee wise sales.

Story

Our dashboard is ready. Now it is time to create a story to showcase the insights found from analyzing the dashboard.

Before creating a new story, it is required that we take screenshots of our findings.

For example, one of the findings which we can include in the story is that the growth of the online channel has been extraordinary for the current year, as compared to the reseller channel, which has grown comparatively less. So to show this finding, we will take snapshots of the KPIs by clicking on the camera button, as shown in following image:

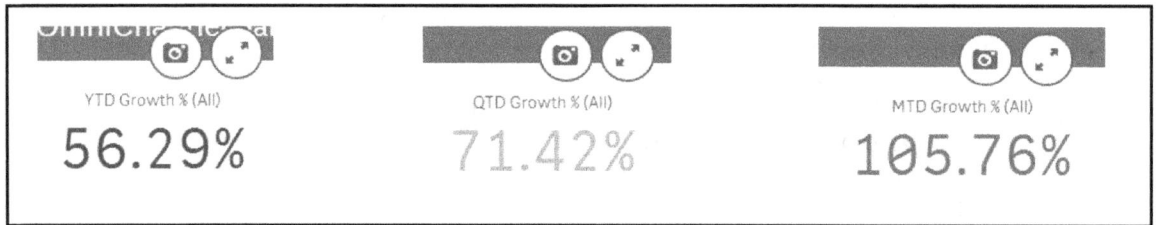

Once you click on the camera button, it will ask you to add the description of the screenshot taken. This helps in identifying the right screenshot from the library.

Once you finish taking screenshots of all the charts and graphs, you can create a new story. For this, you can go to stories, create a new story, and give name as **Monthly Sales Review**, or you can give any name of your choice, as shown in the following image:

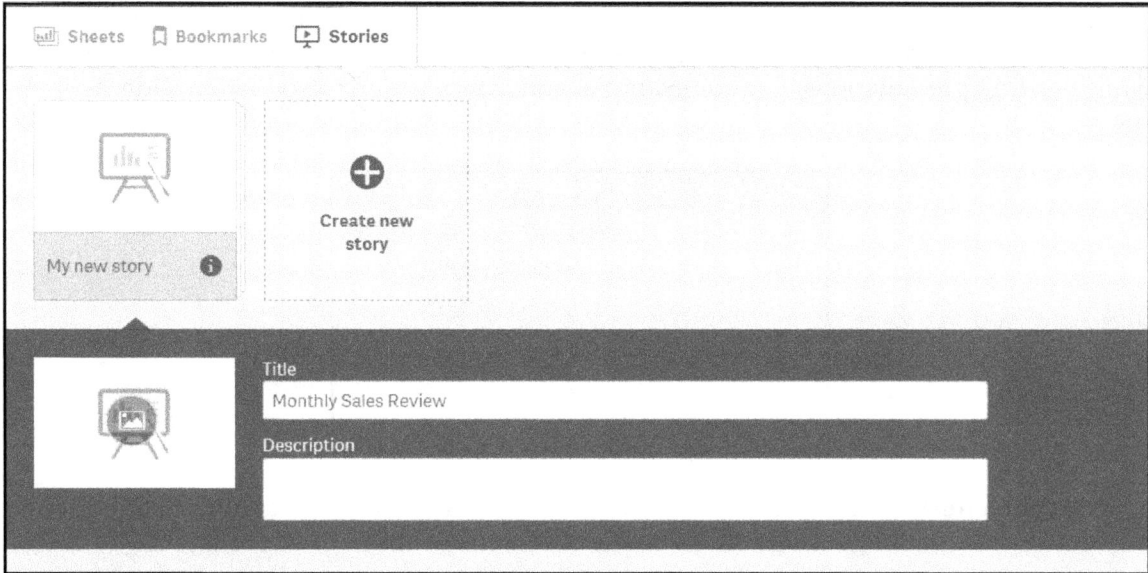

Once the story is created, click on it to open the design view of the story, as shown in the following image:

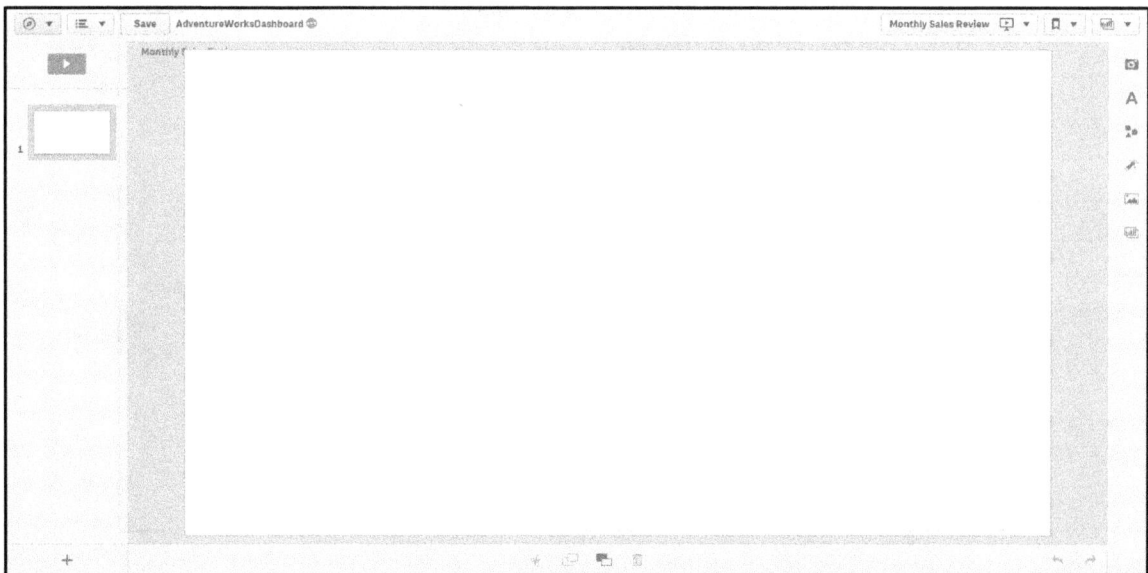

Now you can start creating the story by dragging the screenshots taken of the various charts. It is a good practice to start a story with an introduction page, similar to what we do while creating presentations. For our example, you can create an introduction slide, as shown next:

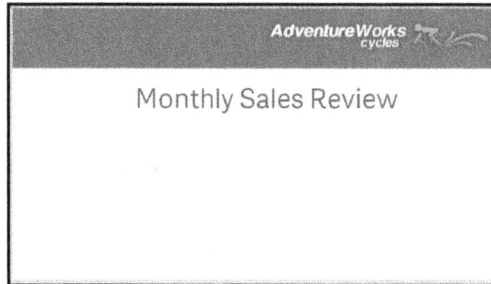

You can put a relevant image or logo of the company in your story, and you can also give a title to the presentation, like shown in the previous screenshot.

Once the introduction slide is ready, you can start putting the screenshots of the relevant analysis in single slide and describe your findings. In our example, we found good insights on omni-channel sales which is presented in the following screenshot:

You can see in the preceding screenshot that we have presented total sales, reseller sales, and online sales. The KPIs show the difference between the values and that provides the action point for the business to think about improving the reseller sales by giving them good discounts.

Another finding related to quota achievement is shown as follows:

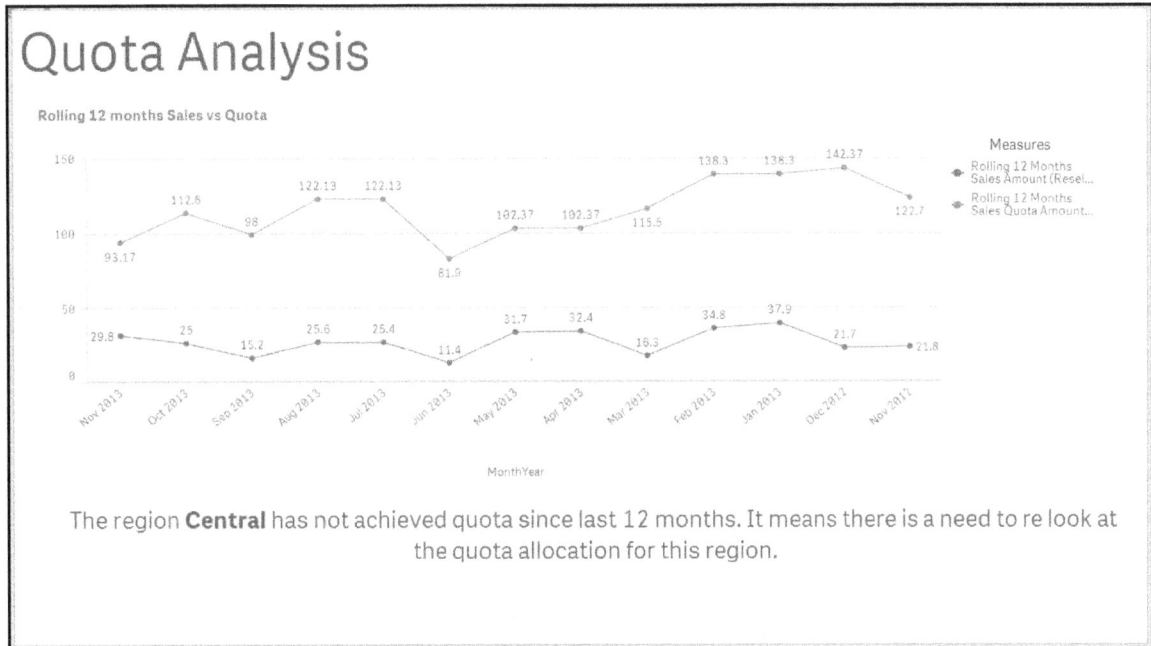

Quota Analysis

Rolling 12 months Sales vs Quota

The region **Central** has not achieved quota since last 12 months. It means there is a need to re look at the quota allocation for this region.

While analyzing the data, we found that the region **Central** has not been achieving the quota for the last 12 months. It is a serious concern for the business and they must find appropriate answers from the sales manager of that region about the same.

Similarly, we found useful analysis of employee performance, which is shown following figure:

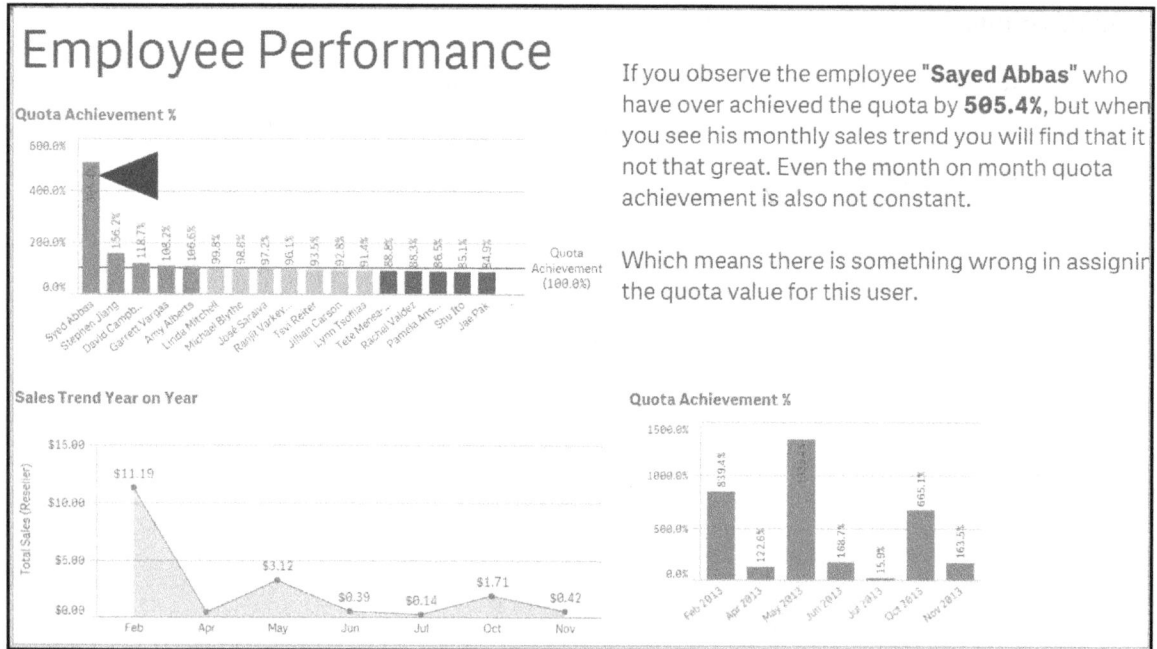

The data shows that there is something wrong in the allocation of quota to some of the employees. One of the examples found was about employee **Syed Abbas**. He has over achieved the quota by almost 505.4 percent, but when the month on month trend is seen for that employee, it is found that the achievement is not consistent. The sales done by him is not great as well. This means that he has not been assigned a proper quota value.

You can thus create multiple stories which depict the insights and also annotate on what can be the action points, and present them to the management.

Post Go-Live Steps

Now that Jim has completed the delivery of the application, he should look at post Go-live steps to increase adoption. The different areas that Jim needs to focus on are as follows:

- Creation of user manual
- Creation of application specific video (this can be similar to the video seen at https://www.youtube.com/watch?v=4X5sjExhoug)

- Creation of frequently asked questions
- Close look at Qlik Sense monitoring apps to check adoption and performance
- Conducting of a refresher end user training
- Ensuring that proper backup strategy has been implemented

Summary

As we come to the end of the book, we hope the readers have enjoyed the journey and could make the most of the concepts that would help them to wear the hat of the consultant.

As consultants, the readers will face varied situations and use cases, and may get chance to work in multiple domains. This chapter looked at a situation where a consultant is exposed to a manufacturing company having both Business to Business (B2B) and Business to Consumer (B2C) models.

The chapter helps the consultants to understand the business challenges and how analytics can help the business users derive better insights and enable taking business decisions. The technical aspects involved in developing dashboards were looked at as well.

Once you are ready with the Qlik Sense application, it's important to plan the roll-out and look at best practices to build user confidence and increase adoption.

Through the medium of the book, we have intended to help all the developers aspiring to be consultants to make the transition smoothly. We hope you have enjoyed the book and we look forward to your valuable feedback!!!

Index